Investment

Strategies

THE GLOBE AND MAIL

Investment

Strategies

Making Them Work for You

STEVEN G. KELMAN
SEYMOUR FRIEDLAND

 I(T)P Nelson

an International Thomson Publishing company

Toronto • Albany • Bonn • Boston • Cincinnati • Detroit • London • Madrid • Melbourne
Mexico City • New York • Pacific Grove • Paris • San Francisco • Singapore • Tokyo • Washington

I(T)P® **International Thomson Publishing**
The ITP logo is a trademark under licence
www.thomson.com

Published in 1999 by

I(T)P® Nelson

A division of Thomson Canada Limited
1120 Birchmount Road
Scarborough, Ontario M1K 5G4
www.nelson.com

Canadian Cataloguing in Publication Data

Kelman, Steven G. (Steven Gershon), 1945–
  Investment strategies

At head of title: Financial times, 198-?-1995; The globe and mail, 1996– .
Following title: How to create your own and make it work for you.
Description based on 1993.
Issues for 1996 – published in the series: The Globe and mail personal finance library.
Issues for 1997 – published by ITP Nelson.
ISSN 1193-9028
ISBN 0-17-606838-4 (1999)

1. Investments – Canada – Periodicals.   2. Finance, Personal – Canada – Periodicals.
I. Friedland, Seymour, 1928–.   II. The Globe and Mail personal finance library.
III. Title.   IV. Series.

HG179.M25   332.6'78'097105   C93-030702-X

Printed and bound in Canada
1 2 3 4 (WC) 02 01 99

Contents

TABLES AND ILLUSTRATIONS

Introduction

Just a few years ago, Canadians could take their money to their bank, trust company or credit union and put it in a five-year guaranteed investment that would pay about 10 per cent annually. That was an acceptable rate for most people. It provided an adequate level of growth in registered retirement savings plans and an acceptable after-tax return when held outside registered accounts.

Today, it is a much different story. The five-year savings rate is about 5 per cent and Canadians have shifted billions of dollars of their savings out of guaranteed investments, as they matured, into other areas of the marketplace. Small differences in interest rates can mean huge differences in results given enough time. For example, $1,000 a year invested for 25 years at 5 per cent will grow to just over $50,000. At 8 per cent you would end up with $79,000 and at 10 per cent $108,000. The slide in interest rates has been bad news for depositors and other lenders. But it has been great news for borrowers, especially those seeking funds to buy their homes or for investment purposes.

The purpose of *Investment Strategies* is to make you aware of your investment alternatives and how they work. It won't show you how to get rich overnight, but it will show you how to accumulate wealth by using the investment alternatives that are widely available in Canada. It will also demonstrate how other investors have increased their wealth by putting money into various investment vehicles and, just as important, will help you avoid the pitfalls that have prevented many people from meeting their financial goals. Even if you have given some thought to financial planning, this book can be a valuable aid. Changes in market values of investments as well as modifications to the tax rules make it necessary to constantly review your goals and financial planning strategies.

A lot of people quite properly consider that those who write books on personal finances have superior expertise in their fields. But beware: Some advisors exploit the public's trust by putting their names on works they did not write.

For this reason I am pleased to see that important segments of the securities industry, indeed the Ontario Securities Commission (OSC), the Investment Dealers Association of Canada and the Financial Planners Standards Council, have clamped down on such people. In recent months, the OSC approved settlement agreements between OSC staff and nine securities and mutual fund salespeople whose names appeared as sole co-authors of different editions of effectively the same book. To paraphrase the settlement documents, their conduct was contrary to the public interest in that they participated in a marketing tool that could have misled existing and potential clients and misrepresented their status as a sole co-author. Each individual agreed to a short suspension. Some agreed to making a payment toward the cost of the investigation. At the time of writing, one of the nine involved who holds a Certified Financial Planner designation was facing disciplinary action from the Financial Planners Standards Council.

The OSC also agreed to a settlement between its staff and the employer of one of the nine salespeople. This investment dealer developed new procedures to avoid the possibility of misrepresentation as to authorship in the future. The Investment Dealers Association of Canada approved these procedures as an appropriate policy for its members. Commenting on the new procedures, OSC Commissioner Glorianne Stromberg said, "The development of these procedures ... is a positive step in endeavouring to ensure that the public is not misled by investment advisors claiming authorship of materials that they have not in fact written, or to which they have made minimal contribution."

Most writers do not appreciate being deprived of the credit, reputation and fame for their astuteness, as well as the financial advantage. Toronto writer and custom home builder, Gary Stuart Weiss, learned that material he had written on investing in foreign real estate had been copied by chartered accountant Lyman MacInnis, and included in two books, *Get Smart! Make Your Money Count* and *Get Smart: Make Your Money Count in the 1990s*. Dr. MacInnis is a past president of the Institute of Chartered Accountants of Ontario and a past chairman of the Canadian Institute of Chartered Accountants. He is a recipient of a Doctor of Laws, *honoris causa*, from the University of Prince Edward Island in part for his contributions as an author. Dr. MacInnis is also a partner at Ernst & Young.

Mr. Weiss was successful in an action against Dr. MacInnis, Deloitte & Touche (where Dr. MacInnis was a partner at the time of the copyright infringement), Prentice-Hall Canada Inc. and Southam Inc. Judge S. Harris, in his Reasons for Judgment, stated that "... the Plaintiff has been deprived of the chance to have his persona and advice receive credit for any success or otherwise which investors using the publications that contained the infringement might have had." Judge Harris found as a fact that Dr. MacInnis copied Mr. Weiss' article.

I find it most incredible that one professional would take the work of another, reproduce it without the author's consent, deprive the author of credit, and then use the work to promote himself and his firm.

I have been writing about personal financial matters since 1976. My level of expertise is such that I was commissioned by the Financial Planners Standards Council to develop its first two professional proficiency examinations and prepare the major portion of the most recent examination. In 1977 and 1978, the *Financial Times of Canada* ran an eight-part series on RRSPs written by me. Dr. MacInnis included portions of this series in the two *Get Smart* books and this is the subject of litigation currently before the courts against Dr. MacInnis, Deloitte & Touche, Prentice-Hall Canada Inc. and Southam Inc.

Steven G. Kelman

About the authors

Born in the United States, Seymour Friedland took his doctorate at Harvard University and came to Canada as professor of finance and economics at York University's faculty of administrative studies. His 40-year teaching career included terms at New York University, Claremont Graduate School, Rutgers State University, the Massachusetts Institute of Technology and Harvard.

He published nine books and numerous articles in academic journals and served as a consultant to many U.S. and Canadian companies, as well as governments. He was chief economist for Dominion Securities Ltd. from 1969 to 1974, business editor of CBC Television's *The Journal* and for many years an associate editor of the *Financial Times*. Many remember him from his appearances as a business and economics commentator on television and radio. In 1980, he was a recipient of a National Business Writing Award. He died on October 15, 1992.

Steven G. Kelman is an investment counsellor and president of Steven G. Kelman & Associates Limited. His company provides specialty communication, analysis, publications and training for the mutual funds industry. Mr. Kelman is the author of *RRSPs and Other Retirement Strategies 1999: Managing RRIFs, LIFs, LIRAs, and RRSPs; Mutual Fund Strategies 1999: Your No-Nonsense Everyday Guide;* and co-author of *Choosing the Best Financial Advisor: Sage Advice* (all published by *ITP Nelson*); and *Investing in Gold*. His articles have appeared in *Investor's Digest, All-Canadian Mutual Fund Guide, the Financial Times of Canada, The Globe and Mail Report on Business,* and in magazines and on the pages of daily newspapers from coast to coast. Mr. Kelman was commissioned by the Financial Planners Standards Council to develop its first two professional proficiency examinations and prepare the major portion of the June 1998 examination. He has acted as a consultant to the Financial Planners Standards Council of Canada on academic issues. He has lectured on financial planning, RRSPs and mutual funds across the country, and is co-author and co-instructor of a proficiency course in Labour Sponsored Investment Funds recognized by securities commissions in five provinces. For several years, he taught a course in applied investments to MBA students at the Faculty of Administrative Studies at Toronto's York University. He has served as chair of the education committee of the Investment Funds

Institute of Canada and his contributions included writing several sections of the revised Canadian Investment Funds Course.

Mr. Kelman is a Chartered Financial Analyst and a member of the Toronto Society of Financial Analysts. After receiving his B.Sc. in 1967 from McMaster University, he graduated with an MBA in 1969 from York University. Mr. Kelman worked as an analyst, then portfolio manager, for a major insurance company before becoming a senior analyst with an investment dealer. In 1975, he joined the *Financial Times* as a staff writer; he became investment editor in 1977. He joined Dynamic Fund Management Ltd. in 1985 and held a number of positions within Dynamic and affiliated companies until the end of 1994, when he left to establish Steven G. Kelman & Associates.

In its August 16, 1996 issue, *Investor's Digest* published the first of Mr. Kelman's several warnings on Bre-X Minerals Ltd. The shares were trading at more than $26 at the time.

Chapter 1

How to Make a Million: Save

It is absurdly easy to become a millionaire. It doesn't take clever gimmicks or blind luck or risks that will keep you awake at night. Becoming a millionaire only takes a bit of knowledge, sound investment strategies and time.

Time is the critical ingredient, for time and the power of compound interest will have the most significant impact on your ability to build your wealth. Compound interest is interest earned and then added to the original investment so that it too begins to earn interest. It's interest on interest.

Suppose $1,000 has been invested at 10 per cent compounded annually. In the first year, interest earnings are 10 per cent of $1,000 or $100. If the first year's interest remains invested, the principal in the second year becomes $1,100, and the second year's interest earnings are $110. In the third year, the principal becomes $1,210, and interest earnings are $121. As long as the interest is not withdrawn, compound interest generates a rapidly ascending curve of wealth.

At the end of five years, the investment will have grown to $1,610.51. With simple interest—where interest is not earned on past interest—the value of the $1,000 at 10 per cent in five years would be only $1,500.

If the interest is compounded semi-annually, rather than just annually, interest in the second six months of the first year would include interest on the first half-year's earnings. With semi-annual compounding, the value of the $1,000 at 10 per cent would be worth $1,628.89 after five years, an increase of $18.38 over annual compounding and $128.89 better than simple interest. Interest that compounds every three months is better still, and monthly compounding better yet.

An easy way to see the impact of time and compounding on your investments is to use the Rule of 72. To determine the time it takes an investment to double, simply divide 72 by the annual interest rate; $1,000 invested at 10 per cent will double in value in 7.2 years. At 5 per cent, it would take 14.4 years for $1,000 to grow to $2,000. At 15 per cent, doubling takes place in just 4.8 years.

How a Single Deposit of $1,000 Can Grow over Time at Different Rates of Return

COMPOUNDED ANNUALLY

YEAR	4%	6%	8%	10%	12%	14%
1	$1,040	$1,060	$1,080	$1,100	$,1,120	$1,140
2	1,082	1,124	1,166	1,210	1,254	1,300
3	1,125	1,191	1,260	1,331	1,405	1,482
4	1,170	1,262	1,360	1,464	1,574	1,689
5	1,217	1,338	1,469	1,611	1,762	1,925
6	1,265	1,419	1,587	1,772	1,974	2,195
7	1,316	1,504	1,714	1,949	2,211	2,502
8	1,369	1,594	1,851	2,144	2,476	2,853
9	1,423	1,689	1,999	2,358	2,773	3,252
10	1,480	1,791	2,159	2,594	3,106	3,707
11	1,539	1,898	2,332	2,853	3,479	4,226
12	1,601	2,012	2,518	3,138	3,896	4,818
13	1,665	2,133	2,720	3,452	4,363	5,492
14	1,732	2,261	2,937	3,797	4,887	6,261
15	1,801	2,397	3,172	4,177	5,474	7,138
16	1,873	2,540	3,426	4,595	6,130	8,137
17	1,948	2,693	3,700	5,054	6,866	9,276
18	2,026	2,854	3,996	5,560	7,690	10,575
19	2,107	3,026	4,316	6,116	8,613	12,056
20	2,191	3,207	4,661	6,727	9,646	13,743

TABLE I

To find the interest rate that would double your investment in a given number of years, divide 72 by the number of years. For example, to double an investment in six years, one must earn 12 per cent. Another example: The population around the Great Lakes is expected to double in the next 40 years. Using the Rule of 72—dividing 72 by 40—we discover that the annual population growth is expected to be 1.8 per cent.

Of course, the rule is only an approximation. In reality, it would take 7.273 years, not 7.2, to double $1,000 at 10 per cent compounded annually. If the compounding period is shorter, the Rule of 72 overstates the length of time needed to double your investment. Compounded monthly, it takes only 6.96 years for $1,000 to double at 10 per cent.

How an Investment of $1,000 a Year Can Grow over Time at Different Rates of Return

COMPOUNDED ANNUALLY

YEARS	4%	6%	8%	10%	12%	14%
1	$1,040	$1,060	$1,080	$1,100	$,1,120	$1,140
2	2,122	2,184	2,246	2,310	2,374	2,440
3	3,246	3,375	3,506	3,641	3,779	3,921
4	4,416	4,637	4,867	5,105	5,353	5,610
5	5,633	5,975	6,336	6,716	7,115	7,536
6	6,898	7,394	7,923	8,487	9,089	9,730
7	8,214	8,897	9,637	10,436	11,300	12,233
8	9,583	10,491	11,488	12,579	13,776	15,085
9	11,006	12,181	13,487	14,937	16,549	18,337
10	12,486	13,972	15,645	17,531	19,655	22,045
11	14,026	15,870	17,977	20,384	23,133	26,271
12	15,627	17,882	20,495	23,523	27,029	31,089
13	17,292	20,015	23,215	26,975	31,393	36,581
14	19,024	22,276	26,152	30,772	36,280	42,842
15	20,825	24,673	29,324	34,950	41,753	49,980
16	22,698	27,213	32,750	39,545	47,884	58,118
17	24,645	29,906	36,450	44,599	54,750	67,394
18	26,671	32,760	40,446	50,159	62,440	77,969
19	28,778	35,786	44,762	56,275	71,052	90,025
20	30,969	38,993	49,423	63,002	80,699	103,768

TABLE II

The real key to making a million

The magic of compounding is much stronger when applied to regular savings, rather than to a single deposit. At a savings rate of 8 per cent compounded monthly, a 32-year-old can be a millionaire at age 65 simply by saving $500 a month. If savings rates were in the 13 to 14 per cent range, hitting the millionaire class would have taken a period of 10 years less. But when rates are about 6 per cent, it would take seven years longer.

Tables I and II show the importance of time and rates of return in reaching your goal. Table I shows how a single deposit will grow over time at differing rates of return. A more comprehensive table appears at the end of this book in Appendix 2. Table II demonstrates how annual investments of $1,000 grow over different time periods and at different rates of return. Again, a more comprehensive table appears in Appendix 1.

Regardless of the interest rate, the real issue is whether you can raise the dollars you need to save each month. A steady savings program is also the key to successfully using the strategies in this book.

The money for that first step into investing can come from only two sources. A fortunate few may inherit the money, but the rest of us have to get it the old-fashioned way—we must earn it and save it. For most of us, then, becoming rich is merely a dream if we cannot save. And the key to saving is controlling expenditures.

Many savers have found that a budget is essential to control spending. That's why a look at how the typical Canadian household spends money is a useful starting point in developing that all-important budget.

The three big expenses for most Canadians are food, shelter and transportation. Depending on where you live—for instance, it costs a lot less for housing in St. John's than in Vancouver—these three necessities of life can consume as much as two-thirds of the take-home pay of typical Canadians.

As earnings increase, these basic expenses take a smaller percentage of income. The family with an income of $65,000 or more is likely to spend a smaller percentage on food, shelter and transportation than will the family with $30,000 of income. And the family with $100,000 will spend an even smaller percentage.

Credit hurts saving

Clearly, savings prospects are improved if you avoid extravagances. And if you avoid extravagant spending, you may also avoid another costly drain on the budget—interest payments on consumer debt.

Canadians owe more than $100 billion of consumer debt, excluding their more than $300 billion in mortgage debt. Some of that borrowed money was used to buy cars but each year more of our debt is tied to credit cards. Still, there are times when it is necessary to borrow. If the borrowing is for a business or investment, such as investing in securities, some or all of the interest may be deductible for income tax purposes. If interest is deductible, a 6 per cent interest rate shrinks to as little as 3.5 per cent for a person whose marginal tax rate is 41 per cent. But without the tax deduction, interest on consumer debt can be a heavy burden, particularly as the interest on an unpaid balance is compounded. That's when compounding turns vicious.

While deposit rates have plunged, your credit card may charge something like 0.05094 per cent daily on unpaid balances. If that's the case, you could be paying an annual interest rate of 20.43 per cent. At that rate your interest costs will exceed the original balance in three years and nine months.

It is much cheaper to go to a bank, trust company or credit union and borrow to pay off your credit card balance—as long as the personal loan rate is less than your card rate. It is cheaper still to operate on a tight budget and owe nothing for spending that is purely for personal consumption. Even at today's relatively low interest rates, it is far better to be a lender than a borrower.

The first thing you should do is create a budget using Your Family Budget (page 7), if only to get a clearer picture of how you spend your money. If you aren't saving anything now, set a target of 10 per cent, then look for areas where you can cut spending to allow for those savings. Your pay slip will show what you pay in taxes each pay period and your cheque records will provide information about where your money goes. You should also keep track of where you spend your pocket money. Don't forget to include all family members on both the income and expenditure sides. Setting aside money each month is the first step toward becoming a millionaire. You must put in place spending limits that will shave a percentage point or two from those categories that can bear the cut.

Don't give up easily. Food costs can be cut by 10 to 40 per cent by seeking out sales, buying no-name products and shopping at food stores that sell out of shipping cartons and have you pack your own groceries.

It may cause some inconvenience, but becoming a millionaire requires savings—and that is not painless. Those nickels and dimes you can save will add up. Remember, $10 a week is more than $500 a year. And $500 a year invested at 5 per cent for 25 years is almost $24,000. That's a far cry from a million, but it's a start.

You're wealthier than you think

Admittedly, preparing a budget is almost as painful as holding to budgeted spending limits. But measuring wealth, particularly if it is your own, is a most gratifying experience. It is also a very useful exercise.

Most of us are wealthier than we think. We rarely look at the things we own and the money we have in Canada Savings Bonds, a few stocks or mutual funds as an investment portfolio, and so we don't try to maximize gains in overall portfolio value. Furthermore, too often we hold a bag of undiversified assets—a risky practice. While diversification is more difficult for individuals than for professional investment managers, the results can be very rewarding.

To assess your wealth, you need to determine your net worth. You can do this by adding up the value of everything you own and subtracting from that everything you owe. But it isn't really that simple; you have to make some adjustments. You may think your furniture is worth a great deal, and in fact your house insurance should be based on its replacement value. But for net worth purposes, it should be given a value of $1. Your RRSP may be worth $50,000, but you have to pay tax on it when you withdraw. So its true value may be as little as $24,000. Whether you use a pretax or after-tax value depends on your circumstances. But most people should use the pretax value because that is the amount that will continue to grow untaxed until retirement when it will be used to generate a stream of income. You can use Your Financial Balance Worksheet (page 9) as a guide to constructing your personal balance sheet. Don't be shy about changing it to suit your circumstances.

If you are a homeowner, your house is probably your biggest asset, although if you recently purchased a house, your assets may only slightly exceed your liabilities or even be less if you bought in those markets where house prices have since fallen from peak levels. Two of the trickier items to estimate on your balance sheet are life insurance and pensions. Term insurance can be ignored because it has no savings component, but the cash surrender value of whole life insurance should be included.

Estimating the value of pensions is also a problem, although this is made easier if your employer sends you pension investment information. Such information usually includes the present value of your pension, which is the amount to include on your personal balance sheet. It

Your Family Budget

	Earner #1	Earner #2	Earner #3
INCOME			
Employment income			
Interest income			
Dividends			
Pension income			
Rental income			
Business income			
Other income			
TOTAL INCOME			
EXPENSES			
Taxes on income			
Mortgage or rent			
Utilities/property taxes			
Home maintenance			
Furniture			
Transportation/car			
Food			
Clothing			
Dental/medical			
Household contribution			
Loan payments			
Education			
Life and disability insurance			
Entertainment			
Charitable donations			
TOTAL EXPENSES			
SAVINGS			
RRSP/PENSION CONTRIBUTIONS			
OTHER INVESTMENTS			

is quite difficult to estimate the value of some government retirement program payments because benefits are partly indexed to the cost of living and are subject to unforeseen legislative changes. Ottawa does, however, provide a statement on Canada Pension Plan benefits.

The value of savings in RRSPs is easier to determine. For your balance sheet, include the current value, which is indicated on the statements sent to you by the financial institution holding your funds.

Once you've compiled a list of your assets, consider whether they are diversified enough. The older the head of the household, the more diversified the portfolio should be. Insufficient diversification means putting too many of your eggs in one basket—a pitfall for older people, who have less time to recover from financial disasters that might result when an investment goes sour. To introduce diversity into a portfolio, it may be necessary to borrow against other assets.

Typically, an undiversified personal balance sheet will consist mainly of pension claims and a house with a small mortgage or no mortgage at all. Borrowing against equity in the home, and using the proceeds to buy financial assets such as stocks and bonds, does more than just increase diversification. It allows the interest expense on the loan to be used as a deduction for income tax purposes. Furthermore, using investment vehicles that produce capital gains and dividends can offer significant tax benefits.

Home mortgages are the largest single liability for most Canadians. In fact, we have more than $300 billion in outstanding residential mortgages. Moreover, it is a huge pile of debt that is extremely expensive because mortgage interest is not deductible when calculating tax liabilities. For example, if you have a 41 per cent marginal tax rate and are paying $5,000 annually in mortgage interest, you must earn $8,475 to cover your after-tax mortgage interest. Those with a 50 per cent marginal tax rate must earn $10,000.

You can save a bundle if you can reduce your mortgage by agreeing to pay it off in less than the usual 25 years through a rapid amortization or by taking advantage of the annual pay-down that most institutions offer. Look at the situation of a homeowner who has $10,000 in savings beyond rainy-day needs. If he or she is in a 41 per cent tax bracket, earning even 8 per cent before taxes on the savings is not as attractive as using the money to reduce the mortgage. That's because the 8 per cent savings rate is reduced to 4.7 per cent after taxes—a lot less than the interest rate being paid on the mortgage.

For higher-income-bracket earners, the results are even more striking. That 8 per cent before-tax savings rate is only 4 per cent after taxes for someone paying a marginal tax rate of 50 per cent. He or she would be far better off using the savings to pay off the mortgage. For

Your Financial Balance Worksheet

	Earner #1	Earner #2
ASSETS		
Bank accounts		
Canada Savings Bonds		
Other cash investments		
GICs		
Bonds		
Mortgage investments		
Annuities		
RRIFs		
Pensions		
RRSPs		
Stocks		
Mutual funds		
Other investments		
Cash value of life insurance		
Collectibles		
Furniture		
Cars		
House		
Cottage		
TOTAL ASSETS		
LIABILITIES		
Mortgages		
Bank loans		
Credit cards		
Investment loans		
Other debt		
TOTAL LIABILITIES		
NET WORTH		

these high-income-bracket earners, a risk-free rate of more than 15 per cent would be necessary to break even after taxes with an 8 per cent mortgage rate. In mid-1998, variable-rate mortgages were available at rates as low as 6.5 per cent, while five-year deposits paid, at most, 5 per cent interest. Unless someone had investments that locked in higher returns on an after-tax basis, it still made sense to pay off a mortgage as quickly as possible.

Most Canadians are well aware of the horrendous mortgage costs they face and attempt to reduce or eliminate the mortgage as soon as possible. For financial well-being, there's no finer aroma than the smell of a paid-up mortgage being burned to a crisp. (In fact, you should keep the discharged mortgage in your safety-deposit box.)

So fill out your balance sheet and tally your worth. After you have completed your balance sheet, review it with the aim of increasing returns and achieving diversification. Then prepare a target balance sheet, setting targets for both the next few years and the distant future. To make sure you're on track, review these targets each year.

Once you know where you are and where you would like to go, you can use the information and strategies in the rest of this book to build an investment program that will help to ensure that your financial life unfolds as you want. The remaining chapters of the book cover taxation of income, methods of putting your financial house in order, the setting of your investment objectives and your range of investment options.

These are the tools you can use to build your wealth. But there are other tools you must use, the most important of which is information. As an investor who wants to make the highest returns possible without ignoring the risks, you must have a fundamental knowledge of events that have an impact on investment.

Chapter 2

A Financial Tool Kit

Most professional investors in Canada make a point of reading the business press to keep themselves informed of developments in the economy, specific industries and individual companies. Basic reading material includes *The Globe and Mail Report on Business* or *The Financial Post* and, possibly, *The Wall Street Journal*. In addition, numerous specialty publications such as *All-Canadian Mutual Fund Guide* and *Investor's Digest* cover the spectrum of investments. Many investors also buy specialty electronic services such as *PALTrak* mutual fund analysis software or search the Internet.

But you have to learn to walk before you run so start with a newspaper that contains financial tables covering the investment areas that interest you, as well as information on economic or industrial developments and business trends. Start slowly and expand your reading as your understanding increases. Don't run out and buy subscriptions to every business publication available—most will end up unread.

The newspapers you choose should keep you informed about interest rate trends and the current rates available. Table III, the money market table, is taken from *The Globe and Mail Report on Business,* and includes several key short-term interest rates. The 91-day treasury bill rate indicates what the federal government is paying for short-term money. The yields on treasury bills (T-bills) are adjusted by the Bank of Canada to reflect its policies toward economic growth and the level at which it wishes to maintain the international value of the dollar.

All short-term rates, including the rate that banks pay on savings accounts, are based on T-bill yields. The Bank of Canada rate is the rate at which certain deposit-taking institutions can borrow funds from the Bank of Canada. But the key yield, as far as individual investors are concerned, is the T-bill rate.

Money Rates

September 16, 1998

ADMINISTERED RATES

| Bank of Canada | 6.00% | Central bank call range | 5.50–6.00% | Canadian prime | 7.50% |

MONEY MARKET RATES (for transactions of $1-million or more)

3-mo. T-bill (when-issued)	5.14%	1-month banker's accept.	5.57%
1-month treasury bills	5.10%	2-month banker's accept.	5.55%
2-month treasury bills	5.16%	3-month banker's accept.	5.55%
3-month treasury bills	5.17%	**Commercial Paper (R-1 Low)**	
6-month treasury bills	5.17%	1-month	5.60%
1-year treasury bills	5.27%	2-month	5.58%
10-year Canada bonds	5.27%	3-month	5.57%
30-year Canada bonds	5.46%	Call money	5.92%

FEDERAL BILL YIELDS

The average yield at this week's auction of $3.2-billion of 97-day Government of Canada treasury bills was 5.149 per cent, down from 5.642 per cent at the previous auction held on Sept. 1.

Accepted yields for the 97-day bills ranged from a high of 5.154 per cent for a price equivalent of 98.64881 to a low of 5.134 per cent for a price equivalent of 98.65399. The average yield of 5.149 per cent provided a price equivalent of 98.65013.

For an offering of $1.6-billion of 182-day treasury bills, accepted yields ranged from a high of 5.169 per cent for a price equivalent of 97.48734 to a low of 5.152 per cent for a price equivalent of 97.49540. The average yield of 5.165 per cent provided a price equivalent of 97.48920.

For an offering of $1.4-billion of 364-day treasury bills, accepted yields ranged from a high of 5.252 per cent for a price equivalent of 95.02306 to a low of 5.239 per cent for a price equivalent of 95.03477 per cent. The average yield of 5.246 per cent provided a price equivalent of 95.02883.

DOW JONES MARKETS

UNITED STATES

NEW YORK (AP) — Money rates for Tuesday as reported by Bridge Telerate as of 4 p.m.:

Bridge Telerate interest rate index: 5.329

Prime Rate: 8.50

Discount Rate: 5.00

Broker call loan rate: 7.25

Federal funds market rate:

High 5.875; low 5.875; last 5.875

Dealers commercial paper:

30–180 days: 5.50-5.20

Commercial paper by finance company: 30–270 days: 5.47–5.09

Bankers acceptances dealer indications: 30 days, 5.49; 60 days, 5.42; 90 days, 5.36; 120 days, 5.33; 150 days, 5.30; 180 days, 5.25

Certificates of Deposit Primary: 30 days, 4.64; 90 days, 4.86; 180 days, 4.96

Certificates of Deposit by dealer: 30 days, 5.53; 60 days, 5.48; 90 days, 5.43; 120 days, 5.42; 150 days, 5.38; 180 days, 5.34

Eurodollar rates: Overnight, 5.875-6.00; 1 month, 5.46875-5.53125; 3 months, 5.40625-5.46875; 6 months, 5.3125-5.375; 1 year, 5.15625-5.21875

London Interbank Offered Rate: 3 months, 5.50; 6 months, 5.41; 1 year, 5.25

Treasury Bill auction results: average discount rate: 3-month as of Sept. 14: 4.740; 6-month as of Sept. 14: 4.755; 52-week as of Sep. 15: 4.505

Treasury Bill annualized rate on weekly average basis, yield adjusted for constant maturity, 1-year, as of Sep. 14: 4.76

Treasury Bill market rate, 1-year: 4.59-4.57

Treasury Bond market rate, 30-year: 5.25

Source: Bridge Information Systems Canada, Inc., AP

TABLE III

Table IV shows the rates that banks and trust companies are willing to pay for minimum deposits, usually of at least $5,000, and for terms ranging from 30 days to five years. Interest rates quoted by an institution can change at any time, depending on deposit levels at the institution. In fact, rates quoted by an institution on large amounts can change hourly to reflect marketplace trends.

It's also a good idea to keep an eye on bond yields so you can see what governments are paying for medium- and long-term funds. Trends in bond yields have a significant impact on mortgage rates and on insurance company annuity rates.

If you invest, or plan to invest, in the stock market, you will require a publication containing stock tables. Those who trade their stocks daily would certainly want to follow their stocks in a daily newspaper with extensive stock coverage. Otherwise, a weekend paper with substantial business coverage will suffice.

Stock tables provide trading information for the most recent period—including the share prices, price changes over the day or week, the number of shares traded and the price range over which the stock has traded during the past 12 months. They also include dividend information. The indicated dividend is the total dividend payment that would be paid over the next 12 months, based on the latest dividend declared by the company. The dividend may be paid quarterly, semi-annually or annually, depending on company policy.

The Toronto and Montreal stock exchange tables included in *The Globe and Mail Report on Business* give earnings information as well as financial ratios useful to investors. Two common ratios are yield and the price-earnings P/E ratio. The yield is the dividend as a percentage of the stock price; the P/E ratio is the stock price divided by the latest 12-month earnings. A P/E ratio of 12.7 means that an investor is paying $12.70 for each $1 of earnings.

The Globe and Mail uses technical analysis to compile its unique stock tables—Stock Trends. These tables are designed to provide investors with an indication of the long-term trend of individual stocks. Various symbols, such as triangles and circles, are used to indicate whether a stock is likely to increase or decrease in value in the coming weeks, while lines, boldfaced type and stars are used to indicate significant increases

Interest Rates

September 14, 1998

Company	Savings account ($1,000 balance)	Chequing account	Min. deposit	30 days	60 days	90 days	120 days	180 days	270 days	Min. deposit	One year	Two years	Three years	Four years	Five years	Var. rate	6 month open	6 month closed	1 year open	1 year closed	2 year closed	3 year closed	4 year closed	5 year closed
Banks																								
Amex Bank of Canada, Markham	0.50	0.25	5,000		4.25	4.25	4.25	4.50	r4.60	1,000	4.55	4.85	4.85	4.95	5.10			7.30	7.50	6.95	7.05	7.15	7.20	7.30
BCI Bank, Toronto	0.35	0.35	5,000	r4.25	r4.25	4.00	4.00	4.15	r4.60	1,000	4.75	5.00	5.00	5.00	5.20	r7.25	5.55	7.30	7.50	6.95	7.05	7.15	7.20	7.30
Bank of Montreal, Toronto	0.25	0.10	5,000	4.00	4.00	4.00	4.00	4.15	4.20	1,000	4.25	4.50	4.60	4.65	4.90	7.50	7.55	7.30	7.50	6.85	7.05	7.15	7.20	7.30
Bank of Nova Scotia, Toronto	0.25	0.05	500	4.00	4.00	4.00	4.00	4.15	4.20	500	4.25	4.50	4.60	4.65	4.90	c6.48	7.55	7.30	7.50	6.85	7.05	7.15	7.20	7.30
CIBC, Toronto	0.35	0.10	5,000	r4.00	r4.00	r4.00	r4.00	4.15	4.20	1,000	4.50	4.50	4.60	4.80	5.05		7.55	7.30	7.50	6.95	7.05	7.15	7.20	7.30
Citibank, Toronto			5,000	r4.25	r4.25	r4.00	r4.00	r4.30	r4.40	5,000	r4.50	r4.75	r4.80	4.80	5.38		7.25	6.80	7.10	6.40	6.25	7.15	7.20	6.50
Citizens Bank of Canada, Vancouver	0.25	0.15	5,000	r4.25	r4.25	r4.50	r4.50	r4.50	r4.75	1,000	5.13	5.38	5.38	5.38	5.38	7.50	7.25	6.80	7.50	6.40	7.05	6.35	6.40	6.50
HongKong Bank, Vancouver			5,000	4.00	4.00	4.00	4.00	4.30	4.40	1,000	4.50	4.75	4.80	4.80	r5.50		7.55	7.30	7.50	6.95	7.05	7.15	7.20	6.40
ING Direct, North York	4.75		1							1	r5.00	r5.00	r5.25	r5.25	r5.50									6.40
Laurentian Bank, Montreal	0.05	0.01	5,000	3.80	3.80	3.80	4.00	4.00	4.20	1,000	4.50	4.75	4.80	4.85	5.05		7.70	7.30	7.50	6.40	7.05	7.15	7.20	7.30
Manulife Bank, Waterloo			25,000	4.90	4.95	4.95	4.95	4.95	4.95	500	5.05	5.05	5.15	5.20	5.30									
National Bank of Greece, Montreal	0.02	0.02	5,000	4.00	4.00	3.80	3.75	4.25	4.38	1,000	4.50	4.75	4.88	4.78	5.25		7.55	7.30	7.50	6.95	7.05	7.15	7.20	7.30
National Bank, Montreal			50,000	3.75	3.75	3.75	4.15	4.15	4.20	50,000	4.35	4.50	4.73	4.78	5.03		7.55	7.30	7.50	6.95	7.05	7.15	7.20	7.30
Republic National Bk NY, Montreal	0.30	0.15	5,000	4.30	4.30	4.25	4.15	4.15	4.20	500	4.35	4.70	4.75	4.75	4.80	7.50	7.55	7.30	7.50	6.95	7.05	7.15	7.20	7.30
Royal Bank of Canada, Montreal	0.35	0.15	5,000	4.00	4.00	4.00	4.00	4.15	4.20	1,000	4.25	4.55	4.60	4.65	4.85	7.50	7.55	7.30	7.50	6.95	7.05	7.15	7.20	7.30
Toronto-Dominion Bank, Toronto																								
Trust Companies																								
AGF Trust Co., Toronto			10,000	r3.25	r3.25	r3.25	r3.25	r3.25	r3.25	5,000	5.10	5.10	5.10	5.25	5.25			7.30		6.95	7.05	7.15	7.20	7.30
Canada Trust, Toronto	1.00		5,000	r4.00	r4.00	r4.00	r4.00	r4.00	r4.40	1,000	4.25	4.50	4.60	4.65	4.90	7.50	7.55	7.30	7.50	6.95	7.05	7.15	7.20	7.30
Citizens Trust, Vancouver			5,000	r4.25	r4.25	r4.50	r4.50	r4.50	r4.75	1,000	5.00	5.25	5.25	5.25	5.25		7.55	7.30						
Co-Operative Trust, Saskatoon			5,000	3.75	3.75	3.75	3.75	4.05	4.15	500	4.75	5.00	5.05	5.10	5.30		7.55	7.30	7.50	6.95	7.05	7.15	7.35	7.45
Effort Trust, Hamilton	1.00	1.00	5,000	3.00	3.00	3.25	3.25	3.25	3.75	5,000	5.00	5.00	5.25	5.38	5.45	7.50	7.55	7.30	7.50	6.57	7.30	7.15	7.40	7.45
Equitable Trust, Toronto			5,000	4.50	5.10	5.10	5.10	5.10	5.10	5,000	5.25	4.00	5.50	4.00	5.55			7.20		7.20	7.30	7.35	7.40	6.58
FirstLine Mortgages, Toronto										1,000	4.50	4.75	4.80	4.85	5.05	c6.29	7.55	7.30		6.95	7.05	6.67	7.20	7.30
Investors Group Trust, Winnipeg																	7.55	7.20		6.95	7.05	7.10	7.20	7.30
Montreal Trust, Montreal	0.35	0.15	1,000	4.00	4.00	4.00	4.00	4.00	4.20	500	4.25	4.50	4.60	4.65	4.90	7.50	7.55	7.30	7.50	6.95	7.05	7.15	7.20	7.30
National Trust, Toronto	0.75	0.63	1,000	4.80	4.80	4.80	4.50	2.30	3.05	1,000	5.13	5.35	5.40	5.40	5.45	7.50	7.55	7.30	7.50	6.95	7.05	7.15	6.45	7.30
Peace Hills Trust, Edmonton			5,000	4.25	4.50	4.50	4.50	2.30	4.20	5,000	4.75	5.00	4.80	4.85	4.90			7.20		6.95	7.05	7.15	6.45	7.30
Peoples Trust, Vancouver	0.30	0.30	5,000	3.63	3.75	4.75	4.75	3.88	4.00	500	5.15	5.00	5.13	5.13	4.90	7.50	7.55	7.30	7.50	6.95	7.05	7.15	7.20	7.30
Royal Trust, Toronto			25,000	4.75	4.75	4.75	4.75	4.30	4.75	1,000	5.00	5.25	5.25	5.35	5.38		7.55	7.30	7.50	6.95	7.05	7.15	7.20	7.30
Standard Life Trust, Montreal	1.00	1.00	5,000	4.30	4.30	4.30	4.30	4.60	4.60	1,000	5.00	5.20	5.25	5.30	5.50	7.50	6.60	7.00	7.00	6.70	6.45	7.30
Sun Life Trust, Toronto																								
Trimark Trust, Toronto			5,000	3.75	3.75	3.75	3.75	4.15	4.20	1,000	4.25	4.50	4.73	4.73	5.03		7.55	7.30	7.50	6.95	7.05	7.15	7.20	7.30
Trust General, Montreal																								
Other Institutions																								
Alberta Treasury Branch, Edmonton			1,000	4.00	4.00	4.00	4.00	4.15	4.20	1,000	4.25	4.50	4.60	4.65	4.90	7.50	7.55	7.30	7.50	6.95	7.05	7.15	7.20	7.30
Avestel Credit Union, Hamilton			500	4.00	4.00	4.00	4.00	4.40	4.40	500	4.50	4.75	4.80	4.85	5.05	7.75	7.55	7.30	7.55	6.95	7.05	7.15	7.20	7.45
CS COOP Credit Union, Ottawa			5,000	r3.00	r3.00	r3.00	r3.00	r3.50	r3.50	1,000	4.50	4.75	4.80	4.85	5.25	7.50	7.70	7.45	7.75	7.20	7.30	7.35	7.45
Canada Life, Toronto	0.25	0.25	1,000	3.75	3.75	3.75	3.75	4.05	4.15	1,000	4.25	4.50	4.60	4.65	4.90		7.55	7.30	7.50	6.95	7.05	7.15	7.20	7.30
Capital City Savings, Edmonton										10,000	r4.75	r5.00	r5.13	r5.13	r4.88									
Commercial Union Life, Scarborough										500	r4.45	r4.45	r4.60	r4.60	r4.85									
Empire Life, Kingston										500	r4.50	r4.40	r4.40	r4.45	r4.88									
Equitable Life, Waterloo	1.00	1.00	5,000	4.00	4.00	4.00	4.00	4.15	4.20	500	r4.25	r4.40	r4.40	r4.45	r4.48		7.50	7.30	7.50	6.95	7.05	7.15	7.20	7.30
Fede Des Caisses De Mtl, Montreal	0.25	0.15	5,000	r4.00	r4.00	r4.00	r4.00	4.15	r4.40	1,000	4.25	4.50	4.60	4.65	4.90	7.50	7.55	7.30	7.50	6.95	7.05	7.15	7.20	7.30
Hepcoe Credit Union, Toronto	0.25	0.15	5,000	4.00	4.00	4.00	4.00	r4.30	5.10	1,000	4.50	r4.75	4.80	r4.85	r5.05	7.50	7.55	7.30	7.50	6.95	7.05	7.15	7.20	7.30
Home Savings & Loan, St. Catharines			1,000	4.00	5.10	5.10	5.10	5.10	r3.34	5,000	5.15	5.30	5.30	5.35	5.45		7.55	7.00		6.60	6.70	6.45	6.45	7.30
London Life, London										1,000	4.25	4.50	4.63	4.63	4.88									
MICAP Mortgage Corp., Toronto										1,000	4.88	5.00	5.13	5.13	5.25	7.50	7.55	7.30	7.50	6.95	7.05	7.15	7.20	7.30
Manulife Financial, Waterloo			5,000							5,000	r4.38	r4.38	r4.38	r4.38	r4.50	7.55	7.30	7.50	6.95	7.05	7.15	7.20	7.30
Maritime Life, Halifax			10,000							10,000	3.75	4.00	4.25	4.25	4.67	7.70	7.45	7.75	7.20	7.30	7.35	7.45
NN Financial, Don Mills			500	4.25	4.25	4.25	4.25	4.25	4.65	500	4.25	4.30	4.50	4.50	4.75									
National Life, Toronto	1.95	1.95													c7.13									
President's Choice Fin'l, Toronto		0.75								500	4.90	5.00	5.05	5.10	5.15		7.40	6.77	6.67	6.54	6.42	6.30	
Prov Ont Savings Office, Oshawa			5,000	3.25	3.38	3.38	3.38			10,000	4.88	4.88	4.88	4.88	r4.63									
Standard Life, Montreal										10,000	4.50	r4.63	r4.63	r4.63	5.13									
SunLife of Canada, Toronto	1.00	1.00	1,000		2.63					1,000	4.75	5.00	5.00	5.00	5.20									
Surrey Metro Savings, Surrey										1,000	r3.85	r3.95	r4.10	r4.20	r4.30									
Transamerica Life, Scarborough			5,000	4.00	4.00	4.00	4.00	4.50	4.50	500	4.50	4.75	4.80	4.85	5.05									
VanCity Savings (BC), Vancouver										5,000	r3.63	r3.88	r4.00	r4.13	r4.13									
Westbury Canadian Life, Hamilton																								

Savings Rates — Interest paid at maturity (30–270 days); Interest paid annually (One year–Five years). Mortgage Rates span 6 month open through 5 year closed.

This survey of rates offered by a sample group of companies was prepared by Cannex Financial Exchanges, Sep. 21, 1998, at 10:15 a.m.
Savings rates are non-redeemable except where indicated by an "r." Variable mortgage rates are open except where indicated by a "c."
Rates are for information purposes only and should be confirmed by the company quoted.

Canadian Indexes

September 16, 1998

TORONTO STOCK EXCHANGE

52 week High	Low	Index	Open	High	Low	Close	Chg	% Chg	Vol (100s)	Div yield	Avg. P/E	Tot. Ret.
7822.25	5530.71	TSE 300	5892.82	5945.93	5848.98	5857.04	−22.36	−0.4	670062	1.82	24.94	12258.90
473.10	317.73	TSE 200	335.48	335.40	333.90	334.39	+1.13	+0.3	330021	0.91	101.93	355.69
475.63	338.52	TSE 100	362.36	366.17	357.62	359.76	−1.89	−0.5	340041	2.01	21.67	403.56
425.37	299.00	TSE 35	330.57	338.14	326.35	328.14	−2.05	−0.6	237382	2.20	23.78	567.87

TSE 300 SUBGROUPS

Index	High	Low	Close	Chg	Vol	Index	High	Low	Close	Chg	Vol
Metals & minerals	2898.65	2849.93	2870.74	+19.95	7227108	Autos & parts	18102.06	17751.43	18027.48	+148.51	212251
Integrated mines	3093.96	3039.31	3062.75	+20.79	2391820	Real estate & const	2105.82	2075.29	2077.59	−15.91	561525
Mining	1332.68	1296.16	1318.13	+10.17	4835288	Transport & envir	5642.58	5555.46	5586.80	+38.94	2791827
Gold & prec minrls	5761.86	5591.12	5591.12	−47.49	5068777	Pipelines	6323.10	6232.81	6285.49	+51.69	614623
Oil & gas	5174.84	5107.79	5111.71	+30.40	24287908	Utilities	6576.04	6383.72	6383.72	−102.72	2943691
Integrated oils	7675.89	7504.13	7520.17	−55.78	1003450	Telephone utils	6547.67	6326.97	6326.97	−129.53	2500241
Oil & gas prdcr	4626.84	4560.87	4577.13	+46.43	21578538	Gas & electrical	5887.49	5836.11	5871.02	+53.31	443450
Oil & gas srvc	1456.23	1407.50	1436.31	+39.55	1705920	Comm & media	13375.55	13142.99	13277.83	+176.93	889078
Paper & forest	3508.38	3475.81	3505.43	+44.96	1623253	Broadcasting	9796.52	9674.78	9740.99	+36.68	328573
Consumer products	9948.52	9836.27	9860.59	+23.74	1139994	Cable & ent	21486.13	20867.40	21076.36	+167.23	154065
Food processing	7506.23	7476.12	7498.82	+15.29	69552	Publishing	15026.17	14680.67	14868.17	+263.77	406440
Tobacco	29107.60	28653.51	28653.51		352098	Merchandising	5189.86	5090.11	5090.11	−28.09	1885201
Distilleries	12189.12	11903.05	12114.49	+161.69	162478	Wholesale	6871.85	6754.05	6754.05	−161.79	83356
Breweries/bev	5035.43	4850.10	4850.10	−166.79	51187	Food stores	15712.26	15583.13	15678.29	+9.55	453278
Household gds	1451.11	1412.06	1446.86	+8.26	59334	Dept stores	1236.45	1198.87	1198.87	−1.42	555995
Biotech/pharm	1321.61	1309.18	1310.26	−8.47	445345	Specialty stores	2046.67	1970.43	2003.83	−23.07	546813
Industrial products	4267.65	4147.05	4172.66	−90.24	10111243	Hospitality	42253.74	39549.78	39549.78	−266.99	245759
Steel	1103.15	1084.87	1089.68	+9.29	672086	Financial services	7428.68	7314.64	7319.54	+9.89	6980844
Fabricating/eng	4410.31	4377.12	4391.06	−1.97	206789	Banks & trusts	7849.51	7700.48	7704.20	−18.77	6034419
Transport equip	63120.63	60305.85	60305.85	−517.97	1486896	Invest co & fund	12108.02	11853.38	11853.38	+12.81	426699
Tech hardware	13408.51	12797.33	12944.69	−583.33	6404061	Insurance	12993.60	12619.79	12713.57	−170.74	31481
Building material	5861.31	5771.35	5824.87	+17.51	152143	Financial mangmt cos	3754.67	3569.34	3719.58	+152.14	488245
Chem & fertilizer	4767.49	4719.91	4722.86	+13.56	490876	Conglomerates	8322.60	8151.38	8278.67	+39.79	881161
Tech software	1725.82	1680.32	1700.97	−27.23	486141						

TSE 100 SUBGROUPS

Index	High	Low	Close	Chg	Vol
Consumer	351.25	344.30	346.03	+1.82	2733844
Industrial	410.46	397.81	401.80	−6.47	11564349
Interest sensitive	530.50	518.21	521.02	−2.20	10095062
Resource	230.70	226.08	226.80		9610871

THE DAY'S TSE 300

The TSE 300 composite index through the day yesterday, showing the change each hour from the previous day's close

9.45 a.m.	5892.82	+13.42	1 p.m.	5904.12	+24.72
10 a.m.	5922.54	+43.14	2 p.m.	5909.03	+29.63
11 a.m.	5910.57	+31.17	3 p.m.	5848.98	−30.42
Noon	5904.08	+24.68	4 p.m.	5857.04	−22.36

MONTREAL EXCHANGE

52-week high	low	Index	Open	High	Low	Close	Chg	% Chg	Vol (100s)	Div yield	Avg P/E
3965.05	2804.59	Mkt portfolio	3078.72	3117.97	3053.19	3056.24	−13.72	−0.5	210847	2.05	21.74
8094.75	4791.38	Banking	5441.85	5518.37	5422.72	5429.09	+1.06	+0.0	65983	2.99	11.30
3015.61	1822.10	Forest prod	2009.10	2034.18	2009.10	2027.34	+23.94	+1.2	16624	2.68	32.33
4311.21	3151.21	Industrial prod	3348.69	3377.01	3273.49	3299.07	−57.84	−1.7	80629	1.30	16.11
2951.05	1456.94	Mining	1748.42	1761.05	1737.89	1737.89			49159	2.12	86.69
3054.50	1890.23	Oil & gas	2229.16	2258.93	2226.22	2226.22	−7.97	−0.4	45192	1.34	30.92
4528.30	3091.27	Utilities	3835.89	3863.51	3816.88	3816.87	−11.66	−0.3	35078	3.53	56.39

VANCOUVER

52-week high	low	Index	Open	High	Low	Close	Chg	% Chg	Vol
843.64	388.08	Composite	409.20	409.13	406.82	407.05	−2.15	−0.5	13632424

ALBERTA

52-week high	low	Index	Open	High	Low	Close	Chg	% Chg	Vol
2611.12	1181.38	Alberta Combin	1745.01	1749.05	1741.16	1748.86	+3.85	+0.2	11382880

Source: Bridge Information Systems Canada Inc.

TABLE V

or decreases in volume of shares traded or price. The tables also include each stock's P/E ratio, book value and cash-flow ratio.

Even if you don't follow individual stocks, you should keep an eye on the major stock market indexes. Virtually every major newspaper with a business section has a market summary graph and table as well as a commentary on the latest developments.

Mutual fund investors can find a daily table of fund prices in most major papers. *The Globe and Mail's* monthly survey of investment funds groups funds according to investment objectives, so you can compare your funds' performance against funds with similar objectives.

If you are an active investor in the U.S. markets, you'll probably want a newspaper with extensive U.S. stock trading information. This information is available in *The Globe and Mail Report on Business, The Wall Street Journal* and *Barron's*, a U.S. financial weekly. You'll also want a daily newspaper with complete tables if your investment interests extend to the options and futures markets. Because prices can be extremely volatile, you must remain well informed in order to make decisions quickly.

Corporate financial statements

Once you're adept at following business news and reading market tables, you should turn your attention to corporate financial statements. To do so, you don't have to become an expert investment analyst, but if you're interested in getting better returns on your investments than you've earned up until now, it's essential that you learn the basics of financial statements.

Even if you plan to keep your money in the largest financial institutions or invest only in corporate bonds, you should learn to read a company's financial report. It is rare for an institution to get into trouble overnight and financial statements can offer valuable warnings of impending difficulties.

By law, every public company must issue an annual report covering financial results for its latest fiscal year. The company must also provide updates through quarterly reports, although these contain less detail. Companies selling securities to the public must issue a prospectus that includes all of the information a person needs to decide whether to invest.

Surprisingly, few people take the time to look at annual reports, which is a shame because the information provided can help investors understand the company. Even if you don't examine the financial statements, the management's discussion and financial review section of the report is helpful because of its description of the company's operations and its essential information about earnings and developments. This review interprets the financial statements for the reader.

An annual report can generally be divided into a number of areas. The first is the report from the board of directors, chairman or president. It usually reviews the company's operations during the year and often gives management's views of the outlook for the company and its industry. Of course, such reports try to show the company in a positive light.

Some investors ignore annual reports and financial statements because they expect their brokerage firm to deal with this information. In fact, the analysts employed by a brokerage house do watch for developments in companies whose shares have been recommended by the firm. Similarly, many people invest in mutual funds in order to have professional managers carry out this investment analysis for them. Even so, it makes sense to understand the basics so you can interpret results yourself—the experts aren't always right.

If you plan to invest in smaller companies, you must learn to conduct your own analysis. While major brokerage houses follow major companies and provide detailed research reports, few provide studies of smaller firms. Sometimes the necessary information is not readily available, in which case it's best to stay away from the company—large or small—as an investment.

Although financial statements may seem intimidating, they are not difficult to understand. Once you've made your way through the report from the president, chairman or board of directors, you'll find four statements you shouldn't ignore. These are:

- the balance sheet;
- the statement of earnings, which shows revenues, expenses and earnings or losses;
- the consolidated statement of retained earnings, which shows the portion of earnings retained or reinvested in the business;
- and the statement of changes in financial position, which shows how the company financed its operations.

The financial statements of ABC Ltd. will help make the value of these statements clearer. The operating statement, corporate balance sheet and statement of retained earnings are fictitious and the statements are simplified. But by examining them you can see the basics that can be applied to analyzing genuine statements.

ABC Ltd. Operating Statement

FOR THE YEAR ENDED DEC. 31

	1998 (000)	1997 (000)
REVENUE		
Sales of products, fees earned	$150,000	$125,000
EXPENSES		
Cost of sales and services	$125,000	$110,000
Depreciation	4,000	3,500
Interest on long-term debt	5,000	4,500
Other interest	2,000	1,500
TOTAL EXPENSES	**136,000**	**−119,500**
Earnings before taxes	14,000	5,500
Taxes	6,000	3,000
NET EARNINGS	**8,000**	**−2,500**
Earnings per share	**$0.80**	**−$0.25**

TABLE VI

On the ABC Ltd. operating statement, the first line includes the revenue that the company received from the sale of its goods or services. From this, you subtract the company's expenses. The cost of goods and services includes the cost of goods sold, labour expenses, heat and light, rent and so on.

ABC Ltd. Statement of Retained Earnings

AS AT DEC. 31

	1998 (000)	1997 (000)
Balance at beginning of year	$19,000	$17,000
Add net earnings	9,000	2,500
Less dividends paid	2,000	500
Balance at end of year	$26,000	$519,000

TABLE VII

Depreciation is an expense that takes into consideration the declining value of equipment because of wear and tear—not a cash expense. For example, if a piece of machinery cost $1 million and has a life span of five years, it would be depreciated by $200,000 each year. That amount would be considered an expense, even though $200,000 wasn't spent. In our example, the total depreciation charged in 1996 is $4 million.

The company may have financed its operations by issuing a bond. The interest paid on this debt is shown separately from interest on short-term debt, usually money borrowed from a bank. Bank borrowings can be repaid at any time and consequently are considered short-term debt and would appear as "other interest."

Subtracting expenses from revenues results in pretax earnings. From these a company will pay taxes, leaving it with net earnings. Often a company will report current and deferred income taxes. Current taxes generally refer to taxes that are required for immediate tax purposes and deferred income taxes are generally segregated for accounting purposes. Earnings per share represents total earnings divided by the number of shares outstanding. In this case, we've assumed that the company has 10 million shares outstanding.

Investors can apply a number of profitability ratios to the income statement. For example, you might look for trends of increased or decreased profitability by comparing the yearly change in the cost of goods sold as a percentage of revenues. Or you could compare this ratio with that of competing companies. Most important is the net profit margin—the percentage of earnings over revenues. Compare this ratio with previous years and with similar companies in order to find trends. When looking at ratios, don't compare companies in different industries since ratios vary widely from industry to industry.

A corporate balance sheet can also provide insight into the health of the company. The balance sheet, a snapshot of the company's financial position, is broken into three sections:

- the company's assets, which are divided into liquid assets, cash and assets that can be quickly turned to cash; and fixed assets, such as buildings and machinery.
- liabilities, which is what the company owes. Current liabilities, such as bank loans, are liabilities that are due within one year. Long-term liabilities, such as bonds and mortgages, refer to debts that are due at some date beyond one year.

- shareholders' equity, which is the difference between assets and liabilities. Shareholders' equity is made up of share capital—the value of shares sold to the public based on the price paid to the company rather than on market value—and retained earnings. Retained earnings are the profits that have been reinvested in the company. An example of a statement of retained earnings is shown in Table VII. This statement shows that of the $9 million profit, $2 million was paid out as dividends, leaving $7 million for reinvestment. Shareholders' equity generally grows by the amount of retained earnings.

ABC Ltd. Balance Sheet

AS AT DEC. 31

	1998 (000)	1997 (000)
ASSETS		
Cash and investments	$20,000	$16,500
Inventory	30,000	10,000
Total current assets	50,000	26,500
Land	8,000	8,000
Buildings	40,500	42,500
Equipment	30,000	36,000
Less accumulated depreciation	12,000	8,000
Net fixed assets	66,500	78,500
Total assets	$116,500	$105,000
LIABILITIES		
Current liabilities	$20,000	$16,000
Bank loans	20,000	16,000
Total current liabilities	50,000	50,000
Long-term debt	70,000	66,000
SHAREHOLDERS' EQUITY		
Share capital	$20,000	$20,000
Retained earnings	26,000	19,000
Total shareholders' equity	46,000	39,000
Total liabilities and shareholders' equity	$116,000	$105,000

TABLE VIII

Again, a number of financial ratios should be examined. One of the most important is the current ratio, which is current assets divided by current liabilities. In the case of ABC Ltd., the current ratio is 1.5 to 1— calculated by dividing $30 million by $20 million. The ratio indicates that the company has more than enough short-term assets available to pay off its current liabilities. Depending on the industry, a ratio of about one to one is reason for concern, although in some cyclical industries investors would require a much higher ratio to ensure that liabilities are met and operations continue during down cycles.

Another important yardstick is the debt-to-equity ratio. In our example of ABC Ltd., the value of outstanding long-term debt exceeds the value of fixed assets, with the ratio being about 1.13 to one. This is acceptable in some industries, such as utilities, where earnings are assured. However, it is not healthy for a company in a cyclical industry.

Analysis of financial ratios is extremely important for people investing in debt such as corporate bonds or in guaranteed investment certificates in excess of what is covered by deposit insurance. If you are investing in corporate bonds, your broker can provide you with the information you need to judge the quality of the issue. But if you are in doubt or cannot understand what you are being told, stick with investments that are backed by government guarantees.

The financial statements in an annual report also include the auditors' report to the shareholders, which states that the company's independent auditors examined the statements in the annual report and are satisfied that they are accurate. Rarely will auditors make a qualified statement indicating concern about a company's viability as an ongoing concern. When they do, it is a warning that should not be ignored. It is not the auditors' job to look for fraud. Instead, they review how the company prepared its statements and decide whether they are reasonable.

The statements also include a series of notes that give substantial information about the company's accounting policies, transactions involving officers and directors, important lawsuits, if any, and information on long-term commitments such as leases. Reading these notes helps to build your understanding of the company.

After you've learned enough about statement analysis to enable you to ask the right questions, you are ready for the next step—learning about the different types of investments offered in Canada.

Debt versus equity

There are two major categories of investment. One is debt, the other is equity. In the case of debt, you lend your money to a government, corporation or individual. In return, you are promised the payment of interest and the return of your principal at the end of a set period. Common examples of debt investments are savings accounts, Canada Savings Bonds and guaranteed investment certificates.

The safety of your money depends on the financial strength of the issuer and whether your funds are insured or guaranteed by a third party. Money on deposit with a bank or trust company is insured up to $60,000 in principal and interest for each institution by the Canada Deposit Insurance Corporation. Credit unions have a similar arrangement. Canada Savings Bonds are guaranteed by the federal government. Some bonds are secured by specific assets, just like a mortgage is secured by property.

Some debt instruments, however, are a great deal safer than others. The subsidiaries of Principal Group that offered investment contracts may have guaranteed these instruments, but their guarantees were worthless when the parent company in Edmonton collapsed.

Here's a good rule to follow: If you aren't going to take the time to analyze the creditworthiness of an issuer of debt, stick with deposits that are backed by a government guarantee or are insured. For amounts above those covered by deposit insurance, stick with the largest banks and trust companies.

Lenders invest in debt. If you invest in equity, such as common stocks, you become an owner and can share in the profits of enterprises. If you choose your investments carefully, you will profit through gains in their value and increased cash flow through dividend payments.

Chapter 3

Tax Rules: Increasing Your Take

As an investor, it is essential that you understand the income tax system and how it applies to investment income. Otherwise you could end up paying more tax than you should.

There are two key points to consider: how different types of investment income are taxed, and what you can and cannot do to split income among family members to reduce your family tax bill.

Since the introduction of tax reform in 1988, Canadians have three tax brackets, down from the previous 10. Federal income tax rates are 17 per cent on the first $29,590 of taxable income, 26 per cent on taxable income from $29,591 to $59,180, and 29 per cent on anything more than $59,180. These brackets increase each year based on a formula tied to inflation. Your federal tax is reduced by tax credits. All taxpayers receive a basic personal tax credit, which replaces the former basic personal deduction. Depending on your circumstances, you may be eligible for other credits, such as those for child support or spousal support.

Although personal tax rates were supposed to drop with the introduction of tax reform, the actual federal tax rates you pay are higher because of surtaxes. These are taxes paid on top of your base federal taxes.

In addition to federal tax, you must pay provincial tax of about 50 to 55 per cent of the federal rate. Provincial taxes vary from province to province. If your top marginal federal tax rate is 26 per cent, your combined top federal-provincial rate will be about 40 per cent, not including surtaxes. If your top federal rate is 29 per cent, your combined federal-provincial rate will be about 50 per cent. You will also face provincial surtaxes—taxes on taxes—which vary from province to province; these depend on your income level and can push your marginal tax rate as high as 54 per cent.

Top Marginal Tax Rates

PROVINCE	RATE	PROVINCE	RATE
Alberta	45.6%	NWT	44.4%
British Columbia	54.2%	Ontario	50.9%
Manitoba	50.1%	Prince Edward Island	50.3%
New Brunswick	50.4%	Quebec	52.6%
Newfoundland	53.3%	Saskatchewan	51.6%
Nova Scotia	49.7%	Yukon Territory	46.6%

The table shows the maximum tax rate you would pay on salary income. The rate of tax that you pay depends on the province in which you live; provincial rates are a percentage of federal rates and vary widely. Moreover, provincial surtaxes, which have pushed top marginal tax rates higher in recent years, vary from province to province and kick in at different levels. For example, the top Ontario rate applies to income over $63,500 while the threshold for New Brunswick is $98,000.

TABLE IX

The taxes you pay on money earned through investment depend not only on your marginal tax rate, but also on the source of the investment income. Interest from Canadian and foreign sources and dividends from foreign corporations are the most heavily taxed, followed by Canadian dividends and capital gains.

You'll pay your full marginal tax rate on interest income and on dividends from foreign companies, whether paid directly to you or through a mutual fund. If you have $1,000 of interest income and your marginal tax rate is 41 per cent, the tax bill comes to $410. Until 1988, the first $1,000 of interest income was exempt from tax because of an investment income deduction that disappeared with tax reform. Interest is taxed in the year earned, whether you receive it or leave it to compound.

Dividends from Canadian corporations are treated differently. This treatment is designed to reflect the fact that dividends are paid from profits that in most cases have already been taxed, and to encourage investors to invest in common and preferred shares. If you receive dividends from Canadian corporations, your tax rate on those payments will be reduced by the federal dividend tax credit.

Calculating the tax on dividends can be complicated. The amount on which you base your federal tax calculation is 125 per cent of the actual

Taxation of Interest and Dividends

	INTEREST	DIVIDEND
Interest received	S100.00	—
Dividend received	—	$100.00
Dividend "gross up"	—	$25.00
Taxable dividend	—	$125.00
Federal tax (29%)	$29.00	$36.25
Less dividend tax credit	—	$16.67
Net federal tax + surtax	$29.87	$20.17
Add provincial tax*	$15.66	$10.57
Total tax paid	$44.66	$30.74
NET RETURN	**S55.34**	**S69.26**

*54% of basic federal tax. Provincial tax rates vary from province to province.

TABLE X

dividend received—known as the "grossed-up" figure. If you receive $100 in dividends, this $100 is increased by 25 per cent to $125, against which you calculate federal tax. From this figure you subtract the dividend tax credit, which is 13.33 per cent of the grossed-up dividend, or 16.67 per cent of the dividend actually received. This amount is then subtracted from your federal tax.

Table X compares the taxation of interest and dividend income. The calculation assumes that the investor pays tax at the top marginal rate and has a provincial tax rate of 54 per cent of the federal rate. Surtaxes are ignored.

In the end, the dividend tax credit reduces the tax you pay on dividends from Canadian corporations so that, on a before-tax basis, $1 of dividends is equal to about $1.26 of interest—a ratio that holds true no matter which federal tax bracket you're in. As a result, a 6.4 per cent after-tax dividend is equal to an 8 per cent interest yield, an 8 per cent dividend is equal to a 10 per cent interest yield and a 12 per cent dividend is equal to a 15 per cent interest yield. The exception is the individual whose income is limited to dividend income. About $21,000 can be earned tax free.

If you live in Quebec, you'll find some variance in your after-tax interest and dividend income because the province sets its own income tax rates, independent of federal rates. A Quebec resident paying the top federal and provincial tax rates would net about $47 from $100 of interest income, $61 from $100 of dividend income.

Capital gains are taxed differently. First, it is comforting to know that not all of the capital gains you earn are taxed. In fact, 25 per cent of capital gains earned is untaxed, leaving only 75 per cent unsheltered from the tax collector's grasp. Therefore, if you have $100 of capital gains, $75 is taxable. If you're paying the top marginal tax rate, that will result in tax of about $38.00 and net earnings of $62.00.

Until the February 22, 1994, federal budget, Ottawa allowed each taxpayer a lifetime capital gains exemption of $100,000. This applied to gross capital gains, as opposed to taxable capital gains, and affected just about any capital gain earned—including stock market profits and profits from selling precious metals. (Gains from the sale of a family's principal residence are exempt from tax and had no bearing on the lifetime exemption.) Ottawa changed the rules regarding real estate capital gains and lifetime capital gains in its February 1992, budget, excluding real estate gains from the lifetime exemption unless it was part of a business or a farm.

Borrowing to invest

Interest on money borrowed for investment can be deducted from your income when filing your tax return. If your marginal tax rate is 50 per cent and you borrow money at 7.25 per cent, your after-tax cost is only 3.625 per cent; if your marginal tax rate is 41 per cent, your after-tax cost of borrowing is 4.278 per cent. Many people are attracted to leveraging—borrowing for investment—because of the relatively low after-tax cost of borrowing. However, it is important to realize that an individual who chooses not to borrow for investment has the use of the funds that would otherwise be paid as interest. Any comparisons of borrowing versus not borrowing to invest must include the use of this capital.

If you are approached to buy mutual funds using borrowed money, make some projections. In these projections, use several rates of return and various different interest rates for your cost of borrowing. By doing this you will have a range of possible results and can understand your potential risks and rewards. You should also determine the cushion you must have to protect yourself against a rise in interest rates or a fall in the market. Before implementing your leverage program, ask yourself whether you could afford to continue with a leverage program if interest rates rose sharply. Similarly, determine the magnitude of a market correction your bank will tolerate before asking you to put up additional security. In fact, you might want to have a generous credit line available to provide additional security.

The two examples in Table XI look at the results of leverage under certain circumstances and specific assumptions. In each case, we've allocated interest rates of 5.75 per cent, which is a recent level and among the lowest prime rates of the past two decades, and 13.75 per cent, the prevailing prime rate of only a few years ago. For rates of return, we are using 10 per cent, 15 per cent, 30 per cent and -20 per cent We've assumed that the investor's marginal tax rate is 50 per cent.

The cost and rates of return are realistic for one-year holding periods and reflect the experience of the past two decades. Just remember that only a handful of funds have managed to produce long-term rates of return in excess of 15 per cent and these are virtually all high-risk funds.

If you wish to make your own projections using longer holding periods, you should consider any taxes that might be payable on capital gains and dividend distributions. These could have a significant impact on your ability to continue your leverage program if you have limited cash flow and must take some profits to meet your tax bill.

We have made one important assumption that you shouldn't overlook. We have assumed that the investor who does not choose a leverage program will invest the cash flow that would otherwise be available for payment of interest. The interest on $100,000 using 5.75 per cent rate is, of course, $5,750, and has an after-tax cost of $2,875, the amount that the investor who does not use leverage has available for investment. Using the higher rate of 13.75 per cent or $13,750, the after-tax cost is $6,875.

If our investors borrow at 5.75 per cent, Table XI shows in the first set of examples a gain of 10 per cent on the capital invested over the year. The leveraged investor receives double the gain—$20,000—and pays twice as much tax but earns double the after-tax profit of $12,500 (excluding interest costs). The investor who doesn't use leverage has an after-tax profit of $6,250 and also has the after-tax value of that interest to invest, about $2,875. Consequently, his or her net worth grows by $9,125 over the year compared with $12,500 for the investor who borrows funds.

Borrowing to Invest—Two Examples

BORROWING TO INVEST AT 5.75% INTEREST

RETURN ON YOUR INVESTMENT	10%		15%		30%		-20%	
	WITHOUT LEVERAGE	WITH LEVERAGE	WITHOUT LEVERAGE	WITH LEVERAGE	WITHOUT LEVERAGE	WITH LEVERAGE	WITHOUT LEVERAGE	WITH LEVERAGE
Equity	$100,000	$100,000	$100,000	$100,000	$100,000	$100,000	$100,000	$100,000
Loan	$0	$100,000	$0	$100,000	$0	$100,000	$0	$100,000
Total Investment	$100,000	$200,000	$100,000	$200,000	$100,000	$200,000	$100,000	$200,000
Capital gain (loss)	$10,000	$20,000	$15,000	$30,000	$30,000	$60,000	($20,000)	($40,000)
Taxable gain (loss)	$7,500	$15,000	$11,250	$22,500	$22,500	$45,000	($15,000)	($30,000)
Tax	$3,750	$7,500	$5,625	$11,250	$11,250	$22,500	($7,500)	($15,000)
After-tax gain (loss)	$6,250	$12,500	$9,375	$18,750	$18,750	$37,500	($12,500)	($25,000)
Cash flow available for investment	$2,875	$0	$2,875	$0	$2,875	$0	$2,875	$0
Increase in equity	$9,125	$12,500	$12,250	$18,750	$21,625	$37,500	($9,625)	($25,000)

Borrowing to Invest

BORROWING TO INVEST AT 13.75% INTEREST

RETURN ON YOUR INVESTMENT	10%		15%		30%		−20%	
	WITHOUT LEVERAGE	WITH LEVERAGE	WITHOUT LEVERAGE	WITH LEVERAGE	WITHOUT LEVERAGE	WITH LEVERAGE	WITHOUT LEVERAGE	WITH LEVERAGE
Equity	$100,000	$100,000	$100,000	$100,000	$100,000	$100,000	$100,000	$100,000
Loan	$0	$100,000	$0	$100,000	$0	$100,000	$0	$100,000
Total Investment	$100,000	$200,000	$100,000	$200,000	$100,000	$200,000	$100,000	$200,000
Capital gain (loss)	$10,000	$20,000	$15,000	$30,000	$30,000	$60,000	($20,000)	($40,000)
Taxable gain (loss)	$7,500	$15,000	$11,250	$22,500	$22,500	$45,000	($15,000)	($30,000)
Tax	$3,750	$7,500	$5,625	$11,250	$11,250	$22,500	($7,500)	($15,000)
After-tax gain (loss)	$6,250	$12,500	$9,375	$18,750	$18,750	$37,500	($12,500)	($25,000)
Cash flow available for investment	$6,875	$0	$6,875	$0	$6,875	$0	$6,875	$0
Increase in equity	$13,125	$12,500	$16,250	$18,750	$25,625	$37,500	($5,625)	($25,000)

TABLE XI

The next columns of the 5.75 per cent example show that the benefit of leverage increases with rates of return. In fact, with these three rates of return, the returns earned exceed the cost of funds, a condition that is not guaranteed. The -20 per cent rate of return shows what can happen in a poor market—a significant loss, in this case 40 per cent of the investor's capital. The loss will be mitigated somewhat if our investor has taxable capital gains against which to apply a capital loss.

The second set of examples in Table XI uses a 13.75 per cent tax rate. It is apparent that the higher the interest rate, the smaller the benefit from leverage. Over the past 10 years, the prime lending rate was in excess of 11 per cent about half the time as viewed monthly.

Before you go into any leverage program, determine what kind of cushion your bank requires in the event of a substantial decline in the value of your holdings or a major jump in the cost of money.

You should also ask any financial adviser recommending a leverage program to show you how someone would have fared on a month-by-month basis over the past 10 years using the specific fund or funds recommended and actual interest rates in place.

You should also consider avoiding any leverage program that is based on the premise that you can cash in units to pay interest on the loan and that your returns will always exceed your cost of funds. A bear market and withdrawals could quickly erode your capital to the point that you would suffer permanent capital loss.

Families and taxes

You should also be aware of how the federal government treats income within a family. In most cases, income is taxed in the hands of the person who earns it, and income from investments is taxed in the hands of the person who provides the capital. In other words, you cannot give your husband or wife (including a common-law spouse after 1992) capital for investment and expect to have the income taxed at his or her marginal tax rate. The federal government will consider the income to be yours and will hold you responsible for the tax on it.

That's the simplest case. Things become more complicated if you provide your husband or wife with financial backing to open a business that he or she will operate. In such a case, you should seek professional accounting and legal advice. If you give or lend funds to your children, grandchildren, nieces or nephews under the age of 18, the rules are again somewhat different. Interest and dividends are taxable in your hands, but capital gains are taxable in the hands of the children. Even more complicated is the fact that interest earned on interest, on which you have paid tax, is taxable in the children's hands.

If you invest child tax-credit cheques on behalf of a child by depositing the payments directly to an account in the child's name, the interest earned is taxable in the child's hands. Because a child can earn several thousand dollars without affecting your ability to claim the child as a deduction, this income can be tax free.

These income-attribution rules only affect spouses and children under age 18. If you give funds to your adult children, the income will be taxed in their hands, but if you lend it to them, or to any other non-arm's-length individual such as a parent, the income is taxable in your hands but any capital gains earned are not. However, the attribution rules won't apply if the loan is made at competitive interest rates. It was common in the past for parents to lend money to their adult children attending university—money that the children would invest to finance their education. Usually, the children would not pay tax on the income. The attribution rules changed in 1988 and ended this strategy.

It is important to note that Ottawa began to recognize common-law marriages for tax purposes beginning in 1993. Under the old rules, if you gave or lent funds to a common-law spouse, any income would be taxed in his or her hands, not yours. This is no longer the case; any income is now taxed in your hands.

The attribution rules make it necessary for families to engage in long-term investment planning if they are to make wise use of their money. Ideally, each spouse should have approximately the same amount of investment assets. If a woman plans to leave the work force to have children, it might make sense for her to save her entire salary and for the couple to use the husband's income to pay expenses. Then, at a later date, he would build up his investment capital. This way, income earned by the wife will likely be taxed at a lower rate than if all the family investment income were taxed in the husband's hands.

At one time, income-splitting was a popular tax-saving strategy, but Ottawa has eliminated most opportunities to split income. However, there are still some ways of selling assets to a family member at fair market value to generate capital that can be invested. Again, if you are considering taking this route, you should seek professional advice.

Moreover, you should consider the impact of your province's family law on your strategy. For instance, in Ontario the matrimonial residence is considered family property regardless of who paid for it. Therefore, a married man or woman who uses an inheritance to pay off the mortgage on the family residence has effectively gifted half of the inheritance to his or her spouse.

Some financial advisors have designed investment schemes over the years that are intended to shift income from one spouse to another, cutting taxes. Some individuals, to their despair, have been reassessed and face taxes, penalties and interest totalling in the six figures. If a scheme sounds too good to be true, pay a tax specialist who has no axe to grind to review the proposal prior to your investing. Ottawa has what is called the general anti-avoidance rule, which allows the federal government to challenge any scheme that appears to be designed solely to avoid taxes.

Chapter 4

First Things First

Before starting your investment program, there are some essential steps you should follow to ensure your financial well-being. One of the first steps is to dispose of all personal debts not used to purchase investment assets such as securities or real assets such as a home or cottage. Personal debts are the biggest barrier to building wealth.

As we discussed earlier, consumer credit is very expensive. The cost of carrying an unpaid balance on a credit card can be as much as 2 per cent a month. On an average balance of $1,000 a month, that adds up to more than $240 a year in interest. Moreover, the interest on personal debt is not deductible from income, which means you must earn a great deal more than $240 to pay that interest. For example, if your marginal tax rate is 41 per cent, more than $400 of your gross income goes to paying the interest on that $1,000. Consequently, it is easy to see why the best investment you can make is to pay down that debt. You will not find a stock market investment that can give you a consistent rate of return that exceeds the cost of consumer debt.

Still, it is unrealistic to expect most people to stay out of debt completely. Credit is necessary in many cases, particularly for big-ticket items such as cars and houses. The trick is to keep debt costs to a minimum, and that means paying off your most expensive forms of credit first. You should, therefore, try to pay off your credit card debt as soon as possible, and then make a habit of paying off balances in full each month. Credit cards should never be used as a source of financing, but instead as a convenient alternative to carrying cash or a chequebook. If it is impossible to pay off the balance, it is better to borrow the necessary funds elsewhere at less cost. You are much better off using a bank personal line of credit, which offers substantially lower interest rates— generally, a percentage point or two above the prime lending rate. This could cut interest expenses by as much as one-half to two-thirds.

If you are in the market for a loan, shop around. The cost of credit varies widely, so if your own bank, trust company or financial institution is not the least expensive, ask it to match the best rate you can find. If it will not, consider going elsewhere. Similarly, mortgage rates can differ among institutions. Even a small fraction of a percentage point can make a significant difference in payments, especially on a large mortgage. Again, your best bet is to shop for the lowest rate possible, particularly if you are buying a new home. Changing mortgage companies to get a lower rate when it's time to renew a mortgage can be expensive because of legal costs (although some institutions will pick up these costs), so shopping at that time may not be as advantageous. In this case, the best route may be to ask your current mortgage holder to match the lowest available rate.

Invest now or pay off your debts?

Of course, you should strive to pay down your debts as quickly as possible. The quicker you do, the more money you'll have in your pocket for savings, investment or spending. However, many people believe they can do better by using their savings to play the stock market, rather than to eliminate debts.

Perhaps they can. But market performance figures suggest that the average investor certainly cannot. Even so, you may be confident you're a member of the minority that can realize a better return on stocks than you would get by paying down debt. Yet even in this case, it makes sense to structure your finances to cut your interest expenses.

First, use your savings or cash flow to pay off debts. Then borrow the funds back to buy stocks or other investments. You'll still owe the same amount but you'll reap additional gains at tax time. Because your loan is now for investments, the interest is deductible from income for tax purposes. But you must be prepared to show that the loan is, in fact, for investment—meaning you must have documentation to prove the money was borrowed and used for an investment. And remember, if you want to deduct interest, your investment must be made with the expectation of producing income in the form of interest or dividends. So while stocks qualify—even if it is unlikely that some will pay dividends—gold bullion does not.

If you plan to restructure your affairs to make your interest deductible, you're probably best off reviewing the procedure with your financial adviser to ensure that you have the proper documentation and that you will not run afoul of Ottawa's anti-avoidance tax rules.

Deciding whether you should borrow for investment is another matter. Certainly, fortunes have been made (and lost) by those who invest with borrowed funds. Most real estate purchases are heavily leveraged, meaning investors provide some of their own capital, but borrow a great deal more. In the case of commercial real estate, deals are often financed 80 per cent or more with borrowed capital.

Stock market purchases can also be leveraged, but stock exchange bylaws limit the portion of borrowed funds to 50 per cent, or even less if you're investing in riskier junior securities. Many sellers of mutual funds also recommend purchasing funds with borrowed money, and a number of financial institutions have arrangements with mutual fund dealers to provide financing of up to $3 for every $1 the client invests.

But markets move down as well as up, and if you are heavily leveraged, a price drop could cause significant problems. For example, if you buy securities with borrowed funds and the price of your investment declines, you must come up with more capital so that the equity in your account meets the minimum under your purchase agreement. In the case of stocks, equity must at least equal the amount owed to your broker. In the case of real estate, the investor must come up with funds to pay interest on debt if the cash flow fails to cover costs.

So while leverage can make you a lot of money, it can also be a losing strategy. If you decide to use borrowed funds for investment, make sure that you understand the risks and have the financial strength to keep yourself above water if your investment goes sour. It's best not to get in over your head when you borrow—if you must borrow at all.

Choosing an investment advisor

Choosing a stockbroker, mutual fund dealer or any other investment professional is one of the most important investment decisions you will make. Even the most sophisticated investors need brokers, if only to execute orders properly and pass on information. Novice investors, meanwhile, must depend heavily on brokers and other investment salespeople for advice, suggestions and guidance about specific securities and an overall investment strategy.

The choice of advisors has become more complicated in recent years with the introduction of specialized financial products such as options and futures on treasury bills, bonds, currencies and stock market indexes. Even traditional financial products such as stocks, bonds and mutual funds have become increasingly complex. As a result, an investor who diversifies—perhaps with a portfolio of stocks, mutual funds, bonds, and maybe even futures and options—can find him- or herself dealing with several investment professionals.

Further complicating matters is the fact that every major bank has a discount brokerage-house affiliate that charges a fraction of the commission charged by a full-service dealer. You can shave costs even more by trading on the Internet. Discounters originally offered bare-bones trading and little else. Generally they have been adding some services in the hopes of attracting additional business in a very competitive market. Still, they appeal mostly to investors who conduct their own research and analysis and who don't want to pay for brokerage-house research.

However, many investors choose to deal with brokerage firms that can provide a variety of services and products, or with those that specialize. The latest twist involves dealers who charge zero commission when buying or selling funds. These dealers receive an annual trailer commission from the fund management company. Trailer commissions can be as much as one percentage point.

Choosing a brokerage firm

Before choosing a brokerage firm, you should decide on your main investment objectives. For example, people whose interests include substantial dealings in bonds are probably wise to consider large, integrated firms. Because of the underwriting business of these firms, they have major bond trading departments and are better equipped to buy and sell bonds than are most small investment dealers.

If stocks are your priority, it's wise to make sure the firm you deal with is a member of the Toronto Stock Exchange (TSE) or, in Quebec, the Montreal Exchange. Such memberships indicate that the firm has direct access to the most important Canadian securities markets.

TSE members dealing with retail investors range in size from small firms with a handful of personnel in a few offices to large firms with offices in major centres across the country. Large firms usually provide a wide variety of research products, ranging from economic analysis to detailed reports on individual industry groups and stocks. However, they cannot be expected to follow many of the smaller publicly traded companies because it would not be a cost-effective use of their analysts' time. They may follow smaller companies as part of an industry group or as a special situation, but their emphasis is almost always on larger, more heavily traded stocks that are more likely to be of interest to clients.

Possible conflicts of interest

The salespeople at large firms are often not allowed to recommend stocks not followed closely by their analysts. As a result, their clients probably will not hear of many investment opportunities. In addition, because these dealers tend to track the same companies, information they distribute is rarely unique and is usually reflected in the price of a stock before clients have access to the research reports.

A second area of concern for investors is the possible conflict between the underwriting and sales departments of major firms. Dealers deny there is a problem, yet it is rare that a brokerage house will issue a negative report on a company that is an important underwriting client of the firm.

Investors should also realize that not all clients receive information at the same time. A firm will be in contact more often with a client who generates $25,000 in yearly commissions than with one whose small portfolio results in $100 in revenues. Large clients, especially portfolio managers with financial institutions, are constantly in touch with brokerage-house analysts and often benefit from analysts' views long before they are printed. Most firms have designed ways to pass on analysts' opinions to retail sales representatives quickly, but small clients still get the last phone call—if they are called at all.

For that reason, small investors who have only a few thousand dollars to invest in stocks and who are unlikely to have large portfolios down the road are probably better off investing in a mutual fund. On the other hand, if you're capable of doing your own analysis and are assertive enough to pester your broker for information, you might consider individual investments. Even then, you should look at the economics of being a small investor in the stock market. If you have only $1,000 and want to split it between two stocks, you'll have to pay two minimum commission fees, which are likely to be at least $50 each unless you go to a discount broker or turn to the Internet. And you'll also have to pay a commission when you sell. If you deal with a firm on the Internet, make sure it is licensed to do business in your province.

Small brokerage houses usually follow the same pecking order when it comes to calling clients. The call made first is the one that is most likely to result in an order. But smaller houses usually have fewer underwriting ties and, therefore, are more inclined to give impartial advice. Smaller dealers may also compensate for offering fewer services by following companies ignored by their larger competitors, bringing their clients superior opportunities for gains. Most firms offer research on individual stocks, but major integrated brokerage houses usually produce much more written information covering the economy, the bond market and preferred shares. Of course, if you do all your own analysis, choose a discount broker to lower your trading costs.

The sales representative

Thousands of people across Canada are licensed to sell securities to the public. Some perform their duties superbly, while some are inept. But, as with most professions, most are adequate for the job.

You should, therefore, give much thought to selecting a broker or other investment advisor. If you know your investment objectives, your first step is to screen a number of dealers to find several that offer the services you require. A phone call to retail sales managers at most firms will get you much of the information you need for a preliminary screening. But face-to-face visits are best. You should be prepared to discuss your investment objectives and financial needs openly. If a firm appears able to provide the services you're looking for, its sales manager will usually try to introduce you to a sales representative with whom you seem compatible. If you have only a few thousand dollars, you will likely be matched to the broker-of-the-day, the person selected to meet most walk-in clients on a particular day.

You should determine how much experience a sales representative has. Since there is no substitute for experience, it is usually desirable to deal with someone who has several years of exposure to the markets, and who has worked in times of both rising and falling prices. Many less experienced brokers were shell-shocked when the market fell in October 1987. After five years of rising prices, it was their first experience with a rapid decline. Today, there are many younger brokers who are now experiencing their first *bear* market.

You should ask for copies of past research reports sent to clients and study them carefully to determine whether the recommendations have helped clients' portfolios outperform the market. Ask the representative whether he or she sticks with the company list or conducts independent research. Find out how the firm deals with sell recommendations of shares of companies that are underwriting clients. In addition, ask the representative for the names of several clients you can contact for an assessment of the firm's and the sales representative's track records.

In your conversations with the representative, determine his or her interests in the market. If the representative has expertise in junior speculative situations and you want a low-risk portfolio, find someone else. In addition, ask whether you can expect much in the way of personal service based on the size of your account. Some firms discourage their employees from taking on new, small accounts because the commissions hardly cover the cost of executing the transaction. No experienced broker can afford the time to service a small account that has little chance of growing.

Placing an order

Clients who understand basic stock market terminology stand a better chance of avoiding confusion when placing orders to buy or sell securities. It is, after all, of utmost importance that your sales representative fully understand your instructions. There should be no confusion about the number of shares being bought or sold.

Unless your order is "at the market"—the best price the broker can get at the time—the client should specify a buying or selling price. Furthermore, you must decide whether the order is a day order—one that must be resubmitted each day until the stock is bought or sold—or an open order that remains in effect until the transaction is complete. Many investors deal with more than one sales representative and it is essential that the order be placed with only one.

Sometimes disputes develop between a representative and a client over what was said. This breakdown of communications can usually be prevented by being explicit when placing an order. (Some brokerage houses tape-record all orders.) You should keep detailed notes that contain the date and time the order was placed and the instructions given to the broker—including whether the order was to buy or sell, the full name of the stock and the price. Make sure you receive progress reports on your orders during the day, particularly on volatile securities, and at the close of trading. If a problem develops, talk to your representative first. If a solution cannot be reached, speak with the office's retail sales manager. If that doesn't work, try the stock exchange involved or, as a last resort, your provincial securities commission. But remember, even though orders are not in writing, they are legally binding contracts.

Types of accounts

Brokerage firms offer clients several types of accounts, including cash accounts, delivery-against-payment accounts (DAP) and margin accounts. With cash accounts, clients pay for their shares on settlement date, which is three business days after a transaction is made. They can either take possession of their share certificates or leave them with the brokerage firm for safekeeping. (In fact, few people request certificates, preferring the computerized record keeping of the industry, which allows for fast settlements of trades.) Discount brokers offer fewer options. Generally, they require that clients have adequate cash in their accounts before placing an order to buy stock. Similarly, they require that shares be in the firm's possession before accepting an order to sell.

In the case of DAP accounts, a broker delivers the securities to the client's bank or trust company in exchange for payment. As a result, DAP accounts are mainly employed by institutional investors, but some individuals also use them. With margin accounts, part of the purchase price of the shares is made with funds borrowed from the brokerage firm. The purchased securities remain in the hands of the firm and can be used as collateral for loans used to finance the firm's operations. Fully paid securities are segregated from those that can be used as collateral.

Each type of account has its pros and cons. However, DAP accounts, although they are inconvenient for brokers and involve some extra expenses for clients, are the safest. Every major bank offers administration and custodian services for investors.

The question then becomes, how safe is safe? Clients, and potential customers, can take some solace in the fact that few major financial disasters have occurred in the Canadian brokerage industry.

Protection limited

Should a firm fail, investors are protected by the Canadian Investor Protection Fund, formerly the National Contingency Fund, established by the brokerage industry to protect clients against losses. It protects clients for up to $250,000 of assets in an account, including $60,000 cash.

If you worry about margin accounts, your only alternative is to use a bank line of credit. Investors who trade frequently on margin do not have an alternative to margin accounts unless they arrange their own bank financing and deliveries. Interest paid on money borrowed to buy shares is deductible for tax purposes, but it is important that detailed records be kept; otherwise, Ottawa may disallow the expense. If you choose a cash or DAP account and plan to keep your shares for some time, they should be fully registered in your name. This assures that you will receive all company information and dividends directly, although investment dealers will collect these on your behalf and credit your account if the shares are in the brokerage firm's, or "street," name. Since early 1988, brokers have been required to send copies of company reports to clients whose holdings are in the broker's name.

Monitoring performance

Once an account has been established, it is important that the client monitor the broker's performance. As a client, you should ensure that you are benefiting from the research you were promised and that you are receiving personal service. You should also monitor the success of your broker's recommendations, and record whether you acted on them. Determine whether they brought higher returns than if you had left your portfolio alone. If you suspect that your representative is making recommendations for your account for the sole purpose of generating commissions—known as "churning"—then it's time to move on. The alternative is to learn to make your own investment decisions or move into a mutual fund.

The funds alternative

If you're a smaller investor, your broker might recommend that you invest in mutual funds, which are also known as investment funds. If you decide that mutual funds are right for you, and you intend to buy from your brokerage firm instead of a mutual fund dealer, make sure that you choose a sales representative who is a specialist.

Anyone can buy into a fund for clients, but it makes sense to use those who closely monitor the objectives and performance of fund management companies. An investment adviser should also help clients to determine how funds can be used as part of a total savings and financial planning program and find funds that meet clients' objectives. The selection criteria for stockbrokers apply equally to those who sell mutual funds. Request client names and check references. Also, determine what type of service you will receive. Will it be a once-a-year telephone call or a more involved relationship?

Financial planners

Some investment professionals call themselves financial planners. Rather than simply selling a financial product, they analyze their clients' financial situations, review their objectives and develop a plan aimed at fulfilling these objectives. A financial planner should look at debt management, life insurance, retirement savings and general investment.

Some financial planners operate on a fee-for-service basis and accept no commissions. However, most do not charge a fee but receive a commission if you buy a financial product through them and an ongoing trailer commission, or service fee, as long as you hold the fund. If you deal with a financial planner, make sure you understand the ground rules—especially how he or she is paid.

First, you should note that anyone can call him- or herself a financial planner. This is a serious problem because it allows people who have no training or experience to hang a shingle suggesting some expertise in the area of finance. As a result, it is important to determine what qualifications a financial planner has. The Certified Financial Planner

(CFP) designation is awarded to those who have completed a series of industry courses. The Canadian Association of Financial Planners also sets minimum standards for membership and awards the Registered Financial Planner (RFP) designation. The industry standard is the Certified Financial Planner designation, which is recognized internationally.

Preparing a will

It is essential that you have a will. Even if you already have one, you should not set it aside and ignore it. You should review it periodically to ensure that it continues to reflect your wishes and conforms to the laws of the province in which you live.

The objective of a will, and estate planning, is to ensure that your assets are distributed according to your wishes after you die, while minimizing the tax bite. Even modest estates require the clarification that a professionally prepared will can provide.

When preparing your will, make sure your lawyer has copies of important investment documents, such as a copy of the beneficiary form you may have signed when you opened an RRSP.

Besides your will, discuss a "power of attorney" with your lawyer.

Life insurance

Life and disability insurance are also key planks in any financial strategy. As such, they should be taken care of before setting up an investment program. First determine how much insurance is necessary to maintain your family's standard of living should anything happen to you.

There are no hard-and-fast rules about adequate coverage, but many advisors suggest life insurance of 10 times annual income, plus enough funds to pay off debts. In fact, many advisors have revised the 10 times figure upward to reflect the decline in interest rates of recent years.

Life insurance is a product offered by dozens of companies. Like any other financial product, quality and price vary widely so it makes sense to shop around and ask agents for comparisons of companies and products. Some agents handle insurance products issued by only one company, others deal with several companies or provide computerized price comparisons of similar products.

Consider the differences between term insurance, insurance that covers you for a specific period, and whole life insurance, insurance that covers you for life and contains a so-called savings element.

A final note: Until recently, few consumers thought about the financial health of an insurance company. However, the confusion following the demise of Confederation Life Insurance Company changed that. The Canadian Life and Health Insurance Compensation Corporation, an industry-owned protection fund, honours life insurance claims up to a maximum of $200,000 (hardly adequate today), health insurance claims up to $60,000, disability and annuity income up to $2,000 a month, and RRSPs up to $60,000.

Chapter 5

Setting Your Investment Objectives

Once you've got your financial house in order, you're ready for the next step—defining your investment objectives and meeting them. This means deciding how much money you'll need on a certain date for a particular purpose and structuring your financial affairs to meet that goal.

The most common investment objectives are building a retirement fund, saving for a child's education, a home or cottage, buying a business or simply building wealth. Some people might even want to speculate with some of their money in hopes of making gains quickly, although it is wise to ensure that your more conservative investment programs are in place before you engage in speculative investing.

Investment objectives can often be divided into short- and long-term objectives. The major difference, obviously, is the period of time the investment will cover. Someone saving $25,000 or $50,000 for the down payment on a house will probably want to use the money within a few years. Conversely, someone saving for a comfortable retirement might expect to wait 20 years or so before making use of the funds—a long-term proposition.

Meeting your goal of a down payment may not be easy. After all, you have to sock away the money. But it is more straightforward than making adequate provisions for retirement. What happens, for instance, if you decide you want to retire in 20 years with an income of $50,000 a year? Thanks to inflation, the major difficulty is determining how large a retirement pot you will need in 20 years to provide $50,000 with today's purchasing power. Even once you know how much you'll need, you'll have to predict the rates of return that you're likely to receive from your investments over the next two decades so you'll know how much to save each year.

What's more, you may have a number of goals in mind, not all of which are complementary. You may want to speed up your mortgage payments, contribute the maximum to your RRSP and set aside funds for your children's education—only to find that doing all three would be an impossible drain on your finances. As a result, you must consider making some trade-offs and establishing priorities.

The level of risk

Timing leads to other important differences, the most crucial being the risk you can afford financially and emotionally. Different types of investments provide different returns. Guaranteed investments are safest because you know the rate of return in advance. If you put your money in a one-year term deposit, you are assured that at the end of the year you'll get all your money back along with the promised interest. But if you sink your money into a mutual fund that invests in Canadian stocks, you have no guarantee on what you will earn.

Historically, long-term investors in such funds, or in diversified portfolios of Canadian common stocks, have realized returns substantially higher than those for guaranteed investments. Some funds have long-term average annual compound rates of return in excess of 15 per cent. But year-to-year rates vary widely and, in fact, the average 10-year annual compound rate of return for Canadian equity mutual funds that invest in larger Canadian companies is about 11 per cent for the period ended June 30, 1998. However, the one-year average is about 16 per cent, the three-year average is about 15 per cent and the five-year average is more than 12 per cent. In most years, they've exceeded the rates available from guaranteed returns, although in some years they've been lower.

It makes sense, then, that the person expecting to need money in a year or so is better off with a guaranteed investment. However, the person with a longer-term horizon, perhaps five to 10 years or longer, is able to accept more risk and volatility in the rate of return each year and should consider investments with growth potential.

For long-term investors, higher compound rates of return make a significant difference in the pool of money created over time. If $1,000 is set aside each year for 20 years at an annual average interest rate of 5 per cent, it will grow to $34,719. But a rate of 10 per cent would result in $63,002 after 20 years. Even for a single investment of $1,000, the difference can be substantial. That single deposit earning 5 per cent would be worth $2,653 after 20 years. At a 10 per cent growth rate, it would be worth $6,727.

If a guaranteed rate of return appeals to you, you can lock away your money for a relatively long period. You might buy government bonds for 20 years or longer. They pay significantly higher rates of return than term deposits or treasury bills, but the rate remains static for the entire period. That's good news if interest rates fall, but if they rise, investors may find themselves wishing they had taken another course of action.

When possible, investors should aim for growth. While growth investments are riskier because their returns are unpredictable, investors are usually compensated over time for this risk through greater gains. Conversely, investors without time on their side should play it safe.

No matter what route you choose, investment options are available to help you meet your goals. For safety, many people choose run-of-the-mill bank accounts. But why not consider alternatives that are just as secure? They include bank premium savings accounts, trust company and credit union accounts, term deposits, treasury bills and money market funds. All are reasonably risk-free but the rates paid vary significantly.

Saving effectively can also involve a great deal more than investing for growth or income. You can use programs and tax breaks that can help to increase returns without increasing risk. Saving for retirement and saving for children's education are two goals for which tax-assisted savings schemes are available.

Saving for retirement

Most people are eager to embark on a savings program that will allow them to live comfortably during retirement. This is recognized by the federal government through tax legislation that encourages companies to implement pension plans and allows individuals to save for retirement through registered retirement savings plans (RRSPs).

Because government pension benefits alone are inadequate for most people during retirement, private pension plans are an excellent way to ensure that the income you need will be available. The trouble is, many companies don't have pension plans. And if they do, the plans may prove to be woefully inadequate. So taking retirement savings into your own hands may be the best solution to financial freedom during your golden years.

If this is the case, there are three cardinal rules to remember: Save as much as you can, start as early as you can, and aim for growth. Starting early is the key, simply because it puts the power of compound interest at your command. The 25-year-old who sets aside $1,000 a year at an 8 per cent annual return will have $186,000 at age 60. The 45-year-old who wants the same amount at age 60 will have to set aside more than $6,000 a year. Furthermore, if the 25-year-old could earn 12 per cent annually, he or she would accumulate $483,000 by age 60—enough to provide an annual income of about $60,000.

It's never too late to start. If you haven't saved for retirement until now, you can still reap the benefits of an improving government regulatory climate for retirement savings. For one thing, pension plans are changing. Ottawa has improved the portability of pension plans and has enhanced survivor benefits.

Even so, this means nothing to those whose employers don't offer pension plans. There are no simple solutions to this dilemma, although the RRSP comes close. It is the most popular tax shelter available to Canadians, and its popularity has grown since the concept was introduced in 1957, especially among those who won't have the benefit of private pension plan payments when they retire.

With an RRSP, you can set aside a portion of your earnings every year and it will not be taxed. Any income earned within an RRSP is allowed to grow untaxed until withdrawn from the plan. As a result, retirement savings through an RRSP grow much more quickly than those that are taxed. And when it comes time to withdraw funds from the plan, the tax collector will likely take a smaller cut because your overall retirement income, and marginal tax rate, will be lower.

Some people invest in off-the-shelf RRSPs similar to guaranteed investment certificates or term deposits offered by banks, trust companies, credit unions, insurance companies and mutual fund distributors. Others use self-directed plans through which they choose their own investments. In fact, there are two types of plans: those that pay a guaranteed rate of return and those in which the returns can't be determined in advance because funds are invested in marketable securities with fluctuating prices.

But before you get carried away with plans to invest in RRSPs, make sure you are aware of the contribution limits. The contribution limit is 18 per cent of your earned income for the previous year, with a dollar limit of $13,500. This limit is reduced by what the federal government refers to as a "pension adjustment." This adjustment includes any contributions made to a pension plan or other tax-assisted retirement plan, such as a deferred profit-sharing plan. In addition, RRSP limits for those who have made past service contributions to their pension plans will be subject to adjustments.

Calculations for RRSP contributions are more complicated than in the past. Employers must file pertinent information about pension contributions with the federal government, which will then calculate how much you can contribute to your RRSP.

You must make your contributions no later than 60 days after year-end to receive a tax break for the year. But starting with the 1991 tax year, you can carry forward unused contributions indefinitely.

When your RRSP matures

You must dispose of your RRSPs by the end of the year in which you reach age 69. You have three basic options when that time comes—or before, if you wish. You can cash in your plan and pay tax on the entire amount, you can purchase an annuity, or you can put your money into a registered retirement income fund (RRIF). Most people choose a RRIF (pronounced "riff"), a life annuity or some combination of the two.

Life annuities, which are available from life insurance companies, provide monthly income for life (you can also get a term annuity). But there are variations on the standard annuity. A popular option is an annuity that pays for a guaranteed period of 10 to 15 years or until both the husband and wife die, whichever is longer.

Annuities pay specified rates of return that depend on your age, or your spouse's age, when you purchase the annuity. Rates also depend on general interest rates at the time and on competition among insurance companies selling the products. Although you will receive a higher income if you take out an annuity when interest rates are high, you really have little control over timing.

Many people shy away from annuities because they involve surrendering control of their investments. RRIFs, on the other hand, allow you to hold the same types of investments that are allowed in RRSPs so investors never relinquish control. In fact, a RRIF is an RRSP in reverse—instead of making contributions, as you do with an RRSP, you withdraw funds from a RRIF.

You can withdraw as much from your RRIF each year as you want. The least you are allowed to withdraw is determined by your age. However, the rules changed in 1993. Under the rules for RRIFs started in 1992 or earlier, minimum RRIF withdrawals are based on the amount of money in a plan at the end of the previous year, divided by the difference between 90 and the RRIF owner's age, or spouse's age, if it is lower. For example, someone who was 71 at the end of 1991 and had $100,000 in a RRIF would have been required to withdraw a minimum of 1/19 or $5,263 in 1992. Under the revised rules, a RRIF can be structured to provide a lifetime income. The new rules require moderately higher minimum withdrawals. For people younger than 71, the old fractions based on age, or spouse's age, 90 will continue to apply.

Saving for children's education

Many families decide that the best way to save for children's education is to start a savings plan at birth. Others decide that the smartest course is to pay off the mortgage as quickly as possible and finance their children's education out of income.

Launching a savings plan when your children are very young makes a great deal of sense. But the way you do it has a significant bearing on how much money you'll have by the time you pack your kids off to university, college or technical school.

If the funds are being put aside by you, the child's grandparents or aunts and uncles, the taxation attribution rules apply and interest and dividends earned on the funds contributed will be taxed at the marginal tax rates of the donors. If structured carefully by keeping the interest separate, any interest earned on interest will be taxed in the child's hands. If the money is invested in stocks or equity mutual funds and capital gains are earned, the capital gains are taxable in the child's hands rather than the donor's.

For many families, Ottawa's decision to stop paying family allowance on a universal basis after 1992 ends one method of saving for children's education. However, the same strategy can be employed by those eligible to receive child tax-credit cheques. Many people establish a separate bank or trust company account in their child's name and use the account only for child tax credit payments. These cheques are taxable in the parent's hands. However, if the money is invested directly on the child's behalf, any income earned on the original contribution is considered the child's. As everyone can earn $6,456 tax free, there is little likelihood that taxes will be paid on income generated from child tax-credit contributions. It may still make sense to open that separate account. It can be used for gifts to the child from people other than parents, grandparents, aunts and uncles, or for inheritances.

And remember, there is no need to leave this money in a savings account. You can invest it in Canada Savings Bonds, GICs, stocks, mutual funds and other financial instruments as long as your purchases are made directly from the child's account. Most people tend to use interest-income investments because they are low-risk or risk-free.

Registered education savings plans

There are also tax-assisted plans in which you can save for children's education. Known as registered educational savings plans (RESPs), they allow tax-free growth of income from contributions to finance post-secondary education.

The maximum annual contribution per child to an RESP is $4,000. The lifetime limit is $42,000. Moreover, effective January 1, 1998, if you save for children's education using an RESP you will get an annual Canadian Education Savings Grant (CESG) of 20 per cent on the first $2,000 that is contributed to an RESP each year to a maximum grant of $400 a year per child up to age 18 or a maximum of $7,200. CESG contributions can be carried forward up to an annual contribution of $4,000 per child.

The capital originally contributed is not deductible from income for tax purposes nor taxable when withdrawn, but income earned on that capital grows tax-free in the RESP until withdrawn to finance a child's education, at which time it and the CESG amounts are taxed in the child's hands. The advantage of an RESP is that students generally have low income, so the tax burden is either non-existent or negligible, depending on the income level. You must close the RESP by the end of February in the year after the year in which the first payment is made.

Consequently the student will be able to spread the income over two tax years.

The introduction of the CESG makes RESPs the best way to save for children's education. If you contribute $2,000 a year for 18 years, you will accumulate $65,500 using a 6 per cent rate of return. With the CESG you accumulate $78,600, giving you an effective rate of return on your $2,000 annual contributions of 8.5 per cent. If you or your family overcontribute to an RESP, there is a 1 per cent a month penalty on the overcontribution. Moreover, the overcontribution, even when withdrawn, counts towards the lifetime limit.

There are two variations of the RESP, both of which have distinct advantages and disadvantages. There are the "scholarship plans" in which your money is pooled with the funds contributed by other parents. The income earned in the plan is then distributed to the children who embark on a post-secondary education. If your child decides against continuing his or her education, you get back the money you put in the plan, but you lose the income earned over the years. In other words, you are gambling that your child will attend a post-secondary institution. Scholarship plans are available only from the firms that sponsor them.

Self-directed RESPs allow you to choose your own investments and are much more flexible. Virtually every bank, mutual fund and insurance company were planning to have RESPs in place by the end of 1998. This type of RESP should probably be your first choice.

When you set up an RESP, consider a family plan for related beneficiaries. That way if one child doesn't continue his or her education, the benefits can be transferred to another child. Family plans can be used when beneficiaries are under 21 years of age at the time the plan was established. Alternatively, they can be set up by transferring one plan to which a contribution has already been made into another.

If the beneficiaries are not pursuing higher education by age 21 and the plan has been running for at least 10 years, a contributor will be allowed to transfer the income to his or her RRSP or spouse's RRSP provided there is RRSP room, to a maximum of $40,000. The amount transferred (to avoid having tax withheld, the amount should be transferred from the RESP to the RRSP directly) must be claimed as an RRSP deduction in the year in which the payment is made. The contributor will pay regular taxes on the RESP but avoids a special 20 per cent charge by rolling the money into an RRSP.

Prior to the introduction of the CESG and new alternatives for reclaiming RESP income, many people saved for their children's education using formal or informal trusts. In effect, these trusts would hold a portfolio of growth stocks or growth mutual funds for your children using your capital. While any interest or dividend income earned would be taxable in your hands, any capital gains would be taxed in your children's hands (and interest earned on interest would be taxed in your children's hands).

Formal trusts can be expensive to set up and administer. Informal trusts, while inexpensive, must be structured in a certain way to work. You should get professional advice before choosing the trust route to save for your children's education.

Chapter 6

As Safe as Money in the Bank

While housing is clearly the favourite investment of Canadians, money in the bank—or trust company or credit union—is a close second, with hundreds of billions of dollars invested in savings accounts, chequing accounts, term deposits and guaranteed investment certificates.

The volatility of interest rates during the late 1970s and early 1980s and, indeed, during the past several years, has made most people sensitive to small differences in interest rates. As a result, competition among financial institutions for savings increased and an array of savings instruments became available. No longer do you have a simple choice of just two accounts—savings and chequing. Now you can choose accounts to meet your specific needs and cash flow.

Look at chequing accounts. Traditionally, a chequing account was used just for writing cheques. You transferred enough money into it each month to cover the cheques you wrote and you neither expected nor received interest. Now it's a different story. You can find chequing accounts that pay interest, provided you maintain a minimum monthly balance. You can find chequing accounts that charge no fees, provided you maintain a minimum monthly balance. You can even get accounts that allow you to pay your bills at the bank without charge, provided you've paid an annual fee. Generally, this last type of account is part of a package that includes a personal line of credit and a credit card named after a precious metal.

Savings accounts have also come a long way. Some pay a low interest rate on the minimum outstanding balance but allow chequing privileges. However, most people who use accounts strictly for savings opt for premium savings accounts that don't allow chequing but pay a higher interest rate.

The type of premium savings account you choose depends largely on your cash-flow needs. Some accounts pay interest on the minimum monthly balance, so if you keep $1,000 in your account for 29 days of one month and let the balance drop to $1 on the 30th day, you get interest for the month on only $1. Others base payments on the minimum daily balance, so if the balance in your account fluctuates widely, the premium daily interest account makes more sense.

You can also keep your money in money market mutual funds that are usually invested in treasury bills and other top-quality short-term debt instruments. The rates paid on these are often several points higher than rates paid on savings accounts.

In addition, you can keep your money in term deposits with a bank or in guaranteed investment certificates (GICs) with a trust company. With these you tie up your money for a specified period, which can be from 30 days to as long as five years.

The rates paid on term deposits and GICs are generally, but not always, higher than the rates paid on savings accounts (for example, during 1990, short-term rates were several points higher than long-term rates). How much higher depends on the amount you deposit and the length of time you are willing to invest. With a term deposit or GIC, you agree to commit your funds for a specific period at a specific rate. If you need your money before the end of the term, you will probably face interest penalties or be forced to sell your GIC at a price that will reflect current interest rates.

If you need the money you have tied up, the best arrangement for conserving interest may be to borrow against the term deposit, GIC or bank account. Let's assume it's close to the end of the month and you need the $15,000 you have in an account that pays a premium rate of interest on your minimum monthly balance. Instead of withdrawing the money, it will save you a few dollars if you borrow the necessary funds for several days. A prearranged personal line of credit is the easiest loan source, but if you don't have one, contact your bank or trust company manager about a loan. Because you're putting up your account as collateral, you should have no difficulty receiving a loan. And if the bank is reluctant to give you the loan or wants to charge you fees, argue. Banks are in business to make money, and branch managers are well aware that they lose if you move your money elsewhere.

When tying up your money for a long time, there are a few details you should watch. In most cases, the interest rate paid by an institution on a longer-term deposit applies to the principal only. Interest earned on interest may be at the institution's deposit rate. Also, when comparing interest rates, make sure you are comparing apples with apples. As you can see in Table XII, the frequency with which your interest is compounded will make a significant difference in the wealth you are able to build over the years.

Value of $1,000 in 10 Years

COMPOUNDED

INTEREST RATE	ANNUALLY	SEMI- ANNUALLY	QUARTERLY	MONTHLY
4%	$1,480	$1,486	$1,489	$1,490
6%	$1,791	$1,806	$1,814	$1,819
8%	$2,159	$1,191	$2,208	$2,220
10%	$2,594	$2,653	$2,685	$2,707
12%	$3,106	$3,207	$3,262	$3,300
14%	$3,707	$3,870	$3,959	$4,022
16%	$4,411	$4,661	$4,801	$4,901

TABLE XII

A 10 per cent rate compounded semi-annually means you are earning 5 per cent interest on your money for the first six months but in the second six months you earn 5 per cent interest on both the money you originally deposited and the interest you earned in the first six months. On a $1,000 deposit you would earn 5 per cent of $1,000 or $50 in the first six months and 5 per cent interest on $1,050, or $52.50, for the next six months. Over one year you would earn $102.50, or an effective interest rate of 10.25 per cent. Invest $1,000 at 10 per cent compounded annually and you'll have only $100 in interest at the end of a year. You should also realize that you are responsible for paying tax on the interest you have accrued even if you haven't received it, as would be the case with some investments that automatically reinvest interest earned.

Deciding on terms

The major investment decision facing many people who keep money on deposit is what term to take. It's not an easy choice, given the volatility of interest rates. If you lock in your money for five years at 6 per cent and rates move up to 10 per cent two years later, you're out of luck—you will continue to get 6 per cent. Conversely, people who left their money in savings accounts at 19 per cent in mid-1982, expecting rates to move higher, saw their returns drop below 10 per cent within a year and to less than 7 per cent within two years. Indeed, with savings rates in mid-1990 at 12 to 14 per cent, investors faced the same decision as they did almost a decade earlier. Rates in fact did decline and savings account rates were less than 2 per cent in mid-1998.

When deciding on terms, you have to choose between buying something like a five-year certificate at the going rate or holding off and buying a three- or six-month certificate because you expect five-year rates to move higher. There is no reliable way to forecast such moves, particularly over the longer term. But there are some general rules governing what constitutes a reasonable rate of return.

The risk-free rate—"risk free" meaning there is no risk to capital as is the case with an insured deposit or a government guarantee—usually hovers around 3 per cent above the rate of inflation. So if you think inflation will be 5 per cent over the next few years, then 8 per cent is a reasonable rate of return. A greater or smaller spread than 3 per cent is a reflection of expectations in the marketplace. Five-year GIC rates in mid-1988 were about 10 per cent when the inflation rate hovered around 4 per cent, reflecting an expectation that inflation might move higher. In mid-1991, when inflation was running at more than 5 per cent, savings rates were about 5.5 per cent while five-year GIC rates were about 9.25 per cent. In mid-1993, with inflation running at 2 per cent, five-year GIC rates had declined to about 6.75 per cent. In mid-1998, with inflation running at just under 2 per cent, five-year GIC rates were about 5 per cent.

If GIC rates are less than 3 per cent above the inflation rate, you are probably better off sticking to short-term deposits and waiting for higher rates. So, if five-year GICs are paying 5 per cent and you expect say, 4 per cent inflation, keep your money in 30-day deposits until longer-term rates move higher or until you are satisfied that the threat of inflation is abating. Conversely, if five-year rates are at 5 per cent and you expect another economic slowdown and a further drop in interest rates, you might want to lock in the longer-term rate.

Sometimes short-term rates move higher than long-term rates, creating what is called an inverted yield curve. This reflects the market's view that long-term interest rates will move lower. To attract short-term money and discourage investors from investing for the long term, deposit-taking institutions raise short-term rates.

If you move into the short end of the market because you expect rates to move up and intend to switch later to five-year deposits, remember that you are speculating. Central banks, such as the Bank of Canada, are responsible for setting interest-rate policies and their interest-rate policies can change overnight. You could find long-term rates moving lower than you expected.

If you prefer short-term savings instruments, don't overlook treasury bills or money market mutual funds. A money market fund is a mutual fund that invests primarily in treasury bills and wholesale bank deposits or top-quality commercial paper and you can expect to earn about two percentage points more than you would with a savings account. If a savings account is paying 2 per cent, you would expect to earn 4 per cent to 4.25 per cent. Treasury bills pay even more and are at least as safe as deposits. However, the T-bills are usually acquired through securities dealers who charge a commission and require a minimum investment of at least $5,000—often as much as $100,000 and even $1 million to get the highest possible rate. Therefore, you should compare the net interest you would receive after commissions with the savings rate or yield available on a money market fund. The net rate on a treasury bill is almost always higher than savings rates of comparable maturities.

Whether a treasury bill pays a superior yield to a money market fund depends on the amount of money you're investing and the commission rate charged by the investment dealer. Banks also sell treasury bills, although the commissions or service fees may prove a great deal higher than those charged by investment dealers. It pays to shop around.

Deposit insurance

Money kept on deposit with a bank or trust company is covered by the Canada Deposit Insurance Corp. (CDIC), while depositors at credit unions are protected by a national insurance system run by the credit unions themselves. The CDIC insures each depositor for up to $60,000 in principal and interest at a specific member institution, and it is compulsory for banks and trust companies that accept deposits to belong.

The $60,000 limit cannot be circumvented by having two accounts at different branches of the same bank. However, if you have one account for yourself and another joint account with your husband or wife, each account is insured up to $60,000. If you have several accounts in trust for each of your children, each account is insured separately because each has a different beneficiary. Your RRSP, if on deposit with a member institution, is insured separately.

Deposit insurance applies to accounts that mature within five years and are denominated in Canadian dollars. Principal and interest are insured up to the date of default. Therefore, if you have a five-year GIC with an institution that fails before the term is up, you get your money back, plus interest owed up to the date of default. The CDIC insures your deposit, but it does not guarantee interest for the term of the deposit.

To avoid difficulties, many people choose to invest only with the largest, strongest financial institutions. Large investors such as mutual funds and pension funds may place millions of dollars with a single institution, but they carefully monitor the financial statements of that institution. If you plan to invest more than the amount covered by deposit insurance with any institution other than the major chartered banks or the largest trust companies, do your homework. While the largest Canadian banks may have their problems from time to time, it is a fair assumption that the regulatory bodies would never allow them to fail under any circumstances.

Deposit insurance does not cover securities other than deposits, such as mutual funds, which are sold by a bank or trust company. Similarly, deposit insurance doesn't cover the mortgage debentures issued by some of the largest chartered banks. They are fully guaranteed by the issuing bank, and that's generally good enough for even the most conservative investor. Otherwise, it's caveat emptor.

The whole area of investor protection is currently being studied by various regulatory bodies. In the years ahead we will likely see arrangements that raise the limits of deposit insurance, and a better system than currently exists for protecting clients of an investment dealer who runs into financial trouble. The life insurance industry has introduced a system to protect policyholders within limits if a life insurance company fails.

Index GICs

Financial institutions have developed a new type of guaranteed investment certificate called an index GIC, which guarantees your capital and provides a portion of the stock market's gains. They are primarily for the RRSP market. They work like this: You tie your money up for a specific period, usually three years or five years. If at the end of that period the stock market is up, you get some portion of the appreciation. If, however, the market is down from the level at which you purchased the instrument, you get your principal back, which has been guaranteed by the financial institution, but no income.

Chapter 7

Bonds, Bills and Debentures

The bulk of personal investments are in debt securities. Virtually all the savings instruments discussed in the last chapter are debt obligations of trust companies, banks and other financial institutions. Most are insured up to the limit of deposit insurance or issued by the strongest financial institutions. As a result, most of them can be considered risk-free.

This chapter deals with a different kind of debt security—the type that is marketed through investment dealers and traded in the marketplace. These marketable debt securities are instruments such as treasury bills, bonds, debentures and mortgage-backed securities.

The major attraction of this type of debt security is its marketability. Given the volatility of interest rates over the past two decades, many investors have decided it is worth opting for a slightly lower rate of return than might be available from a GIC in order to have the ability to sell their investment at any time. If their investments remain liquid, they can move into shorter-term investments such as treasury bills if they believe that interest rates will move higher. And if they see rates moving lower, they can buy long-term bonds to lock in what they feel will prove to be a high return.

The performance of bonds

Bonds are generally safer than stocks. Government bonds have a strong guarantee and corporate bonds must pay interest on their debt before any dividends can be paid on stock. Even if the company goes broke, the investors in the corporation's bonds have first crack at the company assets before stockholders are paid anything—although some lenders get priority over others.

So, bonds should be dull plodders when it comes to generating a return, right? Wrong. At least, not in recent years.

For periods ended June 30, 1998, mutual funds that invest primarily in bonds showed an average compound annual return of 8.4 per cent over the last five years. The best returned 12.6 per cent while the worst eked out 4.7 per cent.

For the same time period, mutual funds that invest primarily in Canadian stocks showed an average return of 12 per cent. The best stock fund generated a 34 per cent return while the worst limped in with an annual compound return of –17 per cent.

The risk difference can be measured by the spread between the best and worst of each type of fund: about 7 percentage points for bonds and more than 50 percentage points for stocks. By investing in stocks five years earlier, you could at best earn about 35 per cent a year—or at worst lose a substantial portion of your capital. With bonds you would almost certainly earn an acceptable return. Chart I compares the average annual returns of Canadian bond mutual funds with average annual returns of mutual funds that invest in shares of large Canadian companies.

If the rewards of the stock game seem worth more than the risk, so be it. Meanwhile, however, the bonds offer a profitable and less uncertain choice for the long-term investor.

Bonds versus Stocks
ANNUAL RETURNS TO JUNE 30

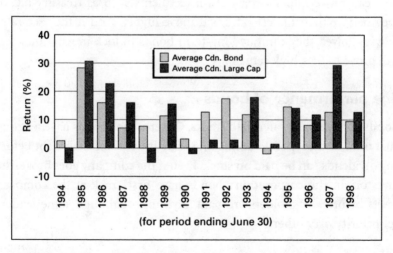

CHART 1

How will bonds perform in the future? No one knows the answer to that nor does anyone know whether stocks can continue their performance of the past. However, it is unlikely that the Canadian bond market will continue to generate double-digit returns over the next few years. Interest rates have declined substantially over the past few years because of the recession and declining inflation rates. With economic recovery, demand for funds by business, government and individuals will almost certainly increase, which will cause rates to rise. That, in turn, would hurt bond prices. In early 1994, bond prices declined sharply as interest rates rose; by early 1995, bond prices had recovered slightly because of an overall decline in rates. They continued to provide good returns through the middle of 1998.

When you buy a bond, you are buying a stream of income and the return of the principal amount of the bond at some point in the future. The market price of a bond reflects interest rate levels at a point in time. If other bonds are available at a higher rate than the coupon rate of your bond, then your bond will trade at a discount to its face value. Conversely, if market interest rates are lower than the coupon rate of your bond, then your bond will trade at a premium to its face or maturity value, normally $1,000.

Bonds that will not mature for many years respond to interest rate changes much more violently than do bonds with less distant maturities. For example, a 5 per cent $1,000 bond that matures in five years would be worth $747 if the market interest rate is 6 per cent. But if interest rates jumped to 10 per cent, the bond's value would drop to $621, a decline of $126.

A $1,000 bond maturing in 10 years would be worth $558 when the market interest rate is 6 per cent, but would drop in value to $386 if the interest rate rises to 10 per cent. That is a decline of $172, a much steeper drop than the $126 decline for the five-year bond.

Today, most bonds outstanding have fixed coupon rates that are 8 per cent or more and trade at premiums to their face values, reflecting the slide in interest rates in recent years.

Your guarantee

Before investing in marketable debt securities you should be familiar with the two basic types: those guaranteed by the federal government and those that are not. Individual investors should generally stick to Government of Canada bonds for two reasons. First and most important, they are backed by Ottawa, so your money is not at risk. Second, they are the most marketable bonds available in Canada. That means that Government of Canada bonds have very narrow spreads between the buying price and selling price. The difference between the bid and ask for $1,000 Government of Canada bonds might be as little as $5. In contrast, if you hold a corporate issue that is not actively traded, the spread could be as much as $50 per $1,000.

Provincial bonds can be considered risk-free as well, as can any other bonds guaranteed by the federal or provincial governments. However, the spreads on these can be wider than those on Government of Canada bonds.

Corporate bonds

Corporate bonds also carry little risk at the time they are issued but a lot can happen to a company over 20 years. Unless you have a large, diversified bond portfolio and are willing to monitor the quality of your holdings frequently, stick to Government of Canada bonds. If you decide to invest in corporate bonds because of their higher interest rates, try to stick to larger issues. The difference in the interest rates on corporate bonds reflects the bonds' quality—lower-quality, higher-risk bonds pay more interest. As with any investment, the higher the promised return, the greater the risk.

Also, the price of thinly traded bonds is usually more volatile than that of larger, broadly traded issues. You may pay less for thinly traded bonds when buying, and you may get more when selling if someone wants them desperately enough. But with a thinly traded bond issue, the selling price is often low.

Within the corporate debt market, investors can also find debentures. Corporate bonds are generally secured by specific assets, while debentures are often secured only by the general credit of the issuer. When buying either bonds or debentures, you risk having problems in the future if the company runs into financial difficulty, even if your debt is secured. Your money could be tied up indefinitely, and the eventual settlement may not be to your liking.

Aside from the risk of default, which you can eliminate by sticking to Government of Canada bonds, there is interest-rate risk. When rates rise, bond prices fall because an investor who wants to buy a bond at current rates will consider an older bond with a lower rate only if the bond's price is discounted to make its yield comparable.

Government bonds

The federal government raises funds by issuing three types of instruments: Canada Savings Bonds, treasury bills and marketable bonds.

A Canada Savings Bond is actually a flexible term deposit with the government rather than a true bond. They typically have a term of seven to 10 years, but the period and the interest rate are based on market conditions and can vary. The rate is adjusted each year, although a minimum is guaranteed for the full term. The bonds can be cashed at any time at full face value plus interest earned to the end of the previous month, with the exception of the first two months.

There are two types of Canada Savings Bonds: those that pay interest annually, and compound interest bonds on which the interest is reinvested. Even if you buy compound bonds, you must declare the earned interest on your income tax return even if you haven't received it. You must declare interest in the year accrued. Specific Canada Savings Bond issues are available for RRSPs and RRIFs.

Treasury bills and marketable bonds differ from savings bonds in that they are not redeemable on demand. But they can be sold through an investment dealer or bank in the bond market. Treasury bills are short-term instruments that mature in 90 to 180 days. They are denominated in amounts of $1,000 and sold at a discount to face value. For example, an investor purchasing a $1,000 treasury bill with 60 days left to maturity earning an annual interest rate of 6 per cent would pay about $990 for the bill. Not only the federal government issues treasury bills. There are also provincial bills that sell at slightly higher yields, reflecting a moderately larger risk.

The commercial paper chase

Major corporations and finance companies issue commercial paper similar to treasury bills in that they mature within one year and are sold at a discount to face value. Yields on commercial paper, even for very sound companies, are higher than for either federal or provincial treasury bills. For instance, 90-day treasury bills were yielding 5.0 per cent in mid-1998, while top-quality 90-day commercial paper was yielding 5.2 per cent. The higher yields may appeal to large investors who monitor the financial strength of borrowers, but most individuals should stay out of this market. Commercial paper is usually subordinated debt, which means that if the company goes belly up, holders of the notes are paid only after secured creditors receive their share.

Some companies issue commercial paper that is guaranteed by a bank. This allows small firms to tap this market for short-term funds. The rates paid reflect the quality of the guarantor.

Lower-quality, high-yielding commercial paper is also available. But be careful. Hundreds of millions of dollars were lost in the 1960s, when Atlantic Acceptance collapsed and its short-term paper became worthless.

Many issues of commercial paper and long-term bonds are rated by Canada's two bond rating services, Dominion Bond Rating Service of Toronto and Canadian Bond Rating Service of Montreal. Also, Moody's Investor Service Inc. and Standard & Poor's Corp., both of the United States, rate Canadian bond issues that are of interest to U.S. investors. If you want to invest in commercial paper, stick to top-quality issues only—those in the top two or three grades of rating classification. All major investment dealers selling commercial paper can supply information on ratings.

Bonds and coupon rates

Bonds issued by governments and corporations have coupon interest rates, which when multiplied by $1,000, the usual maturity value of a bond, tell you the amount of interest paid each year. Payments are usually made semi-annually. For example, the Government of Canada bond maturing June 1, 2010, has a 9.5 per cent coupon, which means it pays $95 interest annually with two payments of $47.50 each. However, the coupon rate does not necessarily indicate the actual return that an investor will receive. In mid-1990, this bond was trading at $927.50. Because of this discount, a buyer would earn a return of almost 10.4 per cent if the bond were held to maturity. This return is made up of interest and capital appreciation of $72.50, which represents the difference between the price paid and the maturity value. Three years later, in mid-1993, this bond was trading at $1,156.50, reflecting the sharp decline in interest rates over the previous two years, and yielding about 7.2 per cent. Now the return a buyer would receive would represent interest, which would be reduced by capital depreciation of $156.60, to maturity. In mid-1995, the bond was trading at $1,081 to yield 8.5 per cent. In mid-1998, it was trading at $1,3422 to yield 5.5 per cent.

There are a number of subtle differences in the rates of return an investor would earn on two bonds issued by the same source and with identical maturity dates, but different coupon rates. For example, a government bond with a 6.5 per cent coupon and maturing in 2004 traded in mid-1994 at about $1,036 to yield 5.9 per cent. A 10.25 per cent bond due in 2004 was trading at about $1,242 to yield 5.8 per cent. The investor will get back $1,000 and while interest income is fully taxable, capital gains are only partially taxed. Therefore, the lower-coupon bond is more valuable, which makes its yield lower and its price higher.

Investors who expect interest rates to decline will often invest in discount bonds. Someone who bought an 8.75 per cent bond when interest rates were 10 per cent and then saw market rates decline from 10 per cent to 8.75 per cent would make a capital gain of $110 on each bond. This capital gain on low-coupon bonds tends to make their prices more volatile than those of bonds with higher coupons. When interest rates fall, all bond prices rise, and when rates rise, bond prices fall. However, a low-coupon bond's price will rise more sharply on falling rates, and drop more precipitously on rising rates, than will the price of a high-coupon bond. The reason lies in the overall income stream of the bond.

A decline in rates increases the ultimate maturity value of the bond more than it increases the value of the interest payments. For example, $10 in interest next year is worth $9.09 today when the interest rate is 10 per cent. And $1,000 of maturity value 10 years from now is worth $385.54 today. If interest rates drop to 5 per cent, the present value of the interest payment will rise to $9.52, an increase of about 4.8 per cent. But the present value of the bond's worth at maturity will shoot up to $613.91, an increase of almost 60 per cent. With a low-coupon bond, most of the present value is in the maturity value, so an increase in interest rates magnifies the value of the capital gain, which is taxed more lightly than interest income, and pushes up low-coupon bond prices sharply. The opposite occurs when interest rates fall and capital gains shrink.

For those who want to take the risky path of speculating on interest rates, choosing bonds by the size of coupon is one possibility. If you believe interest rates will fall sharply in a short period, the best bonds to buy are long-term, low-coupon bonds; they will appreciate most. If you want to hold bonds but are worried about an interest-rate increase, choose high-coupon bonds with a short maturity.

Bond speculators should also be aware of the effect of the term to maturity on bond prices. Long-term bonds respond more strongly to interest-rate changes than do short-term bonds. The reason stems from compound interest; interest-rate changes have a greater impact on payments far in the future than on payments in the near future.

Government of Canada bonds provide a good example of this phenomenon, as shown in Table XIII. The table looks at the change in price between two 10.25 per cent bonds. One of the bonds matures on February 1, 2004. The second matures on March 15, 2014. Bond prices are quoted in points, so a bond quoted at 102.05 means it is trading at $102.05 per $1,000 of face value. As you can see, a drop in market interest rates caused the price on the shorter-term bond to rise by 18.9 per cent while the price on the long-term bond rose by 24.8 per cent. Just as longer-term bonds generally rise more than shorter-term bonds when interest rates fall, they fall more when interest rates rise.

One thing certain

One thing is certain—few investors can accurately predict interest-rate movements. Those who are investing for the long haul should hold bonds with a mixture of coupon rates and terms to maturity, slanting the portfolio in the direction they believe will provide the greatest short-term returns. This reflects an investment portfolio approach to interest-rate risk, with parts of the portfolio geared to generating satisfactory performance, no matter what happens to interest rates. If you choose not to create a diversified bond portfolio, you can invest in a bond mutual fund, which offers the advantages of professional management and a diversified portfolio.

Change in Price of Two 10.25% Bonds

BOND	PRICE DEC. 31, 1994	PRICE AUG. 2, 1998	% CHANGE
10.25% Feb., 2004	$106.70	$122.32	+ 14.6
10.25% Mar. 15, 2014	109.50	148.95	+ 36.0

TABLE XIII

If you prefer your own portfolio, other bond features must be considered. For example, government bonds are almost always non-callable, which means that when you buy a 20-year bond, it will be outstanding for the full 20 years. That isn't the case with corporate bonds. Often a corporate bond has what is known as a call feature, which gives the company issuing the bonds the right to buy them back at a specified price after a specific number of years. If you buy a bond with a call feature, the price you pay is often based on the call date, rather than the maturity date.

Similarly, many corporate bonds have a sinking-fund provision that requires a portion of the bonds to be repurchased each year after a specified number of years. The purpose of a sinking fund is to retire a number of bonds each year to reflect the depreciated value of the asset originally financed by the bonds. A sinking-fund provision protects investors, and the expected diminishing supply of bonds can lead to premium prices.

Strip bonds

Many people buy strip bonds for their RRSPs. A strip bond is created when an investment dealer buys a bond and strips off the coupons and sells them and the principal bond separately. Each coupon sells at a different price depending on when it is paid and the interest rate applied to that term.

In effect, a buyer who holds the bond to maturity knows the rate of return in advance. For example, a 20-year bond with an 8 per cent coupon rate consists of 40 coupons of $40 each, payable every six months, and the principal repayable in 20 years. A buyer of a coupon payable in six months who wants a rate of return of 8 per cent would discount that coupon by 4 per cent and would pay $38.46. The coupon payable in six months would sell at a price of $36.98. The coupon payable in 20 years would sell at a price of $8.33. If, however, the market yield for 20-year coupons was 9 per cent, the price would be $6.88; conversely, if the rate was 7 per cent, the price would be $10.10.

Strip bonds are especially popular when rates are high since they allow investors to lock in a long-term rate of return that is, in effect, risk-free if held to maturity. However, strip coupons are far more volatile than bonds with a stream of income that can be reinvested. Also, the longer the term, the more volatile the bond, as there is more potential for interest-rate changes. For tax purposes, the difference between purchase price and maturity price is considered interest. Thus, they are best used in RRSPs where they would grow untaxed.

Redeemable and extendible bonds

In periods of rising interest rates, it is common to see issues of redeemable and extendible bonds. For example, a government might issue a 20-year bond, redeemable after five years. If you bought one of these bonds you would have the option, just before the end of the five-year period, of keeping the bond or redeeming it for the full face value. If interest rates were higher than the coupon rate, you would likely cash in the bond and reinvest your money elsewhere. The market price of a redeemable bond would be based on the redemption date if market interest rates were higher than the coupon rate, and on the maturity date if market rates were lower than the coupon rate. An extendible bond might be issued for five years with a feature extending it, at the holder's choice, to 15 years.

These bonds appeal to investors who are concerned that interest rates might skyrocket. Without such features, governments would have difficulty attracting long-term money in periods of rising interest rates.

Convertible debentures

Some corporate debentures are convertible into common stock. The issuer may have one of two reasons for offering such debentures: to make the bonds more attractive or to use the bonds to issue equity in a period when the market is nervous about accepting new share issues.

Convertible debentures carry coupons like those of regular debentures, although the interest rates paid would likely be lower than those paid on regular debentures. The lower coupon rate is offset by the provision that allows investors to convert their bonds to common stock at a predetermined price for a specified time period—usually several years. This way the buyer knows that if the stock price goes up, he or she can convert the debenture and realize a capital gain. If the stock price doesn't rise, the investor continues to receive interest until maturity, at which time the principal will be repaid.

The price of a convertible debenture depends on the conversion price relative to the price of the underlying stock. If a $1,000 debenture is convertible into 100 shares and the stock is selling at $15, the debenture would likely trade around $1,500. If the stock fell to $8, the convertible debenture would either trade at $800, plus some premium to reflect the possibility that the stock price might rise, or the price of the debenture based on its coupon rate, whichever is higher. Most companies issuing convertible debentures, as well as the investors who buy them, hope that the price of the company's shares will rise so that the debentures can be converted to stock.

Junk bonds

Another type of bond is the so-called "junk bond," which may yield several points more than other corporate issues. The ability of a company to make the interest payments on these bonds is often questionable and the assets involved often leave little cushion for safety. That's why a buyer may receive several points of interest more than on less risky bonds such as a utility bond. Investors buy junk bonds because of their high coupon rates and because the market will reduce the risk premium paid and the bonds will appreciate in value if the company's profitability improves.

Some junk bonds trade at deep discounts when the issuer is unable to pay the interest. Normally, if a company defaults on interest, the trustee involved in the receivership will try to get its hands on company assets, and the firm is liquidated—making bonds worth much less than their original value. However, there often is another solution that benefits everyone involved, including the holders of junk bonds. All parties may agree to a settlement that will see creditors get more than they would if the company were liquidated. Bondholders speculating on this outcome between the company and its creditors find that their bonds are suddenly worth a great deal more because their share of assets has increased.

Where do you buy bonds?

In Canada, bonds trade "over-the-counter" rather than on an exchange such as the stock market. This means you buy and sell bonds through investment dealers and banks. Most knowledgeable traders deal with investment dealers because the costs are less and the returns are higher. Both investment dealers and banks will sell new government issues at the issued price, without commission.

A dealer with a bond department is probably buying bonds as principal, which means the dealer will buy bonds at one price from you and then either sell them at a higher price to another investor or hold them in inventory. If a dealer buys bonds as principal, the fee is built into the price paid and no additional commission is payable. Alternatively, if you sell a bond, the price received from the dealer is reduced by the dealer's markup.

Some smaller investment dealers don't have bond departments. These companies will likely purchase from or sell to another dealer, and tack on a commission. It is best, however, to work with a dealer that has a specialized bond department with expert staff. But remember, bond trading is a big business, so don't expect much service if you're trading only a few thousand dollars' worth of bonds.

Mortgage-backed securities

Available through investment dealers in denominations of $5,000, mortgage-backed securities are backed by a pool of residential mortgages. Canada Mortgage and Housing Corporation guarantees both principal and interest, and payment takes place on the 15th of each month. Each month's payment is a mixture of principal repayment and interest. Most issues have terms of two to five years, and the yields generally put them among the highest AAA-rated, fixed-income investments available.

Chapter 8

Preferred Shares: The "Bond Stock"

A preferred share can be viewed as a bond that hasn't quite made it in terms of safety, or as a common stock without the profit potential. Investors buy preferred shares because they pay dividends that generally provide an after-tax rate of return greater than that of interest-paying investments such as bonds and GICs.

Because of the dividend income tax credit, on an after-tax basis $1 of dividend income from a Canadian corporation is equal to $1.26 of interest income. This is just a general rule, but usually if your choice is between a bond with a yield of 8 per cent and a preferred share yielding about 6.4 per cent, the preferred share will return more. For people in lower income brackets, the difference in after-tax rate is especially significant. But there are other considerations, such as the safety of your investment. Many people would prefer to take a slightly lower return on a guaranteed investment and worry less. However, when properly chosen, preferreds have a definite advantage over interest-paying securities because of that higher after-tax return. You would not include preferred shares in your RRSP for income because an RRSP cannot take advantage of the dividend tax credit.

Preferred shareholders are, in fact, owners of the company. But they generally don't have a vote on company affairs—a privilege usually reserved for common shareholders. Still, preferred shares have more clout when it comes to dividends. Preferred shareholders receive their share of company profits before common shareholders but after interest due on bonds and other debt securities is paid.

If a company fails, preferred shareholders are entitled to nothing until all creditors, including bondholders, are paid. But preferred shareholders take precedence over common shareholders when a company winds up. Yet this may be of little comfort because companies that go under usually have a liquidation value that is too low to repay even the creditors. In addition, preferred shareholders have somewhat less protection in the event of a takeover than do common shareholders.

Preferred dividends are usually fixed, either in dollars or as a percentage of par (nominal) value.

When earnings are inadequate, the preferred dividend will be skipped. But most preferred share issues have a cumulative feature requiring that all preferred dividends be paid, including those in arrears, before any common stock dividend is declared.

Even though preferred stock issues are safer than common stock, company failure or dividend default should be a concern. If you are buying preferred shares for income, and wish to keep your portfolio as low-risk as possible, you should consider only those issued by the most financially solid companies. The same services that rate commercial paper and bonds also rate preferred shares, so inform your broker that the only preferreds you wish to consider are those with P1 and P2 ratings, the two highest classifications. And make sure your broker informs you of any changes in the ratings of your stock.

In addition to sticking to the strongest companies, diversify your holdings in case one of your investments turns sour. If the fortunes of a company in which you hold preferreds become clouded, you are probably better off selling. The adage that your first losses are your smallest often proves true.

Of course, higher yields are available from preferreds with lower rankings and from shares of companies that are not ranked by the services. These often appeal to sophisticated investors who are willing to assume increased risk as a trade-off for higher returns.

The preferred market can seem complicated for the novice because of the different types of shares available. What they have in common, at least when issued by major companies, is that they trade on stock exchanges just like common stocks. The following are some of the types of preferred shares available.

- **Straight preferreds:** These do not carry a maturity date and are, in effect, a perpetual security. Prices of straight preferreds are most sensitive to changes in interest rates. They can be volatile in periods of sharply changing rates, but are extremely attractive in periods of high rates—particularly if it appears that rates will fall.

- **Retractable preferreds:** These give the holder the right to redeem the shares at a specific date for par value. This is an attractive provision because it protects investors against a sharp increase in interest rates. Retractable preferreds are a good choice in periods when the direction of rates is uncertain.
- **Floating-rate preferreds:** These have an interest rate that floats with changes in the prime rate. Floating-rate preferreds are the best bet during periods of rising interest rates.
- **Fixed floating-rate preferreds:** These have a fixed rate for several years, then a floating rate. These give investors some protection against rising rates.
- **Convertible preferreds:** These are convertible into common stock. Convertibles, particularly those issued by utilities, are popular with those who invest for income. In the short term, the convertible preferred pays a higher dividend than the common share. But in the longer term, there is a high probability that the common dividend will increase to a point that exceeds the preferred dividend. At that point, investors would convert their convertible preferreds to common shares.

The fact that preferred dividends are more certain than common stock dividends is a big plus for investors who want to maximize after-tax income. Even so, not every investor holds preferreds for income. Some buy those with dividends in arrears as speculative investments, hoping for capital gains if the company pays past dividends. But whatever the reason for investing, don't lose sight of the fact that shares of any sort are not as safe as government bonds. As a result, you must monitor your holdings carefully. If you're not prepared to do this, consider investing in preferreds through a mutual fund whose professional manager will decide what stocks have the best potential.

Chapter 9

Common Stocks: The Inside Story

To many people it isn't that important whether gambling is legalized in Canada. After all, they can always take a chance on the stock market.

But stocks don't have to be a gamble. Thousands of individual and institutional investors who play or invest in the stock markets are rewarded with long-term profits far above what they would earn in guaranteed investments and bonds. However, to be successful you must know how the markets work.

Stock price movements on organized Canadian exchanges—the Toronto Stock Exchange, the Montreal Exchange, the Vancouver Stock Exchange and the Alberta Stock Exchange—and on the major American exchanges are continuously reported and updated during each trading day. With the exception of the Alberta exchange, the exchanges publish indexes of price movements that chronicle the aggregate ups and downs of the market.

Common shares, which represent ownership of a company, constitute by far the largest portion of listed stocks. Prices of common shares may change throughout each trading day. Share prices reflect the general outlook for the stock market; investor expectations about a firm's profits, dividends and other developments that affect the company; and the prospects for the industry that the firm is involved in. Common share prices are generally much more volatile than prices of bonds or preferred shares, and some stocks are more erratic than others. For example, shares of a telephone utility that pays a high dividend will be more stable than shares of a penny mine with unknown prospects and whose share price reflects speculators' expectations.

Stock markets move in cycles, with prices and investor expectations rising and falling in response to changes in the economic outlook, interest rates, exchange rates, the rate of inflation and other economic variables. At a somewhat less august level, rumours of takeover attempts or changes in the performance of large firms have been enough to cause at least short-run market fluctuations. However, if you have a diversified portfolio of stocks and hold them for some time, you can expect to earn a rate of return that is several percentage points higher than if you invest in guaranteed investments.

Some investors choose to invest in only a single stock or a small number of stocks in hopes of quickly making a substantial profit. Some succeed, but portfolios with only a few stocks tend to be more volatile than widely diversified portfolios. The Toronto Stock Exchange 300 composite index reflects the prices of the 300 TSE-listed stocks with the largest market capitalizations. Market capitalization is the value of the shares traded on the exchange, or the price of the shares multiplied by the number of shares outstanding. Therefore, a company with 10 million shares outstanding and a stock price of $25 has a market capitalization of $250 million.

Over the 10 years ended June 30, 1998, the TSE total return index, which is the gain in the TSE 300 index plus stock dividends, recorded an average annual compound return of 11 per cent, about 4 percentage points more than you would have earned holding treasury bills. Using a June 30, 1997 ending date, the 10-year rate was 8.8 per cent, marginally more than you would have earned by holding treasury bills. Using a June 30, 1988 ending date, we see that the 10-year return was 16 per cent—about five percentage points above the treasury bill return. For the 10 years ended June 30, 1992, the return was 13.5 per cent, more than three points above the treasury bill return. Chart II shows the year-by-year performance for periods ended June 30 of the Toronto Stock Exchange total return index and the rate of return on federal treasury bills. The total return index is a good representation of what you would have earned by holding a broadly based stock portfolio.

Market cycles vary in length. Rising periods are called bull markets and falling markets are known as bear markets. Bear markets generally are shorter than bull markets and losses are usually made back in relatively short periods. However, bear markets can be severe, especially if you need your money in the middle of one. The deepest bear market in Canada took place between November 1980 and July 1992 when the index fell 44 per cent. It rose 202 per cent in the subsequent five years.

Stocks versus T-Bills
TOTAL RETURNS FOR PERIODS ENDED JUNE 30

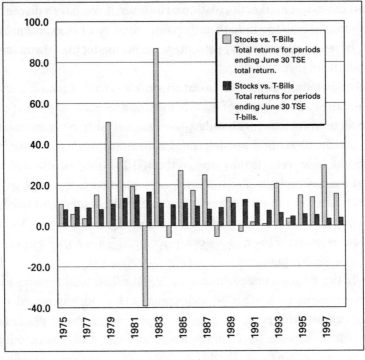

CHART II

However, segments of the market can have performance that differs dramatically from the composite index. For example, in the 36 months ended June 30, 1998, the TSE gold and silver index lost half its value. In contrast, the TSE financial services index more than tripled in value.

Investment techniques

There are many different strategies and techniques for investing in the stock market. One that has proven consistently profitable over the years is creating a diversified portfolio of shares in senior companies with solid histories of earnings, strong balance sheets and good prospects for the future. Good prospects for earnings are very important and, indeed, many companies that were considered blue chip in the 1980s failed to participate in the stock market recovery of 1993 because their earnings prospects were poor. This kind of diversification spreads risk among many companies. You then constantly monitor your holdings, adding new investments that appear to have better-than-average prospects and selling those that no longer meet your expectations. You can do this by conducting your own analysis, by depending on your broker for advice or by using professional management through a mutual fund. Some brokerage houses, investment counselling firms and trust companies also have investment management divisions that will look after your portfolio.

Of course, it is impossible for small investors to purchase a diversified portfolio of shares of senior companies because of commission costs. Addressing this, the Toronto Stock Exchange offers an investment product that gives investors diversification based on the TSE 35 index. Called an index participation unit, each unit represents a fraction of one share of each of the 35 companies represented in the index. The shares of the companies themselves are held by a custodian. Dividends paid by the companies flow through to holders of index participation units.

Another stock market investment technique, as we've already mentioned, is to hold only a few stocks in hopes of making gains far greater than those you would receive from a diversified portfolio. This method suits some investors well, while others lose most of their capital. People who use this technique specialize in trying to choose stocks before their prices start to rise and in unloading their dogs before they start to bark.

What separates the winners from the losers are their methods of picking stocks. Winners tend to use detailed analyses of companies, often confining their research to firms that are not widely followed by the investment industry in hopes of finding an undiscovered bargain. The share price of widely followed companies generally reflects all the known information, so it's difficult to stay ahead of the crowd when investing in these issues.

Benjamin Graham's legacy

The most successful method of investment analysis—perhaps at once the simplest and the most complicated—is the method developed by American analyst Benjamin Graham more than 60 years ago. Simply put, it involves searching for value—the share price should be below the value of the company's assets as represented by each share, after deducting liabilities. Although many variations of the method exist, including careful consideration of earnings trends and developments that may enhance a company's earnings, it all comes down to buying value.

The Benjamin Graham method is not always the most exciting way of assessing stocks. It requires patience, but it usually proves profitable over the long term. And you won't get badly burned, particularly if you remember to sell when a stock's price rises above its underlying value. Other methods involve buying into a falling market and selling when prices are rising. However, most stock market investors find it emotionally difficult to move against the crowd. Indeed, this "contrary" approach takes more discipline than the Graham approach. Even so, a follower of Graham is just as likely to be buying near the bottom and selling near the top.

Some investors play interest-rate cycles. When interest rates move up sharply, stock prices usually move lower; declining interest rates are usually associated with rising stock markets. But playing interest rates can be extremely tricky. Rates can move higher because of demand for funds by growing companies, so selling on this basis can be costly in terms of potential profits.

Technical analysis is another way to predict market behaviour and choose stocks. This technique looks not at balance sheets and income statements, but at charts of market and individual stock performance, trading volumes, various ratios of advancing stocks versus declining stocks and so on. Many people are skeptical about technical analysis, yet virtually every brokerage house employs a highly paid technical analyst whose job is to produce observations that individuals and brokers can consider when making investment decisions.

Timing purchases

If you knew when the stock market has hit its peak or its bottom, you would not need this book. You could buy stocks when prices are at their lowest and sell when they are at their highest—and you'd be very wealthy. But you can't do it. Even the pros are not consistently accurate in calling the direction of markets. According to the American Statistical Association, which has been conducting an ongoing evaluation of forecasting accuracy, a 50 per cent accuracy rating is par for the course—about the same odds as accurately calling heads or tails when flipping a coin.

Since it's not possible for you to buy at the bottom of the market and sell at the top, other rules have been developed. None of these works perfectly but at least two are better than buying in a hot market and selling when prices tumble, which is the apparent strategy of the emotional investor.

Buy-and-hold is one strategy. Simply put your money into a well-diversified portfolio consisting of 15 or more stocks spread among different industry groups, and only make changes when the condition of one of the companies deteriorates. Otherwise, ignore the day-to-day twitches of the market. When the long-term market trend is bullish, as it has been for the past 10 years or so, buy-and-hold pays off both in money returns and lack of anxiety.

Another strategy, somewhat more conservative, is to dollar-average. To dollar-average, you must put the same amount of money into a diversified portfolio regularly, perhaps every month or every three months. When prices are rising, you will automatically buy fewer stocks. When the market is falling, and share prices are lower, you will be able to buy more stocks. As a result, when market prices are fluctuating, the average cost of your shares tends to be lower than with a buy-and-hold strategy.

Which strategy is better? When markets are strong, buy-and-hold appears better. When markets are fluctuating with either a few sharp down periods, as in October 1987, or many small down periods, dollar-averaging is superior.

If you take the view that the stock market will outperform money market funds over the long term and you can invest for the long term, then the buy-and-hold strategy works best. For example, if you invested $180,000 in the TSE 300 at the end of June 1983, you would have accumulated $847,631 at the end of 15 years. If, however, you had put $1,000 in the TSE and invested the remaining $179,000 in money market funds, and then invested $1,000 each month in the TSE, you would have accumulated $693,338 at June 30, 1998.

Which strategy do you choose? It depends on how averse you are to losing money. If you hate losing money, dollar-averaging is better. In a bull market, it generates positive returns but they'll be smaller than with buy-and-hold. In a bear market, it will generate the smallest losses and, often, as in the 1930s, a gain. If you are more of a gambler, try buy-and-hold. It is still better than buying on hunches but it does expose you to sharp declines in the market.

The reality is that few of us have huge lump sums available for investment and instead invest a portion of our income on a monthly basis, effectively following a dollar-averaging strategy.

Selling under dollar-averaging

Adopting the right strategy for buying stocks is one trick to achieving a profitable portfolio. Selling strategies are even more obscure. But the time comes when an investor needs the proceeds from the portfolio for retirement expenses, tuition needs for children or just to spend on something else.

Selling at the top of the market or just when prices are beginning to slide is optimal. The trouble is that, at the top, most investors fail to recognize they're sitting on a peak. Even when prices begin to slide, there is always hope that the slide is a temporary "technical" adjustment, and that prices will recover in the near future. So, the investor holds on to his or her stocks and doesn't sell until the decline becomes precipitous and pessimism dominates the market. This kind of emotional selling is the other side of the coin to emotional buying: It leads to selling at lower prices than necessary.

Dollar-averaging techniques also work for selling. However, they require some modification. If one simply sold a constant dollar amount of shares over the cycle, most shares would be sold when stocks are cheap and the fewest number would be sold when prices are high—not an ideal outcome.

Instead, the seller should sell those shares where the difference between market price and average cost of the shares is largest. If share A was bought at $100 and now has a selling price of $150, while share B was bought at $80 and now sells at $120, the investor would sell share A before selling share B because the gain spread on A is $50 while it is only $40 on B. The selling program can continue even if the price falls below average cost and the stocks are sold at a loss, as long as the stocks sold first are those where the loss is least—where the difference between acquisition cost and selling price is smallest. However, the regularity of the sales should persist: In other words, there should be no wholesale dumping. Sales should continue on a constant dollar of sales each month according to acquisition cost.

This rule is based on the assumption that the inherent quality of the stock has not changed. Stocks issued by companies that have deteriorated should be sold immediately if the investor believes that the weakness is permanent and will lead to further weaknesses.

This selling policy will probably result in the portfolio losing its diversification. At the bottom of the cycle, the remaining stocks will be what are called cyclical stocks—stocks that are very sensitive to economic and market conditions. However, as the market turns up, these stocks usually show the strongest recovery and the investor will realize better gains than if the cyclicals had been dumped during the downswing of the cycle. Further, the disinvestment process will unload the "concept" or "trendy" stocks early in the game when their prices are highest, which is just when everyone is becoming emotionally high on the stocks.

Beating the market

As many stock pros have known for years, it is possible to beat the market. Still, for many years, a strong argument was made that it was impossible to buy an undervalued stock. All stocks, the story went, reflect all the available information so that they are properly priced. This is called the "efficient markets hypothesis." What made it work, the argument goes, is arbitrage, where a knowledgeable investor would sell a stock when its market price was above its true value, and buy a stock selling at a price below value. The sales would push down the stock price and the purchase of "cheap" stocks would push up prices. All of this supposedly happens so fast that no one could make an abnormally high profit on a stock.

A second and related argument was called the "perfect capital markets theory." Under this theory, a stock's price was determined by its riskiness. If a stock seemed cheap, based on price and earnings, it probably was riskier than other similar stocks. An expensive stock was probably safer.

These arguments, which started among academic finance experts, became pervasive. Indeed, market index funds, where the composition of the portfolio mimicked the TSE 300, for instance, is a reflection of the theories. An index fund makes no attempt at stock selection: It simply holds stocks that follow the stock market index and the returns are then supposed to be as good as you can get without taking unnecessary risks. According to these arguments, fund managers who spend money on securities analysis were wasting both money and time. The market tells all.

In the last several years, empirical investigations, often done by the same people who erected the two theories originally, have called into question the effectiveness of the theories. There are just too many exceptions to the theory to support its original claims of supremacy.

However, investors can use a number of indicators to find bargains. Several of these indicators, such as the price-to-earnings ratio, price-to-book-value ratio and intrinsic value, are thoroughly studied and often used; others do not have a rational explanation, at least not yet. Where there is no rational explanation, the investor using the indicators is acting on the historic repetition alone. There's nothing wrong with that except that, while financial history does repeat itself sometimes, it does not do so all of the time. Here's a look at a few of these bargain indicators.

The price-to-earnings (P/E) ratio: Buy stocks with low ratios of market price to earnings per share and, according to the studies, you should do far better than the market. This is part of Benjamin Graham's formula for choosing undervalued stocks. The notion has been around a long time and it makes some sense.

If a company is making high earnings and its price is still low, the chances are that the market will eventually recognize it. Meanwhile, a company with a high price-to-earnings ratio is likely to be a favourite, but an increasingly expensive one. When the trendiness of the high P/E stocks fades, so do the prices. At the very least, this strategy should keep you out of overvalued stocks.

The price-to-book-value ratio: Sometimes this is called the Value Line effect, after the investment service that popularized it. Pick stocks with a low ratio of price to book value per share. Book value per share is the total of assets less liabilities and preferred shares, all divided by the number of shares outstanding. Low price-to-book-value ratio stocks do significantly better than stocks selling at a high ratio of price to book value.

This effect has been borne out by many studies. It has nothing to do with risk. However, it may be related to the size of the firm and low price-to-earnings ratio. Once your stock's price starts rising faster than its book value, it becomes a candidate for sale.

Intrinsic value and mean reversion: For most of us, finding a value for a stock different from the market price is no simple matter. But this value, called the stock's intrinsic value, is significant. Intrinsic value is based on such things as expected earnings growth, industry growth and the hidden value of such things as real estate that may be worth far more than the value shown on the balance sheet. Press your broker and he or she can likely get some estimate of intrinsic value from the firm's research team.

If your broker tells you that the intrinsic value equals the market price, don't bother buying it unless you want to do no better than average. But if he or she convinces you that the intrinsic value of the stock exceeds its price, give it some thought. While you are thinking, check whether the price has been at or above the intrinsic value over the past year or so. If it has, it becomes an excellent buy candidate. The reason for this is that stocks tend to move toward their intrinsic value.

A stock that has lost favour in the market but retains a high intrinsic value is likely to show superior price appreciation as its price reverts to the mean. Substantial evidence supports this argument, and in markets where investors tend to buy trendy stocks only to move on to other stock trends, it is a great way to avoid the crowd and make money at the same time.

Find a stock that is priced well above its intrinsic value and you have a strong candidate for sale. If all goes well, many of your intrinsic value bargains will become selling candidates as price rises toward intrinsic value.

Small is beautiful: In comparing firms that involve the same degree of risk, it has been found that the returns tend to be significantly higher for firms that have a small total value of equity than for firms that have a large equity capitalization.

In Canadian stock markets, there is evidence that portfolios of small firms show better monthly return than do portfolios of large firms of equal risk. Similar results have been found in Australia, Japan, the United Kingdom and the United States.

Although this effect works most of the time, it doesn't always. Between 1969 and 1973, for example, small-firm portfolios underperformed portfolios with large companies. Again, there is no convincing evidence explaining this effect. It may have something to do with the growing dominance of large institutional investors who tend to overlook small companies. On the other hand, the effect has been recorded for nearly 50 years and the institutional investors were less dominant in the stock market in the 1950s than today. Still, if you had invested $1,000 in the average Canadian large-cap fund at the end of June 1993, you would have had $1,874 at the end of five years. If you had invested in the average small-capitalization fund, you would have had $1,763.

The January effect: This is a dominant seasonal effect. Firms whose shares drop in December tend to rebound strongly in January. Therefore, buying a portfolio of these cheap stocks in December should generate above-average returns in January and maybe longer.

Some claim that this is a tax effect: Investors sell to establish losses at the end of the year and then buy back into their positions during January. In Canada, however, the January effect is discernible prior to 1972, when there was no capital gains tax on stock sales. Another argument against the tax sell-off explanation is that some studies have shown that January-effect stocks can continue to outperform the market for as long as three years.

There have been some suggestions that the January effect reflects the effect of year-end bonuses or pension contributions made at the end of the year and invested by pension funds in January. Still, the January effect is not fully understood but it is persistent.

Day-of-the-week effect: Sell on Tuesday through Friday, but buy on Monday. Studies going back to 1928 indicate that this is a way to improve the rate of return on your portfolio. There isn't an explanation for this but it is pervasive.

The monthly effect: Buy toward the end of the month and sell during the first half of the month. Studies have shown that from the last day of the preceding month into the first half of the next month, stocks tend to register most of their gains. In the second half of the month, returns are lower and even negative. So buy when stocks are cheap—in the second half of the month—and do your selling during the first half of the month when prices tend to rise.

The reasons behind this monthly swing are even more obscure. Still, it seems to work.

All shares are not equal

Investors should also be aware that there are different types of common stock, especially when it comes to voting privileges. At one time, common shareholders had one vote for each share held. This has changed and a number of companies now have two classes of common shares, one of which is a subordinated share for voting. The regular common shares generally carry more votes per share than the subordinated common shares. As a result, control of the company's affairs often lies with a group of investors who have substantial voting power but less than a majority of the equity in the company.

This normally isn't a problem for investors, except when a takeover offer is made. Securities law requires that when a premium price of 15 per cent or more is paid for a control block of shares, a comparable offer must be made to all holders of that class of shares. This means that a takeover offer at a substantial premium to the market price will be made to the common shareholders, but not to the holders of subordinated common shares. Some companies with subordinated shares have what are called "coattail" provisions that are designed to protect holders of these shares in the event of a takeover. However, the market tends to discount the price of subordinated shares, even when there is a coattail.

There have been a number of cases in which companies have been bought out, or offers made, with the common shareholders who control the company getting a better deal than other shareholders. As a result, some institutional investors have a policy of buying only shares that control the vote, even though it means paying a premium. If you decide to invest in a company that has two classes of common shares, check how the coattail, if there is one, protects you. If you're not sure, play it safe and choose the shares that will benefit from a takeover offer.

In the end, consistent profits are made by being careful, avoiding excessive greed and doing a lot of homework. Certainly, the investor who buys a stock simply because he or she believes there exists a greater fool who will pay more for the stock, is often the greater—and poorer—fool him- or herself.

Unfortunately, many people get their first taste of the stock market by buying the penny dreadfuls—over-the-counter stocks only sold over the telephone by dealers who are not members of any exchange and make a living peddling paper and preying on people's greed and dreams.

If you are determined to try to get rich quickly, you must develop expertise in a specific area of the market, most likely in natural resources, and be prepared for massive ups and downs. Big money can be made, but luck is as much a part of it as is skill. And don't forget the adage about not putting all your eggs in one basket. Speculate with only those savings you can afford to lose without affecting your lifestyle and long-term goals.

Employee purchase plans

Many companies offer stock-purchase plans to encourage employees to become owners in their enterprises. Some plans are good, others are much better. When investing in your company stock, always remember that your investment portfolio should be diversified. You shouldn't put everything in one stock, particularly if your industry is cyclical and you may need to cash out when the industry is in the dumps. Remember, too, that such stocks are long-term investments. If you think you'll need your money in a year or so, stay out of the plan.

There are several variations. Many companies have a matching program in which a percentage of the employee's income is used to purchase shares issued by the company's treasury. The purchase is matched by the company so, in effect, you are getting shares at half price. However, the purchases that the company makes on your behalf are a taxable benefit.

Some companies give employees interest-free loans to buy shares. If you are offered shares at $20 each and the stock doubles, you could make a lot of money. But what happens if the company's fortunes turn and the stock plummets to 10 cents? You will owe the company the value of the loan. And even if the company forgives the loan, Revenue Canada will consider it a taxable benefit and you will have to pay tax on the value of the loan even though the stock is worth only a fraction of your purchase price.

Other companies give employees options to buy stock at a specific price for a specific time period. The advantage of the option is that you exercise it only if the stock goes up. Twenty-five per cent of the gain is tax-free. The remainder is taxed as income.

Another variation is the option loan plan. The option is granted at some price higher than the market price of the stock. Once the share price rises above the exercise price, the option is exercised and financed by a loan from the company. Any subsequent profits are capital gains.

Chapter 10

Mutual Funds: Suitable for Everyone

For many people, mutual funds are the best way to invest—whether the investment is in stocks, bonds, mortgages, treasury bills or a combination of investment vehicles.

A mutual fund is a pool of investments that is owned by many people and managed by professional portfolio managers. Investors become part of these pools, which are also known as investment funds, by buying units of the funds. The value of each unit represents the total value of the fund's investment portfolio divided by the number of shares outstanding. Most Canadian mutual funds are open-ended, which means that the number of outstanding shares changes as investors buy and sell units.

There is also a handful of "closed-end" funds that have a fixed number of shares. These shares generally trade on a stock exchange. While the value of an open-end fund unit is based on the underlying value of the portfolio divided by the number of units, the value of a closed-end fund share reflects whatever the market is willing to pay for it. In other words, the market value of a closed-end fund share may be lower or higher than the value of its underlying assets.

The pools of capital are invested by professional fund managers in a portfolio of securities, with the types of securities purchased reflecting the fund's objectives. For example, a fund with the goal of long-term growth within the framework of the Canadian economy would invest in common shares of Canadian companies. A fund whose objective is to earn current income might hold bonds or mortgages.

Mutual funds are extremely popular, with an estimated two million Canadians holding about $323 billion in the country's more than 1,700 mutual funds. There are several reasons for this popularity. First, mutual funds provide investors with an opportunity to diversify their investments. Because money is spread among many securities, investors are unlikely to suffer great financial losses if one investment goes sour. Most mutual funds invested in stocks usually own shares of at least 20 companies.

A second important reason for the popularity of mutual funds is professional management. In a mutual fund, investors' money is managed by a full-time investment professional whose job is to select and maintain a portfolio of securities that meets the fund's objectives. Professional management often gives investors higher returns than they could earn on their own.

In addition, mutual funds offer a selection of investment opportunities that is not generally available to individuals. For example, some funds hold bonds payable in foreign currencies but issued by Canadian government agencies or corporations—instruments that most individual investors simply don't have the capital to buy. Even investors who usually invest directly in securities can benefit from mutual funds, particularly if they want to invest a portion of their money in specific markets, such as Japan or Europe, and reap the rewards of global diversification and professional management.

Another big plus for mutual funds is liquidity. Investors can redeem shares of most funds on any business day, and the proceeds will be in their hands within a week.

Types of funds

Mutual funds fall into two main categories: growth and income. Within each of these categories are a variety of types, ranging from those that invest in a wide range of securities to those that concentrate on sectors such as precious metals or energy stocks. Some of these funds meet Revenue Canada's Canadian-content requirements for registered retirement savings plans, while others invest internationally.

Most growth funds that are eligible for RRSPs invest in a broad spectrum of Canadian common shares covering many industries. But there are also RRSP-eligible specialty funds that focus on smaller sectors of the Canadian economy. Even within the international group of funds, investors can choose specialty funds such as health funds or funds that concentrate their holdings in a single geographical area.

Fixed-income funds include bond funds, mortgage funds, preferred-share funds, money market funds and funds that combine two or more of these investments. Bond, mortgage and money market funds that confine their investing to the Canadian markets are RRSP-eligible.

Preferred-share funds invest primarily in dividend-paying preferred shares, and are usually purchased by investors who want high after-tax returns outside the shelter of an RRSP. Proceeds from such funds are eligible for the federal dividend tax credit, which effectively reduces the tax rate on dividends so that after-tax rates of return from preferred shares are competitive with those for bonds. However, the dividend tax credit cannot be used within an RRSP.

Money market funds invest in short-term debt securities such as government treasury bills, in deposits with major financial institutions and in corporate debt. Consequently, their rates of return are stable.

Of course, some funds are involved in a number of areas. There are several dozen balanced funds, or "managed-asset-mix" funds, that combine growth and income investments, with the mix of these vehicles changing according to market conditions.

Mutual funds are available through a number of sources. Some are offered through independent mutual fund dealers and stockbrokers who deal in funds offered by several fund management groups. Others are offered directly by their managers through affiliates or direct sales forces. All major banks and trust companies offer their own families of funds, while major insurance companies offer mutual funds or segregated funds that are similar to mutual funds. Bank-affiliated discount investment dealers offer their own plus others' mutual fund families.

Funds sold through a sales force are generally sold one of two ways: with an acquisition fee or commission that is paid to either a dealer or salesperson and which reduces the amount of capital available for investment; or with a redemption fee that declines with the time the investment is held.

Given the choice, most investors choose the redemption fee alternative because it appears less expensive and because all of an investor's money is invested in the fund. Front-end loads or acquisition fees can be as high as 9 per cent on paper, with a sliding scale of reductions for larger purchases. The realities are that most transactions are done at much lower levels. Indeed, because these commissions are negotiable, some firms charge zero commission to their clients. These dealers, however, receive a trailer commission from the fund management company. This trailer is a percentage of the management fee and can be as much as 1 per cent of the assets on an annual basis.

If you buy a fund with a redemption fee, the fund company pays the broker or dealer who sold you the fund a sales commission. The redemption fee declines over time. For example, if you redeem the fund within a year of purchase you will be charged a fee of about 5 per cent; different funds have different schedules. If you redeem in the second year, you could be charged 4.5 or 5 per cent, again depending on the fund. If you redeem after, say, seven years, you might not be subject to any redemption fee. Some fund groups allow you to switch among funds within the group without triggering redemption fees. You only pay redemption fees if you withdraw your money from the fund group.

If you invest $1,000 in a fund that charges a front-end commission and you require a lot of advice, don't expect a huge reduction in the commission. But if you invest $50,000 and require little service or information from a financial advisor, you should be able to negotiate a lower fee.

Funds sold directly by fund management companies, as well as bank and trust company funds, are generally "no-load" funds, meaning they are sold without a commission. With no-load funds, all your money goes to work for you.

Some no-load funds have staff members who offer advice on funds while trust companies and banks have improved the quality of information they provide to investors. Of course, don't expect an employee of a no-load organization to provide you with information on funds offered by competitors.

The rate of return you can earn from a fund depends on the type of fund, market conditions, the length of time you hold the fund and the skills of the fund manager.

Generally speaking, funds that invest for growth provide the highest long-term rates of return—often exceeding 12 per cent annually or more over a period of 10 to 20 years. In the short term, however, there is no way of predicting rates of return for a growth fund. Consequently, they should not be purchased with the view of making money over a very short period.

The Globe and Mail, The Financial Post and several other newspapers publish surveys of investment fund performance every month. You can also purchase compute software such as *PALTrak* for analyzing mutual funds.

Funds can be categorized by volatility of their monthly rate of return. The least volatile funds are money market funds. Their monthly rates of return are the most stable and rarely vary widely on a month-to-month basis. In contrast, specialty funds such as energy funds, gold funds, resource funds or funds that invest in specific markets, such as Japan, tend to have monthly rates of return that can vary widely. Broad-spectrum Canadian equity funds tend to be less volatile than specialty funds. Balanced or asset-allocation funds that combine stocks and bonds tend to be less volatile than equity funds but more volatile than bond funds. Bond funds are generally more volatile than money market funds but less volatile than those holding stocks.

If you want a stable rate of return, you will often have to settle for lower overall performance. If you want certainty, the only option is a money market fund. Because money market funds invest only in short-term instruments, you can redeem shares at any time and collect everything you invested, plus interest. Money market funds have historically paid about two percentage points more than premium savings accounts, but that rate of return is dwarfed by the long-term performance of growth funds. Still, money market funds offer excellent investment potential for those with short-term savings objectives—such as a down payment on a home.

Bond funds and other income funds usually provide medium- and long-term rates of return that fall between those of money market and growth funds. They are more volatile than money market funds but less volatile than growth funds because the income generated by the under-lying assets stabilizes returns. They are best suited to people who want current income in their portfolios or who want more stability than they would have with growth funds.

Even though growth funds offer the best long-term returns, you should consider market conditions before making a purchase. If conditions suggest that stock prices are expensive, you may want to put your money elsewhere. Most equity fund managers will protect investors by building up cash reserves when stock prices seem high. But if you are nervous about market conditions, you may want to choose a more conservative fund or a mixture of fund types. You might also consider funds with a mixture of asset types—balanced or managed-asset-mix funds—that make these decisions for you. These funds are designed to invest in growth assets when they are expected to perform best and in income assets when that is prudent.

Most investors buy funds entirely on past performance. Undoubtedly, historical performance is important because it shows how a manager has performed relative to competitors under identical market conditions. But there is a pitfall: You should make sure the person responsible for that stellar past performance is still running the fund. If not, past performance may be misleading. A fund's volatility ranking can also provide valuable performance clues. Top-performing funds with high volatility ratings often perform poorly in down markets.

When judging funds, look at various time periods. It is surprising how investors' conclusions can change when judging the performance of funds over different periods.

Also look at relative costs. Each fund discloses its management expense ratio—all expenses as a percentage of assets. These can vary widely among funds with similar objectives.

Chapter 11

Real Estate: Perils, Problems and Promise

If you're like most Canadians, the largest single investment you'll ever make, excluding your RRSP and pension, will be in real estate—your family home. Following close behind, your next largest financial venture will probably be another property, either for vacations or as an investment.

Real estate has been a financial winner for thousands of Canadians in many parts of the country over the past few decades. But the road has not always been smooth. In most parts of the country, real estate prices have been volatile. Some years ago, prices plunged in Alberta when the bottom fell out of oil prices. Some people walked away from their mortgages because they owed more than their homes were worth. High interest rates in 1990 triggered sharp declines in some markets, such as Toronto, where prices had soared beyond the reach of even affluent buyers. A few years later, mortgage rates fell to their lowest levels since the 1960s and prices bounced back in part. Vancouver house prices have been the highest in the country from time to time, fuelled by immigration from the rest of the country as well as abroad. Recent concerns about construction quality hurt some segments of the condominium market.

Even with regional ups and downs, the forces that have pushed prices higher in many markets remain intact. These forces include a sharp shift in demographics that has increased the number of young families and singles reaching home-purchasing age along with speculative and inflationary forces and relatively low interest rates.

Yet even with this history as a profitable investment, many people choose to be renters—and for good reason. Despite price increases, renting is still one of the best bargains in town. Monthly rents across Canada run at 50 per cent to 75 per cent of the cost of owning.

The better-paid, and presumably more financially sophisticated, Canadians are the homeowners. Indeed, the vast majority of high-income Canadian families own their own homes. Are these people crazy to own instead of saving money by paying rent? More to the point, should you buy a house? Or if you are already an owner, should you sell your house and rent instead?

You must never ignore the emotional and lifestyle influences in this decision, but financially at least part of the answer lies in where rents are headed. The vacancy rate in rental housing in most urban areas is low, which means that few rental apartments or houses are available.

Rent controls and hefty construction and maintenance costs make the building of new rental units risky. Once a building is constructed, there isn't any difficulty renting it if rates are competitive with existing rent-controlled structures, except in markets with low vacancy rates, where new units rent at much higher prices. However, it is just about impossible to keep rents moving up as quickly as maintenance and financing costs.

As a result, it seems unlikely that the existing rental structure will prevail. Within the next few years, unless there is general price deflation, the existing rental structure may fall apart. Alternatively, buildings will deteriorate to the point that even fewer acceptable rental units will be available and new units put on the market will carry much higher rents.

Yet soaring rents do not automatically mean it will be better to own than to rent. The reason is that, as rents rise, many renters will find home ownership attractive, and the subsequent demand will push up housing prices.

Where are housing prices headed?

Both housing prices and rental rates declined sharply in many markets during the last recession and have rebounded with lower interest rates and economic growth. What happens next? Answer correctly and you'll be rich. When monthly rental costs are lower than ownership costs, the only economic justification for owning rather than renting is the expectation that housing prices will rise. The expected price increase promises a tax-free capital gain for the homeowner but the value of that gain must offset the higher monthly ownership costs.

Two factors suggest that the future rise in housing prices will be significantly smaller than it has been in the past. These factors are demographic patterns and the current low inflation environment in which wages do not rise rapidly—limiting the ability of people to pay up for homes.

The impact of demographics

Most families have been having fewer children since the middle 1960s. The drop in family size has been so marked that, despite immigration, government officials believe that Canada is approaching zero population growth. This isn't a guess. The number of births per family has been dropping and shows no sign of increasing. This isn't a short-term fluke either. Except for the post-Second-World-War baby boom, family size has been gradually decreasing since the turn of the 20th century.

The early fruits of these smaller families are now in their twenties and early thirties. They are the next generation of house buyers, but their numbers are small. Already, the number of single-person households is rising dramatically and, according to government statistics, these people are not good candidates for home ownership.

Gradually, the percentage of the population from which new homeowners have traditionally been drawn, those aged 25 to 44, will

Population by Age Group

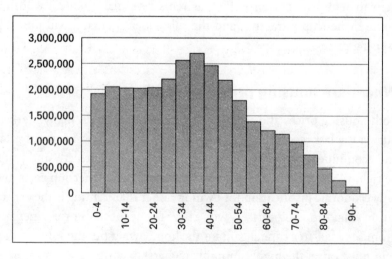

CHART III

diminish. The peak population group, aged 35 to 39, was 8.93 per cent of the population in 1997. As Chart III indicates, the number of potential home buyers entering home buying age will shrink. Meanwhile, there is an increase in the middle-aged segment of the population, who already own their homes and may be thinking of selling as their children leave home and retirement nears.

These demographic factors do not spell doom for housing price increases. But they do indicate that one of the major sources of housing demand is shrinking. We may even see a housing surplus early in the next century.

Trends in wages and housing prices

Another negative factor is the trend in wages compared to the costs of shelter. When wages drop below housing costs, then the cost of housing—whether rents or the price of homes—tends to flatten. This happened in the early 1970s. By the mid-1970s, housing costs again began to rise more rapidly than wages, and flattened once again between 1979 and 1982. Since then, a gap has again gradually developed between housing costs and wages. Over the next few years, it seems likely that house prices and rents will increase less rapidly than they have in the past few years.

So there are two reasons to be pessimistic about housing prices in the next few years. Over the long term, shifting demographics will cut into the growth of demand for housing. And, in the short term, it is unlikely that wages will be able to support a rapid rise in housing prices.

Does that mean that housing prices will drop dramatically? No. Even if inflation is totally abolished, housing prices are at worst likely to remain flat in the next few years. In the longer run, if inflation is flat and demand for housing shrinks, prices may gradually decline relative to the inflation rate. It also does not mean that housing prices will not boom in specific areas as bubbles of demand appear. But these bursts of prices are hard to predict and, overall, the long-term rate of price appreciation may be less than the historic average of 8 per cent.

One grim memory should deepen your appreciation of the fact that housing prices do not always rise. In 1958, the price of a home was about the same as it had been in 1928.

Should you buy or rent?

With today's low inflation rates, it may be unreasonable to expect 8 per cent appreciation in the long term. Of course, different locations can offer different rates of appreciation. On average, however, it is unlikely that prices will rise more rapidly than the inflation rate—and that may not be enough if mortgage rates return to double-digit levels from current levels of 6 per cent to 8 per cent. Does it make much sense to pay interest on an investment that appreciates by a lower rate annually?

There are three crucial variables in the economics of the decision to buy a home. The first is the amount of money needed to buy a home, including the down payment, financing and legal fees, and renovation costs. The second is the monthly difference between ownership payments and rental payments. Ownership payments include mortgage costs, taxes, property insurance and maintenance. If you are a tenant, don't forget to include heat and other utilities as part of your rental costs if they are paid separately. The third variable is the expected price of the home at the time you expect to sell, less the mortgage outstanding at that time.

Though an oversimplification, your profit from owning a home will be the difference between the cost of buying the house and the money you'll have in your pocket after you've sold it and paid off the mortgage. On average, Canadians stay in a home for nine years, so let's look at whether it would be more profitable to buy or rent over that period of time. Over those nine years, all of the money that went into buying the home—the down payment, fees and taxes—could have been invested had you decided to rent instead of buy. A down payment of $100,000 invested at an annual after-tax return of 5 per cent, with all income reinvested, would be worth over $155,000 in nine years.

You must add to your $155,000 the value of investing the monthly difference in ownership payments and rent payments. At today's mortgage rates and tax rates, that could easily amount to $200 a month. If we use the 5 per cent after-tax interest rate, that $200 a month could be worth about $28,000 in nine years.

All together, you could have had $183,000 in investment funds—the $155,000 value of the down payment plus the $28,000 from the difference between the monthly payments when renting and buying—at the end of nine years if you rent instead of buy.

The question then is: Will the value of the house increase by $183,000 or more in nine years? If you think so, then buy the house. If you think not, rent.

If the house's original price was $350,000, it would have to be worth at least $533,000 in nine years to make it a reasonable investment. That is an annual rate of appreciation of 4.8 per cent compared to the historic average rate of increase of 8 per cent. As interest rates rise, the decision tends to shift against buying for two reasons. The monthly cost of buying rises, and the return on invested funds if you rent also tends to rise. That means that the rate of appreciation on the house has to be higher than if interest rates were lower.

Should you sell your home?

Suppose you already own your home and it has risen dramatically in value since you bought it. Should you sell it and rent? Or is it better to hold on to the house and hope for even greater gain?

Deciding whether to sell requires exactly the same analysis as was used to determine whether you should buy. The cost of holding on to your home equals the net proceeds you would receive if you sold it. Remember, net proceeds are the selling price less sales commission and the cost of paying off your mortgage. You should also subtract from the price any legal fees involved in the sale and any renovation costs that would be needed beyond what might have to be done in a rented home.

The remainder of the analysis is identical to that followed by a home buyer. You combine the future value of the expected net receipts from selling the house with the future value of the monthly savings by renting instead of keeping your home. The total is the minimum amount by which your home must increase in value if you are to keep it.

You can use Table XIV to determine the annual rate of appreciation at which your house must increase in value by dividing the value of the house in five years by its original cost. Once you determine how quickly your house must rise in value, you have to decide if this is reasonable considering historic patterns and current conditions, including the probable path of inflation. Finally, you must consider local market conditions. For instance, a market that has seen huge increases recently may stabilize or even turn down.

How Quickly Will Your House Increase in Value?

VALUE OF YOUR HOME IN FIVE YEARS DIVIDED BY ORIGINAL COST	ANNUAL GROWTH RATE
$1.105101	1%
1.10408	2
1.15927	3
1.21665	4
1.27628	5
1.3382	6
1.4026	7
1.4639	8
1.5386	9
1.6105	10
1.6851	11
1.7623	12
1.842	13
1.925	14

TABLE XIV

Buying a home

After pondering the question of renting versus buying and considering your personal desires, you may decide that you do want to buy. The next questions you must answer are when and how. Do you buy a home now or do you wait and risk the possibility that inflation—even at a moderate rate—will push up the value of homes at a faster pace than your savings?

There are no easy answers. Housing prices fluctuate like the prices of other goods and services. And while the general trend of housing prices is upward, prices have fallen in some areas.

Before taking the plunge, consider your career path and, if you are married, your desire to have children and whether you will remain a household with two incomes. All of these have a bearing on whether a family can afford to carry a home without suffering a serious change in lifestyle. A person whose income is likely to grow by leaps and bounds in future years can probably risk assuming a large mortgage to buy a home. As a young working couple, you should include both incomes in your calculations but don't neglect to consider whether you could carry the home on one income if you decide to have a family and one parent will stay at home with the children. If you can't, are you better off buying a less expensive home?

There are various ways of financing the purchase of a home. Because a large down payment results in smaller mortgage payments, it usually makes sense to make as large a down payment as possible. In some cases, this also allows a repayment schedule that will increase your equity more rapidly.

Some people buy their homes with moderate down payments, choosing to keep as much of their savings as possible in bank and trust company deposits or in certificates and stocks. This makes little sense because mortgage rates exceed deposit rates. Also, because interest is taxed as income, the after-tax return from fixed income investments is dwarfed by the mortgage rate.

Mortgage interest is generally not tax-deductible. Therefore, you should consider paying off your mortgage as a risk-free investment. In fact, you probably couldn't get an after-tax rate of return exceeding your mortgage rate from any investment. If you have investments and a mortgage and feel you want both, consider selling your investments and paying off your mortgage. Then borrow against the equity in your home and buy a similar investment portfolio back. You'll still own a comparable portfolio and owe the same amount of money as before. But now your loan is for investment purposes and the interest is deductible from income for tax purposes.

How much money will the bank lend you?

Lenders look at two figures when considering a mortgage: your down payment relative to the value of the home and your income. Institutions usually won't lend more than 75 per cent of a property's value unless the amount above 75 per cent is insured.

With mortgage insurance, an institution will lend up to 95 per cent of the property's value. High-ratio mortgages, as they are called, are more expensive because of the additional cost of the insurance premium. An alternative to a high-ratio mortgage is a second mortgage, which makes sense if you are buying a home and assuming an existing mortgage with favourable terms or getting a first mortgage from the vendor at below market rates. While second mortgages are available from mortgage brokers, your bank or trust company is the first place you should try.

Many lenders have also put a ceiling on the values of properties against which they will lend 75 per cent, especially in markets where house prices have skyrocketed in recent years. Lenders are concerned that if housing prices fall they might find the values of some properties falling below the values of their loans.

Shop for a mortgage

In recent years the mortgage market has been a strong area for lenders. As a result, financial institutions are competitive and will usually come up with terms to suit your needs. For instance, some will rewrite an existing mortgage when a house is sold, raising the loan amount and adjusting the payment to reflect a blend of current interest rates and the rate in effect when the mortgage was originally arranged.

New homes generally have financing in place when you buy. But if the home is a resale, the vendor will often take back a mortgage. However, you would probably be better off arranging your own financing before making an offer for a home if the existing financing is inadequate. By arranging your own funds, you can make an unconditional offer and possibly get the house at a lower price.

It's best to shop for financing before you make an offer on a house. See your bank, trust company or credit union manager to discuss your intentions and to determine the size of the loan for which you will qualify. The general rule followed by some institutions is that mortgage payments, property taxes and heating expenses should not exceed 32 per cent of your gross income. Those amounts, plus other consumer debt such as car payments, should not exceed 37 per cent.

Your choice of term

Your mortgage will probably be amortized over 25 years. But the term over which interest rates are fixed will be less—one to five years in most cases, although some pundits expect to see 25-year terms. People who believe that rates will remain low or move lower usually go for short terms, while people who are nervous about the direction of rates usually opt for longer terms.

Your choice of term should reflect not only your view on the direction of rates but also your ability to take risk. Sometimes you might be better off locking in a rate for a longer term if only to have the peace of mind that your mortgage payments won't change for several years, no matter what happens to interest rates. If your mortgage comes up for renewal in a period of high rates and you think they might tumble, find out whether the mortgageholder will give you an open mortgage or a floating-rate mortgage. With these you'll be able to renegotiate your mortgage to a longer-term fixed rate when rates fall.

If you need a mortgage or have one coming up for renewal, it pays to shop well in advance to find the best deals. It might not pay to move from one lender to another, especially since you are likely to incur legal fees and have to pay for an appraisal of your home. However, some institutions will pay a portion of the costs involved in moving a mortgage from another lender. If you find a rate lower than the one your lender has offered, see if your lender will match the competing bid.

Before buying a home, inspect it thoroughly so you're aware of any faults or potential repairs. Many people use inspection services, which for a few hundred dollars look over the house, reporting on the condition of its electrical system, plumbing, heating system and other features.

Selling a home, like selling any other investment, also incurs costs. But a house is one of the few investments you can sell on your own. However, it is a difficult, time-consuming task. Most people who decide to sell turn to a real estate broker. With dozens of firms to choose from in most cities, finding the real estate broker who's best for you can be wearisome.

The quest for competence

Finding a competent real estate broker and agent is extremely important. A poor choice could mean your home will sit on the market for months because it is listed at an unrealistically high price. Conversely, you don't want your home sold at a price substantially below its value.

When properly chosen, a broker will get you the best possible price quickly. The agent will screen out sightseers and show the house to more potential buyers than a homeowner can. A good broker can also come up with financing to help potential buyers make a deal. But it's expensive to use a broker. Commissions range from 3.5 to 6 per cent of the selling price for an exclusive listing, with the rate dependent on the value of the home and market conditions. Including the home under a multiple listing service costs another percentage point but it exposes your home to many brokers and their clients. Don't expect to negotiate the commission rate, even though technically it is negotiable. Despite growing pressures to change, in reality, rates in most markets are fixed.

When the time comes to choose a broker, talk with three or four before making your decision. Ask each broker to come to your home to appraise its value and discuss how he or she proposes to sell it. The brokers you invite should have plenty of experience selling homes in your neighbourhood. It doesn't matter whether the firms are national, independent franchise operations or a trust company. It does matter that they are successful at selling homes in your area.

If you're not familiar with a firm's roster of agents, call the owner or manager and insist that the agent sent to deal with you is experienced and has sold extensively in your neighbourhood. It is also important that the agent be experienced in selling your type of home. It makes little sense to have someone who specializes in rambling mansions if your home is a modest bungalow.

Agents should be prepared to suggest a selling price, supported by recent sales figures of homes in your area. You should be made aware of listing prices, selling prices and how long the homes were on the market. You should also be shown listings of homes that didn't sell because of high prices.

An agent who does not arrive properly prepared, or who cannot back up an evaluation with data, should be rejected. Similarly, reject any agent who does not ask about existing mortgages and who has no suggestions about financing. Financing arrangements can often make or break a sale.

Most homes have mortgages held by banks, trust companies or insurance companies. A good agent will first determine whether the holder would be willing to rewrite the mortgage for the purchaser. Many financial institutions will do this routinely, so be wary of any agent who suggests a financing alternative before checking to see what can be done with the existing mortgage.

The agent should also present a strategy for selling your home. Most will ask for an exclusive listing, which may be for 90 days. In return for this, the broker will spend some money advertising your home. Determine the firm's advertising policy and look at recent issues of the daily newspaper to determine whether homes listed with the firm get good exposure. On any given day a firm may advertise only a few of the homes it has listed in a neighbourhood, but its agents would probably show several homes to anyone responding to an advertisement.

Once you make your choice, the agent will ask you to sign a listing agreement. This is a binding contract appointing the firm as your agent for a limited time, so your lawyer should examine the agreement before you sign it. Many listing agreements state that a commission is payable for procuring an acceptable offer. In other words, the broker is paid even if the deal doesn't close. Many lawyers insist that this clause be changed so the commissions are paid only if the actual sale takes place. If the deal doesn't close, the vendor should be entitled to keep the deposit made by the potential buyer. This compensates for lost time and legal expenses.

Do-it-yourself sale

Many people are capable of selling their own homes, but this can be a time-consuming task and individuals often make errors in assessing the values of their homes. However, the saving on commission is reason enough to consider acting as your own broker. Remember, however, that in private sales the buyer often thinks he should get the benefit of commission savings.

If you decide to bypass a broker, set a realistic price. This can be determined by checking recent sales in your neighbourhood. It makes sense to hire an independent appraiser, who for a fee of $200 to $300 will give you a written report on the value of your home. The appraisal itself can be an excellent sales tool. Check with the mortgage departments of banks, trust companies and insurance companies for names of appraisers they use. Most institutions will accept an appraisal as proof of value for mortgage financing. You can then take the appraisal to the institution that holds the mortgage on your property to determine the amount it would lend to a purchaser who meets its requirements.

You should also advertise your home. A simple sign on your lawn is essential, but make sure it says "By Appointment Only" so you can control who comes in and when. Your newspaper advertisements—budget at least $500 for a long-term campaign—should list the location of your home, type of home', the number of rooms and outstanding features.

To leave room for haggling, your asking price should be about 5 per cent higher than the price you expect to get. Make sure your lawyer knows what you're doing and show him or her every offer you are considering. Remember, once your signature appears on the offer, it becomes a binding contract. In addition, let your lawyer know about any outstanding liens against your property so arrangements can be made to deal with them before your home is sold. Any offer should be accompanied by a deposit, around 10 per cent of the selling price. Your lawyer will hold the deposit in trust until the sale closes.

A cottage as an investment

The economics of buying a cottage or a resort condominium as a vacation home involves an analysis identical to buying your residence, with one important difference—75 per cent of the capital gain on selling a second home will be taxable. You should also be aware that the increase in the value of vacation homes does not necessarily follow the same pattern as price movements on residences.

Again, demographics is a major factor in explaining the differences. Back in the 1950s and 1960s, Canada's population was surging and it moved beyond traditional city limits as city property values rose. Businesses were also moving from urban areas in search of less expensive land and lower taxes, so they pulled even more people in their wake as workers were tempted to move to the countryside to be closer to work.

In the past decade, explosive population growth has slowed, reducing the pressure on land values in some cities. Furthermore, urban areas have found themselves stuck with empty factory sites because of the combination of high land costs and high taxes. Cities are rapidly developing programs to keep and attract new businesses and jobs. These changes should result in a slowing of the movement to rural areas and a lower rate of price increase for vacation properties, if not a decrease in some areas.

Another factor has been the slow growth of real personal income. Traditional first-home buyers—those in their twenties and thirties—are having difficulty buying a first home, never mind a summer cottage or ski chalet. The blight on real income growth has also hit older families, impeding their ability to buy a second home.

All these factors combine to make the outlook for second-home price appreciation far less optimistic than it was a decade ago, although the lifetime exemption on capital gains has improved the attractiveness of a second home as an investment.

Commercial property

As a pure investment, commercial property is more interesting than a second home. Commercial income-producing property includes stores, office buildings, warehouses and residential rentals. Residential rental properties in provinces such as Ontario, where rent controls are in effect, are generally avoided by investors these days.

However, consider the advantages of commercial property. All expenses, including mortgage interest, real estate taxes and capital cost allowances are tax-deductible from gross income.

If your major business is real estate management, losses incurred in conducting a commercial property business are deductible from other income in determining personal taxes. However, you should get advice from a tax professional before assuming you can integrate losses from real estate investment into other personal income. A retired person is likely to qualify, as might a spouse who has a source of personal income, such as that from a trust, and whose only work outside the home is managing the properties.

The value of commercial property

One long-standing rule for determining the value of commercial property dictates that the price should not be more than 10 times net income from the property before financing charges and income taxes. Net income is gross income less all cash expenses, including maintenance and property taxes but excluding mortgage payments.

For example, an older property with a small store and a doctor's office upstairs might generate income of $5,000 a month, or $60,000 a year. Maintenance and other cash expenses, including real estate taxes, could be $45,000 annually. So a first approximation of the value of the property is $150,000—10 times the $15,000 difference between gross income and cash expenses.

If we assume there is a $112,500 mortgage at 8 per cent, the investment profile of the property for the first year would be as follows: $60,000 gross income less $45,000 cash expenses, $7,500 capital cost allowance and $9,000 for interest payments on the mortgage. At the end of the year, there would be a net loss of $4,300 before income taxes. But this loss doesn't mean that the investor is out of pocket this money. It simply means that for tax purposes, no income tax is due.

In fact, the building has generated a positive cash inflow of $3,200. The capital cost allowance is simply a bookkeeping charge against income and does not reflect a cash outlay.

The capital cost allowance is 5 per cent of the unamortized value of the building. A $150,000 building has a capital cost allowance of $7,500 in the first year. In the second year, capital costs would drop to 5 per cent of the unamortized value, which is $150,000 less the first year's capital cost allowance, or $150,000 minus $7,500. Capital cost allowance in the second year amounts to 5 per cent of $142,500, or $17,125. In the third year, the capital cost allowance would be 5 per cent of $135,375, or $6,768.75.

Keep in mind that capital cost allowance is allowed only on the buildings and equipment, not on land. If the land were part of the investment, its cost would have to be deducted from the cost of the investment to find the depreciable asset investment base on which the 5 per cent would be charged.

Investment analysis of commercial property

The analysis of commercial property is identical to that for home ownership. Legal and closing fees, as well as any renovation costs, must be added to the owner's investment. Let's assume in our $150,000 store and office property that these fees total $10,000, to which must be added the down payment of $32,500 for combined initial costs of $47,500.

These initial costs of $47,500 would be worth about $60,625 in five years at an after-tax interest rate of 5 per cent. Suppose that the monthly flows total $3,200 a year with no income tax liability on building income over a five-year period.

At an after-tax interest rate of 5 per cent, the cash flows would be worth about $18,570. Unlike the housing example, where the cash flow of owning versus renting was negative, this cash flow is positive since you would not have received the cash if you had not bought the commercial property. Therefore, the $18,570 should be deducted from the $60,625 initial costs. The property must appreciate by at least $42,055 to make the investment worthwhile. The price of the building after five years must be $192,055, an annual appreciation rate of 5.1 per cent. The investment should be undertaken if, in your judgment, that rate of appreciation is the minimum rate of appreciation expected. It should be noted that as interest rates fall, the values of cash flows increase.

In the analysis, remember that the cash flows were assumed to be positive. If they were negative, instead of deducting the cash flow from the acquisition costs you must add them to your costs. If there had been a negative cash flow of $4,300 a month for five years on our store and doctor's office, the present value of $212,076 would be added to the $47,500 initial cost. To make the investment acceptable, the building now must be worth $488,606.35 in five years—a jump of 325 per cent or 26.6 per cent a year. Unless there are special circumstances that might generate such extraordinary results, perhaps the opening of a subway station nearby, a reasonable investor would be justified in rejecting this investment. Negative cash flows do not necessarily mean the investment is bad. They do mean that the value of the property must increase over the investor's planning horizon, and the larger the negative numbers, the larger the required increase.

Of course, many people live in the small apartment buildings or duplexes that they own. Their investment analysis is essentially the same as for commercial property. The difference is that you cannot deduct the capital costs, real estate taxes or mortgage interest for that part of the home in which you live. In a duplex, for example, these deductible costs would be halved if the owner lived in half the house. On the other hand, only half of the capital gain would be taxable when the property is sold.

Should you be a landlord?

The answer to this depends on the price you pay for the property, the level of rent you can expect, expected capital appreciation and expected rent increases—in other words, can you expect to make a profit by being a landlord? The analysis is similar to the one for commercial property. However, many individuals apparently jump into the real estate game without doing proper analyses.

An example is the condominium market in Toronto in recent years. Individual investors were encouraged to put the minimum down payment on condominiums before construction even began on the expectation that by the time the building was completed and they had to take possession, the condo's price would have risen by 10 to 20 per cent. These investors hoped to sell their properties and make a hefty profit. In reality, prices did not surge ahead. Moreover, there were many, many other investors in the same situation. To protect their investment and avoid losses, the investors took possession and placed their units on the rental market. In many cases, the rental income covered only a fraction of the carrying costs. With rent increases restricted by rent control, it will be many years before these investments break even on a cash-flow basis.

The situation can become even worse—the tenant could stop paying rent. It can take a landlord many months to evict a tenant, a period during which the landlord receives no income. When the tenant is finally evicted, it is unlikely the landlord will recover lost income. The bottom line is that being a landlord has become a high-risk business, one in which the potential rewards do not compensate for the high risks.

Real estate syndicates

Small investors can participate in large real estate projects through real estate syndicates. Generally, these take the form of limited partnerships in which investors can purchase partnership units and own an interest in apartment buildings, hotels, office buildings and shopping plazas. Investors participate in the profits or losses of the partnership and receive a portion of capital gains, if any, should the property be sold at some time in the future. Depending on the specific issue, the minimum investment ranges from $10,000 to $150,000.

The rule with real estate syndicates is *caveat emptor*. In many cases, the returns promised in early years consist of losses from the project, which investors can use to reduce their taxable income. Often cash flow from the project is inadequate to cover mortgage payments and other expenses in the early years so the general partner guarantees any shortfalls for the first five years. Future profits are often based on expected rent increases and capital gains.

Before signing up for any real estate syndicate, look at what you are getting for your money. Examine any appraisals critically to determine whether the price you are paying for the property is inflated. Determine what portion of the price covers fees, including the cost of the cash-flow guarantee. These can make a project very expensive. Read the fine print. In some cases, the cash-flow guarantees are actually loans made by the general partner. These have to be repaid, generally when the project must be refinanced. Look closely at the definition of cash flow so you fully understand what is included and what is excluded.

The prospectus will almost certainly include a table showing cash-flow projections. Do the projections make sense? While real estate has been an excellent investment in recent years in many areas of the country, there is no way of knowing whether revenues will continue to climb. You should also determine whether you have any additional liability besides your initial investment. For example, projects may have to be refinanced after five years. If the cash flow is inadequate to cover the costs at that time, what liabilities do you face? You also have to look at the liquidity of your investment should you wish to sell it at some time in the future. Generally, there is no market for units of a specific project or at best a very limited market.

Actual liquidity often depends on the type of project. For example, some are offerings of specific suites in condominium projects. While cash flows to cover costs are guaranteed by the general partner who is responsible for renting and maintaining the units, you are responsible for mortgage payments. If the building has not appreciated when the mortgage comes up for renewal and rents have not escalated substantially, you could find yourself having to subsidize the carrying costs. And if you and other investors in the complex decide to sell at the same time, you could drive down prices and suffer a capital loss.

If you are seriously considering an investment in a real estate syndicate, do some in-depth analysis. Play with the projections provided. Determine where you will stand if cash flows grow at a lower rate than the promoter projects or if the property appreciates at a moderate rate or not at all.

Examine the general partner's financial strength and see how it has performed on other projects. The general partner's financial strength is very important because you depend on it for cash-flow guarantees. If the guarantor fails, the guarantee is worthless. And make sure you know how much money you have at risk. You may be required to put only

$10,000 up front, but you could be on the hook for $150,000. Read the fine print. Finally, never buy any property without inspecting it first yourself or having it inspected by an independent party. Brochures may provide illustrations of a building, but an inspection of the property and the surrounding area can tell you a lot about the quality of a neighbourhood and whether rents charged in the project are competitive.

A final but very important warning. If the deal is structured as a tax shelter designed to provide maximum losses over the next several years and a capital gain when the property is sold, watch out. Properties with a history of losing money generally will not appreciate; therefore, a capital gain is unlikely. Moreover, losses stemming from projects structured to lose money with little reasonable expectation of profit are likely to be rejected by Revenue Canada. This, in fact, has been the experience of some investors who bought real estate tax shelters and now find that, as well as owing money to the banks that financed their investments, Revenue Canada has rejected their deductions and wants back taxes, interest and penalties.

Chapter 12

Options: Heaven or Hell in the Market

So you're looking for an investment that will double your money overnight—or at least within a week.

It's rare for stocks to perform that well. But the doubling of investors' money is fairly common in the options markets. Options can be a speculator's paradise, or they can be a place to quickly lose your shirt in a few days. Ironically, conservative investors use options as a vehicle to reduce risk. Indeed, some analysts blame the volatility of stock markets—particularly the sharp price declines of October 1987—on institutional use of options and futures contracts to hedge exposure through a computer strategy called "program trading."

Options are the right to buy or sell a specific security, currency or commodity at a given price until a set date. There are options on stocks, bonds, currencies, stock market indexes, gold, silver and bonds. Much of the growth in options trading in Canada is a relatively recent development. Options were first introduced on the Toronto Stock Exchange in 1975 for blue-chip stocks such as Bell Canada. In 1987, the TSE introduced options on a new market index, the Toronto 35, giving institutional investors a new instrument for hedging their portfolios. Even so, the options market is still "thin," which means there isn't a massive amount of trading. However, it has been picking up.

There are two types of options—calls and puts. A call option on a stock gives the holder the right to buy 100 shares of a specific stock, the underlying security, at a fixed price until a given date. A put option gives the right to sell the shares at a specified price by a certain date. For example, an XYZ Ltd. February $17.50 call option gives the holder the right to buy 100 shares of XYZ Ltd. at $17.50 until the third Friday in February.

Maturity dates for options are standard. There are three maturity cycles:

- January, April, July and October
- February, May, August and November
- March, June, September and December

Each option trades in one cycle only, and the longest option contract is nine months. Exercise prices are also standard but several options can be available on the same stock with the same maturity date and with different exercise prices. This would happen if a stock price were to move sharply. New options would be created using $2.50 intervals for stocks selling below $50.

Since 1990 in the United States and 1992 in Canada, investors have been able to trade longer-term options called LEAPS, which stands for long-term equity anticipation securities. These give holders the right to buy in the case of calls, or sell in the case of puts, the underlying shares for up to two years.

Options contracts are issued by a clearing corporation such as the Canadian Derivatives Clearing Corp., which is responsible for guaranteeing that all parties involved meet their obligations. You can trade options through any stockbroker registered to deal in options.

The option itself is liquid and marketable. Its value is called the premium, which consists of the difference between the stock price and the exercise price, plus the value that the market places on the time remaining before the option expires. With our XYZ Ltd. example, if the stock trades at $19 and the $17.50 call option trades at $3, the option price, or premium, is made up of $1.50 in difference between the price of the stock and the exercise price plus $1.50 in time value placed on the option by the market. The time value can quickly disappear as the option approaches maturity.

If you buy an option at $3 and the stock price moves almost immediately to $22, you would expect the option to appreciate by about $3 as well, so you would double your money. Compare your potential return with what you would have gained by buying the stock. However, if you bought the stock and it failed to move, you would dispose of the option prior to the exercise date at $1.50—the difference between the stock price and the exercise price. This means you would lose half your money, plus whatever commissions you must pay.

Playing the options market can be risky, and many people quickly lose all their capital. But the potential rewards are great, and that's what entices investors. A good general rule is to not use more than 10 to 20 per cent of your total investment capital when buying options. And if you're going to speculate in options on stocks, stick to options on securities that have historically been more volatile than the general market. For example, if you buy call options because you think the market will go higher, go for options on stocks that tend to do better than the market when it is rising. Conversely, if you are buying put options, go for options on underlying securities that tend to tumble hard when the general market moves lower.

Some people participate in the options market in a more conservative way. They "write" options to reduce the risk of losing money on their portfolios. In other words, they sell options against stocks they own.

For example, ABC Ltd. may trade at $20. An investor buying at this price might decide to sell an August $22 call option contract against the holding at $2. This investor has now reduced his or her cost by $2, which acts as a cushion if the stock declines. If the stock moves up, but doesn't exceed $22, the investor won't see the option exercised, so he or she will not only have the premium but will also keep the stock. If the stock moves above $22 at the exercise date, the option will be exercised and the investor's broker will turn over the shares to the options exchange or clearing corporation at $22, making for the investor a profit of $4 before commissions.

You can, of course, purchase an option to cover your liability. For instance, if the stock price fell to $18, the premium would fall too. An investor might purchase the option back at a fraction of its previous sale price and then sell another option on it, exercisable at a lower price.

You shouldn't be too concerned if a call option is exercised against you. The price of the premium is usually great enough that the likelihood of your shares being called is slim. And if the shares are called, you will earn a significant return on your capital.

You can also sell options without owning the underlying security. However, this is extremely risky because your exposure is unlimited, while your maximum profit is the premium you've received. For example, you might sell an option that can be exercised at $20, only to find that a takeover offer is suddenly made at $60 a share. Your option could be called, forcing you to buy shares at $60 to satisfy your obligation. Few brokers recommend writing "naked calls" because it's a dangerous strategy for the client and the broker if something goes sour.

Options trading has become much more sophisticated in recent years with the development of computer programs that calculate potential profits using assumptions about where the markets might move. Options departments at most major brokerage firms use these programs for their retail and institutional clients.

Program trading is an extension of these facilities. With program trading, a large financial institution attempts to hedge against swings in the value of its portfolio by using futures contracts and general index options. For instance, a portfolio manager might sell an index option or futures contract against the value of the portfolio to lock in profits. If the index fell, the gain in the price of the futures or the premium from the option would offset any decline in the value of the portfolio.

In thin markets, the values of options and futures get out of line with the values of underlying securities. Picture a system where computers monitor portfolios, options and futures prices and trigger trades to take advantage of price differences. This trading activity is known as arbitrage. Now imagine what happens when a computer triggers trades in a thin, volatile market. Buying and selling pressures send prices even more out of line, thus increasing the volatility of the market. Some people in the investment business view program trading as a problem. In the United States, measures have been taken to reduce the volatility by restricting the magnitude of price movements caused by program trading.

Individual investors can use options to stabilize their returns or as an alternative to holding stocks. For example, if you have realized substantial paper profits and are worried about the market moving lower, you might use some of your gain to buy call options and participate in further price moves up that might occur in the near future. Alternatively, you might sell call options against your portfolio, giving you a cushion if prices decline.

You can play the same game with put options. Rather than selling your shares, paying a commission and possibly using up some of your lifetime capital gains exemption, you could continue to hold the stock and buy put options. If your shares continue to rise, your profits will grow and the put options you bought will be worthless when they expire. But if the stocks reverse, your put options will appreciate in value, offsetting any declines. When you use call and put options to lock in profits, consider your costs as insurance.

You can also sell put options. But by doing this, you commit yourself to buying a specific stock at a specific price, even if it is well below the market price. Selling put options is a strategy you might use if you want to buy a specific stock but believe that it is too expensive. By selling a put option you can potentially get the stock at a lower price if it pulls back. And if it doesn't, you're still ahead of the game because you've received a premium for your efforts.

Buying put options is an alternative to "short selling," which involves borrowing shares from your broker, then selling them with the intention of buying them back at a later date at a lower price. In this case, the difference in price at which you borrow and the price at which you buy represents your profit. Selling short incurs unlimited liability, while buying puts limits your risk to the cost of the put.

Similarly, you can use index options to protect your entire portfolio. The TSE 35 Index was created specifically to allow the trading of options and futures based on a basket of liquid, widely held stocks found in many institutional portfolios.

Options can also be used for some fairly conservative strategies. You could, for instance, put 95 per cent of your money in treasury bills and 5 per cent in call or put options. If properly used, this strategy will protect your capital while giving you an opportunity to participate in market movements. You don't have to tie this type of strategy to stock options; you can also use bond options if your objective is to profit from moves in interest rates.

There are numerous strategies that use more than one option to limit potential losses in options trading. The thing to remember is that any strategy that limits losses usually puts a ceiling on profits. For example, you might write one call and one put against the same security. You would earn two premiums, thereby reducing your cost and earning a profit if the price increases. You could lose, however, if the stock fell sharply and you were "put," meaning you would have to buy more shares as the puts were exercised.

Options strategies are quite complex and many investors make the mistake of ignoring commissions when they calculate their potential returns. Commissions can be significant and should be included in any calculation, although they will vary, depending on what type of dealer you choose. You can do business with a full-service dealer or a discounter with low commissions. If you need advice, information and the use of a dealer's option expertise, the full-service dealer will prove good value. Just make sure the broker you choose has extensive experience in options and the firm has the latest technical equipment to give you the information you need to make the best decision.

You should also familiarize yourself with the language of options and learn some of the terms involved. Most dealers can provide you with literature on options, and some offer seminars on the topic.

You'll encounter phrases such as in-the-money options, intrinsic value, opening-purchase transaction, opening-sale transaction and straddles. Here are some explanations of terms used in options trading:

- **In-the-money option:** In the case of a call option, this is an option for which the stock price is higher than the exercise price. In the case of a put option, the stock price is lower.
- **Out-of-the-money option:** In the case of a call option, this is an option for which the stock price is lower than the exercise price. For a put option, the stock price is higher than the exercise price.
- **Intrinsic value:** The difference between the stock and exercise prices when an option is in the money.
- **Opening-purchase transaction:** A transaction in which an investor buys an option.
- **Opening-sale transaction:** A transaction in which an investor writes an option. The writer is the seller of an option contract.
- **Straddle:** A strategy that involves buying or selling both puts and calls. A straddle is an order to buy or sell the same number of put and call options on the same underlying stock for the same exercise price and expiration date.
- **Time spread:** Also known as calendar spread and horizontal spread, this refers to the practice of holding options with the same exercise price but with different expiration dates.
- **Price spread:** This involves the holding of options with different exercise prices but with the same expiration date.
- **Diagonal spread:** A combination of time spread and price spread.

Chapter 13

Commodities, Currencies and Futures

Stories abound of people starting off with next to nothing and becoming millionaires in a matter of days by playing the futures markets. There are also plenty of stories about people losing everything in the futures markets. They're true, too. They just aren't as popular as the tales of success.

Depending on whom you listen to, the futures markets are either one of the few places where huge fortunes can be made overnight or they're a path to financial disaster where you can lose your shirt in minutes. In fact, both can happen. But many novices jump into commodities without fully considering how risky they can be. When things go wrong, you can lose not only your investment money, but just about everything you own. If you want to dabble in the futures markets, it is imperative that you understand what futures are and the purpose of the markets.

Special delivery

A futures contract is an obligation that covers the delivery of a specific amount of a commodity, currency or security at a specified future date at a specific price. The amounts are standard, such as 112,000 pounds of sugar, 100 ounces of gold or 12.5 million Japanese yen.

You can also invest in stock index futures that involve a cash settlement, rather than delivery of a stock portfolio. One type of futures contract is based on the Toronto Futures Exchange's index of 35 stocks. You aren't required to deliver a basket of 35 stocks, but you must settle with an amount of cash based on the index's closing value on the third Friday of the month.

Even if you buy commodity futures, you needn't worry about having 112,000 pounds of sugar dumped on your lawn—unless you really want delivery. Instead, your broker would automatically buy or sell an offsetting contract prior to the delivery date.

The original hedge

Futures markets were established to allow commodity producers, such as farmers, mining companies and lumber companies, and commodity purchasers, such as food processing companies, metal fabricators and lumber dealers, to hedge against price swings. The major North American commodity exchanges are in Winnipeg, Chicago and New York, and they deal with a variety of commodities, including grains, meats, cotton, lumber, coffee, sugar, livestock and metals such as gold and silver. In addition, exchanges trade in currencies and interest-rate futures as well as stock market futures. In Canada, the Toronto Futures Exchange and the Montreal Exchange specialize in contracts tied to securities and precious metals.

The large players in the markets are hedgers. A farmer who is worried that the price of wheat might be lower at harvest time might decide to sell some of his anticipated production in the futures market. But the farmer will not necessarily deliver wheat on the contract date; instead, he is likely to buy another contract to cancel the one sold. If his prediction of lower prices is correct, he will buy a contract at a price lower than that for which he sold a contract. The difference, the profit, will help to offset the low prices received for his crop.

However, if the farmer is wrong and prices move higher at harvest time, he will take a loss in the futures market. But the farmer will still get more for the crop, so in the long term hedging allows him to stabilize his income. Similarly, users of commodities may want to lock in a price months or even a year in advance of taking delivery by buying futures contracts to hedge against wide price swings.

Something for everyone

Who uses futures markets to hedge? Everyone from major gold producers to the operators of small businesses who want protection against changing currency values. A Canadian retailer who buys merchandise in New York may worry that the Canadian dollar will tumble before the goods are delivered. He could lock in an exchange rate using the futures market. Importers can also deal with their banks in what is known as the forward market, whereby a bank will specify an exchange rate for a specific amount and a specific date.

But to be efficient, the market requires a large number of participants. There aren't enough farmers and food processors to give the market liquidity, but there are enough speculators. They trade in futures not because they want to hedge, but because they are trying to make a financial killing.

A matter of leverage

Futures markets are risky because of the leverage involved. Unlike stock markets, where investors have to put up at least half the value of a stock when they make a purchase, futures markets require only a small portion of the total value of a contract. It is possible to buy a contract valued at about $100,000 (U.S.)—most contracts are quoted in U.S. funds, including some traded in Canada—with only $2,000 tied up as margin or good-faith money.

If the value of a $100,000 futures contract tumbles by, for instance, 5 per cent in a given day, a trader who is "long," or obligated to buy, would have to come up with an additional $5,000 to maintain his or her margin position. If the trader doesn't have the necessary funds, the position will be sold out by the broker and the trader will lose his or her initial investment and be responsible for the difference.

How do people make millions? They do it by pyramiding their positions. If a commodity goes up in price by 5 per cent, a trader would then buy additional contracts with his or her new equity and continue to add more as the price rises. But if the trend reverses, watch out. Equity will quickly evaporate, leaving the trader responsible for additional losses.

The risks inherent in commodities futures markets are underlined by the fact that a broker will allow you to open a trading account only after you've read and signed some detailed forms that spell out the risks. That doesn't mean everybody reads the forms carefully before signing. Many investors begin to understand the risks only when they face substantial losses.

Beginner's luck

The biggest pitfall facing beginners in the futures markets is lack of experience. Although individuals with beginner's luck may make money in the beginning, they don't always hang on to it. At the end of 1979 it was possible to buy a gold contract for about $500 (U.S.) an ounce. A few weeks later, gold peaked at $850 (U.S.). As prices rose, some investors used their growing equity to finance additional purchases. When the trend reversed, they lost heavily. Similarly some investors made a killing in mid-1998, correctly predicting that the Canadian dollar would lose ground against the U.S. dollar.

Even the experts get burned. Take the rapid price decline of silver, which tumbled in early 1980 from $50 (U.S.) an ounce to about $12 (U.S.). Brokers and players, including the legendary Hunt brothers of Texas, lost hundreds of millions of dollars.

Both silver and gold fell sharply—gold to below $300 (U.S.) an ounce in early 1985 and silver to less than $6 (U.S.). However, fortunes were made by those who were able to ride the downtrend.

Many beginners think they can protect themselves by issuing stop-loss orders. These are orders to liquidate positions if the price reaches a certain level with the aim of limiting losses. While stop-loss orders are something speculators should consider, they must also realize that such orders don't always limit risk. A commodity price can decline for a number of days without any futures trading taking place. When the stop-loss is finally executed, the loss may greatly exceed the amount originally projected.

Because of the potential volatility of commodities markets—for example, the sharp rise in orange juice futures on news of a heavy, unexpected frost—mechanisms have been put in place to restrict price movements, including limits on how far a price is allowed to move up or down in a day.

Who should play?

If you intend to play the futures markets, make sure you understand the risks, that you can live with them and, most important, that you can afford them. There are no hard and fast rules about who should or should not get involved with commodities or other futures. But anyone interested should first realize that for every winner there is a loser, and in some cases the person on the other side of the trade is a lot more knowledgeable about the factors affecting the price of a specific commodity. If you want to trade in coffee or sugar, for example, odds are that the trader for a food processing company who may be on the other side of the trade will almost certainly know more about the relevant markets than you do.

Then there's the matter of cost. Most brokers want only clients who can afford the risks. Some won't take clients who have a net worth of less than $250,000, excluding their homes and cars. These people should probably restrict the futures portion of their holdings to 10 per cent, and they should be prepared to lose that 10 per cent. Many experienced futures brokers will also refuse to accept as clients people who seem unable to handle the stress that trading commodities futures produces. And if you have a history of losing money in the stock market, stay out of futures; you'd probably end up losing even more—possibly everything you own.

Many beginners make the same errors, which explains why most investors lose money on commodities. Using the pyramiding strategy unsuccessfully is one of those errors. Many traders and brokers tend to pyramid positions, which increases the trader's risk. A minor setback puts the trader in a major loss position. Another common error is holding too large a position in one area of the market. The markets are simply too volatile for investors to put all their eggs in one basket.

The key decision

If you decide to invest in commodities, your key decision will be your choice of broker. With a good broker you might make money—possibly a great deal of money. More important, a good broker won't let you get into a position where you could lose everything.

Most brokerage houses will check your credit rating. Don't withhold information about other commodity accounts because you are embarrassed about your previous losses. The industry is small enough that your omission will be discovered. And remember, you make the decisions, not your broker. His or her job is to advise and guide you, and to try to keep you out of trouble. But you're the one who places the order and accepts the consequences.

Of course, you should check out your broker thoroughly. Deal only with an established firm. Most are affiliated with major stock brokerage houses or are members of futures exchanges, including the Toronto Futures Exchange.

The research provided by brokers to their clients is fairly standard and consists of industry studies, technical analysis of trends and news reports of developments that affect prices. Some firms have computerized trading models that can be used to provide trading discipline with the objective of cutting losses and letting profits ride.

Some people may want to consider buying units, or shares, of one of the commodity funds offered from time to time by major brokerage houses. They offer the advantages of professional management, diversification and limited risk. With these funds you can't lose more than you put in.

Before launching a futures program, ask yourself, "How much can I lose?" not "How much can I make?" Of course, you can lower your risk by putting up more margin in the form of U.S. government treasury bills. But most people who play the commodities futures markets are interested in speculating rather than limiting risk.

As with options, there are numerous trading strategies you can follow to limit your risk. Most futures dealers can provide detailed information on how such trading strategies can be used to your advantage.

Gold and Silver: Money That Is Real

It's difficult for some people to understand why gold, silver and other precious metals are considered investments. After all, gold doesn't pay dividends or interest.

On the other hand, there are many people who can't understand why anyone would sink all his or her money into securities issued or guaranteed by governments, given the history of paper money around the world. Indeed, inflation has eroded the value of paper money in most countries over the years.

The fact is that precious metals have proven to be a store of value through periods of inflation, political upheaval, war and social unrest. Also, gold is a historical and universal medium of exchange. While some countries' central banks have been selling their gold, others have committed to maintaining a portion of their exchange reserves as gold bullion. But putting everything you own into precious metals can be risky if the prices that people are willing to pay for those metals get out of whack with reality.

Take the events of late 1979 and early 1980. People were lining up at banks, coin dealers and precious metals dealers to buy gold and silver. Inflation was higher than interest rates, so people who put their money in banks to earn interest were losing, even before taxes. As a result, people flocked to buy tangibles. In less than a decade, gold moved from about $40 (U.S.) an ounce to its early 1980 high of $850 (U.S.). Silver followed a similar pattern, peaking at $50 (U.S.) an ounce. (Gold and silver prices are quoted worldwide in U.S. dollars in both troy ounces and metric weights.)

Then the bubble burst and prices plunged. In mid-1992, gold was trading at about $340 (U.S.) an ounce. Silver was trading at around $4 (U.S.). One year later, gold was at $400 (U.S.) an ounce and silver was at

$5 (U.S.). Undoubtedly, fortunes have been made by traders who have caught the many swings in precious metals since the early 1970s, when the U.S. government decided to stop selling gold at $35 (U.S.) an ounce and no longer redeem its silver certificate $1 (U.S.) bills for silver dollars. But fortunes have been lost by people who misunderstood the markets and allowed greed to rule their decisions.

If you put everything you own into gold and silver, you become a gambler, betting that currencies and securities that pay interest will lose much of their value—like the German mark did in the 1920s. However, if you put 5 to 15 per cent of your assets in precious metals, you can classify yourself as a hedger, holding precious metals as a hedge against a sharp increase in inflation or political turbulence.

Gold, silver and other tangible investments, such as diamonds, rise in inflationary periods when people are worried that the purchasing power of their money is being eroded. They rise most when the spread between nominal interest rates and inflation is shrinking or when inflation exceeds nominal interest rates. They do poorly when people can do better by putting their money in interest-bearing securities.

Sometimes politics helps gold and silver. Worries about political unrest in different parts of the world often send money looking for havens. Sometimes that haven is the U.S. dollar, at other times it's gold.

Inflation hasn't been a big problem lately, so gold and silver have been in the doldrums. But many investors continue to hold a portion of their assets in precious metals as a hedge against inflation.

Shopping for gold

There are several ways to buy gold. You can buy the metal itself in the form of wafers and bars, or in coins such as the Canadian Maple Leaf. You can also buy gold certificates, which are backed by the assets of the issuer but not necessarily by gold itself. You can buy the shares of gold mining companies and you can even invest in gold through mutual funds that hold the metal itself, shares in gold mining companies or both.

Gold shares tend to outperform gold bullion when prices are rising. But bullion tends to fall less than gold shares when bullion prices decline. Many people prefer bullion because it is a tangible investment.

Bullion is sold in bars and wafers in a wide range of weights from five grams to standard bars of 400 ounces. The gold prices quoted in newspapers generally apply to 400-ounce purchases and sales. Bullion has a number of advantages for the investor. It is easily marketable worldwide and it is probably the least expensive way of buying gold because commissions and other charges are small. Also, it can be purchased in some provinces without paying sales tax. The disadvantages of holding gold bullion include storage and insurance fees, and possible assay charges if you sell after the gold has been in your possession.

Banks and dealers that sell gold to the public quote prices based on 400-ounce bars. On a given day they may bid for gold at one price, perhaps $288 (U.S.) an ounce and sell it at another, maybe $291.50 (U.S.). But few people have the resources to buy 400-ounce bars. Instead, they purchase smaller amounts and pay a bit more per ounce to cover manufacturing charges. These bar charges range from about $1.10 an ounce for a 100-ounce bar to $3.35 for a one ounce wafer to $15 an ounce for a five-gram wafer, or 0.161 ounces. You do not pay a premium when you sell.

Poor man's gold

Silver is sometimes described as "poor man's gold." Its price tends to be more volatile and, because of the metal's widespread industrial use, it may not always move with gold. Silver can also be more susceptible than gold to movement by groups of buyers. That was the case in 1979 and early 1980, when a group tried to corner the silver market and its value increased fivefold before crashing.

Like gold, silver can be bought as wafers, bars, coins and certificates. Also, most precious metals funds invest in silver as well as gold. The prices quoted for silver by dealers are for 1,000-ounce bars, but you can buy smaller sizes, ranging from one ounce to 100 ounces. A one-kilogram bar, which contains 32.150 fine ounces of silver, is also available. The premium for a one-ounce wafer is about $3 (U.S.), which makes a small purchase proportionately expensive.

Commissions and fees

Besides the premiums and assay charges on gold and silver, you have to consider other possible charges. There may be delivery fees, and even a small commission. One bank recently quoted a commission of 0.25 per cent on transactions of less than $5,000 and 0.125 per cent on transactions beyond that. Storage charges are about 0.375 per cent on the first $50,000 of gold bullion held and 0.125 per cent on the balance. For silver, charges are fractionally higher.

Bullion is available from bullion dealers, a handful of stock brokerage houses and some banks and trust companies. You should choose your dealer with care, and the novice is best off dealing with a bank or trust company. Remember, however, that they are dealers and are not responsible for dispensing advice on price trends.

Certificates and coins

If you don't want to take delivery of your gold or silver, you can buy certificates. They can be converted into bullion, with delivery usually taking place within 30 days. They are also negotiable outside of Canada at certain institutions. However, they aren't always backed by bullion. Instead, they are backed by the general assets of the institution from which the certificates are purchased. That's why you should buy certificates only from stable institutions, such as the major Canadian chartered banks, which have precious metals departments.

Certificates are usually sold in minimum amounts of 10 ounces of gold and 50 ounces of silver. Storage and administration charges are minor—only a few cents a day for each 100 ounces. However, you could face manufacturing charges if you trade your certificate for the real thing.

One advantage of certificates is that you can buy them in fractional weights, calculated to three decimal places. This means that you can purchase $1,000 of gold, which at the time of writing would entitle you to a certificate for 3.47 ounces.

Coins and certificates for coins are also popular. Until the mid-1980s, the South African Krugerrand one-ounce gold coin was the favourite of gold bugs worldwide. But its popularity has waned at the hands of the Canadian Maple Leaf and coins issued by the United States, Mexico, China and Australia. Few major dealers still sell the Krugerrand. But people holding them have no trouble getting full value if they sell. After all, gold is gold, no matter what is stamped on it.

The Canadian Maple Leaf gold coins are available in one-ounce, half-ounce, quarter-ounce and one-tenth-ounce sizes and are readily marketable anywhere in the world. The coins trade at a premium above the price of bullion. For example, you would be able to buy a one-ounce

Maple Leaf coin for about $296.64 if bullion is trading at $288.00. That's a premium of about 3 per cent. You could sell a Maple Leaf for about $292.74 when bullion is selling at about $287 an ounce, a premium of about 2 per cent. If you live in certain provinces, you will also have to pay sales taxes on gold coins (but not GST, as gold and silver bullion are exempt). For example, Ontario and British Columbia charge 8 per cent and Quebec charges 9 per cent. There is no sales tax on coins in Alberta.

You can also buy what are known as numismatic coins. They sell at prices above the value of the bullion they contain, and appeal to collectors. Their price reflects their scarcity as well as their gold content, but they are less marketable than bullion coins.

Playing gold stocks

Gold share prices reflect gold price expectations as well as companies' production, profits, dividend payments and the outlook for new discoveries. The gold stocks market is highly specialized, but it can be divided into three major categories:

- Senior companies, which are major producers and generally have large market capitalizations;
- Intermediate companies, which are medium producers of about 200,000 ounces annually;
- Junior companies, which are exploration plays that have yet to produce gold. There are also those companies that have yet to discover gold, but which have promising properties.

The prices of shares in companies that produce and pay dividends tend to be less volatile than those of junior exploration companies. Yet they are still more volatile than the prices of most other stocks, with the junior stocks extremely volatile. If you want to invest in the junior gold stocks, you should first decide whether you can afford the risks. If you can't, stay away.

Gold mutual funds make sense for investors who want a diversified precious metals portfolio. As with other mutual funds, the advantage is professional management.

As virtually every investor is aware, the biggest boom-and-bust gold story of the decade is Bre-X Minerals Ltd., whose shares commanded a market capitalization of $6 billion on expectations that a property in Indonesia in which it held an interest was the world's largest gold deposit with reserves of 200 million ounces. The stock became worthless when independent studies concluded there was no pot at the end of this rainbow.

While many institutional and retail investors as well as brokerage analysts lost money and reputation, others avoided the stock for various reasons including concerns about title to the property and the values being placed on it by the marketplace. While about 150 mutual funds held the shares, few held large positions. The few that did were precious metals funds whose unit-holders were or should have been prepared for volatility.

Precious stones

In the past decade or so, diamonds and other gemstones have grown increasingly appealing to investors, particularly during periods of high inflation. However, their prices can be very volatile just like gold and silver. Diamonds are a highly specialized area of investment, and are definitely not for the beginner.

There are two key points to remember. First, no two diamonds are alike, even if they are in the same class and are of the same weight. And, unlike commodities, gold and stocks, diamonds are not sold in an auction market.

Diamonds differ from gold in that you cannot obtain a price quote over the telephone or buy and sell at the same price throughout the world. To determine a diamond price, you must obtain an appraisal. Moreover, the spreads between the bid price and ask price are substantial. Unlike gold, where the markup is usually less than 1 per cent, the markup on diamonds can be 100 to 200 per cent. In other words, the price has to double for you to break even, unless you can buy at cost. On top of that, unless you're buying smuggled diamonds, you're paying a hefty federal tax and duty.

Diamonds do have their uses as investments, particularly in parts of the world where people are looking for hedges against political upheaval. After all, it's easier to flee a country with $100,000 of diamonds than with $100,000 of gold.

If you want to invest in diamonds, stick to top-quality stones of about one carat. Larger ones may prove difficult to sell because the market is thin. Buy only from reputable dealers. More than one person has purchased industrial-grade stones thinking they were jewellery quality. Others have been fooled into buying synthetic stones, believing them to be the real thing. Some experts suggest that investors buy and store their stones outside Canada to avoid paying duties and sales taxes.

You can also invest in coloured stones, such as emeralds, rubies or sapphires, but the market for these gems is more fragmented than the diamond market, and there are no standard grading systems.

Chapter 15

The Art of Investing in Art

The 1980s were a bonanza for astute art investors as prices soared. In early 1989, the Getty Museum paid $35.2 million (U.S.) for a portrait of a Florentine duke painted by Jacopo Pontormo, an old master, more than 450 years ago. The sale broke the previous old master record price of $10.5 million that had been set in 1985 by Andrea Mantegna's *Adoration of the Magi.*

In 1990, the highest price ever paid for an art object was set when Christie's sold Vincent van Gogh's *Portrait of Dr. Gachet* for $82.5 million (U.S.); Sotheby's set a new high for paintings by Auguste Renoir when it sold *Au Moulin de la Gallett* for $78.1 million (U.S.). The recession has temporarily ended the art boom. More attention, though, is being paid to paintings that don't sell at an auction.

But how did the seller fare?

During booms, auction houses profit. The normal auction-house toll is 10 per cent charged to both buyer and seller. If neither buyer nor seller were given a concession by Christie's, the auction house pocketed over $7 million (U.S.) just for marketing the sale of Pontormo's painting. And market it they did, with plenty of press releases speculating on whether the Getty would go for it.

The painting was sold to the Getty Museum by the estate of Chauncey D. Stillman, a New York investor and philanthropist. Stillman had bought the painting in 1937 for $37,000 (U.S.). If we ignore the auction-house fee, the Stillman estate pocketed a pretax gain of over $35 million (U.S.).

That impressive sum shrinks to something mere mortals can understand when we calculate the rate of return earned over the 52 years that elapsed between the 1937 purchase and the 1989 sale. Stillman earned

11.7 per cent annually on his $37,000 (U.S.) investment—good, but not much better than the 11.1 per cent performance of the TSE 300 for the same period. And remember, the 11.7 per cent was earned with a record-breaking painting while the 11.1 per cent was earned on a basket of typical stocks.

But who computes compound rates of return? Certainly not the throngs that once filled the New York auction halls of Christie's and Sotheby's in November 1988. They paid $433 million (U.S.) for impressionist, modern and contemporary art, twice the take from auctions a year earlier.

Jasper Johns, a 59-year-old American painter, saw his *False Start* bring $17.1 (U.S.) million. In 1960, it sold for $3,150 (U.S.). In fact, that was a startling rate of appreciation—almost 36 per cent compounded annually. And Johns is a contemporary painter whose name may not even be in the art history books 400 years from now.

But the Johns price, and the oversized compound rate, reflected art fever, a fever that reached such an unprecedented pitch because two well-heeled collectors, S.I. Newhouse, the American publishing tycoon, and Hans Thulin, a Swedish property developer, were both determined to have *False Start*. It was their battle of bids that caused the price to soar.

In the end, Newhouse won. Thulin had to console himself with a $7 million all-American white flag by Johns and a $6.3 million giant collage by Rauschenberg, another contemporary painter.

Question: Will either Newhouse or Thulin achieve an 11 per cent return on the swollen prices they paid? The record suggests they will not. These days even the auction houses have problems.

The Canadian experience

Canadians are not immune to art fever. In mid-1993, the National Gallery of Canada unveiled seven recent purchases and a selection of 244 pieces purchased for $3.4 million. The number of purchases, their significance and their average price of just under $14,000 were overshadowed by the $1.9 million paid for Mark Rothko's *No. 16*. In fact, the seven pieces, which included Lawren Harris's $410,000 *Decorative Landscape,* represented the bulk of the $3.4 million.

The record price for a Canadian painting was $520,000 paid by an anonymous bidder in 1995 for James Wilson Morrice's impressionist painting *Bull Ring, Marseilles*. Commission raised the cost to $572,000. In November 1989, Clarence Gagnon's *Ice Harvest* sold for $495,000, the previous record auction price for a piece of art in Canada. In May 1990, Jean Paul Riopelle's *Composition* fetched $420,000, and in May 1994, his *Tryptique* sold for $462,000.

In that auction of May 1990, *Lynn Valley* by Group of Seven painter Frederick Varley sold for $363,000. Just four years earlier, the painting had sold for $85,000. The annual return of almost 44 per cent was extraordinary.

Rules for buying

You'd be foolish to expect that kind of return on your art investments—they're much like winning a lottery. There's little anyone can do to ensure a high return on art. It's said you can never go wrong buying high quality—this might be true esthetically but it's not true financially.

If your aim is high returns, you're better off timing your art purchases. Art prices move in cycles much as do stock prices. Unfortunately, just as with stock market investing, when prices are falling, we wait for them to go lower; when prices are rising, we all climb on the bandwagon.

Of course, most of us are not in the league of art buyers who are able to pay millions for a painting. Neither do we have to come up against the tycoons in bidding wars. But do we have a chance at making a reasonable return on an art investment?

The hype artists

Art as an investment is pushed by art auction houses and fancy dealers. Without high art prices, art sellers could not afford expensive rented premises and the good things in life. So, although good dealers and auction-house people usually know a fair amount about art, they clearly have a vested interest. But art is what counts, not money. So the suave dealer peddling a $10,000 piece of art can become downright contemptuous if you ask what the investment prospects are for his or her treasure. The dealer may well reply: "If you are interested in money, buy bonds." For some reason, he or she will seldom refer to the stock market, where the risks more closely reflect the art market.

The world of art is in many ways like the world of stocks. Just as there are established artists and new artists, there are established stocks and new issues. There are stocks for which there are always buyers, although not always at the best price, and there are stocks for which the market disappears at the first sign of a cloud.

What the art dealer wants to do, as does the auctioneer who wears formal dress to peddle paintings, is to intimidate you. Your $10,000 is as real to the dealer as it is to you. But the major difference is this: Until you have bought the painting, the $10,000 is yours, not the dealer's. You could like the painting but feel that unless the price of the piece will appreciate by at least the rate paid by your friendly bank, it is beyond your means.

Of course, dealers don't have the slightest notion of how fast the price will rise, or if it will rise at all. So they take the noble posture of being above mere money. Still, the dealer and everyone involved in selling art have to rely on hype that implies fast returns if they are to make sales.

One of the schemes used by art dealers is announcements of record prices. The art auction season, which traditionally runs from late October through late May, but actually extends as long as the major art auction companies believe that they can attract enough money to make an auction profitable, has become the focus of the announcements.

Dealers often view auction houses as competition, even though their relationship is symbiotic with auction houses providing at least some degree of liquidity to the art market. If there were no auction houses, it would be even more difficult for collectors to unload their treasures. Dealers would have to provide liquidity themselves or sell less at lower prices. Auction houses also serve as a means through which dealers can efficiently adjust inventories.

Auction houses and dealers both benefit from announcements of record prices, even though the announcements are made by auction houses. The most potent announcement is the establishment of the highest price ever achieved for a painting widely viewed as a masterpiece, or the highest price for a work painted by a particular master. The news media report the record price, and dealers and auction houses let their clients know.

The problem with the record announcement approach is that to get a world record price you need a very unusual and beautiful piece of art.

These, by definition, are rare. So the auction houses often lack items of rarity and beauty.

Trying to create gold from dross

Caught in a booming art market, some greedy dealers and auction houses work rapidly to bring new artists to the $100,000 range and more. They also attempt to revive the fortunes of long-dead artists whose work has fallen out of favour. They even work to make a market for the work of long-dead artists who never were in favour.

The arguments used by some dealers to sell old works that are now of small value, never were of value, and probably never will be of value should have a familiar ring to investors in penny stocks.

To keep the ball rolling, living artists, even relatively young ones, may form the subject of an announcement of a record price. Despite the fact that the auction tradition and the tradition at the grander art galleries favour dead artists, there are often announcements on the works of some living artists for whom there are enough well-heeled enthusiasts.

Buying a living artist's work as an investment is like grubstaking a prospector. Either is risky but acceptable if you don't overspend. Neither the artist nor the prospector is likely to have any real success.

Crass causes

What is usually ignored is that one needs more than a masterpiece to generate an announcement of a record price. Inflation, particularly if combined with low interest rates, is a big help.

Art is an international commodity of global appeal and it is not an accident that Europeans dominate the art markets when the Euro-currencies are strong. Japanese dominate, despite cultural differences, when the yen rises. And Americans buy everything in sight if the U.S. dollar is strong.

Currency movements can be a major factor in record prices. If an auction is held in yen instead of dollars, after the yen has appreciated, prices might fall. As a result, as an investor you should try to make purchases when the Canadian dollar is strong, and let others buy when the dollar is in the doldrums.

The penny paintings

Most new artists will not make rewarding financial investments even if you like their work. Of course, if the promoter—the art dealer in this case—has a good track record, you may buy a few more so-called penny paintings or pay a bit more than you might otherwise. But unless you have good connections, it may be hard to buy into an attractive deal.

Otherwise, the pennies in art can be far more satisfying than the penny stocks issued in Vancouver. If you like the art and paid little for it, who really cares if it appreciates?

After the pennies come works by the juniors—local artists who have had a number of shows and who are usually represented by a reasonably prestigious dealer. The work of a junior can cost well in excess of $10,000, but some good ones are available for around $5,000. It would be encouraging to say that the prices of these works will certainly appreciate—and some dealers say exactly that. But the truth is that the worth of most will dwindle.

Better dead than alive

Even junior artists who should be seniors mess up the deal if they stay alive. They can paint junk and sell works they should have burned, as did Picasso. In time, if the junior's work becomes blue chip, the world will be willing to distinguish between the good and the bad. But few juniors make that jump.

The risky blue chips

The blue chips—particularly Canadian blue chips—are generally bad investments. Even if you bought a painting by Tom Thomson, the father of the Group of Seven, for $20 in 1918 and sold it for $35,000 in 1988, your rather handsome gain is a lot less impressive than it sounds. When translated into a compound rate of return, the annual yield on the investment is 11.125 per cent. Although it is somewhat better than the yield on most financial investments, it is a lot riskier.

Who in 1918, or even 1928, would have foreseen that the commanding position painters such as A.Y. Jackson, A.J. Casson and the other members of the Group of Seven would hold in Canada that they have attained over the past two decades? Few investors did. Furthermore, converting a Thomson into cash during the Great Depression of the 1930s, when you might well have preferred cash to art, was virtually impossible. The return was not only risky, but the investment was also highly illiquid.

That's all behind us, so perhaps an investor should buy a Thomson today. Indeed, many investors are doing exactly that. The argument is that if we ignore the problem with fakes that grows in parallel with the price of the artist's work, there won't be any more Thomsons painted. Furthermore, many of the holders, such as museums, will keep their Thomsons off the market. Thus, we really are dealing with a shrinking number of Thomsons. Still, it is not impossible to imagine a time when Thomson or the Group of Seven are viewed as simply regional examples of post-impressionism. Such a view could bring prices down appreciably.

Indeed, the only art that is truly of investment quality, comparable to government bonds or stocks of blue-chip companies, are the best examples of the international masters. Their value is not distorted by regionalism because the works are well known and have been heavily reviewed. They have stood the test of time. If you cannot get top examples from the work of the 18th-century masters, settle for those top-drawer artists of the 19th century. But be careful of the 20th century; there is too much chance of trendiness that pushes prices above value. Who knows how Picasso's works will stand the test of real time?

Of course, most of us cannot afford the hundreds of thousands of dollars involved in buying a single example of such work. We may be decorating by buying works of imitators or preening ourselves by buying inferior examples of the work of first-class artists in a kind of autograph hunting. We may be showing off as art collectors. We may even really be collectors.

All of these things may be great fun but they are not investing. Someone with limited dollars can get much better returns, albeit with less pleasure, in the securities markets.

Chapter 16

Tax Shelters: Easing the Pain

Everyone likes to keep their taxes to a minimum. Indeed, because of the way that taxation has increasingly bitten into incomes, cutting taxes has become a prime ambition for many Canadians.

Tax avoidance—as opposed to tax evasion—is legal and involves the use of a variety of measures allowed by Ottawa to reduce taxes. For instance, RRSPs and pension plans are popular tax shelters. Investing in Canadian dividend-paying shares to get the dividend tax credit is another widely used method of cutting the amount you pay to Revenue Canada. Similarly you can reduce the tax burden on investment income if you save for your children's education by using an RESP.

There are other ways people can shelter income, although some tax shelters are quite complex and not suitable for most families of moderate means. Moreover, the federal government has been cutting back on tax shelters. In 1985, it virtually ended income-splitting plans between spouses and between parents and minor children. The most common strategy involved low-interest or no-interest loans between husbands and wives, whereby one spouse would lend funds to the other if the borrowing spouse had substantially lower income. The borrower would invest the funds and any interest earned would then be taxed at his or her marginal tax rate, which was usually much lower than that of the lending spouse.

With these spousal loans, families could circumvent Ottawa's attribution rules, which require that within a family, tax on investment income must be paid by the person who supplied the capital, not the person whose name is on the bank account or share certificates. The February 1992 federal budget ended income-splitting between common-law spouses effective 1993.

Although most income-splitting devices are gone, some are still left. If one spouse makes a loan to the other to buy or invest in a business to be managed by the spouse to whom the money is lent, the profits are taxed in the hands of the spouse operating the business.

You cannot make low- or no-interest loans to children 18 and over for investment purposes. Until the change, these loans made sense for those with children at university because the children could earn investment income that was lightly taxed due to tuition deductions. In effect, you had shifted investment income to be taxed at your children's marginal rates from your higher one. You can, however, give money to your children without tax consequences.

The risk is always there

Other types of shelters have allowed individuals to invest in specific industries to reduce taxes. Ottawa has reduced the attractiveness of this type of issue in recent years. Provincial legislation, however, may give rise to regional tax shelters.

Another method of sheltering money from taxes is to invest with borrowed funds through a limited partnership in a venture that is losing money. You can write off your share of the losses from the limited partnership against other income and deduct the interest you pay for tax purposes. You are, of course, at risk for the money that you've borrowed. Ideally, the venture will eventually be sold and you will recover your after-tax costs or, better still, make a handsome profit.

The truth of the matter is that shelters are usually risky. However, some are a lot riskier than others and there are ways to separate those with good investment potential from those without. First, use the investment's prospectus to determine your after-tax costs. In other words, if you put up $10,000 and get $6,000 back from Ottawa, your after-tax cost is $4,000. Then determine, also from the prospectus, the after-tax value of the investment. For example, if you sold the shelter at the earliest possible time that allowed you a full tax write-off, what would you get? If the value of your $4,000 investment is, say, $5,000 after taxes when sold, it would appear to be a good prospect.

It is important to understand what you own when you buy a shelter and what that holding is worth. Too many investors have used borrowed money to buy a shelter, and then spent the tax refund while under the impression that the value of their investment was equal to the value of their loan. They then find that when it comes time to repay the loan, on liquidation of the investment, that the amount borrowed exceeded the after-tax value of the investment.

If you're in the market for tax shelters, you should look at the investment aspects of any proposal before you look at the tax implications. If it doesn't look good from an investment perspective, it should be avoided. The tax-shelter benefits should be considered the icing on the cake.

Marketability is another important factor. It is often quite difficult to get out of a shelter once you're in because in many cases there is no secondary market. Moreover, few shelters provide a mechanism for liquidity after a set period. In the past, some flow-through limited partnerships rolled into mutual funds that could be redeemed for full market value at any time. Others distributed the shares in which the partnership invests and these can be sold like other stocks.

In addition, you should be careful about how you finance your purchase. Interest on funds borrowed for investment is deductible for tax purposes, so many people have in the past borrowed to buy shelters in the hope of increasing their tax deductions and sheltering a major portion of their income from taxes. Problems arose when their investments failed to bring the promised returns and they found themselves in debt. As noted in the chapter on real estate investment, Revenue Canada has challenged some of these schemes, alleging their sole purpose was to cut taxes, not earn income.

Provincial stock savings plans

Some provinces have provincially sponsored tax shelters, the most successful and best known being the Quebec Stock Savings Plan. Introduced in 1979, the plan allows Quebec residents a tax break for investing in Quebec-based public companies.

The plan encourages Quebec residents to become investors rather than savers. As with any other investment, the tax aspect is an added bonus. Any shares considered should be able to stand on their own as investments.

Labour-sponsored funds

Labour-sponsored venture funds are offered in some provinces. These invest in small business ventures and should be considered high-risk investments. They are heavily marketed during January and February when people are making RRSP decisions. In most participating provinces, investors who buy $3,500 of these funds receive a federal tax credit of $525 and an additional provincial matching credit. This amount will rise in 1999 to $5,000 and $750. However, as with any investment, the tax break should be viewed as a bonus. If the investment can't stand scrutiny, it should be avoided. In short, labour-sponsored investment funds provide a means for small investors to invest in venture capital. Venture capital is risk capital.

Offshore bank accounts

Tax avoidance is legal, tax evasion is not. If you can't tell the difference, get professional advice from a tax accountant or tax lawyer. Many people talk about moving their money offshore. That's easy enough. But if the assets are still yours, then the income is taxable in Canada. Some people set up complex schemes that provide for their assets to be held by a trust outside the country in which income compounds for their benefit. Generally, they give up or appear to give up control of their assets to keep the strategy from violating the tax rules.

As far as secret accounts are concerned, more than a few Canadians have been burned when their advisors made poor if not improper investment decisions. These people had no recourse. Moreover, if you die your estate could have a horrendous time getting at your assets. Even if your executors could locate them, and could get access to them, they would have to face tax ramifications that you sought had to avoid, assuming they did not intend to carry on with your scheme.

Chapter 17

Strategies: Do What Works Well

You might have heard a long-term investor described as "a short-term investor whose stock went down." There's some truth to this. Indeed, many people make the mistake of holding their losers indefinitely in hopes that they will rise in price. Sometimes the losers do recover, but people holding investments that have lost value should ask whether they can do better investing their money elsewhere.

That's what this chapter is about: demonstrating some of the strategies you can use to structure your investments to meet your objectives and make the most of your money.

It pays to diversify

Strategy No. 1 is diversification—in other words, don't put all your eggs in one basket. It's a fact of financial life that if you put everything in one security and the company has difficulties, you will have serious problems as well. And putting all your money into a company you think is stable can also be a recipe for disaster; even blue-chip companies can have problems. You might recall when Royal Trustco was considered a blue-chip stock and paid handsome dividends—before it fell on hard times.

Of course, by diversifying you won't make the killing in the market that you would if you put everything in one stock that skyrockets. But steady growth is preferable to watching your fortune go down the tubes.

Just how much you diversify depends on how much risk you are willing to take. Even splitting your money between two growth investments significantly reduces risk, so try to introduce some variety into your holdings or at least limit the portion of your assets with which you speculate.

Another point worthy of consideration is diversification across different classes of assets. Many people diversify within one asset group, such as the stock market. But not venturing outside that asset group can be a mistake; no single class of asset is best all the time.

Take the stock market as an example. Although it performed extremely well over the past 10 years, if you had all your money in the Asian market or resource shares over the past year, you took a short-term beating. Similarly, there have been times when guaranteed investment certificates and long-term bonds have been poor investments, and periods when treasury bills have been a costly choice because of falling interest rates.

By spreading your investments among different types of assets, such as gold, interest- and dividend-producing instruments, stocks and real estate, your returns are likely to be more stable than if you put everything into growth investments.

Manage your investments

Another secret to success is managing your investments well. To achieve maximum returns, you must constantly re-evaluate your holdings in light of current and anticipated economic and market conditions. For example, long-term government bonds may be safe, but you don't want to hold them if it looks like interest rates are ready to skyrocket. And you don't want a heavy equity position when stocks are a poor value relative to other investments.

Be prepared to change the mix of assets you hold to take advantage of opportunities while preserving capital. You must constantly monitor your individual holdings within asset groups to ensure that each security continues to meet your criteria for holding on to that investment.

Even if you've delegated the management of your assets to a professional—through mutual funds, for instance—you must be aware of their status so you can determine whether your manager's performance is satisfactory. However, don't be too quick to make changes. You may want to judge professional results over a few years, or even a full market cycle, rather than over a couple of months.

Taxes and speculation

To make the most of your investments, any strategy must take full advantage of government-approved methods of saving to meet specific objectives. Your RRSP, for instance, is the best way to save for retirement because of the generous tax breaks.

You should also keep the speculative portion of your portfolio within limits. There is nothing wrong with speculating, but it should only be done with money you can afford to lose. Don't, for example, gamble with your retirement prospects by speculating with your RRSP funds. Don't speculate at all if the loss of the funds involved will affect your lifestyle and destroy your chances of meeting other financial objectives.

Future Value of an Annual Investment of $1,000 Made at the Beginning of the Year

	1%	2%	3%	4%	5%	6%	7%	8%	9%	10%
1	$1,010	$1,020	$1,030	$1,040	$1,050	$1,060	$1,070	$1,080	$1,090	$1,100
2	$2,030	$2,060	$2,091	$2,122	$2,153	$2,184	$2,215	$2,246	$2,278	$2,310
3	$3,060	$3,122	$3,184	$3,246	$3,310	$3,375	$3,440	$3,506	$3,573	$3,641
4	$4,101	$4,204	$4,309	$4,416	$4,526	$4,637	$4,751	$4,867	$4,985	$5,105
5	$5,152	$5,308	$5,468	$5,633	$5,802	$5,975	$6,153	$6,336	$6,523	$6,716
6	$6,214	$6,434	$6.662	$6,898	$7,142	$7,394	$7,654	$7,923	$8,200	$8,487
7	$7,286	$7,583	$7,892	$8,214	$8,549	$8,897	$9,260	$9,637	$10,028	$10,436
8	$8,369	$8,755	$9,159	$9,583	$10,027	$10,491	$10,978	$11,488	$12,021	$12,579
9	$9,462	$9,950	$10,464	$11,006	$11,578	$12,181	$12,816	$13,487	$14,193	$14,937
10	$10,567	$11,169	$11,808	$12,486	$13,207	$13,972	$14,784	$15,645	$16,560	$17,531
11	$11,683	$12,412	$13,192	$14,026	$14,917	$15,870	$16,888	$17,977	$19,141	$20,384
12	$12,809	$13,680	$14,618	$15,627	$16,713	$17,882	$19,141	$20,495	$21,953	$23,523
13	$13,947	$14,974	$16,086	$17,292	$18,599	$20,015	$21,550	$23,215	$25,019	$26,975
14	$15,097	$16,293	$17,599	$19,024	$20,579	$22,276	$24,129	$26,152	$28,361	$30,772
15	$16,258	$17,639	$19,157	$20,825	$22,657	$24,673	$26,888	$29,324	$32,003	$34,950
16	$17,430	$19,012	$20,762	$22,698	$24,840	$27,213	$29,840	$32,750	$35,974	$39,545
17	$18,615	$20,412	$22,414	$24,645	$27,132	$29,906	$32,999	$36,450	$40,301	$44,599
18	$19,811	$21,841	$24,117	$26,671	$29,539	$32,760	$36,379	$40,446	$45,018	$50,159
19	$21,019	$23,297	$25,870	$28,778	$32,066	$35,786	$39,995	$44,762	$50,160	$56,275
20	$22,239	$24,783	$27,676	$30,969	$34,719	$38,993	$43,865	$49,423	$55,765	$63,002
21	$23,472	$26,299	$29,537	$33,248	$37,505	$42,392	$48,006	$54,457	$61,873	$70,403
22	$24,716	$27,845	$31,453	$35,618	$40,430	$45,996	$52,436	$59,893	$68,532	$78,543
23	$25,973	$29,422	$33,426	$38,083	$43,502	$49,816	$57,177	$65,765	$75,790	$87,497
24	$27,243	$31,030	$35,459	$40,646	$46,727	$53,865	$62,249	$72,106	$83,701	$97,347
25	$28,526	$32,671	$37,553	$43,312	$50,113	$58,156	$67,676	$78,954	$92,324	$108,182
26	$29,821	$34,344	$39,710	$46,084	$53,669	$62,706	$73,484	$86,351	$101,723	$120,100
27	$31,129	$36,051	$41,931	$48,968	$57,403	$67,528	$79,698	$94,339	$111,968	$133,210
28	$32,450	$37,792	$44,219	$51,966	$61,323	$72,640	$86,347	$102,966	$123,135	$147,631
29	$33,785	$39,568	$46,575	$55,085	$65,439	$78,058	$93,461	$112,283	$135,308	$163,494
30	$35,133	$41,379	$49,003	$58,328	$69,761	$83,802	$101,073	$122,346	$148,575	$180,943
31	$36,494	$43,227	$51,503	$61,701	$74,299	$89,890	$109,218	$133,214	$163,037	$200,138
32	$37,869	$45,112	$54,078	$65,210	$79,064	$96,343	$117,933	$144,951	$178,800	$221,252
33	$39,258	$47,034	$56,730	$68,858	$84,067	$103,184	$127,259	$157,627	$195,982	$244,477
34	$40,660	$48,994	$59,462	$72,652	$89,320	$110,435	$137,237	$171,317	$214,711	$270,024
35	$42,077	$50,994	$62,276	$76,598	$94,836	$118,121	$147,913	$186,102	$235,125	$298,127
36	$43,508	$53,034	$65,174	$80,702	$100,628	$126,268	$159,337	$202,070	$257,376	$329,039
37	$44,953	$55,115	$68,159	$84,970	$106,710	$134,904	$171,561	$219,316	$281,630	$363,043
38	$46,412	$57,237	$71,234	$89,409	$113,095	$144,058	$184,640	$237,941	$308,066	$400,448
39	$47,886	$59,402	$74,401	$94,026	$119,800	$153,762	$198,635	$258,057	$336,882	$441,593
40	$49,375	$61,610	$77,663	$98,827	$126,840	$164,048	$213,610	$279,781	$368,292	$486,852

	11%	12%	13%	14%	15%	16%	17%	18%	19%	20%
1	$1,110	$1,120	$1,130	$1,140	$1,150	$1,160	$1,170	$1,180	$1,190	$1,200
2	$2,342	$2,374	$2,407	$2,440	$2,473	$2,506	$2,539	$2,572	$2,606	$2,640
3	$3,710	$3,779	$3,850	$3,921	$3,993	$4,066	$4,141	$4,215	$4,291	$4,368
4	$5,228	$5,353	$5,480	$5,610	$5,742	$5,877	$6,014	$6,154	$6,297	$6,442
5	$6,913	$7,115	$7,323	$7,536	$7,754	$7,977	$8,207	$8,442	$8,683	$8,930
6	$8,783	$9,089	$9,405	$9,730	$10,067	$10,414	$10,772	$11,142	$11,523	$11,916
7	$10,859	$11,300	$11,757	$12,233	$12,727	$13,240	$13,773	$14,327	$14,902	$15,499
8	$13,164	$13,776	$14,416	$15,085	$15,786	$16,519	$17,285	$18,086	$18,923	$19,799
9	$15,722	$16,549	$17,420	$18,337	$19,304	$20,321	$21,393	$22,521	$23,709	$24,959
10	$18,561	$19,655	$20,814	$22,045	$23,349	$24,733	$26,200	$27,755	$29,404	$31,150
11	$21,713	$23,133	$24,650	$26,271	$28,002	$29,850	$32,824	$33,931	$36,180	$38,581
12	$25,212	$27,029	$28,985	$31,089	$33,352	$35,786	$38,404	$41,219	$44,244	$47,497
13	$29,095	$31,393	$33,883	$36,581	$39,505	$42,672	$46,103	$49,818	$53,841	$58,196
14	$33,405	$36,280	$39,417	$42,842	$46,580	$50,660	$55,110	$59,965	$65,261	$71,035
15	$38,190	$41,753	$45,672	$49,980	$54,717	$59,925	$65,649	$71,939	$78,850	$86,442
16	$43,501	$47,884	$52,739	$58,118	$64,075	$70,673	$77,979	$86,068	$95,022	$104,931
17	$49,396	$54,750	$60,725	$67,394	$74,836	$83,141	$92,406	$102,740	$114,266	$127,117
18	$55,939	$62,440	$69,749	$77,969	$87,212	$97,603	$109,285	$122,414	$137,166	$153,740
19	$63,203	$71,052	$79,947	$90,025	$101,444	$114,380	$129,033	$145,628	$164,418	$185,688
20	$71,265	$80,699	$91,470	$103,768	$117,810	$133,841	$152,139	$173,021	$196,847	$224,026
21	$80,214	$91,503	$104,491	$119,436	$136,632	$156,415	$179,172	$205,345	$235,438	$270,031
22	$90,148	$103,603	$119,205	$137,297	$158,276	$182,601	$210,801	$243,487	$281,362	$325,237
23	$101,174	$117,155	$135,831	$157,659	$183,168	$212,978	$247,808	$288,494	$336,010	$391,484
24	$113,413	$132,334	$154,620	$180,871	$211,793	$248,214	$291,105	$341,603	$401,042	$470,981
25	$126,999	$149,334	$175,850	$207,333	$244,712	$289,088	$341,763	$404,272	$478,431	$566,377
26	$142,079	$168,374	$199,841	$237,499	$282,569	$336,502	$401,032	$478,221	$570,522	$680,853
27	$158,817	$189,699	$226,950	$271,889	$326,104	$391,503	$470,378	$565,481	$680,112	$818,223
28	$177,397	$213,583	$257,583	$311,094	$376,170	$455,303	$551,512	$668,447	$810,523	$983,068
29	$198,021	$240,333	$292,199	$355,787	$433,745	$529,312	$646,439	$789,948	$965,712	$1,180,882
30	$220,913	$270,293	$331,315	$406,737	$499,957	$615,162	$757,504	$933,319	$1,150,387	$1,418,258
31	$246,324	$303,848	$375,516	$464,820	$576,100	$714,747	$887,449	$1,102,496	$1,370,151	$1,703,109
32	$274,529	$341,429	$425,463	$531,035	$663,666	$830,267	$1,039,486	$1,302,125	$1,632,670	$2,044,931
33	$305,837	$383,521	$481,903	$606,520	$764,365	$964,270	$1,217,368	$1,537,688	$1,942,877	$2,455,118
34	$340,590	$430,663	$545,681	$692,573	$880,170	$1,119,713	$1,425,491	$1,815,652	$2,313,214	$2,947,341
35	$379,164	$483,463	$617,749	$790,673	$1,013,346	$1,300,027	$1,668,994	$2,143,649	$2,753,914	$3,538,009
36	$421,982	$542,599	$699,187	$902,507	$1,166,498	$1,509,191	$1,953,894	$2,530,686	$3,278,348	$4,246,811
37	$469,511	$608,831	$791,211	$1,029,998	$1,342,622	$1,751,822	$2,287,225	$2,987,389	$3,902,424	$5,097,373
38	$522,267	$683,010	$895,198	$1,175,338	$1,545,165	$2,033,273	$2,677,224	$3,526,299	$4,645,075	$6,118,048
39	$580,826	$766,091	$1,012,704	$1,341,025	$1,778,090	$2,359,757	$3,133,522	$4,162,213	$5,528,829	$7,342,858
40	$645,827	$859,142	$1,145,486	$1,529,909	$2,045,954	$2,738,478	$3,667,391	$4,912,591	$6,580,496	$8,812,629

Future Value of a Single Investment of $1,000 Made at the Beginning of the Year

	1%	2%	3%	4%	5%	6%	7%	8%	9%	10%
1	$1,010	$1,020	$1,030	$1,040	$1,050	$1,060	$1,070	$1,080	$1,090	$1,100
2	$1,020	$1,040	$1,061	$1,082	$1,103	$1,124	$1,145	$1,166	$1,188	$1,210
3	$1,030	$1,061	$1,093	$1,125	$1,158	$1,191	$1,225	$1,260	$1,295	$1,331
4	$1,041	$1,082	$1,126	$1,170	$1,216	$1,262	$1,311	$1,360	$1,412	$1,464
5	$1,051	$1,104	$1,159	$1,217	$1,276	$1,338	$1,403	$1,469	$1,539	$1,611
6	$1,062	$1,126	$1,194	$1,265	$1,340	$1,419	$1,501	$1,587	$1,677	$1,772
7	$1,072	$1,149	$1,230	$1,316	$1,407	$1,504	$1,606	$1,714	$1,828	$1,949
8	$1,083	$1,172	$1,267	$1,369	$1,477	$1,594	$1,718	$1,851	$1,993	$2,144
9	$1,094	$1,195	$1,305	$1,423	$1,551	$1,689	$1,838	$1,999	$2,172	$2,358
10	$1,105	$1,219	$1,344	$1,480	$1,629	$1,791	$1,967	$2,159	$2,367	$2,594
11	$1,116	$1,243	$1,384	$1,539	$1,710	$1,898	$2,105	$2,332	$2,580	$2,853
12	$1,127	$1,268	$1,426	$1,601	$1,796	$2,012	$2,252	$2,518	$2,813	$3,138
13	$1,138	$1,294	$1,469	$1,665	$1,886	$2,133	$2,410	$2,720	$3,066	$3,452
14	$1,149	$1,319	$1,513	$1,732	$1,980	$2,261	$2,579	$2,937	$3,342	$3,797
15	$1,161	$1,346	$1,558	$1,801	$2,079	$2,397	$2,759	$3,172	$3,642	$4,177
16	$1,173	$1,373	$1,605	$1,873	$2,183	$2,540	$2,952	$3,426	$3,970	$4,595
17	$1,184	$1,400	$1,653	$1,948	$2,292	$2,693	$3,159	$3,700	$4,328	$5,054
18	$1,196	$1,428	$1,702	$2,026	$2,407	$2,854	$3,380	$3,996	$4,717	$5,560
19	$1,208	$1,457	$1,754	$2,107	$2,527	$3,026	$3,617	$4,316	$5,142	$6,116
20	$1,220	$1,486	$1,806	$2,191	$2,653	$3,207	$3,870	$4,661	$5,604	$6,727
21	$1,232	$1,516	$1,860	$2,279	$2,786	$3,400	$4,141	$5,034	$6,109	$7,400
22	$1,245	$1,546	$1,916	$2,370	$2,925	$3,604	$4,430	$5,437	$6,659	$8,140
23	$1,257	$1,577	$1,974	$2,465	$3,072	$3,820	$4,741	$5,871	$7,258	$8,954
24	$1,270	$1,608	$2,033	$2,563	$3,225	$4,049	$5,072	$6,341	$7,911	$9,850
25	$1,282	$1,641	$2,094	$2,666	$3,386	$4,292	$5,427	$6,848	$8,623	$10,835
26	$1,295	$1,673	$2,157	$2,772	$3,556	$4,549	$5,807	$7,396	$9,399	$11,918
27	$1,308	$1,707	$2,221	$2,883	$3,733	$4,822	$6,214	$7,988	$10,245	$13,110
28	$1,321	$1,741	$2,288	$2,999	$3,920	$5,112	$6,649	$8,627	$11,167	$14,421
29	$1,335	$1,776	$2,357	$3,119	$4,116	$5,418	$7,114	$9,317	$12,172	$15,863
30	$1,348	$1,811	$2,427	$3,243	$4,322	$5,743	$7,612	$10,063	$13,268	$17,449
31	$1,361	$1,848	$2,500	$3,373	$4,538	$6,088	$8,145	$10,868	$14,462	$19,194
32	$1,375	$1,885	$2,575	$3,508	$4,765	$6,453	$8,715	$11,737	$15,763	$21,114
33	$1,389	$1,922	$2,652	$3,648	$5,003	$6,841	$9,325	$12,676	$17,182	$23,225
34	$1,403	$1,961	$2,732	$3,794	$5,253	$7,251	$9,978	$13,690	$18,728	$25,548
35	$1,417	$2,000	$2,814	$3,946	$5,516	$7,686	$10,677	$14,785	$20,414	$28,102
36	$1,431	$2,040	$2,898	$4,104	$5,792	$8,147	$11,424	$15,968	$22,251	$30,913
37	$1,445	$2,081	$2,985	$4,268	$6,081	$8,636	$12,224	$17,246	$24,254	$34,004
38	$1,460	$2,122	$3,075	$4,439	$6,385	$9,154	$13,079	$18,625	$26,437	$37,404
39	$1,474	$2,165	$3,167	$4,616	$6,705	$9,704	$13,995	$20,115	$28,816	$41,145
40	$1,489	$2,208	$3,262	$4,801	$7,040	$10,286	$14,974	$21,725	$31,409	$45,259

	11%	12%	13%	14%	15%	16%	17%	18%	19%	20%
1	$1,110	$2,120	$1,130	$1,140	$1,150	$1,160	$1,70	$1,180	$1,190	$1,200
2	$1,232	$1,254	$1,277	$1,300	$1,323	$1,346	$1,369	$1,392	$1,416	$1,440
3	$1,368	$1,405	$1,443	$1,482	$1,521	$1,561	$1,602	$1,643	$1,685	$1,728
4	$1,518	$1,574	$1,630	$1,689	$1,749	$1,811	$1,874	$1,939	$2,005	$2,074
5	$1,685	$1,762	$1,842	$1,925	$2,011	$2,100	$2,192	$2,288	$2,386	$2,488
6	$1,870	$1,974	$2,082	$2,195	$2,313	$2,436	$2,565	$2,700	$2,840	$2,986
7	$2,076	$2,211	$2,353	$2,502	$2,660	$2,826	$3,001	$3,185	$3,379	$3,583
8	$2,305	$2,476	$2,658	$2,853	$3,059	$3,278	$3,511	$3,759	$4,021	$4,300
9	$2,558	$2,773	$3,004	$3,252	$3,518	$3,803	$4,108	$4,435	$4,785	$5,160
10	$2,839	$3,106	$3,395	$3,707	$4,046	$4,411	$4,807	$5,234	$5,695	$6,192
11	$3,152	$3,479	$3,836	$4,226	$4,652	$5,117	$5,624	$6,176	$6,777	$7,430
12	$3,498	$3,896	$4,335	$4,818	$5,350	$5,936	$6,580	$7,288	$8,064	$8,916
13	$3,883	$4,363	$4,898	$5,492	$6,153	$6,886	$7,699	$8,599	$9,596	$10,699
14	$4,310	$4,887	$5,535	$6,261	$7,076	$7,988	$9,007	$10,147	$11,420	$12,839
15	$4,785	$5,474	$6,254	$7,138	$8,137	$9,266	$10,539	$11,974	$13,590	$15,407
16	$5,311	$6,130	$7,067	$8,137	$9,358	$10,748	$12,330	$14,129	$16,172	$18,488
17	$5,895	$6,866	$7,986	$9,276	$10,761	$12,468	$14,426	$16, 672	$19,244	$22,186
18	$6,544	$7,690	$9,024	$10,575	$12,375	$14,463	$16,879	$19,673	$22,901	$26,623
19	$7,263	$8,613	$10,197	$12,056	$14,232	$16,777	$19,748	$23,214	$27,252	$31,948
20	$8,062	$9,646	$11,523	$13,743	$16,367	$19,461	$23,106	$27,393	$32,429	$38,338
21	$8,949	$10,804	$13,021	$15,668	$18,822	$22,574	$27,034	$32,324	$38,591	$46,005
22	$9,934	$12,100	$14,714	$17,861	$21,645	$26,186	$31,629	$38,142	$45,923	$55,206
23	$11,026	$13,552	$16,627	$20,362	$24,891	$30,376	$37,006	$45,008	$54,694	$66,247
24	$12,239	$15,179	$18,788	$23,212	$28,625	$35,236	$43,297	$53,109	$65,032	$79,497
25	$13,585	$17,000	$21,231	$26,462	$32,919	$40,874	$50,658	$62,669	$77,388	$95,396
26	$15,080	$19,040	$23,991	$30,167	$37,857	$57,414	$59,270	$73,949	$92,092	$114,475
27	$16,739	$21,325	$27,109	$34,390	$43,535	$55,000	$69,345	$87,260	$109,589	$137,371
28	$18,580	$23,884	$30,633	$39,204	$50,066	$63,800	$81,134	$102,967	$130,411	$164,845
29	$20,624	$26,750	$34,616	$44,693	$57,575	$74,009	$94,927	$121,501	$155,189	$197,814
30	$22,892	$29,960	$39,116	$50,950	$66,212	$85,850	$111,065	$143,371	$184,675	$237,376
31	$25,410	$33,555	$44,201	$58,083	$76,144	$99,586	$129,946	$169,177	$219,764	$284,852
32	$28,206	$37,582	$49,947	$66,215	$87,565	$115,520	$152,036	$199,629	$261,519	$341,822
33	$31,308	$42,092	$56,440	$75,485	$100,700	$134,003	$177,883	$235,563	$311,207	$410,186
34	$34,752	$47,143	$63,777	$86,053	$115,805	$155,443	$208,123	$277,964	$370,337	$492,224
35	$38,575	$52,800	$72,069	$98,100	$133,176	$180,314	$243,503	$327,997	$440,701	$590,668
36	$42,818	$59,136	$81,437	$111,834	$153,152	$209,164	$284,899	$387,037	$524,434	$708,802
37	$47,528	$66,232	$92,024	$127,491	$176,125	$242,631	$333,332	$456,703	$624,076	$850,562
38	$52,756	$74,180	$103,987	$145,340	$202,543	$281,452	$389,998	$538,910	$742,651	$1,020,675
39	$58,559	$83,081	$117,506	$165,687	$232,925	$326,484	$456,298	$635,914	$883,754	$1,224,810
40	$65,001	$93,051	$132,782	$188,884	$267,864	$378,721	$533,869	$750,378	$1,051,668	$1,469,772

Survey of Annual Fund Performance for 12-Month Periods Ended June 30

Funds are listed by category:
  Divers=Diversified;
  SC=Small capitalization;
  LC=Large capitalization;
  FinSer=Financial Services;
  PrMet=Precious Metals;
  LSV=Labour Sponsored Investment Fund;
  SAA=Strategic Asset Allocation;
  TAA=Tactical Asset Allocation.

Table prepared using PAL*Trak*
© Copyright Portfolio Analytics Limited, 1998

% RETURN AT YEAR END

FUND NAME		FUND CATEGORY	JUN98	JUN97	JUN96	JUN95	JUN94	JUN93	JUN92	JUN91	JUN90	JUN89
20/20 Canadian Resources	CdnEq	Resource	-21.9	16.3	28.6	-3.4	-9.2	117.1	2.8	-11.8	15.8	-6.1
20/20 RSP Aggr Smaller Co	CdnEq	Growth	20.7	8.0	-	-	-	-	-	-	-	-
20/20 RSP Aggressive Eq	CdnEq	Growth	24.0	1.8	57.5	19.6	-	-	-	-	-	-
ABC Fundamental-Value	CdnEq	Value	6.6	32.5	16.2	4.7	38.2	66.5	0.9	27.1	6.2	-
AGF Canadian Equity	CdnEq	Divers	0.7	11.0	17.4	7.8	1.2	19.5	0.4	-1.3	-9.0	9.2
AGF Canadian Growth	CdnEq	Divers	12.7	24.3	4.7	13.8	7.9	9.7	2.9	7.7	1.9	-
AGF Dividend	CdnEq	Dividend	19.1	39.1	12.1	19.5	3.6	14.5	7.4	6.4	2.9	14.0
AGF Growth Equity	CdnEq	Growth	6.4	21.3	21.6	2.4	3.0	59.0	14.1	2.4	-4.1	4.6
AGF High Income	CdnEq	Dividend	6.6	12.1	9.3	10.8	3.6	6.6	14.9	7.9	-	-
AGF Intl Grp-Canada Class	CdnEq	Divers	-2.4	-	-	-	-	-	-	-	-	-
AIC Advantage	CdnEq	FinSer	25.4	82.9	38.9	24.8	10.1	30.3	17.0	14.5	-8.0	11.7
AIC Advantage Fund II	CdnEq	Divers	28.2	-	-	-	-	-	-	-	-	-
AIC Diversified Canada	CdnEq	Growth	32.4	64.6	32.7	-	-	-	-	-	-	-
AIM Canadian Premier	CdnEq	Divers	18.8	16.6	15.6	10.7	-2.5	17.5	4.3	-1.4	-	-
AIM GT Canada Growth	CdnEq	Growth	25.1	13.7	33.9	-	-	-	-	-	-	-
APEX Canadian Growth (AGF)	CdnEq	Divers	3.1	15.0	13.4	9.3	10.5	9.9	-0.8	3.6	-0.1	13.2
APEX Canadian Stock	CdnEq	Divers	10.9	-	-	-	-	-	-	-	-	-
Acuity Pld Cdn Equity	CdnEq	Divers	31.4	70.0	16.6	12.2	-3.8	-	-	-	-	-
Acuity Pld High Income	CdnEq	Dividend	31.2	14.5	11.4	10.8	11.8	-	-	-	-	-
All-Canadian Capital Fund	CdnEq	Divers	4.9	-0.2	4.9	16.9	7.8	22.2	0.4	3.3	2.8	7.0
All-Canadian Compound	CdnEq	Divers	4.8	-0.2	4.3	16.6	8.1	21.6	0.5	3.3	2.8	7.0
All-Canadian Consumer Fund	CdnEq	Consum	6.3	16.0	0.1	11.0	5.7	-	-	-	-	-
All-Canadian Resources Co.	CdnEq	Resource	-11.6	-19.9	1.9	11.8	11.3	54.9	-7.4	-8.9	-15.4	-2.7
Allstar AIG Canadian Eq	CdnEq	LCDivers	12.9	27.8	9.7	9.5	-2.4	8.2	3.0	2.3	-5.3	-
Altafund Investment Corp.	CdnEq	Divers	-18.6	25.2	22.7	0.5	2.3	57.5	15.9	-	-	-
Altamira Capital Growth	CdnEq	LCGrowth	15.6	14.0	4.0	14.8	6.6	20.8	19.7	3.1	6.3	12.0
Altamira Dividend	CdnEq	Dividend	21.3	28.7	13.9	-	-	-	-	-	-	-
Altamira Equity	CdnEq	Divers	1.2	12.9	14.0	12.5	0.4	52.9	42.4	13.6	18.0	32.7
Altamira Prec & Strat Metal	CdnEq	PrMetl	-35.6	-28.9	40.7	-	-	-	-	-	-	-
Altamira Resource	CdnEq	Resource	-33.6	3.4	13.8	-10.8	-5.7	108.8	46.9	8.6	4.6	8.1
Altamira Special Growth	CdnEq	SCGrowth	2.5	19.4	22.5	-2.7	-9.8	54.1	34.5	14.2	-4.6	14.6
Associate Investors	CdnEq	Value	34.6	38.8	13.8	10.3	0.2	12.8	4.3	4.7	-	-
Atlas Cdn Dividend Growth	CdnEq	Dividend	15.0	-	-	-	-	-	-	-	-	-
Atlas Cdn Emerging Growth	CdnEq	SCGrowth	-22.2	14.0	31.9	-	-	-	-	-	-	-
Atlas Cdn Large Cap Growth	CdnEq	LCDivers	20.2	34.2	15.9	13.8	1.9	6.9	-1.5	3.6	-0.8	13.5
Atlas Cdn Large Cap Value	CdnEq	LCDivers	14.4	21.7	5.9	-	-	-	-	-	-	-
Atlas Cdn Small Cap Growth	CdnEq	SCDivers	5.0	-	-	-	-	-	-	-	-	-
Atlas Cdn Small Cap Value	CdnEq	SCDivers	0.8	29.5	10.3	-	-	-	-	-	-	-
Azura Growth RSP Pooled	CdnEq	Growth	6.6	18.6	-	-	-	-	-	-	-	-
BNP (Canada) Equity	CdnEq	Divers	14.5	30.5	13.4	14.1	-2.8	19.5	4.9	-	-	-
BPI Canadian Equity Value	CdnEq	Value	8.9	21.8	21.0	3.7	-3.7	30.6	-	7.5	-0.1	-
BPI Canadian Mid-Cap	CdnEq	Divers	3.5	-	-	-	-	-	-	-	-	-
BPI Cdn Opportunities RSP	CdnEq	Divers	-19.6	4.1	-	-	-	-	-	-	-	-

% RETURN AT YEAR END

FUND NAME	FUND CATEGORY		JUN98	JUN97	JUN96	JUN95	JUN94	JUN93	JUN92	JUN91	JUN90	JUN89
BPI Cdn Resource Fund Inc	CdnEq	Resource	-31.1	-20.9	33.8	-7.6	-9.4	102.3	9.8	7.4	0.5	2.7
BPI Cdn Small Companies	CdnEq	SCDivers	-24.0	0.2	54.2	10.8	-1.6	52.1	7.4	10.8	-9.8	3.4
BPI Dividend Income	CdnEq	Dividend	18.3	25.4	15.3	16.3	1.6	6.2	3.9	9.8	0.1	9.3
BPI High Income	CdnEq	Dividend	10.7	-	-	-	-	-	-	-	-	-
Batirente Sec Actions	CdnEq	Value	17.0	32.5	10.2	10.2	-	-	-	-	-	-
Beutel Goodman Cdn Equity	CdnEq	Divers	12.5	24.4	7.5	15.2	8.3	9.6	-3.3	-	-	-
Beutel Goodman Small Cap	CdnEq	SCDivers	3.4	38.6	25.1	-	-	-	-	-	-	-
Bissett Canadian Equity	CdnEq	Divers	23.0	41.5	19.7	15.9	0.2	32.5	4.4	5.3	1.9	12.2
Bissett Dividend Income	CdnEq	Dividend	17.2	33.9	18.8	16.8	3.5	12.9	5.3	2.9	-0.6	8.4
Bissett Income Trust	CdnEq	Dividend	-1.1	-	-	-	-	-	-	-	-	-
Bissett Small Capital	CdnEq	SCDivers	6.8	43.3	27.5	7.3	6.7	101.7	-	-	-	-
C.I. Canadian Growth	CdnEq	Divers	14.8	11.8	9.8	13.5	7.3	-	-	-	-	-
C.I. Canadian Resource	CdnEq	Resource	-26.9	-	-	-	-	-	-	-	-	-
C.I. Canadian Sector	CdnEq	Divers	11.4	10.9	9.2	13.2	6.4	31.7	-7.1	-6.5	-7.4	7.4
C.I. Dividend	CdnEq	Dividend	16.9	-	-	-	-	-	-	-	-	-
C.I. Harbour Sector	CdnEq	Value	4.1	-	-	-	-	-	-	-	-	-
CCPE Growth R	CdnEq	LCDivers	10.5	27.6	9.5	15.4	4.8	10.5	-1.8	3.5	-2.6	18.9
CDA Aggressive Equity (A)	CdnEq	SCGrowth	5.9	23.4	19.0	-4.4	-	-	-	-	-	-
CDA Canadian Eq (Trimark)	CdnEq	Divers	1.4	-	-	-	-	-	-	-	-	-
CDA Common Stock(Altamira)	CdnEq	Divers	9.3	12.3	9.0	10.2	3.2	23.0	3.8	5.0	-1.7	16.2
CDA Special Equity (KBSH)	CdnEq	SCDivers	15.0	-	-	-	-	-	-	-	-	-
CIBC Canadian Equity	CdnEq	Divers	19.4	26.6	7.0	10.7	-4.7	18.5	-6.2	1.4	2.8	-
CIBC Canadian Index	CdnEq	Divers	15.5	-	-	-	-	-	-	-	-	-
CIBC Canadian Resources	CdnEq	Resource	-28.0	5.8	8.3	-	-	-	-	-	-	-
CIBC Capital Appreciation	CdnEq	Divers	12.7	21.3	-	5.7	-6.2	44.2	-	-	-	-
CIBC Dividend	CdnEq	Dividend	17.0	23.4	9.5	11.5	-1.4	18.1	-	-	-	-
CIBC Energy	CdnEq	Resource	-16.6	-	-	-	-	-	-	-	-	-
CIBC Precious Metal	CdnEq	PrMetl	-27.5	-	-	-	-	-	-	-	-	-
CT Canadian Equity Index	CdnEq	Divers	14.8	-	-	-	-	-	-	-	-	-
CT Dividend Income	CdnEq	Dividend	17.2	27.9	16.1	0.8	-5.3	45.5	-	5.6	-2.3	-
CT Special Equity	CdnEq	SCGrowth	4.8	18.5	13.9	9.6	0.8	30.1	7.2	2.9	-0.4	14.5
CT Stock	CdnEq	LCDivers	12.5	30.9	7.3	-	-	-	5.2	-	-	-
CUMIS Life Cdn Growth Eq	CdnEq	Divers	2.4	-	-	-	-	-	-	-	-	-
Caldwell Canadian Equity	CdnEq	LCValue	2.5	-	-	-	-	-	-	-	-	-
Cambridge Growth	CdnEq	SCDivers	-29.0	-34.5	25.8	-8.1	-4.4	42.8	9.2	6.3	4.4	12.4
Cambridge Precious Metals	CdnEq	PrMetl	-47.2	-48.7	84.8	-16.5	-19.9	202.4	-	-	-	-
Cambridge Resource	CdnEq	Resource	-45.6	-40.3	63.9	-8.1	-14.8	81.3	-17.3	-8.4	-7.8	-2.3
Cambridge Special Equity	CdnEq	SCGrowth	-22.5	-47.1	12.8	12.6	-0.5	18.5	-17.4	-19.3	-1.7	17.7
Canada Life Cdn Equity	CdnEq	LCDivers	9.6	27.5	13.8	13.1	0.3	18.5	4.7	0.7	-5.2	16.5
Canada Life S-2	CdnEq	Divers	10.6	27.9	4.1	6.1	-5.1	20.9	5.8	2.4	-4.8	15.4
Canadian Protected	CdnEq	Divers	9.6	0.6	16.5	13.5	-1.8	30.7	4.3	6.4	6.4	5.8
Cdn Anaes. Mutual Accum.	CdnEq	Divers	10.6	25.1	-	-	-	16.3	-3.2	-2.1	0.6	11.9
CentrePost Canadian Equity	CdnEq	Divers	2.6	19.1	19.4	7.0	-15.0	60.5	6.6	6.4	-	-

% RETURN AT YEAR END

FUND NAME	FUND CATEGORY		JUN98	JUN97	JUN96	JUN95	JUN94	JUN93	JUN92	JUN91	JUN90	JUN89
Chou RRSP	CdnEq	SCValue	43.9	30.6	20.4	2.6	3.1	9.0	5.3	-0.7	-5.5	15.3
Clarington Canadian Equity	CdnEq	Divers	8.0									
Clarington Cdn Small Cap	CdnEq	SCDivers	3.2									
Clean Environment Equity	CdnEq	Growth	29.0	31.5	19.4	12.4	5.0	31.2				
Co-Operators Canadian Eq	CdnEq	Divers	20.1	27.7	7.8	12.1	4.2	18.8				
Colonia Life Equity	CdnEq	Divers	19.2	32.7	6.9	6.8	-3.3	14.4				
Colonia Life Special Gth	CdnEq	SCGrowth	6.7	40.3	38.8	16.1						
Cornerstone Cdn Growth	CdnEq	Divers	4.9	16.8	19.2	17.2	-3.9	18.6	12.9	3.4	-8.5	13.0
Cote 100 EXP	CdnEq	SCDivers	15.0	28.6	23.9	26.5						
Cote 100 REA - action	CdnEq	SCDivers	8.8	13.7								
Cote 100 REER	CdnEq	Divers	16.9	31.0	19.0	14.8	5.5					
Cundill Security A	CdnEq	SCValue	17.8	22.9	10.6	18.6	17.9	25.2	-16.2	-1.8	-4.5	9.7
Cundill Security B	CdnEq	SCValue	17.3									
Desjardins Distinct Eqty	CdnEq	LCDivers	11.7	32.1	12.1	14.1	1.9	22.3	4.6	4.8	-3.0	13.6
Desjardins Dividend	CdnEq	Dividend	21.2	28.4	12.3	13.6						
Desjardins Environment	CdnEq	Divers	16.2	35.9	7.7	15.7	0.2	10.6	1.9			
Desjardins Equity	CdnEq	Divers	9.9	29.0	9.6	15.0	-3.1	20.3	-0.8	3.2	-4.7	15.3
Desjardins Growth	CdnEq	Growth	16.9	20.1	13.1	11.0						
Dominion Equity Resource	CdnEq	Resource	-18.9	28.3	10.8	-19.2	-17.6	163.0	2.1	-7.3	3.1	-37.9
Double Gold Plus	CdnEq	PrMetl	-16.0	6.7	-5.2	-6.9	20.0	19.8	-3.6	-18.4	-13.2	-3.8
Dynamic Cdn Growth	CdnEq	Divers	-5.8	20.8	13.7	4.6	1.7	106.8	6.4	16.3	-4.6	4.1
Dynamic Dividend	CdnEq	Dividend	10.9	20.4	11.6	10.7	3.0	14.6	9.6	7.2	2.0	10.1
Dynamic Dividend Growth	CdnEq	Dividend	6.1	29.5	16.1	13.6	5.2	13.6	9.7	-2.7	0.2	9.2
Dynamic Fund of Canada	CdnEq	Divers	6.2	27.2	7.0	4.2	-6.9	51.9	5.9	2.3	1.2	12.5
Dynamic Precious Metals	CdnEq	PrMetl	-37.4	-23.9	27.4	-0.4	23.1	75.0	-1.9	-3.6	3.1	-12.7
Dynamic Quebec	CdnEq	Divers	11.7									
Dynamic Small Cap	CdnEq	SCDivers	17.0									
Elliott & Page Equity	CdnEq	Divers	3.6	17.7	20.0	17.5	-2.0	28.0	13.1	8.6	-6.4	20.7
Empire Elite Equity	CdnEq	LCDivers	8.1	32.0	13.4	9.6	-1.7	22.0	9.4	1.2	-2.0	10.3
Empire Equity Growth #3	CdnEq	LCDivers	10.8	36.2	15.0	10.4	3.5	26.8	1.3	6.1	-4.1	18.2
Empire Premier Equity	CdnEq	LCDivers	10.0	35.2	13.9	10.4	1.6	21.7	4.4	3.0	-1.8	14.6
Equitable Life Cdn Stock	CdnEq	Divers	6.4	26.2	11.1	14.7	4.1	11.6				
Equitable Life Common Stck	CdnEq	Divers	6.9	31.1	14.8	18.6	6.9	14.5	1.7	1.5	-5.6	10.9
Ethical Growth	CdnEq	LCDivers	13.7	31.9	15.2	17.1	-1.7	19.2	-0.8	7.3	4.0	16.0
Ethical Special Equity	CdnEq	SCDivers	4.5	19.7								
FIRM Canadian Growth	CdnEq	Divers	15.7									
FMOQ Canadian Equity	CdnEq	Divers	30.9	24.4	9.4	18.5						
Ficadre Actions	CdnEq	Divers	4.8	24.0	15.3	16.0	3.0	12.3	2.3	-2.8	-15.0	8.5
Fidelity Capital Builder	CdnEq	Growth	5.2	14.9	12.8	7.5	-2.9	26.5	-2.1	13.9	1.3	14.3
Fidelity Cdn Gth Company	CdnEq	SCGrowth	22.9	28.4	20.1							
Fidelity True North	CdnEq	Divers	16.1									
First Canadian Div Income	CdnEq	Dividend	31.7	40.4	13.8							
First Canadian Eq Index	CdnEq	Divers	14.7	28.2	12.3	12.9	2.4	17.6	0.2	-0.5	-3.7	11.0

% RETURN AT YEAR END

FUND NAME	FUND CATEGORY		JUN89	JUN90	JUN91	JUN92	JUN93	JUN94	JUN95	JUN96	JUN97	JUN98
First Canadian Growth	CdnEq	Divers	-	-	-	-	-	-	14.6	13.2	32.8	16.0
First Canadian Resource	CdnEq	Resource	-	-	-	-	-	-	5.7	14.1	9.1	-32.5
First Canadian Special Gth	CdnEq	SCGrowth	-	-	-	-	-	-	2.1	21.5	30.6	4.9
First Cdn Precious Metals	CdnEq	PrMetl	-	-	-	-	-	-	-	-	-	-39.3
First Heritage	CdnEq	Resource	0.4	-5.1	-11.2	-3.8	57.5	-3.7	5.4	10.9	2.1	-19.4
Fonds D'Investissement REA	CdnEq	SCDivers	-	-	-	-	-	-3.0	-0.6	11.9	29.7	25.3
GBC Canadian Growth	CdnEq	SCGrowth	-	10.4	15.2	16.9	49.0	-4.1	9.7	21.7	33.9	18.3
GS Canadian Equity	CdnEq	Value	-	-	-	-	-	-	-	-	29.5	6.5
General Trust Cdn Equity	CdnEq	LCDivers	10.9	-5.8	3.6	-2.3	12.8	-1.1	14.7	12.3	30.5	0.0
General Trust Growth	CdnEq	SCDivers	25.2	-10.5	2.7	15.9	45.6	-2.6	4.4	9.9	27.8	11.8
Global Strategy Canada Gth	CdnEq	Value	-	-	-	-	18.2	0.7	10.4	10.9	26.4	7.0
Global Strategy Cdn Opport	CdnEq	Divers	-	-	-	-	-	-	-	-	-	14.6
Global Strategy Cdn Sm Cap	CdnEq	SCDivers	-	-	-	-	-	-	-	11.0	44.5	-1.0
Global Strategy Gold Plus	CdnEq	PrMetl	-	-	-	-	67.2	22.0	16.0	44.1	-25.5	-43.5
Goldtrust	CdnEq	PrMetl	-18.2	3.1	-3.2	-6.1	-	-	-11.2	14.4	-23.3	-27.5
Goodwood Fund	CdnEq	Value	-	-	-	-	-	-	-	-	-	38.6
Great-West Cdn Eq (G) A	CdnEq	Growth	9.9	1.8	3.7	6.8	33.0	-3.0	5.9	12.9	24.7	7.6
Great-West Cdn Eq (G) B	CdnEq	Growth	-	-	-	-	-	-	-	13.1	25.0	7.9
Great-West Cdn Res (A) A	CdnEq	Resource	-	-	-	-	-	-	-	-	13.1	-23.7
Great-West Cdn Res (A) B	CdnEq	Resource	-	-	-	-	-	-	-	-	13.4	-23.5
Great-West Eq Index (G) A	CdnEq	Divers	11.2	-3.9	0.0	-0.8	17.9	1.6	12.3	10.9	26.6	13.1
Great-West Eq Index (G) B	CdnEq	Divers	-	-	-	-	-	-	-	11.1	26.9	13.3
Great-West Equity (M) A	CdnEq	Divers	-	-	-	-	-	-	-	-	23.7	13.4
Great-West Equity (M) B	CdnEq	Divers	-	-	-	-	-	-	-	-	24.0	13.7
Great-West Equity (S) A	CdnEq	Value	-	-	-	-	-	-	-	-	31.1	10.2
Great-West Equity (S) B	CdnEq	Value	-	-	-	-	-	-	-	-	31.5	10.5
Great-West Gth Equity (A)A	CdnEq	Growth	-	-	-	-	-	-	-	-	23.2	4.6
Great-West Gth Equity (A)B	CdnEq	Growth	-	-	-	-	-	-	-	-	23.5	4.9
Great-West Lg Company(M)A	CdnEq	Divers	-	-	-	-	-	-	-	-	18.8	9.8
Great-West Lg Company(M)B	CdnEq	Divers	-	-	-	-	-	-	-	-	19.1	10.1
Great-West Smaller Co.(M)A	CdnEq	Divers	-	-	-	-	-	-	-	-	14.7	12.2
Great-West Smaller Co.(M)B	CdnEq	Divers	-	-	-	-	-	-	-	-	15.0	12.5
Green Line Blue Chip Eq.	CdnEq	LCDivers	15.2	-1.0	1.8	4.2	10.9	0.1	9.1	14.0	31.1	10.2
Green Line Canadian Equity	CdnEq	Divers	-	-5.6	1.3	-1.7	26.3	1.7	11.0	9.4	35.9	11.2
Green Line Canadian Index	CdnEq	Divers	11.5	-3.5	0.5	-0.2	19.1	2.7	14.0	12.6	28.4	15.4
Green Line Dividend	CdnEq	Dividend	14.1	-0.1	13.4	11.7	13.8	1.4	7.7	7.9	37.9	23.5
Green Line Energy	CdnEq	Resource	-	-	-	-	-	-	-	10.3	45.2	-38.5
Green Line Precious Metals	CdnEq	PrMetl	-	-	-	-	-	-	-	56.5	-15.6	-32.1
Green Line Resource	CdnEq	Resource	-	-	-	-	-	-	-1.9	19.8	10.4	-35.5
Green Line Value	CdnEq	Value	-	-	-	-	-	-	9.3	22.1	39.8	4.5
GrowSafe Canadian Equity	CdnEq	Value	-	-	-	-	-	-	12.5	10.0	26.7	3.0
Guardian Enterprise C	CdnEq	SCGrowth	2.5	5.7	1.5	-1.8	26.5	-0.2	6.7	45.8	32.0	-4.6
Guardian Enterprise M	CdnEq	SCGrowth	-	-	-	-	-	-	-	-	31.2	-5.3

% RETURN AT YEAR END

FUND NAME	FUND CATEGORY		JUN98	JUN97	JUN96	JUN95	JUN94	JUN93	JUN92	JUN91	JUN90	JUN89
Guardian Growth Equity C	CdnEq	Divers	4.4	35.1	18.8	2.5	1.2	41.4	7.2	4.2	6.5	-
Guardian Growth Equity M	CdnEq	Divers	3.8	34.4	-	-	-	-	-	-	-	-
Guardian Mnthly High Inc C	CdnEq	Dividend	-5.6	-	-	-	-	-	-	-	-	-
Guardian Mnthly High Inc M	CdnEq	Dividend	-6.0	-	-	-	-	-	-	-	-	-
Guardian Monthly Divid C	CdnEq	Dividend	0.0	16.1	8.8	9.4	1.0	12.5	10.1	5.7	1.6	7.7
Guardian Monthly Divid M	CdnEq	Dividend	-0.6	15.6	-	-	-	-	-	-	-	-
Harbour Fund	CdnEq	Value	5.2	-	-	-	-	-	-	-	-	-
Hongkong Bank Dividend Inc	CdnEq	Dividend	21.1	32.0	14.8	-	-	-	-	-	-	-
Hongkong Bank Equity	CdnEq	Divers	12.8	31.4	14.8	0.6	4.7	43.8	-1.3	1.9	-	-
Hongkong Bank Sml Cap Gth	CdnEq	SCGrowth	6.5	27.5	25.8	-	-	-	-	-	-	-
ICM Equity	CdnEq	Divers	8.6	16.7	13.6	13.7	9.3	20.9	3.9	6.0	-3.6	13.9
IG BG Canadian Small Cap	CdnEq	SCDivers	1.9	-	-	-	-	-	-	-	-	-
IG Beutel Goodman Cdn Eq	CdnEq	Divers	13.3	-	-	-	-	-	-	-	-	-
IG Sceptre Canadian Equity	CdnEq	Divers	10.5	-	-	-	-	-	-	-	-	-
Ideal Equity	CdnEq	Divers	20.1	27.0	18.4	15.8	4.0	14.3	4.2	5.0	0.9	7.7
Imperial Gth Cdn Equity	CdnEq	LCDivers	9.4	27.9	9.9	11.4	1.5	19.3	5.4	3.1	-5.9	27.4
Ind. Alliance Ecoflex A	CdnEq	LCValue	2.2	24.6	8.8	19.5	6.1	-	-	-	-	-
Ind. Alliance Stock 2	CdnEq	Divers	4.1	-	-	-	-	-	-	-	-	-
Ind. Alliance Stocks	CdnEq	LCValue	3.1	25.4	9.4	20.1	6.6	26.2	1.9	4.3	5.1	14.1
Industrial Dividend Growth	CdnEq	Dividend	21.7	33.5	14.0	10.3	7.1	40.0	-8.3	-8.7	-4.4	2.7
Industrial Equity	CdnEq	SCValue	-29.7	2.6	6.9	-7.6	3.6	91.9	-0.2	-12.6	-13.0	-2.9
Industrial Growth	CdnEq	Divers	-5.8	16.6	9.5	7.5	4.2	32.5	-8.8	-1.5	-2.5	8.4
Industrial Horizon	CdnEq	Divers	15.4	21.9	8.3	11.7	6.2	21.5	-2.3	0.5	-1.7	10.0
Infinity Canadian	CdnEq	Growth	25.3	-	-	-	-	-	-	-	-	-
Infinity Income	CdnEq	Dividend	0.5	-	-	-	-	-	-	-	-	-
Infinity Wealth Management	CdnEq	FinSer	25.3	-	-	-	-	-	-	-	-	-
InvesNat Canadian Equity	CdnEq	Divers	0.5	30.1	12.7	15.2	-2.1	20.5	4.9	3.4	1.4	-
InvesNat Dividend	CdnEq	Dividend	8.9	14.9	11.4	9.7	2.4	28.6	4.8	6.6	1.0	9.1
Investors Canadian Equity	CdnEq	Divers	3.6	25.5	12.4	8.8	5.3	-	-	-	-	-
Investors Cdn Natural Res	CdnEq	Resource	-8.1	-	-	-	-	-	-	-	-	-
Investors Cdn Small Cap	CdnEq	SCDivers	14.6	-	-	-	-	-	-	-	-	-
Investors Dividend	CdnEq	Dividend	21.5	26.1	10.2	10.0	0.6	11.3	12.0	10.6	1.5	12.9
Investors Ret. Gth. Port	CdnEq	Divers	8.2	22.9	13.3	9.3	6.3	18.2	2.3	2.7	1.0	-
Investors Retirement	CdnEq	Divers	5.8	24.4	13.0	10.5	5.3	18.1	-0.8	1.9	-2.7	12.7
Investors Summa	CdnEq	Divers	24.3	31.9	17.1	10.9	3.2	14.3	5.7	1.8	-3.2	12.4
Ivy Canadian	CdnEq	LCValue	17.4	25.6	14.8	15.7	3.8	-	-	-	-	-
Ivy Enterprise	CdnEq	SCDivers	13.6	21.1	20.0	-	-	-	-	-	-	-
Jones Heward Fund Limited	CdnEq	Divers	13.2	23.2	7.6	7.3	-5.1	41.8	8.8	4.4	-9.7	10.7
Lasalle Equity	CdnEq	Divers	16.2	14.8	-	-	-	-	-	-	-	-
Leith Wheeler Cdn Equity	CdnEq	Value	19.9	46.7	7.3	10.1	24.7	-	-	-	-	-
Lion Knowledge Industries	CdnEq	SCDivers	-8.7	-16.7	36.7	36.9	-1.5	-	-	-	-	-
London Life Cdn Equity	CdnEq	Divers	18.2	28.3	12.7	9.8	-	27.2	-	-	-	-
Lotus Group Cdn Equity	CdnEq	Growth	5.4	27.1	37.1	-7.0	-	-	-	-	-	-

% RETURN AT YEAR END

FUND NAME		FUND CATEGORY	JUN98	JUN97	JUN96	JUN95	JUN94	JUN93	JUN92	JUN91	JUN90	JUN89
MAXXUM Cdn Equity Growth	CdnEq	Divers	6.6	13.8	17.7	22.7	-7.9	50.5	8.7	-1.0	-4.0	10.7
MAXXUM Dividend	CdnEq	Dividend	21.2	33.8	14.4	16.7	9.6	35.0	6.0	5.5	-11.6	7.9
MAXXUM Natural Resource	CdnEq	Resource	-31.2	-15.8	48.1	18.6	-7.8	125.5	14.2	-6.5	14.4	18.7
MAXXUM Precious Metals	CdnEq	PrMetl	-34.1	-27.7	68.8	8.0	15.4	62.6	2.9	-15.8	12.3	2.1
MB Canadian Equity Growth	CdnEq	LCDivers	12.2	43.4	18.9	14.9	1.6	24.0	6.5	2.5	-2.1	18.9
MD Dividend	CdnEq	Dividend	15.8	18.7	12.0	12.8	2.4					
MD Equity	CdnEq	Divers	15.4	28.0	8.1	4.8	11.0	29.3	-1.8	0.9	-0.4	11.1
MD Select	CdnEq	Divers	7.3	32.8	19.0	5.2						
MLI AGF Canadian Eq GIF	CdnEq	Divers	0.5									
MLI Fidelity Cap Build GIF	CdnEq	Divers	4.7									
MLI Fidelity True NorthGIF	CdnEq	Divers	15.5									
MLI GT Glo Canada Gth GIF	CdnEq	Divers	24.4									
MLI Trimark Select Cdn Gth	CdnEq	Divers	0.3									
Mackenzie Sentinel Cda Eq	CdnEq	Divers	-0.7	16.0	7.5	5.6	13.3	46.0	-7.6	-6.2	-4.3	6.1
Manulife Cabot Blue Chip	CdnEq	LCDivers	15.9	23.8	15.2	20.0						
Manulife Cabot Cdn. Equity	CdnEq	LCDivers	16.8	24.5	15.2	23.9						
Manulife Cabot Cdn. Growth	CdnEq	SCDivers	-0.4	26.8	33.0	-6.2						
Manulife Cabot Emer Growth	CdnEq	SCGrowth	-3.9	21.8	31.6	-5.0						
Manulife VistaFd 1 Cap.Gns	CdnEq	Divers	-11.9	9.6	11.3	9.3	-2.7	35.3	8.3	2.3	0.3	11.8
Manulife VistaFd 2 Cap.Gns	CdnEq	Divers	-12.6	8.8	10.4	8.5	-3.4	34.2	7.5	1.5	-0.4	11.0
Manulife VistaFnd 1 Equity	CdnEq	Divers	11.3	12.6	9.9	11.3	-0.5	21.5	5.1	3.7	-1.9	10.5
Manulife VistaFnd 2 Equity	CdnEq	Divers	10.4	11.7	9.2	10.5	-1.2	20.6	4.3	2.9	-2.7	9.7
Marathon Equity	CdnEq	SCGrowth	-23.6	16.2	39.5	35.6	11.3	105.7	26.9	-7.3	-5.9	35.6
Marathon Resource	CdnEq	Resource	-38.4									
Maritime Life Aggr Eq A&C	CdnEq	Growth	7.1									
Maritime Life Aggr Eq B	CdnEq	Growth	7.1									
Maritime Life Cdn Eq A&C	CdnEq	LCDivers	14.8	21.9	13.6							
Maritime Life Cdn Equity B	CdnEq	LCDivers	14.8									
Maritime Life Divid Inc A	CdnEq	Dividend	22.1	26.0	8.9							
Maritime Life Divid Inc B	CdnEq	Dividend	21.3									
Maritime Life Divid Inc C	CdnEq	Dividend	21.9									
Maritime Life Growth A&C	CdnEq	Divers	10.8	31.6	12.5	11.3	-2.6	26.5	-1.1	-1.0	-4.0	13.5
Maritime Life Growth B	CdnEq	Divers	10.7									
Mawer Canadian Equity	CdnEq	LCDivers	17.8	29.2	5.8	14.8	-2.8	21.4	-3.9	7.8	11.2	9.4
Mawer New Canada	CdnEq	SCValue	6.2	23.2	24.8	4.6	16.0	49.0	6.1			
McElvaine Investment Trust	CdnEq	Divers	31.0									
Mclean Budden Equity Gth	CdnEq	Divers	9.9	39.6	16.4	12.7	1.0	19.6	6.0	1.3	-3.6	
Merrill Lynch Cdn Equity	CdnEq	Divers	-1.2	20.3								
Metife Mvp Equity	CdnEq	LCDivers	16.2	24.7	8.0	9.5	1.1	13.4	-3.3	-1.4	-0.5	12.9
Metife Mvp Growth	CdnEq	SCGrowth	16.6	28.6	18.6	6.4	10.6	57.2	0.0			
Middlefield Growth	CdnEq	Resource	-8.0	20.7	10.5	-4.8	-10.2					

% RETURN AT YEAR END

FUND NAME	FUND CATEGORY		JUN98	JUN97	JUN96	JUN95	JUN94	JUN93	JUN92	JUN91	JUN90	JUN89
Millennia III Cdn Eq 1	CdnEq	LCDivers	9.1	27.4	-	-	-	-	-	-	-	-
Millennia III Cdn Eq 2	CdnEq	LCDivers	8.8	27.2	-	-	-	-	-	-	-	-
Millennium Income	CdnEq	Dividend	-4.7	-	-	-	-	-	-	-	-	-
Millennium Next Generation	CdnEq	SCDivers	13.3	25.5	50.2	14.1	-	-	-	-	-	-
Monarch Canadian	CdnEq	Divers	7.1	-	-	-	-	-	-	-	-	-
Monarch Canadian Sector	CdnEq	Divers	6.8	-	-	-	-	-	-	-	-	-
Montrusco Select Cdn Eq	CdnEq	Divers	10.3	25.4	14.6	16.5	8.5	18.5	1.3	5.5	1.2	15.3
Montrusco Select Growth	CdnEq	Divers	-1.9	41.1	35.1	17.1	-4.0	30.6	28.2	23.9	2.2	7.9
Multiple Opportunities	CdnEq	SCDivers	-8.4	-13.5	58.2	28.2	46.3	66.6	-2.1	-3.9	27.3	-35.9
Mutual Alpine Equity	CdnEq	Divers	0.6	-	-	-	-	-	-	-	-	-
Mutual Alpine Resources	CdnEq	Resource	-25.6	-	-	-	-	-	-	-	-	-
Mutual Equifund	CdnEq	Divers	8.4	28.0	16.4	14.7	0.8	15.3	-2.0	-1.9	-8.2	20.3
Mutual Premier Blue Chip	CdnEq	LCDivers	11.0	27.3	14.4	13.3	1.0	-	-	-	-	-
Mutual Premier Growth	CdnEq	SCGrowth	-1.8	25.3	18.6	19.0	2.6	-	-	-	-	-
Mutual Summit Dividend Gth	CdnEq	Dividend	19.6	-	-	-	-	-	-	-	-	-
Mutual Summit Equity	CdnEq	Divers	14.1	-	-	-	-	-	-	-	-	-
NAL-Canadian Equity	CdnEq	Divers	2.2	17.9	20.7	16.4	-4.5	20.3	-0.8	4.1	-0.8	12.0
NAL-Equity Growth	CdnEq	Divers	10.6	33.4	14.2	-	-	-	-	-	-	-
NN Canadian 35 Index	CdnEq	LCDivers	16.9	28.4	11.3	16.0	3.2	8.4	-1.0	1.2	-2.3	-
NN Canadian Growth	CdnEq	LCDivers	14.8	27.3	10.6	7.0	0.5	16.8	-0.9	4.7	-6.5	9.9
NN Dividend	CdnEq	Dividend	10.7	22.5	13.3	14.1	-	-	-	-	-	-
National Equities	CdnEq	LCDivers	15.3	35.0	12.6	12.9	3.9	21.4	1.0	6.6	-4.6	10.3
National Trust Cdn Equity	CdnEq	LCDivers	15.0	33.9	7.0	11.9	-4.3	18.5	5.2	6.6	0.8	10.8
National Trust Cdn Index	CdnEq	Divers	16.0	-	-	-	-	-	-	-	-	-
National Trust Dividend	CdnEq	Dividend	35.1	35.4	13.7	6.2	4.1	-	-	-	-	-
National Trust Special Eq	CdnEq	SCGrowth	6.1	20.2	16.1	-0.4	-0.9	-	-	-	-	-
Navigator Value Inv Retire	CdnEq	SCGrowth	-21.9	14.2	37.1	21.9	31.1	-	-	-	-	-
North West Life Ecoflex A	CdnEq	Divers	2.2	-	-	-	-	-	-	-	-	-
Northwest Dividend	CdnEq	Dividend	9.9	41.8	19.0	15.0	1.7	14.2	-	-	-	-
Northwest Growth	CdnEq	Divers	11.7	22.5	15.9	-	-	-	-	-	-	-
O'Donnell Cdn Emerging Gth	CdnEq	SCGrowth	-21.1	12.0	-	-	-	-	-	-	-	-
O'Donnell Growth	CdnEq	SCGrowth	1.3	16.3	-	-	-	-	-	-	-	-
O.I.Q. Ferique Actions	CdnEq	LCDivers	10.9	28.4	12.1	17.6	2.6	16.7	1.1	6.5	-0.3	13.1
O.I.Q. Ferique Croissance	CdnEq	Divers	7.0	11.6	-	-	-	-	-	-	-	-
OTGIF Diversified	CdnEq	Divers	16.7	32.0	13.2	12.2	1.4	17.2	-3.1	-0.8	-0.8	16.9
OTGIF Growth	CdnEq	SCGrowth	10.7	24.3	9.8	8.2	1.7	17.6	-4.2	-0.6	0.9	16.9
Optima Strat-Cdn Equity	CdnEq	Value	15.8	47.2	12.8	19.7	-	-	-	-	-	-
Optimum Actions	CdnEq	Divers	13.3	34.6	10.1	9.7	-	-	-	-	-	-
PH & N Canadian Eq Plus	CdnEq	Divers	9.7	32.4	11.7	18.3	6.4	16.5	0.6	1.1	5.2	17.9
PH & N Canadian Equity	CdnEq	Divers	11.5	32.3	12.9	17.6	5.7	16.1	-1.2	1.3	4.1	18.2
PH & N Cdn Eq Plus Pens Tr	CdnEq	Divers	15.6	33.7	15.4	15.3	7.6	14.7	1.9	1.9	3.6	14.9
PH & N Dividend Income	CdnEq	Dividend	36.6	47.9	12.9	17.2	5.4	14.7	5.7	5.3	3.5	14.7
PH & N Vintage	CdnEq	Growth	11.5	40.5	18.5	21.2	4.9	23.0	8.2	10.5	13.3	17.2

% RETURN AT YEAR END

FUND NAME		FUND CATEGORY	JUN98	JUN97	JUN96	JUN95	JUN94	JUN93	JUN92	JUN91	JUN90	JUN89
Pacific Total Return	CdnEq	Divers	1.9									
Perigee Equity Fund B	CdnEq	LCDivers	22.9	30.7	14.3	14.6	-0.1	17.9	1.3	1.1	-9.0	24.5
Perigee Nth American Eq Tr	CdnEq	LCDivers	24.7	30.9	14.0	14.5	1.1	17.0	2.5	0.9	-7.6	20.5
Pret et Revenu Canadien	CdnEq	Divers	8.5	26.3	14.4	16.8	-0.8	21.5	8.9	4.2	-4.3	13.7
Pret et Revenu Dividendes	CdnEq	Dividend	8.6	41.5	21.8							
Primus Canadian Equity	CdnEq	Divers	13.2									
Pursuit Canadian Equity	CdnEq	Growth	20.3	38.3	12.0	14.6	-3.1	31.1	5.8	10.3	-8.9	-2.2
Quebec Growth Fund Inc.	CdnEq	Growth	38.0	46.8	18.9	2.1	-2.8	38.8	45.8	13.5	-31.2	13.2
Quebec Prof Cdn Equity	CdnEq	Divers	13.8	27.3	12.3	13.1	-1.7	14.3	-0.3	4.7	-4.0	14.7
Resolute Growth	CdnEq	SCGrowth	14.8	-17.7	68.9	4.9						
Royal&SunAlliance Intl Eq	CdnEq	Divers	13.2	23.2	12.1	11.7	5.0	27.5	-1.4	-6.3	0.1	10.2
Royal&SunAlliance Mny Mrkt	CdnEq	SCGrowth	0.5	14.8	17.4	1.0	0.7					
Royal Asian Growth	CdnEq	SCGrowth	-5.7	7.1	19.2	0.6	0.9					
Royal Canadian Equity	CdnEq	Dividend	31.5	41.9	12.4	15.1	2.2					
Royal Canadian Growth	CdnEq	Resource	-14.6	37.6	9.3	-11.2	-7.7	115.6	3.6	-7.4	9.4	5.2
Royal European Grth	CdnEq	SCDivers	-1.1	16.5	21.1							
Royal Global Bond	CdnEq	Value	16.1	30.9	13.2	12.0	5.0	12.8	4.0	11.6	-7.6	
Royal Premium Money Market	CdnEq	PrMetl	-30.4	-19.4	79.5	34.1	1.0	40.9	0.6	-3.1	1.1	14.9
SSQ - Actions Canadiennes	CdnEq	Divers	11.9	27.1	15.0	15.4	-3.6	15.9	2.9	8.3	-13.5	9.1
Saxon Small Cap	CdnEq	SCDivers	21.0	35.8	15.8	2.3	6.9	38.3	6.0	-1.9	-5.4	2.0
Saxon Stock	CdnEq	Divers	13.4	25.8	11.8	24.3	-2.0	51.9	-0.1	1.6	-0.1	13.4
Sceptre Equity Growth	CdnEq	Divers	0.3	30.4	38.1	22.7	23.8	15.0	-2.2	3.2	-2.2	10.1
Scotia Ex. Canadian Growth	CdnEq	Divers	8.2	23.2	23.0	19.7	5.9	17.7	-0.2	5.8	-2.4	9.9
Scotia Ex. Cdn Blue Chip	CdnEq	Dividend	7.4	24.5	9.4	7.9	-3.0	16.7	7.9	7.6	1.4	10.1
Scotia Ex. Dividend	CdnEq	PrMetl	23.1	31.4	14.2	10.4	2.6	13.2	6.0	9.3		
Scotia Ex. Precious Metals	CdnEq	Value	-36.1	-18.7	41.5	3.3						
Scudder Canadian Equity	CdnEq	Divers	26.2	47.3								
Spectrum Utd Canadian Eq	CdnEq	SCDivers	12.4	29.1	12.8	11.1	5.5	29.2	8.5	9.6	-4.2	16.1
Spectrum Utd Canadian Gth	CdnEq	LCValue	-6.1	18.2	25.7	20.6	4.6	43.9	10.7	3.3	-11.8	13.1
Spectrum Utd Canadian Inv	CdnEq	Resource	18.6	34.5	13.9	14.4	-0.1	10.2	-2.7	-1.4	0.4	15.4
Spectrum Utd Cdn Resource	CdnEq	Divers	-28.6									
Spectrum Utd Cdn Stock	CdnEq	Dividend	15.6	27.5	9.5	10.2	3.9	14.5	-1.4	2.5	-4.2	10.1
Spectrum Utd Dividend	CdnEq	Dividend	16.6	20.0	10.1	11.2	2.5	9.7	4.9	8.9	1.9	12.7
Standard Life Cdn Dividend	CdnEq	Divers	38.3	44.6	16.3							
Standard Life Equity	CdnEq	Resource	19.5	28.8	13.3	15.1	4.5					
Standard Life Natural Res	CdnEq	Divers	-20.1	6.2	17.4							
Stone & Co Flagship Stock	CdnEq	Divers	12.8	26.7								
Strategic Val Cdn Eq Value	CdnEq	LCDivers	4.4									
Strategic Val Cdn Equity	CdnEq	SCGrowth	13.3	26.7	9.1	10.2	-0.5	16.8	1.3	1.6	-11.1	17.0
Strategic Val Cdn Small Co	CdnEq	Dividend	15.0	18.4	0.4	11.4	11.7	24.6	1.8	3.4		
Strategic Val Dividend	CdnEq	Divers	15.6	25.0	9.2	11.0	1.0	11.0	8.0	6.2	1.8	14.0
Sunfund	CdnEq	Divers	22.3	31.6	10.7	14.0	2.4	16.5	-1.1	4.1	-3.0	13.0
Tal/Hyper Small Cap Cdn Eq	CdnEq	SCGrowth	10.2	38.2	17.7	9.1						

% RETURN AT YEAR END

FUND NAME	FUND CATEGORY		JUN98	JUN97	JUN96	JUN95	JUN94	JUN93	JUN92	JUN91	JUN90	JUN89
Talvest/Hyper Cdn Eq Gth	CdnEq	Growth	24.5	-	-	18.7	1.3	10.6	2.4	10.6	-1.3	8.8
Talvest Canadian Eq. Value	CdnEq	Divers	11.2	23.5	7.3	-	-	-	-	-	-	-
Talvest Dividend	CdnEq	Dividend	10.8	22.3	15.8	15.0	-	-	-	-	-	-
Talvest New Economy	CdnEq	Growth	8.2	6.6	-	-	-	-	-	-	-	-
Templeton Canadian Stock	CdnEq	Divers	8.5	28.7	11.1	9.9	10.4	10.9	-0.6	-3.4	-1.0	-
Tradex Canadian Growth	CdnEq	Divers	7.5	-	-	-	-	-	-	-	-	-
Tradex Equity	CdnEq	Divers	12.0	35.8	19.4	17.8	5.8	20.6	-3.3	0.6	1.0	12.1
Trans-Canada Dividend	CdnEq	Dividend	4.5	10.0	16.1	15.0	6.9	5.2	-7.0	5.1	-2.0	10.9
Trans-Canada Value	CdnEq	Value	-18.8	21.9	11.6	-3.9	-0.4	35.2	-11.8	1.4	-1.0	11.0
Trimark Canadian	CdnEq	Divers	0.9	24.5	13.7	11.4	10.7	22.8	8.0	5.1	3.1	16.9
Trimark RSP Equity	CdnEq	Value	-2.0	23.0	10.8	12.9	8.8	17.5	6.6	8.0	1.4	-
Trimark Select Cdn Growth	CdnEq	Value	0.9	24.3	10.4	13.5	9.2	-	-	-	-	-
Universal Canadian Growth	CdnEq	Divers	12.6	34.7	20.2	-10.2	-0.1	177.2	-9.5	-14.0	-3.6	-
Universal Cdn Resource	CdnEq	Resource	-25.7	16.3	11.0	20.3	5.4	37.5	-5.3	-0.9	-2.6	-8.7
Universal Future	CdnEq	Divers	12.7	19.6	30.9	15.6	-	-	-	-	-	11.0
Universal Precious Metals	CdnEq	PrMetl	-33.0	-20.8	20.4	3.6	-4.1	56.4	26.8	14.6	-	-
University Avenue Canadian	CdnEq	Divers	-0.3	-3.8	-	-	-	-	-	-	-	-
Valorem Cdn Equity-Value	CdnEq	Divers	9.2	-	-	-	-	-	-	-	-	-
Value Contrarian Cdn Eq	CdnEq	Divers	27.0	-	-	-	-	-	-	-	-	-
Westbury Cdn Life A	CdnEq	LCDivers	21.0	31.9	13.4	17.6	0.7	23.1	6.7	6.3	5.6	11.3
Westbury Cdn Life Eq Gth	CdnEq	LCValue	15.9	29.7	10.9	10.9	-1.2	18.0	-1.2	-3.0	-	-
YMG Emerging Companies	CdnEq	SCDivers	6.2	-	-	-	-	-	-	-	-	-
YMG Growth	CdnEq	Divers	4.4	41.9	10.0	-2.5	1.6	15.7	-4.8	5.4	0.1	12.8
ABC Fully-Managed	Balan	CdnSAA	6.6	27.3	22.4	7.8	20.2	38.2	-1.1	17.7	5.3	22.5
AGF American T.A. Alloc	Balan	GblTAA	24.5	17.2	10.9	17.6	4.6	23.4	17.6	4.7	4.2	-
AGF Cdn T.A. Asset Alloc	Balan	CdnTAA	15.5	22.0	10.0	10.3	4.6	10.6	9.6	8.9	3.1	-
AGF European Asset Alloc	Balan	GblTAA	45.9	27.6	12.5	6.7	6.8	-	-	-	-	-
AGF Growth & Income	Balan	CdnTAA	2.4	12.4	25.7	11.4	25.1	14.5	10.5	1.7	-2.5	10.3
AGF World Balanced	Balan	GblTAA	17.2	14.5	16.0	-10.7	-	14.9	18.7	-11.6	10.5	4.0
AIC Income Equity	Balan	CdnSAA	-	-	-	-	-	-	-	-	-	-
AIM Canadian Balanced	Balan	CdnTAA	13.8	13.5	8.8	6.1	5.6	-	-	-	-	-
AIM GT Canada Income	Balan	CdnSAA	11.9	27.7	-	-	-	-	-	-	-	-
AIM GT Global Grwth & Inc	Balan	GblSAA	26.3	16.3	10.7	11.7	6.4	15.5	7.2	4.5	0.5	11.3
APEX Balanced (AGF)	Balan	CdnTAA	5.9	8.6	8.2	-	-	-	-	-	-	-
APEX Growth & Income	Balan	CdnSAA	7.7	-	-	-	-	-	-	-	-	-
Acadia Balanced	Balan	CdnSAA	-7.4	23.3	3.9	-	-	-	-	-	-	-
Acuity Pld Cdn Balanced	Balan	CdnSAA	30.4	34.7	11.5	19.6	5.3	-	-	-	-	-
Acuity Pld Conserv AA	Balan	CdnSAA	27.6	25.6	5.7	0.9	-3.9	-	-	-	-	-
Acuity Pld Global Balanced	Balan	GblSAA	45.7	3.8	11.4	10.8	-2.6	-	-	-	-	-
Altamira Balanced	Balan	CdnTAA	11.3	11.4	7.5	10.5	-4.4	33.4	9.1	-1.0	-5.0	8.6
Altamira Glo Diversified	Balan	GblSAA	12.1	9.3	23.0	0.4	17.9	7.3	12.2	-10.2	-9.3	5.7
Altamira Growth & Income	Balan	CdnTAA	-2.9	3.9	6.4	6.6	8.8	18.4	18.3	10.7	3.5	10.3

% RETURN AT YEAR END

FUND NAME	FUND CATEGORY		JUN98	JUN97	JUN96	JUN95	JUN94	JUN93	JUN92	JUN91	JUN90	JUN89
Asset Builder I	Balan	CdnTAA	17.4	25.2	9.7	14.5	-	-	-	-	-	-
Asset Builder II	Balan	CdnTAA	22.8	30.8	10.0	14.2	-	-	-	-	-	-
Asset Builder III	Balan	CdnTAA	24.3	33.0	11.0	13.1	-	-	-	-	-	-
Asset Builder IV	Balan	CdnTAA	23.5	33.3	10.9	12.0	-	-	-	-	-	-
Asset Builder V	Balan	CdnTAA	22.6	33.6	11.2	11.8	-	-	-	-	-	-
Atlas Canadian Balanced	Balan	CdnSAA	15.8	23.4	11.6	15.6	1.0	10.0	7.6	6.5	-	-
Azura Balanced Pooled	Balan	GblSAA	8.8	15.1	-	-	-	-	-	-	-	-
Azura Balanced RSP Pooled	Balan	CdnSAA	6.4	17.0	-	-	-	-	-	-	-	-
Azura Conservative Pooled	Balan	CdnSAA	6.9	13.1	-	-	-	-	-	-	-	-
BPI Canadian Balanced	Balan	CdnSAA	10.0	10.5	11.3	6.7	-2.4	21.0	11.6	6.2	-0.2	10.7
BPI Global Balanced RSP	Balan	CdnSAA	19.2	14.8	4.0	8.1	10.2	30.1	10.3	1.0	-0.2	0.7
BPI Income & Growth	Balan	CdnSAA	40.3	-	-	-	-	-	-	-	-	-
Beutel Goodman Balanced	Balan	CdnSAA	10.7	19.3	9.2	14.0	5.2	11.2	8.4	9.5	-	-
Beutel Goodman Private Bal	Balan	GblSAA	18.5	27.3	13.0	12.2	6.2	18.3	14.1	-	-	-
Bissett Retirement	Balan	CdnSAA	16.2	25.9	16.3	14.9	1.9	20.4	-	-	-	-
C.I. Canadian Balanced	Balan	CdnSAA	10.8	11.1	10.3	13.7	8.4	-	-	-	-	-
C.I. Canadian Income	Balan	CdnSAA	7.5	17.8	13.9	-	-	-	-	-	-	-
C.I. International Bal	Balan	GblSAA	18.7	18.0	14.5	-	-	-	-	-	-	-
C.I. Intl. Balanced RSP	Balan	CdnSAA	14.5	17.1	14.9	12.1	2.8	11.7	8.6	7.6	2.3	14.5
CCPE Diversified	Balan	CdnSAA	9.0	21.3	12.9	14.1	0.8	12.4	10.2	8.5	2.7	13.9
CDA Balanced (KBSH)	Balan	CdnSAA	9.2	20.8	12.9	-	-	-	-	-	-	-
CGO&V Balanced	Balan	CdnSAA	8.4	-	-	-	-	-	-	-	-	-
CGO&V Hazelton	Balan	GblSAA	9.7	-	-	-	-	-	-	-	-	-
CIBC Balanced	Balan	CdnTAA	16.9	21.1	9.3	12.7	-2.8	13.1	6.7	8.7	3.2	12.0
CT Balanced	Balan	CdnSAA	10.7	20.4	10.5	11.6	-0.5	18.7	9.4	8.3	2.2	17.9
CT Retirement Balanced	Balan	CdnSAA	12.3	-	-	-	-	-	-	-	-	-
CUMIS Life Balanced	Balan	CdnSAA	1.1	-	-	-	-	-	-	-	-	-
CUMIS Life Global Balanced	Balan	GblSAA	6.6	-	-	-	-	-	-	-	-	-
Caldwell Associate	Balan	CdnTAA	3.7	24.7	11.5	15.6	16.8	6.1	8.0	-	-	-
Caldwell International	Balan	GblSAA	1.4	6.4	11.0	11.6	20.0	1.0	-	12.7	2.2	8.5
Cambridge Balanced	Balan	CdnSAA	-28.9	-18.8	9.9	-4.2	-2.4	36.6	10.8	6.1	-0.7	13.0
Canada Life Managed	Balan	CdnSAA	9.7	20.3	11.5	13.3	-0.1	15.4	10.9	10.3	5.4	9.9
Capstone Investment Trust	Balan	CdnSAA	20.1	18.2	17.4	7.0	3.6	16.2	2.9	-	-	-
CentrePost Balanced	Balan	CdnSAA	4.3	15.9	16.3	12.8	-5.4	-	-	-	-	-
Clarington Canadian Bal	Balan	CdnSAA	9.0	-	-	-	-	-	-	-	-	-
Clarington Canadian Income	Balan	CdnSAA	10.6	-	-	-	9.1	28.5	-	-	-	-
Clean Environment Balanced	Balan	CdnTAA	23.5	28.9	10.7	9.5	1.3	15.2	-	-	-	-
Co-Operators Balanced	Balan	CdnTAA	17.9	22.9	11.3	19.2	-	-	-	-	-	-
Colonia Strategic Balanced	Balan	CdnSAA	13.2	22.9	-	-	-	-	-	-	-	-
Cornel Equilibree	Balan	CdnSAA	14.4	19.5	9.5	15.4	-0.1	17.5	12.9	10.7	3.9	12.5
Cornerstone Balanced	Balan	CdnSAA	7.0	13.8	14.8	14.8	-4.2	14.4	5.9	6.5	2.0	9.2
Desjardins Balanced	Balan	CdnSAA	9.7	20.8	9.9	13.1	1.0	14.6	8.6	8.5	0.9	12.2
Desjardins Distinct Dvrsd	Balan	CdnSAA	11.2	22.0	10.5	14.8	0.8	17.6	10.9	8.7	-	-

% RETURN AT YEAR END

FUND NAME	FUND CATEGORY		JUN98	JUN97	JUN96	JUN95	JUN94	JUN93	JUN92	JUN91	JUN90	JUN89
Desjardins Diver Audacious	Balan	CdnSAA	7.9	15.0	10.0	-	-	-	-	-	-	-
Desjardins Divers Moderate	Balan	CdnSAA	6.5	11.1	9.1	-	-	-	-	-	-	-
Desjardins Divers Secure	Balan	CdnSAA	4.9	6.8	7.2	-	-	-	-	-	-	-
Desjardins Divers. Ambitious	Balan	CdnSAA	10.1	-	-	-	-	-	-	-	-	-
Desjardins Quebec	Balan	CdnSAA	23.0	-	-	-	-	-	-	-	-	-
Desjardins World Balanced	Balan	GblTAA	9.8	12.7	-	-	-	-	-	-	-	-
Dynamic Global Partners	Balan	GblTAA	2.9	19.0	12.9	5.5	6.7	40.5	14.4	5.9	4.1	-
Dynamic Partners	Balan	CdnTAA	5.1	17.8	8.0	9.6	1.6	38.9	8.3	1.9	1.3	9.2
Dynamic Team	Balan	CdnTAA	-0.8	15.5	13.9	7.0	2.4	26.1	9.1	9.0	-0.9	12.5
Elliott & Page Balanced	Balan	CdnSAA	5.9	14.6	13.9	14.3	-	-	-	-	-	-
Elliott & Page Global Bal	Balan	GblSAA	10.6	11.6	6.2	-	-	-	-	-	-	-
Empire Asset Allocation	Balan	CdnTAA	7.9	21.8	9.1	6.2	-	-	-	-	-	-
Empire Balanced	Balan	CdnSAA	7.2	21.5	10.3	11.5	-0.1	15.5	8.7	8.1	3.3	-
Equitable Life Asset Allc	Balan	CdnTAA	10.1	18.0	7.6	-	-	-	-	-	-	-
Ethical Balanced	Balan	CdnSAA	19.9	24.1	8.7	16.6	0.7	10.4	5.7	11.5	-	-
FMOQ Fonds De Placement	Balan	GblSAA	30.4	26.0	16.1	18.0	2.3	18.7	15.4	13.9	7.7	7.8
FMOQ Omnibus	Balan	GblSAA	21.8	21.4	11.6	17.0	2.3	14.0	11.2	12.0	3.9	10.4
Ficadre Equilibre	Balan	CdnTAA	7.3	16.5	13.1	14.7	2.4	6.3	11.2	5.4	0.9	9.0
Fidelity Cdn Asset Alloc	Balan	CdnSAA	20.0	31.4	13.6	-	9.3	-	-	-	-	-
Fidelity Glob Asset Alloc	Balan	GblSAA	20.1	24.5	14.8	2.6	-5.6	-	-	-	-	-
First Canadian Asset Alloc	Balan	CdnTAA	9.8	19.1	9.9	15.0	-0.5	12.3	9.2	8.4	-0.6	10.1
GS Canadian Balanced	Balan	CdnSAA	14.8	28.4	-	12.4	-	13.2	9.5	7.6	-1.3	12.0
General Trust Balanced	Balan	CdnSAA	5.8	19.7	10.9	-	-	-	-	-	-	-
Global Mgr-Tactical Growth	Balan	GblTAA	15.3	-	-	-	-	-	-	-	-	-
Global Strategy Income Pls	Balan	CdnSAA	16.2	29.4	14.0	11.2	5.7	18.0	-	-	-	-
Global Strategy World Bal	Balan	GblSAA	14.6	9.4	9.1	-	-	-	-	-	-	-
Great-West Balanced (B) A	Balan	CdnSAA	11.5	18.2	-	-	-	-	-	-	-	-
Great-West Balanced (B) B	Balan	CdnSAA	11.8	18.5	-	-	-	-	-	-	-	-
Great-West Balanced (M) A	Balan	CdnSAA	1.9	21.8	-	-	-	-	-	-	-	-
Great-West Balanced (M) B	Balan	CdnSAA	2.1	22.1	-	-	-	-	-	-	-	-
Great-West Balanced (S) A	Balan	CdnSAA	9.2	21.2	-	-	-	-	-	-	-	-
Great-West Balanced (S) B	Balan	CdnSAA	9.5	21.6	-	-	-	-	-	-	-	-
Great-West Divers (G) A	Balan	CdnSAA	12.3	17.8	9.3	9.8	-0.8	15.7	9.1	6.0	2.7	10.6
Great-West Divers (G) B	Balan	CdnSAA	12.6	18.1	9.5	-	-	-	-	-	-	-
Great-West Equity/Bd (G) A	Balan	CdnSAA	9.3	20.0	10.4	9.6	-2.9	21.2	11.5	8.8	1.9	10.8
Great-West Equity/Bd (G) B	Balan	CdnSAA	9.6	20.3	10.6	-	-	-	-	-	-	-
Great-West Gth & Inc (A)A	Balan	CdnSAA	-0.4	9.4	-	-	-	-	-	-	-	-
Great-West Gth & Inc (A)B	Balan	CdnSAA	-0.2	9.6	-	-	-	-	-	-	-	-
Great-West Gth & Inc (M)A	Balan	CdnSAA	13.4	22.4	-	-	-	-	-	-	-	-
Great-West Gth & Inc (M)B	Balan	CdnSAA	13.7	22.8	-	-	-	-	-	-	-	-
Green Line Balanced Growth	Balan	CdnSAA	12.6	22.7	14.8	14.2	-4.2	10.6	10.0	5.3	-0.3	12.5
Green Line Balanced Income	Balan	CdnSAA	10.0	23.4	11.5	11.3	-0.7	9.3	8.2	6.6	-1.6	-
Greystone Managed Wealth	Balan	CdnSAA	17.8	23.1	5.2	9.6	-	-	-	-	-	-

% RETURN AT YEAR END

FUND NAME		FUND CATEGORY	JUN98	JUN97	JUN96	JUN95	JUN94	JUN93	JUN92	JUN91	JUN90	JUN89
GrowSafe Canadian Balanced	Balan	CdnSAA	7.1	14.7	9.2	9.5	-	-	-	-	-	-
GrowSafe Intl Balanced	Balan	GblSAA	12.1	13.5	12.1	3.0	-	-	-	-	-	-
Guardian Cdn Balanced C	Balan	CdnSAA	3.3	13.7	8.7	10.9	3.5	13.1	12.3	12.2	5.8	9.7
Guardian Cdn Balanced M	Balan	CdnSAA	2.6	13.1	-	-	-	-	-	-	-	-
Guardian Gth & Income C	Balan	CdnSAA	7.1	-	-	-	-	-	-	-	-	-
Guardian Gth & Income M	Balan	CdnSAA	7.1	-	-	-	-	-	-	-	-	-
Guardian Intl Balanced C	Balan	GblSAA	4.4	13.2	14.2	3.1	-	-	-	-	-	-
Guardian Intl Balanced M	Balan	GblSAA	3.7	12.4	-	-	-	-	-	-	-	-
Harbour Gth & Income	Balan	CdnSAA	4.4	-	-	-	-	-	-	-	-	-
Hemisphere Value	Balan	CdnSAA	7.6	13.6	8.8	-	-	-	-	-	-	-
Hongkong Bank Balanced	Balan	CdnTAA	10.4	20.8	13.7	8.5	2.2	20.6	14.7	6.6	-0.5	10.9
ICM Balanced	Balan	CdnSAA	9.2	14.6	13.9	15.7	4.0	18.9	14.9	10.8	-	-
IG Beutel Goodman Cdn Bal	Balan	CdnSAA	11.2	-	-	-	-	-	-	-	-	-
IG Sceptre Cdn Balanced	Balan	CdnSAA	9.2	-	-	-	-	-	-	-	-	-
Ideal Balanced	Balan	CdnSAA	14.7	20.5	10.0	16.3	0.9	12.3	14.2	9.9	1.5	8.4
Imperial Gth Diversified	Balan	CdnSAA	9.1	22.3	9.2	12.9	0.8	11.3	10.1	7.4	2.5	12.3
Ind. Alliance Divers 2	Balan	CdnTAA	1.8	19.3	8.7	16.6	2.8	17.6	7.4	12.4	-	-
Ind. Alliance Diversified	Balan	CdnTAA	8.8	18.5	8.1	16.0	2.3	19.9	6.5	-	4.4	-
Ind. Alliance Ecoflex D	Balan	CdnTAA	7.8	24.3	7.4	12.9	-0.5	16.5	13.3	8.8	-	-
Industrial Balanced	Balan	CdnSAA	3.2	17.9	7.9	15.7	-4.1	-	-	-	-1.4	12.6
Industrial Income Class A	Balan	CdnSAA	5.8	32.6	12.3	12.7	11.4	26.1	-7.3	-9.7	-7.8	-
Industrial Pension	Balan	CdnSAA	14.6	20.7	10.1	13.5	-3.0	13.4	10.2	10.1	-0.8	3.5
InvesNat Retirement Bal	Balan	CdnSAA	5.8	22.0	15.8	9.9	-	-	-	-	-	-
Investors Asset Allocation	Balan	CdnTAA	13.2	18.0	12.7	8.6	8.8	17.1	9.5	5.2	4.9	-
Investors Growth Plus Port	Balan	GblSAA	17.2	15.4	8.2	11.4	-0.8	8.9	11.8	11.7	3.6	-
Investors Income Plus Port	Balan	CdnSAA	11.8	21.2	9.1	10.5	4.3	21.5	6.4	8.1	-0.6	11.6
Investors Mutual	Balan	CdnSAA	13.2	15.4	9.0	10.6	3.8	14.1	7.0	6.7	3.4	-
Investors Ret. Plus Port	Balan	CdnSAA	8.2	23.9	18.0	14.2	-1.0	-	-	-	-	-
Ivy Growth & Income	Balan	CdnSAA	16.6	15.0	6.4	10.2	-2.6	-	-	-	-	-
Jones Heward Cdn Balanced	Balan	CdnSAA	10.4	19.9	7.4	14.9	-2.0	24.0	12.4	7.8	-0.3	8.7
Lasalle Balanced	Balan	CdnSAA	9.9	26.1	9.1	13.5	4.5	17.4	10.4	7.1	2.1	12.6
Leith Wheeler Balanced	Balan	CdnSAA	15.4	18.9	11.4	11.1	-0.5	13.6	12.0	11.7	-1.2	8.0
London Life Diversified	Balan	CdnSAA	14.6	20.2	11.6	7.5	-0.5	18.9	11.7	5.7	0.8	12.4
Lotus Group Balanced	Balan	CdnSAA	13.1	21.2	10.3	15.8	-4.8	24.4	8.2	7.6	0.4	9.0
MAXXUM Canadian Balanced	Balan	CdnSAA	9.2	25.2	15.3	14.8	3.2	26.6	14.2	9.5	-2.3	13.7
MB Balanced Growth Pension	Balan	CdnSAA	12.8	23.0	12.1	14.3	4.4	17.9	12.8	8.7	4.1	14.5
MD Balanced	Balan	CdnSAA	12.1	-	-	-	-	-	-	-	-	-
MLI AGF Gth & Income GIF	Balan	CdnSAA	2.0	-	-	-	-	-	-	-	-	-
MLI Fidelity Cdn AA GIF	Balan	CdnSAA	19.3	-	-	-	-	-	-	-	-	-
MLI Trimark Select Bal GIF	Balan	CdnSAA	3.7	-	-	-	-	-	-	-	-	-
Manulife VistaFd 1 Divers	Balan	CdnSAA	8.9	11.9	8.8	13.4	-1.7	17.7	9.5	6.4	0.5	10.7
Manulife VistaFd 2 Divers	Balan	CdnSAA	8.1	11.1	8.0	12.5	-2.5	16.8	8.7	5.6	-0.3	9.9
Maritime Life Balanced A&C	Balan	CdnSAA	13.2	18.2	10.5	13.9	0.4	13.5	5.7	8.7	0.7	11.2

% RETURN AT YEAR END

FUND NAME	FUND CATEGORY	JUN98	JUN97	JUN96	JUN95	JUN94	JUN93	JUN92	JUN91	JUN90	JUN89
Maritime Life Balanced B	Balan CdnSAA	13.1	21.7	10.3	14.9	-0.7	14.2	11.2	10.0	2.5	9.4
Mawer Canadian Diver Invst	Balan CdnTAA	11.5	22.9	10.0	15.1	-0.1	14.9	12.4	9.4	2.8	10.2
Mawer Cdn Balanced RSP	Balan CdnSAA	13.7	11.6	8.7	12.3	-	-	-	-	-	-
McDonald Canada Plus	Balan CdnSAA	8.0	-	-	-	-	-	-	-	-	-
Mclean Budden Balanced	Balan CdnSAA	11.6	24.7	13.4	15.3	-0.2	15.1	12.5	9.5	2.1	-
Members Mutual	Balan CdnSAA	-5.2	19.2	-	-	-	-	-	-	-	-
Merrill Lynch Cap Asset	Balan GblSAA	21.7	19.0	-	-	-	-	-	-	-	-
Merrill Lynch World Alloc	Balan GblSAA	5.7	-	-	-	-	-	-	-	-	-
Metlife Mvp Balanced	Balan CdnSAA	11.8	17.9	8.2	10.3	-0.3	10.8	6.1	5.5	2.2	11.0
Millennia III Cdn Bal 1	Balan CdnSAA	8.6	20.4	-	-	-	-	-	-	-	-
Millennia III Cdn Bal 2	Balan CdnSAA	8.4	20.0	-	-	-	-	-	-	-	-
Millennium Diversified	Balan CdnSAA	15.6	21.3	15.5	11.4	-	-	-	-	-	-
Montrusco Select Balanced	Balan CdnSAA	9.0	19.4	13.8	13.4	6.6	17.0	12.5	10.6	2.8	12.4
Montrusco Select Balanced+	Balan CdnSAA	12.5	27.5	16.1	12.3	18.7	-	-	-	-	-
Mutual Diversifund 40	Balan CdnTAA	12.3	20.3	12.4	13.7	0.1	13.5	7.3	6.3	-2.8	14.0
Mutual Premier Diversified	Balan CdnSAA	10.2	21.0	13.6	13.0	-	-	-	-	-	-
Mutual Summit Growth & Inc	Balan CdnSAA	14.0	-	-	-	-	-	-	-	-	-
NAL-Balanced Growth	Balan CdnSAA	10.6	24.5	11.6	-	-	-	-	-	-	-
NAL-Canadian Diversified	Balan CdnSAA	6.5	14.6	16.2	15.7	-3.8	17.2	7.0	7.7	0.4	11.1
NN Asset Allocation	Balan CdnSAA	13.9	20.5	13.2	12.4	0.7	15.0	7.4	5.8	0.3	7.4
NN Elite	Balan GblSAA	5.2	11.2	6.2	-	-	-	-	-	-	-
National Balanced	Balan CdnSAA	11.6	24.2	11.2	12.5	0.5	15.5	12.1	9.5	-	-
National Trust Balanced	Balan CdnSAA	15.5	24.0	10.5	14.6	-1.8	15.0	-	-	-	-
North West Life Ecoflex D	Balan CdnTAA	7.8	-	-	-	-	-	-	-	-	-
Northwest Balanced	Balan CdnTAA	11.2	15.5	12.6	-	-	-	-	-	-	-
O'Donnell Balanced	Balan CdnSAA	3.6	-	-	-	-	-	-	-	-	-
O.I.Q. Ferique Equilibre	Balan CdnSAA	20.6	23.3	11.3	16.0	2.1	14.5	9.7	12.3	3.6	15.2
OTGIF Balanced	Balan CdnSAA	12.8	22.8	11.3	13.0	1.8	18.5	4.5	7.5	3.3	14.0
Optimum Equilibre	Balan CdnSAA	10.8	16.5	10.2	15.8	-0.4	14.3	12.6	8.5	0.0	12.3
PH & N Balance Pension Tr	Balan CdnSAA	12.3	22.6	13.2	14.6	5.0	14.4	11.7	9.5	5.7	-
PH & N Balanced	Balan CdnSAA	10.7	21.8	11.9	15.1	4.4	14.3	-	-	-	-
Pret et Revenu Eq Retraite	Balan CdnTAA	8.2	17.6	14.5	16.0	-0.1	13.3	15.3	8.9	3.7	10.0
Protected American	Balan CdnTAA	10.5	-3.5	4.5	4.2	-3.2	36.9	6.4	9.1	8.3	-
Quebec Prof Balanced	Balan CdnSAA	9.0	14.2	10.5	12.6	0.3	10.6	13.9	14.0	3.6	10.8
Quebec Prof Gth & Income	Balan CdnSAA	8.1	16.2	10.3	-	-	-	-	-	-	-
Royal&SunAlliance Cdn Gwth	Balan CdnTAA	11.9	17.3	10.5	10.0	3.6	19.5	13.0	4.3	3.9	9.8
Royal Energy	Balan CdnSAA	12.4	21.7	9.2	13.1	-0.1	13.3	7.9	11.8	-	-
Royal Trust Adv. Growth	Balan CdnSAA	11.6	18.1	9.9	10.5	2.3	14.2	11.0	8.4	3.3	12.0
Royal Trust Adv. Income	Balan CdnSAA	9.5	17.2	11.2	9.0	3.1	16.0	8.5	5.8	2.9	10.7
Royal U.S. Equity	Balan CdnSAA	10.9	16.3	8.7	11.1	1.7	12.4	12.6	10.3	4.3	11.4
SSQ - Equilibre	Balan CdnTAA	12.4	20.0	14.0	14.7	-0.6	13.9	-	-	-	-
Saxon Balanced	Balan CdnSAA	10.7	20.7	9.6	22.8	-1.0	38.6	6.1	3.9	-8.0	3.9
Sceptre Balanced Growth	Balan CdnSAA	8.2	24.9	20.9	10.2	7.7	13.2	10.2	8.7	0.9	11.7

% RETURN AT YEAR END

FUND NAME	FUND CATEGORY		JUN98	JUN97	JUN96	JUN95	JUN94	JUN93	JUN92	JUN91	JUN90	JUN89
Scotia Ex. Balanced	Balan	CdnSAA	9.0	15.6	12.3	11.8	4.1	14.1	8.2	9.2	8.4	-
Scotia Ex. Total Return	Balan	CdnTAA	8.1	24.0	11.8	9.5	9.0	20.2	15.3	11.4	1.4	-
Spectrum Utd Asset Alloc	Balan	CdnTAA	13.3	18.5	9.6	11.3	1.6	-	-	-	-	-
Spectrum Utd Cdn Bal Port	Balan	CdnSAA	9.3	17.1	14.8	13.2	1.6	20.7	11.3	10.4	-0.1	-
Spectrum Utd Diversified	Balan	CdnSAA	12.6	21.6	9.0	13.2	-2.4	13.6	8.8	7.3	-0.1	10.2
Spectrum Utd Global Diver	Balan	GblSAA	15.2	10.5	14.0	11.7	2.6	16.3	12.4	7.8	2.3	-
Standard Life Balanced	Balan	CdnSAA	14.5	22.1	12.3	14.6	-0.9	-	-	-	-	-
Stone & Co Flagship Gth&In	Balan	CdnSAA	8.7	-	-	-	-	-	-	-	-	-
Strategic Val Cdn Balanced	Balan	CdnSAA	9.4	20.5	8.5	12.2	-0.8	9.7	7.6	7.8	2.9	-
Strategic Val Glo Bal RSP	Balan	GblSAA	4.4	-	-	-	-	-	-	-	-	-
Strategic Val Global Bal	Balan	GblSAA	15.1	11.2	8.1	7.0	8.8	15.6	7.2	-2.6	-	10.2
Talvest Canadian Asset All	Balan	CdnSAA	16.1	20.9	9.4	10.5	3.4	12.4	7.6	8.4	3.2	9.1
Talvest Global Asset Alloc	Balan	GblSAA	9.0	11.9	9.4	0.1	19.7	11.2	17.6	-8.0	14.9	6.1
Templeton Balanced	Balan	CdnSAA	8.9	26.8	10.9	12.4	7.6	10.9	7.3	-	-	-
Templeton Cdn Asset Alloc	Balan	CdnTAA	6.7	19.9	11.7	-	-	-	-	-	-	-
Templeton Global Balanced	Balan	GblSAA	8.5	19.8	11.6	-	-	-	-	-	-	-
Templeton Intl Balanced	Balan	GblSAA	5.6	18.4	-2.8	-	-	-	-	-	-	-
Trans-Canada Pension	Balan	CdnTAA	-0.4	42.9	9.2	9.8	2.6	36.2	-9.5	6.4	1.4	10.2
Transamerica Bal Inv Gth	Balan	CdnSAA	7.1	14.9	11.4	12.6	3.6	13.1	10.3	12.0	6.2	5.8
Trimark Income Growth	Balan	CdnSAA	0.8	20.2	11.8	16.6	6.0	18.4	12.4	7.2	2.6	13.2
Trimark Select Balanced	Balan	CdnSAA	4.4	21.7		15.4	5.3	17.9	12.2	10.1	-	-
Universal Canadian Bal	Balan	CdnSAA	19.4	-	-	-	-	-	-	-	-	-
Universal World Asst Alloc	Balan	GblTAA	22.3	5.9	7.6	-3.1	-	-	-	-	-	-
Universal World Bal RRSP	Balan	GblSAA	5.7	23.2	17.4	4.1	-	-	-	-	-	-
Valorem Diversified	Balan	CdnSAA	13.3	-	-	-	-	-	-	-	-	-
Westbury Cdn Life Balanced	Balan	CdnTAA	12.9	21.8	9.7	14.3	0.8	8.8	5.6	9.8	1.5	12.0
YMG Balanced	Balan	CdnSAA	-1.7	19.2	8.0	7.9	3.0	7.9	3.5	-	-	-
Zweig Global Managed Asset	Balan	GblSAA	20.9	13.6	-	-	-	-	-	-	-	-
AGF Cdn Asset Alloc Serv	Alloc	TAA	3.4	9.1	10.7	11.7	0.9	18.4	12.6	8.5	-	-
Great-West Advanced Port	Alloc	SAA	11.6	-	-	-	-	-	-	-	-	-
Great-West Advanced Port B	Alloc	SAA	11.9	-	-	-	-	-	-	-	-	-
Great-West Aggress Port B	Alloc	SAA	13.9	-	-	-	-	-	-	-	-	-
Great-West Aggressive Port	Alloc	SAA	13.6	-	-	-	-	-	-	-	-	-
Great-West Balanced Port	Alloc	SAA	10.9	-	-	-	-	-	-	-	-	-
Great-West Balanced Port B	Alloc	SAA	11.2	-	-	-	-	-	-	-	-	-
Great-West Conserv Port	Alloc	SAA	9.0	-	-	-	-	-	-	-	-	-
Great-West Conserv Port B	Alloc	SAA	9.3	-	-	-	-	-	-	-	-	-
Great-West Moderate Port	Alloc	SAA	10.3	-	-	-	-	-	-	-	-	-
Great-West Moderate Port B	Alloc	SAA	10.6	-	-	-	-	-	-	-	-	-
MatchMaker Balanced 1	Alloc	SAA	9.6	15.1	-	-	-	-	-	-	-	-
MatchMaker Balanced 2	Alloc	SAA	11.9	18.9	-	-	-	-	-	-	-	-
MatchMaker Growth 1	Alloc	SAA	6.3	20.9	-	-	-	-	-	-	-	-

% RETURN AT YEAR END

FUND NAME	FUND CATEGORY		JUN98	JUN97	JUN96	JUN95	JUN94	JUN93	JUN92	JUN91	JUN90	JUN89
MatchMaker Growth 2	Alloc	SAA	4.2	22.4	-	-	-	-	-	-	-	-
MatchMaker Security 1	Alloc	SAA	7.5	9.1	-	-	-	-	-	-	-	-
MatchMaker Security 2	Alloc	SAA	10.7	12.4	-	-	-	-	-	-	-	-
Reg MatchMaker Balanced 1	Alloc	SAA	9.7	16.5	-	-	-	-	-	-	-	-
Reg MatchMaker Balanced 2	Alloc	SAA	10.6	18.7	-	-	-	-	-	-	-	-
Reg MatchMaker Growth 1	Alloc	SAA	4.6	21.7	-	-	-	-	-	-	-	-
Reg MatchMaker Growth 2	Alloc	SAA	6.2	23.2	-	-	-	-	-	-	-	-
Reg MatchMaker Security 1	Alloc	SAA	5.4	5.7	-	-	-	-	-	-	-	-
Reg MatchMaker Security 2	Alloc	SAA	7.4	9.9	-	-	-	-	-	-	-	-
STAR Cdn Bal Gth & Income	Alloc	SAA	10.2	20.0	-	-	-	-	-	-	-	-
STAR Cdn Conserv Inc & Gth	Alloc	SAA	9.3	-	-	-	-	-	-	-	-	-
STAR Cdn Long-Term Growth	Alloc	SAA	10.5	-	-	-	-	-	-	-	-	-
STAR Cdn Maximum Eq Gth	Alloc	SAA	10.3	25.6	-	-	-	-	-	-	-	-
STAR Cdn Maximum L-T Gth	Alloc	SAA	10.5	-	-	-	-	-	-	-	-	-
STAR Fgn Bal Gth & Income	Alloc	SAA	13.7	10.0	12.4	-	-	-	-	-	-	-
STAR Fgn Maximum Eq Gth	Alloc	SAA	5.4	16.9	-	-	-	-	-	-	-	-
STAR Fgn Maximum L-T Gth	Alloc	SAA	1.4	12.4	14.7	-	-	-	-	-	-	-
STAR Inv Bal Gth & Income	Alloc	SAA	10.5	15.8	9.9	-	-	-	-	-	-	-
STAR Inv Conserv Inc & Gth	Alloc	SAA	13.0	13.3	14.2	-	-	-	-	-	-	-
STAR Inv Long-Term Growth	Alloc	SAA	11.6	18.6	11.2	-	-	-	-	-	-	-
STAR Inv Maximum L-T Gth	Alloc	SAA	6.5	10.6	13.6	-	-	-	-	-	-	-
STAR Reg Bal Gth & Income	Alloc	SAA	7.4	17.5	11.7	-	-	-	-	-	-	-
STAR Reg Conserv Inc & Gth	Alloc	SAA	9.1	13.6	11.3	-	-	-	-	-	-	-
STAR Reg Long-Term Growth	Alloc	SAA	6.1	18.3	12.7	-	-	-	-	-	-	-
STAR Reg Maximum Eq Gth	Alloc	SAA	7.7	24.0	-	-	-	-	-	-	-	-
STAR Reg Maximum L-T Gth	Alloc	SAA	9.2	15.2	15.2	-	-	-	-	-	-	-
20/20 Managed Futures Val.	Spcty	Other	-34.2	11.2	18.8	-	-	-	-	-	-	-
AIM GT Glbl Infrstructure	Spcty	GlobST	12.0	12.2	22.6	-	-	-	-	-	-	-
AIM GT Global Health Care	Spcty	GlobST	18.8	19.3	-	-	-	-	-	-	-	-
AIM GT Global Telecom	Spcty	GlobST	27.2	-1.2	41.7	-	-	-	-	-	-	-
AIM Global Health Sciences	Spcty	GlobST	27.9	13.9	57.5	41.4	-	16.2	-	-	-	-
AIM Global Technology	Spcty	GlobST	30.9	-	-	-	-	-	-	-	-	-
Acuity Pld Envir Sc & Tech	Spcty	GlobST	30.3	15.5	15.0	5.0	-	5.1	-	-	-	-
Allstar Adrian Day Gold Pl	Spcty	GlPrMt	-54.2	-	-	-	-	-	-	-	-	-
Altamira Science & Tech	Spcty	GlobST	45.7	4.5	-	-	-	-	-	-	-	-
C.I. Glo Health Sci Sector	Spcty	GlobST	17.6	-	-	-	-	-	-	-	-	-
C.I. Glo Technology Sector	Spcty	GlobST	40.6	-	-	-	-	-	-	-	-	-
C.I. Glo Telecom Sector	Spcty	GlobST	71.1	-	-	-	-	-	-	-	-	-
CIBC Global Technology	Spcty	GlobST	32.0	14.6	-	-	-	-	-	-	-	-
Clarington Glo Communica.	Spcty	GlobST	43.1	-	-	-	-	-	-	-	-	-
Dynamic Cdn Real Estate	Spcty	CdnRE	6.1	-	-	-	-	-	-	-	-	-
Dynamic Global Millennia	Spcty	GlobST	-9.0	29.6	33.4	-5.8	25.1	-8.3	-0.4	-11.4	16.4	3.7

% RETURN AT YEAR END

FUND NAME		FUND CATEGORY	JUN98	JUN97	JUN96	JUN95	JUN94	JUN93	JUN92	JUN91	JUN90	JUN89
Dynamic Global Prec Metal	Spclty	GlPrMt	-32.8	-1.6	-	-	-	-	-	-	-	-
Dynamic Real Estate Equity	Spclty	GlobRE	13.0	40.4	42.8	-	-	-	-	-	-	-
Fidelity Focus Health Care	Spclty	GlobST	34.4	-	-	-	-	-	-	-	-	-
Fidelity Focus Technology	Spclty	GlobST	22.9	-	-	-	-	-	-	-	-	-
First Cdn Global Sci & Tec	Spclty	GlobST	42.2	-	-	-	-	-	-	-	-	-
Friedberg Currency	Spclty	Crrncy	46.5	10.7	22.1	-	-	-	-	-	-	-
Friedberg Diversified	Spclty	Crrncy	-8.2	-	-	-	-	-	-	-	-	-
Goldfund Limited	Spclty	GlPrMt	-32.1	-24.9	6.7	-10.9	65.5	34.6	-7.8	-1.1	3.4	-20.4
Great-West Real Estate(G)A	Spclty	CdnRE	14.0	3.5	2.7	-0.5	-13.4	-5.5	-4.1	-4.3	11.5	9.9
Great-West Real Estate(G)B	Spclty	CdnRE	14.3	3.7	2.9	-	-	-	-	-	-	-
Green Line Health Sciences	Spclty	GlobST	24.3	-	-	-	-	-	-	-	-	-
Green Line Science & Tech	Spclty	GlobST	22.1	10.9	23.4	70.1	-	-	-	-	-	-
Hillsdale LS American Eq	Spclty	Crrncy	17.1	-	-	-	-	-	-	-	-	-
Horizons Multi-Asset	Spclty	Other	1.1	15.1	5.0	-1.8	-	-	-	-	-	-
Investors Real Property	Spclty	CdnRE	8.9	4.4	4.0	2.6	-2.1	-0.3	2.1	5.3	7.3	11.6
Middlefield Cdn Realty	Spclty	CdnRE	-2.1	-	-	-	-	-	-	-	-	-
O'Donnell World Prec Metal	Spclty	GlPrMt	-40.7	-	-	-	-	-	-	-	-	-
Optima Strat-Real Estate	Spclty	GlobRE	13.7	25.5	-	-	-	-	-	-	-	-
Royal Dividend	Spclty	CdnRE	-24.6	4.1	-1.7	9.3	-2.9	-0.4	-1.9	8.6	7.6	-
Royal Life Science & Tech	Spclty	GlobST	14.2	18.7	18.4	21.8	-	-	-	-	-	-
Spectrum Utd Glo Telecomm	Spclty	GlobST	31.8	2.6	-	-	-	-	-	-	-	-
Tal/Hyper Glo Health Care	Spclty	GlobST	16.7	-	-	-	-	-	-	-	-	-
Tal/Hyper Glob Sci & Tech	Spclty	GlobST	44.6	-	-	-	-	-	-	-	-	-
Trimark Discovery	Spclty	GlobST	12.8	13.2	-	-	-	-	-	-	-	-
Universal World Sci & Tech	Spclty	GlobST	34.3	-	-	-	-	-	-	-	-	-
YMG Hedge	Spclty	Other	19.8	-	-	-	-	-	-	-	-	-
20/20 Aggressive Growth	USEq	Divers	28.8	-0.9	26.9	27.2	-	8.7	9.9	-2.5	5.0	21.2
AGF Intl Grp-American Gth	USEq	LgCap	44.9	35.1	17.8	24.9	22.1	9.7	11.8	4.7	8.2	15.2
AGF Intl Grp-Special U.S.	USEq	Divers	6.7	2.5	13.3	17.7	20.8	7.8	-	-	-	-
AIC American Advantage	USEq	Divers	-	-	-	-	-	-	-	3.7	-	-
AIC Value	USEq	LgCap	28.4	57.0	26.6	23.7	27.2	9.1	16.6	-	-	-
AIM American Aggress Gth	USEq	Divers	-	-	-	-	-	-	-	-	-	-
AIM American Premier	USEq	LgCap	37.5	26.2	-6.0	18.7	8.8	3.1	-	-	-	-
AIM GT America Growth	USEq	LgCap	32.8	3.9	6.8	-	-	-	-	-	-	-
APEX U.S. Equity	USEq	Divers	32.4	-	-	-	-	-	-	-	-	-
Altamira Select American	USEq	SmCap	17.2	7.3	23.4	20.3	40.7	17.2	24.1	-	-	-
Altamira US Larger Company	USEq	LgCap	32.4	17.5	20.1	31.0	-	1.9	-	-	-	-
Atlas Amer Large Cap Gth	USEq	LgCap	23.4	34.8	21.4	22.8	10.9	-	12.2	6.0	9.1	5.6
Atlas American Advan Value	USEq	LgCap	21.4	28.7	19.1	-	-	-	-	-	-	-
Atlas American RSP Index	USEq	Divers	25.0	-	-	-	-	-	-	-	-	-
BPI American Equity Value	USEq	LgCap	42.8	25.6	18.5	18.6	17.1	7.3	9.8	7.4	7.0	-
BPI American Small Comp	USEq	SmCap	10.8	24.4	20.7	30.9	53.2	17.2	4.6	6.6	13.1	-17.9

% RETURN AT YEAR END

FUND NAME	FUND CATEGORY		JUN89	JUN90	JUN91	JUN92	JUN93	JUN94	JUN95	JUN96	JUN97	JUN98
Beutel Goodman American Eq	LgCap	USEq	-	-	-	7.9	11.3	30.1	16.9	10.8	24.1	18.2
Beutel Goodman Private Fgn	Divers	USEq	-	-	8.8	12.8	16.3	23.6	11.7	17.4	33.4	31.9
Bissett American Equity	LgCap	USEq	8.1	4.0	6.8	12.6	7.6	13.2	19.8	20.1	21.5	22.1
C.I. American	LgCap	USEq	-	-	-	-	16.5	-	21.6	21.2	23.3	24.7
C.I. American RSP	LgCap	USEq	-	-	-	-	-	-	-	-	22.7	27.9
C.I. American Sector	LgCap	USEq	-	-	-	-	16.0	-	21.1	20.6	22.3	22.5
CCPE US Equity	Divers	USEq	-	-	-	-	-	-	-	10.2	36.3	35.7
CDA U.S. Equity (KBSH)	Divers	USEq	-	-	-	-	-	-	-	-	-	24.3
CIBC North Amer Demograph	Divers	USEq	-	-	-	-	-	-	-	-	-	41.4
CIBC U.S. Index RRSP	Divers	USEq	-	-	-	-	-	-	-	-	-	36.2
CIBC U.S. Small Companies	SmCap	USEq	-	-	-	-	-	-	-	-	5.2	19.8
CIBC US Equity	LgCap	USEq	-	-	-	16.6	3.6	16.9	11.6	24.6	20.5	35.0
CT AmeriGrowth	LgCap	USEq	-	-	-	-	0.4	-	25.4	24.4	28.5	26.0
CT U.S. Equity	LgCap	USEq	-	-	-	4.8	0.6	19.4	19.0	10.7	23.9	22.3
CT U.S. Equity Index	Divers	USEq	-	-	-	-	-	-	-	-	-	35.9
Caldwell American Equity	LgCap	USEq	-	-	-	-	-	-	-	-	-	16.0
Cambridge American Growth	SmCap	USEq	-	-	-	-	1.4	4.7	6.1	-18.2	28.8	14.2
Century DJ	LgCap	USEq	5.2	17.7	3.3	4.7	2.8	7.2	2.4	6.2	4.9	4.4
Clarington U.S. Equity	Divers	USEq	-	-	-	-	-	-	-	-	-	36.1
Clarington US SmallerCo Gw	Divers	USEq	-	-	-	-	-	-	-	-	-	32.9
Co-Operators U.S. Equity	LgCap	USEq	-	-	-	-	-	-	51.8	24.3	38.7	30.1
Cornerstone US	LgCap	USEq	11.4	15.1	0.5	10.9	7.8	13.7	17.0	19.2	34.0	34.2
Cote 100 US	Divers	USEq	-	-	-	-	-	-	-	-	-	-6.5
Desjardins American Market	Divers	USEq	-	-	-	-	-	-	-	-	24.0	29.4
Dynamic Americas	Divers	USEq	16.4	7.5	-4.0	11.8	4.3	15.7	3.1	36.8	32.6	28.8
Elliott & Page Amer Gth	LgCap	USEq	8.9	14.7	-0.9	8.4	8.6	15.7	16.9	11.3	36.3	35.6
Ethical North Amer Equity	LgCap	USEq	9.3	-3.6	3.2	6.4	3.6	14.1	22.9	18.5	36.7	55.9
Fidelity Focus Consum Ind	Divers	USEq	-	-	-	-	-	-	-	-	-	43.8
Fidelity Focus Financ Serv	Divers	USEq	-	-	-	-	-	-	-	-	-	49.5
Fidelity Growth America	LgCap	USEq	-	-	-	-	8.6	28.4	26.8	17.1	25.0	34.5
Fidelity Small Cap America	SmCap	USEq	-	-	-	23.2	-	-	25.6	11.0	24.6	27.5
First Canadian US Growth	LgCap	USEq	-	-	-	-	-	-	22.8	0.1	33.5	34.8
First Canadian US Value	Divers	USEq	-	-	-	-	-	-	-	-	-	36.1
First Cdn US Eq Index RSP	Divers	USEq	-	-	-	-	-	-	-	-	-	25.6
First Cdn US Special Gth	Divers	USEq	-	-	-	-	-	-	-	-	33.9	28.3
FirstTrust DJIATarget10 96	Divers	USEq	-	-	-	-	-	-	-	-	-	21.5
FirstTrust DJIATarget10 97	Divers	USEq	-	-	-	-	-	-	-	-	-	20.4
Fonds de Croissance Select	Divers	USEq	-	-	-	-	-	-	15.4	22.9	34.5	26.6
Formula Growth	Divers	USEq	7.8	-1.4	-6.3	33.0	9.2	60.9	31.7	40.1	11.3	35.5
Franklin US Small Cap Gth	SmCap	USEq	-	-	-	-	-	-	-	-	-	24.5
GS American Equity	Divers	USEq	-	-	-	-	-	-	-	-	32.5	30.9
Global Mgr-US Bear	Divers	USEq	-	-	-	-	-	-	-	-15.8	-19.4	-21.6
Global Mgr-US Geared	Divers	USEq	-	-	-	-	-	-	-	41.0	56.6	49.3

% RETURN AT YEAR END

FUND NAME	FUND CATEGORY		JUN98	JUN97	JUN96	JUN95	JUN94	JUN93	JUN92	JUN91	JUN90	JUN89
Global Mgr-US Index	USEq	Divers	27.9	29.2	22.3	-	-	-	-	-	-	-
Global Strategy US Equity	USEq	Divers	28.8	22.9	24.2	-	-	-	-	-	-	-
Great-West US Equity (G) A	USEq	LgCap	30.8	24.4	13.5	-	-	-	-	-	-	-
Great-West US Equity (G) B	USEq	LgCap	31.1	24.7	13.7	-	-	-	-	-	-	-
Green Line US Blue Chip Eq	USEq	LgCap	36.0	-	-	-	-	-	-	-	-	-
Green Line US Index	USEq	Divers	29.1	33.4	24.5	24.3	11.2	0.6	11.8	5.4	14.0	17.7
Green Line US Mid-Cap Gth	USEq	Divers	37.3	16.0	27.9	22.8	-	-	-	-	-	-
GrowSafe US 21st Century	USEq	Divers	45.2	-	-	-	-	-	-	-	-	-
GrowSafe US 500 Index	USEq	Divers	34.6	31.6	-	-	-	-	-	-	-	-
Guardian American Equity C	USEq	LgCap	18.2	21.7	14.5	22.9	22.7	11.8	16.0	4.2	11.3	12.3
Guardian American Equity M	USEq	LgCap	17.4	21.1	-	-	-	-	-	-	-	-
Hongkong Bank U.S. Equity	USEq	Divers	33.0	33.4	17.5	-	-	-	-	-	-	-
Ind. Alliance Ecoflex S	USEq	Divers	42.9	-	-	-	-	-	-	-	-	-
Ind. Alliance US Equity	USEq	Divers	44.0	-	-	-	-	-	-	-	-	-
Industrial American	USEq	LgCap	21.0	22.2	11.6	12.0	19.4	11.0	10.5	-1.1	7.7	8.3
Infinity International	USEq	Divers	30.2	-	-	-	-	-	-	-	-	-
Investors US Growth	USEq	LgCap	44.0	37.4	18.8	12.8	18.6	15.9	21.7	8.1	7.7	15.8
Investors US Opportunities	USEq	Divers	27.7	-	-	-	-	-	-	-	-	-
Jones Heward American	USEq	LgCap	35.9	28.3	10.9	2.0	26.2	2.6	9.4	3.6	5.2	20.9
Leith Wheeler US Equity	USEq	Divers	17.6	22.4	15.4	22.0	-	-	-	-	-	-
London Life US Equity	USEq	Divers	36.7	35.8	18.5	7.3	18.3	4.9	14.3	-3.0	-7.5	18.6
MAXXUM American Equity	USEq	LgCap	41.0	26.7	30.6	25.6	10.3	9.4	18.2	5.4	21.4	22.4
MB American Equity	USEq	LgCap	27.3	41.1	21.6	23.5	-	9.6	-	-	-	-
MD US Equity	USEq	Divers	57.2	33.3	21.1	-	-	-	-	-	-	-
MLI AGF American Grth GIF	USEq	Divers	43.7	-	-	-	-	-	-	-	-	-
MLI Fidelity Gth Amer GIF	USEq	Divers	33.1	-	-	-	-	-	-	-	-	-
MLI GT Glo America Gth GIF	USEq	Divers	33.2	-	-	-	-	-	-	-	-	-
Manulife Vistafd1 Am Stock	USEq	Divers	23.3	16.5	18.3	-	-	-	-	-	-	-
Manulife Vistafd2 Am Stock	USEq	Divers	22.4	15.6	17.4	-	-	-	-	-	-	-
Marathon Perf Large Cap US	USEq	LgCap	-	-	-	-	-	-	-	-	-	-
Margin of Safety	USEq	Divers	17.8	29.9	18.1	9.5	14.1	7.6	3.9	16.2	5.3	-
Maritime Life Am Gth&IncAC	USEq	LgCap	26.3	25.2	19.6	13.8	-	-	-	-	-	-
Maritime Life Am Gth&Inc B	USEq	LgCap	26.2	-	-	-	-	-	-	-	-	-
Maritime Life Discovery AC	USEq	SmCap	22.6	-	-	-	-	-	-	-	-	-
Maritime Life Discovery B	USEq	SmCap	23.3	-	-	-	-	-	-	-	-	-
Maritime Life S&P 500 A&C	USEq	Divers	24.7	28.0	24.0	-	-	-	-	-	-	-
Maritime Life S&P 500 B	USEq	Divers	24.7	-	-	-	-	-	-	-	-	-
Mawer US Equity	USEq	LgCap	34.3	29.2	20.1	17.0	-	4.6	-	-	-	-
McDonald New America	USEq	LgCap	16.2	14.6	-	-	-	-	-	-	-	-
Mclean Budden American Gth	USEq	LgCap	27.3	36.0	19.3	23.1	8.4	6.2	15.3	15.1	17.6	-
Metlife Mvp US Equity	USEq	Divers	41.9	30.9	21.5	14.3	-	7.2	-	-	-	-
Millennia III Amer Eq 1	USEq	LgCap	24.9	16.7	-	-	-	-	-	-	-	-
Millennia III Amer Eq 2	USEq	LgCap	24.5	16.5	-	-	-	-	-	-	-	-

% RETURN AT YEAR END

FUND NAME	FUND CATEGORY		JUN98	JUN97	JUN96	JUN95	JUN94	JUN93	JUN92	JUN91	JUN90	JUN89
Montrusco Select NTx US Eq	USEq	Divers	30.2	34.6	19.0	18.0	19.8	3.0	3.9	5.0	17.6	13.9
Montrusco Select Strat US	USEq	Divers	18.8	33.8	-	-	-	-	-	-	-	-
Montrusco Select Tax US Eq	USEq	Divers	18.1	33.7	16.7	20.0	19.6	4.1	2.4	6.4	16.8	14.3
Montrusco Select U.S. Gth	USEq	Divers	0.8	-	-	-	-	-	-	-	-	-
Mutual Amerifund	USEq	LgCap	30.1	34.3	16.3	13.5	17.1	9.2	6.4	-2.6	3.5	10.4
Mutual Premier American	USEq	LgCap	28.4	33.4	15.3	12.2	-	9.0	-	-	-	-
NAL-U.S. Equity	USEq	Divers	34.9	35.9	9.6	17.9	-	-	-	-	-	-
NN Can-Am	USEq	Divers	24.1	27.2	22.9	24.9	-	-0.5	-	-	-	-
NN Can-Daq 100	USEq	Divers	33.7	-	-	-	-	-	-	-	-	-
National Trust American Eq	USEq	LgCap	40.7	26.4	18.8	11.2	-	4.9	-	-	-	-
National Trust U.S. Index	USEq	Divers	37.1	-	-	-	-	-	-	-	-	-
Navigator American Growth	USEq	Divers	25.3	-	-	-	-	-	-	-	-	-
Navigator American Value	USEq	LgCap	28.4	24.3	19.2	-	-	-	-	-	-	-
North West Life Ecoflex S	USEq	Divers	42.9	-	-	-	-	-	-	-	-	-
O'Donnell Amer Sector Grth	USEq	LgCap	21.5	5.5	-	-	-	-	-	-	-	-
O'Donnell U.S. Mid-Cap	USEq	Divers	34.9	17.4	-	-	-	-	-	-	-	-
O.I.Q. Ferique America	USEq	Divers	37.0	33.4	-	-	-	-	-	-	-	-
Optima Strat-US Equity	USEq	LgCap	38.5	40.0	30.2	14.3	-	-	-	-	-	-
PH & N Pooled US Pension	USEq	LgCap	26.7	32.0	30.2	13.5	24.8	13.8	12.9	10.5	19.4	13.8
PH & N US Equity	USEq	LgCap	24.8	30.4	28.6	12.6	23.2	12.4	12.8	9.7	17.6	13.1
Pret et Revenu Americain	USEq	Divers	18.0	-0.2	38.6	19.0	7.6	4.6	20.4	3.1	13.6	11.2
Primus U.S. Equity	USEq	Divers	39.5	-	-	-	-	-	-	-	-	-
Royal Monthly Income	USEq	Divers	40.3	34.9	-	-	-	-	-	-	-	-
Royal US Gth Strategic Idx	USEq	LgCap	20.7	32.1	12.7	19.8	19.6	8.7	12.9	1.8	18.2	16.1
SSQ - Actions Americaines	USEq	LgCap	25.9	26.7	29.1	21.1	9.7	5.9	9.8	10.1	33.0	-
Scotia CanAm Growth	USEq	LgCap	25.4	28.9	24.3	24.9	-	-	-	-	-	-
Scotia Ex. American Gth	USEq	Divers	30.5	18.0	10.6	16.7	16.7	11.3	8.3	6.8	11.4	-5.9
Scudder US Growth & Income	USEq	Divers	27.1	-	-	-	-	-	-	-	-	-
Spectrum Utd American Eq	USEq	LgCap	31.7	24.3	29.9	20.4	7.0	2.0	13.8	8.4	3.4	25.7
Spectrum Utd American Gth	USEq	Divers	40.4	11.2	38.2	28.9	22.7	7.3	13.1	12.6	2.2	19.8
Spectrum Utd Optimax USA	USEq	Divers	30.3	19.0	15.9	19.4	-	-	-	-	-	-
Standard Life US Equity	USEq	LgCap	30.7	30.7	17.8	-	-	-	-	-	-	-
Strategic Val American Eq	USEq	LgCap	29.1	17.4	15.1	19.3	18.2	8.6	8.6	-4.3	1.6	15.6
Tal/Hyper Value Line US Eq	USEq	LgCap	26.5	22.8	23.7	31.5	35.7	-3.3	16.9	-	-	-
Templeton Mutual Beacon	USEq	Divers	22.0	-	-	-	-	-	-	-	-	-
Universal US Emerg Growth	USEq	SmCap	20.2	-6.7	43.3	41.9	44.1	3.6	-	-	-	-
University Avenue Growth	USEq	Divers	33.0	11.5	13.9	10.3	-6.3	-0.5	-6.1	2.0	0.6	18.1
University U.S. Small Cap	USEq	Divers	26.5	-	-	-	-	-	-	-	-	-
Valorem U.S. Equity-Value	USEq	Divers	22.0	-	-	-	-	-	-	-	-	-
Zweig Strategic Growth	USEq	Divers	29.0	16.9	18.5	9.7	27.3	13.1	-	-	-	-
20/20 Aggr Global Stock	FgnEq	Global	27.3	7.1	-	-	-	-	-	-	-	-
20/20 Emerging Mkts Value	FgnEq	Emerg	-43.8	18.9	4.1	-12.9	-	-	-	-	-	-

% RETURN AT YEAR END

FUND NAME	FUND CATEGORY		JUN98	JUN97	JUN96	JUN95	JUN94	JUN93	JUN92	JUN91	JUN90	JUN89
20/20 India	FgnEq	India	-16.8	-15.0	-22.0	-	-	-	-	-	-	-
20/20 Latin America	FgnEq	Latin	-35.9	67.3	9.6	3.5	-	-	-	-	-	-
ABC American-Value	FgnEq	NrthAm	34.4	31.4	-	-	-	-	-	-	-	-
AGF International Value	FgnEq	Global	18.2	31.1	13.8	11.1	15.4	21.9	5.5	5.1	10.0	-
AGF Intl Grp-Asian Growth	FgnEq	PacRim	-53.6	3.7	5.2	12.0	38.7	21.2	-	-	-	-
AGF Intl Grp-China Focus	FgnEq	China	-47.4	31.2	-2.4	-4.2	-	-	-	-	-	-
AGF Intl Grp-European Gth	FgnEq	Europe	52.1	15.5	17.0	15.7	-	-	-	-	-	-
AGF Intl Grp-Germany	FgnEq	German	43.8	36.1	14.9	-	-	-	-	-	-	-
AGF Intl Grp-Germany M	FgnEq	German	46.8	38.4	16.0	-	-	-	-	-	-	-
AGF Intl Grp-Intl Stock	FgnEq	IntlEq	15.4	-	-	-	-	-	-	-	-	-
AGF Intl Grp-Japan	FgnEq	Japan	-13.7	8.9	11.0	-22.3	21.8	32.9	-12.9	-16.8	16.0	-6.8
AGF Intl Grp-World Equity	FgnEq	Global	16.2	19.5	9.0	-1.8	-	-	-	-	-	-
AGF RSP Intl Equity Alloc	FgnEq	Global	15.2	16.4	26.9	0.4	-	-	-	-	-	-
AIC World Equity	FgnEq	IntlEq	33.6	27.3	7.4	8.1	3.0	-	-	-	-	-
AIM Europa	FgnEq	Europe	56.7	33.1	2.6	-	-	-	-	-	-	-
AIM GT Glbl Ntrl Res	FgnEq	Global	-7.6	5.2	33.4	-	-	-	-	-	-	-
AIM GT Global Theme Class	FgnEq	Global	29.6	-	-	-	-	-	-	-	-	-
AIM GT Latin Amer Grwth	FgnEq	Latin	-21.1	43.6	28.0	-	-	-	-	-	-	-
AIM GT Pacific Growth	FgnEq	PacRim	-48.2	25.2	15.3	-	-	-	-	-	-	-
AIM Global RSP Index	FgnEq	Global	20.2	-	-	-	-	-	-	-	-	-
AIM International	FgnEq	Global	17.8	25.2	3.4	-5.6	36.0	20.4	10.5	-13.2	17.8	-1.9
AIM Korea	FgnEq	Korean	-66.2	-20.7	-18.2	-0.1	32.8	8.6	-	-	-	-
AIM Nippon	FgnEq	Japan	-29.5	-2.2	40.3	-29.1	11.2	-	-	-	-	-
AIM Tiger	FgnEq	PacRim	-55.6	17.7	-9.9	-13.2	38.1	16.8	13.3	-8.9	-	-
APEX Asian Pacific	FgnEq	PacRim	-39.4	-2.1	8.9	0.4	-	-	-	-	-	-
APEX Global Equity	FgnEq	Global	25.3	-	-	-	-	-	-	-	-	-
Acuity Pld Global Equity	FgnEq	Global	24.3	33.9	26.0	15.8	-3.6	-	-	-	-	-
Allstar AIG Asian	FgnEq	PacRim	-53.7	-	-	-	-	-	-	-	-	-
Altamira Asia Pacific	FgnEq	PacRim	-38.5	-5.3	-5.3	-16.1	31.4	-	-	-	-	-
Altamira European Equity	FgnEq	Europe	40.6	24.6	16.1	11.1	-	-	-	-	-	-
Altamira Glo Small Company	FgnEq	Global	10.1	-	-	-	-	-	-	-	-	-
Altamira Global Discovery	FgnEq	Global	-30.4	26.4	11.0	-	-	-	-	-	-	-
Altamira Japanese Opp	FgnEq	Emerg	-26.9	-6.7	23.7	-	-	-	-	-	-	-
Altamira Nth Amer Recovery	FgnEq	NrthAm	12.2	32.8	8.2	6.8	-	-	-	-	-	-
Atlas European Value	FgnEq	Europe	38.3	27.8	16.5	11.5	25.9	15.2	15.8	-7.3	-	-
Atlas Global Value	FgnEq	Global	9.6	17.6	10.7	1.3	-	-	-	-	-	-
Atlas Intl Emerg Mkts Gth	FgnEq	Emerg	-10.7	-	-	-	-	-	-	-	-	-
Atlas Intl Large Cap Gth	FgnEq	IntlEq	27.9	-	-	-	-	-	-	-	-	-
Atlas Intl RSP Index	FgnEq	IntlEq	11.9	-	-	-	-	-	-	-	-	-
Atlas Latin American Value	FgnEq	Latin	-11.4	35.4	21.3	-22.2	-	-	-	-	-	-
Atlas Pacific Basin Value	FgnEq	PacRim	-20.2	-8.3	9.8	-16.7	-	-	-	-	-	-
Azura Growth Pooled	FgnEq	Global	6.9	-	-	-	-	-	-	-	-	-
BPI Asia Pacific	FgnEq	PacRim	-44.5	15.5	-	-	-	-	-	-	-	-

% RETURN AT YEAR END

FUND NAME	FUND CATEGORY	JUN98	JUN97	JUN96	JUN95	JUN94	JUN93	JUN92	JUN91	JUN90	JUN89
BPI Emerging Markets	FgnEq Emerg	-15.9	31.2	14.8	4.6	23.1	5.3	18.4	-2.5	17.8	11.3
BPI Global Equity Value	FgnEq Global	29.3	24.1	16.1							
BPI Global Opportunities	FgnEq Global	49.2	38.2	6.3	1.7						
BPI Global Small Companies	FgnEq Global	7.6	22.0			43.1					
BPI Intl Equity Value	FgnEq IntlEq	37.3									
Beutel Goodman Intl Equity	FgnEq IntlEq	1.5	16.1	14.3	-3.7	37.5					
Bissett International Eq	FgnEq IntlEq	14.3	15.7	8.8	7.9						
Bissett Multinational Gth	FgnEq Global	27.4	37.6	23.2							
C.I. Emerging Markets	FgnEq Emerg	-8.9	15.6	5.3	-10.8	30.5	13.4				
C.I. Emerging Mkts Sector	FgnEq Emerg	-9.2	15.0	4.6	-10.8	29.9					
C.I. Glo Consumer Prod Sec	FgnEq Global	24.0									
C.I. Glo Financial Ser Sec	FgnEq Global	40.3									
C.I. Global	FgnEq Global	24.3	20.3	13.8	-0.3	19.6	17.3	21.7	2.2	10.8	2.9
C.I. Global Equity RSP	FgnEq Global	14.9	16.8	16.8	-2.8						
C.I. Global Resource Sect	FgnEq Global	-21.6									
C.I. Global Sector	FgnEq Global	23.4	19.0	13.1	-0.5	19.5	17.3	19.7	3.2	10.4	2.2
C.I. Latin American	FgnEq Latin	-25.1	24.0	13.3	-15.0						
C.I. Latin American Sector	FgnEq Latin	-25.5	23.5	12.8							
C.I. Pacific	FgnEq PacRim	-49.3	21.3	5.1	-3.7	36.3	24.6	15.4	-7.0	22.1	2.0
C.I. Pacific Sector	FgnEq PacRim	-49.7	20.5	4.7	-4.0	35.7	24.2	15.3	-7.0	20.6	1.8
CCPE Global Equity	FgnEq Global	12.4	14.9	15.0							
CDA Emerging Markets(KBSH)	FgnEq Emerg	-35.8	-0.9	5.3							
CDA European (KBSH)	FgnEq Europe	37.6	18.5	21.0							
CDA Global (Trimark)	FgnEq Global	7.4									
CDA Intl Equity (KBSH)	FgnEq IntlEq	3.6	11.8	21.2							
CDA Pacific Basin (KBSH)	FgnEq PacRim	-24.9	9.9	23.1							
CGO&V International	FgnEq IntlEq	2.0									
CIBC Emerging Economies	FgnEq Emerg	-12.6	23.5								
CIBC European Equity	FgnEq Europe	33.2	13.4								
CIBC Far East Prosperity	FgnEq PacRim	-35.0	2.6	9.7	3.3						
CIBC Global Equity	FgnEq Global	27.5	20.4	11.5	1.9	14.7	9.4	23.4	-10.7	13.4	5.4
CIBC Intl Index RRSP	FgnEq IntlEq	11.2									
CIBC Japanese Equity	FgnEq Japan	-5.4	13.2								
CIBC Latin American	FgnEq Latin	-19.4									
CT AsiaGrowth	FgnEq PacRim	-35.1	-2.1	25.4	-11.9						
CT Emerging Markets	FgnEq Emerg	-38.3	17.8	5.7							
CT EuroGrowth	FgnEq Europe	32.3	31.2	17.1	6.0						
CT GlobalGrowth	FgnEq Global	9.0									
CT International	FgnEq IntlEq	26.0	14.5	14.4	-7.0	25.0	11.6	3.1	-8.1	26.0	30.0
CT International Eq Index	FgnEq IntlEq	12.1									
CT North American	FgnEq NrthAm	13.7	24.5	9.8	4.4	-1.0	29.8	5.0	1.6	-0.2	11.9
Cambridge Americas	FgnEq Amrcas	44.6	-2.0	27.4	7.5	-1.6	21.3	12.6	-0.2	10.0	2.9
Cambridge China	FgnEq China	-16.7	-21.3	4.2	12.4						

% RETURN AT YEAR END

FUND NAME	FUND CATEGORY		JUN98	JUN97	JUN96	JUN95	JUN94	JUN93	JUN92	JUN91	JUN90	JUN89
Cambridge Global	FgnEq	Global	-39.5	-45.1	8.7	7.5	8.5	18.9	8.7	-6.9	-2.7	6.5
Cambridge Pacific	FgnEq	PacRim	-45.6	-24.7	-7.0	0.3	14.3	19.5	-0.4	1.4	12.1	-50.3
Canada Life AsiaPacific Eq	FgnEq	PacRim	-28.2	2.3								
Canada Life European Eq	FgnEq	Europe	32.2	26.1								
Canada Life US & Intl	FgnEq	Global	18.4	28.6	17.1	13.0	17.4	18.7	19.7	3.0	13.3	17.5
Capstone Intl Invest Tr	FgnEq	Global	23.1	-1.1	27.4	6.1	13.0	19.1	12.9	4.5	14.5	10.4
CentrePost Foreign Equity	FgnEq	Global	23.1	28.0	7.2	19.8	20.9					
Champion Growth	FgnEq	NrthAm	20.5	33.7	12.8	12.3						
Chou Associates	FgnEq	NrthAm	22.9	42.1	21.1	14.4	4.8	24.2	17.0	5.1	-4.1	18.6
Clarington Global Oppor	FgnEq	Global	27.3									
Clean Environment Intl Eq	FgnEq	NrthAm	43.1	25.6	17.3	3.4						
Cornerstone Global	FgnEq	Global	14.4	19.5	17.3	9.1	20.5	13.7	10.5	1.3	19.0	7.9
Cote 100 Amerique	FgnEq	NrthAm	12.7	21.0	27.0	15.2	4.9					
Cundill Value A	FgnEq	Global	-5.8	14.1	12.8	11.3	23.4	25.1	9.7	-5.7	1.6	10.4
Cundill Value B	FgnEq	Global	-6.2									
Desjardins International	FgnEq	Global	12.2	13.5	16.9	1.7	24.9	16.3	15.3	-2.1	15.8	17.1
Dynamic Europe	FgnEq	Europe	39.0	40.5	17.2	9.4	21.2	-1.3	8.1	-17.4		
Dynamic Far East	FgnEq	PacRim	-28.9	23.4	8.0	1.6						
Dynamic Global Resource	FgnEq	Global	-17.8	15.0	57.2							
Dynamic International	FgnEq	Global	11.1	25.7	17.9	6.2	8.5	28.2	9.5	10.9	-9.6	-2.6
Dynamic Latin American	FgnEq	Latin	-17.1									
Elliott & Page Asian Gth	FgnEq	PacRim	-31.0	4.1	10.2							
Elliott & Page Emerg Mkt	FgnEq	Emerg	-27.3	22.5	3.5							
Elliott & Page Global Eq	FgnEq	Global	17.0	18.9	17.2							
Empire International Gth	FgnEq	Global	11.5	26.4	10.5	7.4	15.7	16.7	17.3	3.2	13.2	
Equitable Life Intl	FgnEq	Global	16.4	16.8	27.3							
Ethical Pacific Rim	FgnEq	PacRim	-57.9	31.0	10.4							
FMOQ International Equity	FgnEq	Global	27.6	18.7	12.0	-10.9						
Fidelity Emerg Mkts Ptf	FgnEq	Emerg	-47.7	-11.7	29.4							
Fidelity European Growth	FgnEq	Europe	45.4	24.9	17.1	15.4	22.7	6.6				
Fidelity Far East	FgnEq	PacRim	-38.7	20.5	17.5	9.0	24.7	29.1				
Fidelity Focus Nat Resourc	FgnEq	NrthAm	6.9									
Fidelity Intl Portfolio	FgnEq	Global	24.1	26.2	17.2	4.9	19.7	23.2	10.3	-7.4	22.8	11.6
Fidelity Japanese Growth	FgnEq	Japan	-21.1	-1.7	10.4	-24.4						
Fidelity Latin Amer Growth	FgnEq	Latin	-19.2	43.3	24.6	-27.0						
First American	FgnEq	NrthAm	6.6	-5.2	3.4	5.8	-7.4	32.9				
First Canadian Emerg Mkt	FgnEq	Emerg	-28.2	19.3	4.9							
First Canadian Europe Gth	FgnEq	Europe	35.1	23.8	10.8							
First Canadian FarEast Gth	FgnEq	PacRim	-43.8	12.5	14.0							
First Canadian Intl. Gth	FgnEq	IntlEq	12.3	7.6	17.3	-5.6	26.2					
First Canadian Japan Gth	FgnEq	Japan	-34.2	-11.4	11.8							
First Canadian NAFTA Adv	FgnEq	NrthAm	15.1	25.2	14.8							
First Cdn Latin America	FgnEq	Latin	-28.6									

% RETURN AT YEAR END

FUND NAME	FUND CATEGORY	JUN98	JUN97	JUN96	JUN95	JUN94	JUN93	JUN92	JUN91	JUN90	JUN89
FirstTrust Glo Target15 97	FgnEq IntEq	-3.6	-	-	-	-	-	-	-	-	-
FirstTrust Pharma 96	FgnEq Global	49.8	-	-	-	-	-	-	-	-	-
FirstTrust Pharma 97	FgnEq Global	44.8	-	-	-	-	-	-	-	-	-
FirstTrust Technology 97	FgnEq NrthAm	19.7	-	-	-	-	-	-	-	-	-
GBC International Growth	FgnEq IntEq	11.7	9.4	9.5	-10.8	13.6	11.8	2.0	-12.5-	-	-
GBC North American Growth	FgnEq NrthAm	18.7	10.1	23.0	17.9	4.6	36.3	25.0	-5.5	-1.8	16.1
GFM Emerg Mkts Country $US	FgnEq Emerg	-29.9	19.6	8.4	-	-	-	-	-	-	-
GS International Equity	FgnEq Global	16.8	15.8	-	-	-	-	-	-	-	-
Global Mgr-German Bear	FgnEq German	-38.7	-40.1	-24.5	-	-	-	-	-	-	-
Global Mgr-German Geared	FgnEq German	107.9	70.2	22.4	-	-	-	-	-	-	-
Global Mgr-German Index	FgnEq German	46.7	26.5	7.6	-	-	-	-	-	-	-
Global Mgr-Hong Kong Bear	FgnEq China	35.4	-26.0	-18.7	-	-	-	-	-	-	-
Global Mgr-Hong Kong Geard	FgnEq China	-75.7	64.2	20.3	-	-	-	-	-	-	-
Global Mgr-Hong Kong Index	FgnEq China	-42.1	36.7	15.4	-	-	-	-	-	-	-
Global Mgr-Japan Bear	FgnEq Japan	4.7	-3.8	-52.3	-	-	-	-	-	-	-
Global Mgr-Japan Geared	FgnEq Japan	-58.9	-26.1	79.8	-	-	-	-	-	-	-
Global Mgr-Japan Index	FgnEq Japan	-37.1	-13.7	21.0	-	-	-	-	-	-	-
Global Mgr-UK Bear	FgnEq Europe	-19.1	-10.5	-9.9	-	-	-	-	-	-	-
Global Mgr-UK Geared	FgnEq Europe	52.2	59.6	19.3	-	-	-	-	-	-	-
Global Mgr-UK Index	FgnEq Europe	29.6	36.6	10.5	-	-	-	-	-	-	-
Global Strategy Asia	FgnEq PacRim	-53.8	3.0	9.1	0.3	-	-	-	-	-	-
Global Strategy Diver Asia	FgnEq PacRim	-49.8	-1.9	1.9	2.1	-	-	-	-	-	-
Global Strategy Diver Euro	FgnEq Europe	39.6	28.9	13.6	8.6	6.0	-	-	-	-	-
Global Strategy Diver Jap	FgnEq Japan	-30.8	-12.7	9.7	-19.0	-	-	-	-	-	-
Global Strategy Divers Latin	FgnEq Latin	-20.1	46.1	11.0	-15.3	-	-	-	-	-	-
Global Strategy Divers World	FgnEq Global	18.6	19.9	14.4	-	-	-	-	-	-	-
Global Strategy Euro Plus	FgnEq Europe	33.9	23.9	16.3	-	-	-	-	-	-	-
Global Strategy Japan	FgnEq Japan	-34.0	-14.8	9.6	-	-	-	-	-	-	-
Global Strategy Latin Amer	FgnEq Latin	-19.4	40.2	15.2	-8.1	-	-	-	-	-	-
Global Strategy World Comp	FgnEq Global	14.6	13.3	40.0	-	-	-	-	-	-	-
Global Strategy World Eq	FgnEq Global	17.5	15.8	20.0	-	-	-	-	-	-	-
Globeinvest Emerg Mkt Ctry	FgnEq Emerg	-30.8	17.0	-	-	-	-	-	-	-	-
Great-West Intl Eq (P) A	FgnEq IntEq	20.0	19.8	14.9	-	-	-	-	-	-	-
Great-West Intl Eq (P) B	FgnEq IntEq	20.3	20.1	15.2	-	-	-	-	-	-	-
Great-West Nth Amer Eq(B)A	FgnEq NrthAm	15.2	24.3	-	-	27.8	-	-	-	-	-
Great-West Nth Amer Eq(B)B	FgnEq NrthAm	15.5	24.6	-	-	-	-	-	-	-	-
Green Line Asian Growth	FgnEq PacRim	-49.9	11.5	3.9	-	-	-	-	-	-	-
Green Line Emerging Mkts	FgnEq Emerg	-31.3	12.6	11.7	8.0	-	-	-	-	-	-
Green Line European Growth	FgnEq Europe	38.7	27.2	22.8	-8.1	-	-	-	-	-	-
Green Line Global Select	FgnEq Global	14.3	15.2	21.1	6.4	-	-	-	-	-	-
Green Line Intl Equity	FgnEq IntEq	8.0	13.0	12.3	-5.6	27.5	-	-	-	-	-
Green Line Japanese Growth	FgnEq Japan	-25.4	-2.5	10.5	-	-	-	-	-	-	-
Green Line Latin Amer Gth.	FgnEq Latin	-12.7	30.8	17.2	-	-	-	-	-	-	-

% RETURN AT YEAR END

FUND NAME	FUND CATEGORY		JUN98	JUN97	JUN96	JUN95	JUN94	JUN93	JUN92	JUN91	JUN90	JUN89
Greystone Managed Global	FgnEq	Global	31.0	22.2	23.3	0.9	-	-	-	-	-	-
GrowSafe European 100	FgnEq	Europe	37.3	-	-	-	-	-	-	-	-	-
GrowSafe Japanese 225	FgnEq	Japan	-35.8	-	-	-	-	-	-	-	-	-
Guardian Asia Pacific C	FgnEq	PacRim	-40.8	1.9	10.5	-	-	-	-	-	-	-
Guardian Asia Pacific M	FgnEq	PacRim	-41.3	1.3	-	-	-	-	-	-	-	-
Guardian Emerging Mkts C	FgnEq	Emerg	-28.7	10.7	12.7	-	-	-	-	-	-	-
Guardian Emerging Mkts M	FgnEq	Emerg	-29.3	10.3	-	-	-	-	-	-	-	-
Guardian Global Equity C	FgnEq	Global	15.4	13.6	17.5	4.0	26.2	6.4	0.7	-12.1	10.0	8.8
Guardian Global Equity M	FgnEq	Global	15.1	12.9	-	-	-	-	-	-	-	-
Hansberger Asian	FgnEq	PacRim	-59.8	1.4	2.2	-2.3	-	-	-	-	-	-
Hansberger Asian Sector	FgnEq	PacRim	-60.1	0.7	1.9	-	-	-	-	-	-	-
Hansberger Dev Markets Sec	FgnEq	Emerg	-42.4	-	-	-	-	-	-	-	-	-
Hansberger Developing Mkts	FgnEq	Emerg	-41.7	11.5	-	-	-	-	-	-	-	-
Hansberger European	FgnEq	Europe	25.2	27.4	7.1	7.1	13.7	-4.6	-	-	-	-
Hansberger European Sector	FgnEq	Europe	23.6	26.4	6.8	6.9	13.3	-	-	-	-	-
Hansberger Glo Small Cap	FgnEq	Global	-6.7	16.3	-	-	-	-	-	-	-	-
Hansberger Glo Small Cap S	FgnEq	Global	-7.5	-	-	-	-	-	-	-	-	-
Hansberger International	FgnEq	IntlEq	-8.1	16.5	-	-	-	-	-	-	-	-
Hansberger Intl Sector	FgnEq	IntlEq	-8.7	-	-	-	-	-	-	-	-	-
Hansberger Value	FgnEq	Global	-9.7	24.0	-	-	-	-	-	-	-	-
Hansberger Value Sector	FgnEq	Global	-10.3	-	-	-	-	-	-	-	-	-
Hongkong Bank Asian Growth	FgnEq	PacRim	-47.0	4.3	7.1	8.8	-	-	-	-	-	-
Hongkong Bank Emerging Mkt	FgnEq	Emerg	-32.8	12.7	1.3	-	-	-	-	-	-	-
Hongkong Bank European Gth	FgnEq	Europe	44.7	26.3	17.1	-	-	-	-	-	-	-
ICM International	FgnEq	IntlEq	7.9	21.0	15.6	2.7	25.8	-	-	-	-	-
Imperial Gth N.A. Equity	FgnEq	NrthAm	24.2	20.0	15.3	18.9	11.8	21.1	8.2	-12.1	-5.7	12.1
Ind. Alliance Ecoflex E	FgnEq	Emerg	-36.7	-	-	-	-	-	-	-	-	-
Ind. Alliance Ecoflex I	FgnEq	IntlEq	9.0	23.9	-	-	-	-	-	-	-	-
Ind. Alliance Emerging Mkt	FgnEq	Emerg	-36.2	-	-	-	-	-	-	-	-	-
Ind. Alliance Intl.	FgnEq	IntlEq	9.8	24.6	-	-	-	-	-	-	-	-
InvesNat European Equity	FgnEq	Europe	45.9	20.0	12.2	9.8	27.6	-7.9	-	-	-	-
InvesNat Far East Equity	FgnEq	PacRim	-42.2	10.7	14.2	-	-	-	-	-	-	-
InvesNat Japanese Equity	FgnEq	Japan	-30.5	-13.5	9.2	-	-	-	-	-	-	-
Investors European Growth	FgnEq	Europe	38.3	24.3	13.5	13.2	18.6	-2.0	24.5	-6.4	20.5	3.0
Investors Global	FgnEq	Global	22.9	15.6	17.0	5.1	23.4	8.4	14.3	-1.1	7.1	-
Investors Growth Portfolio	FgnEq	Global	19.9	23.5	15.2	7.1	17.7	22.5	8.5	-9.4	-1.7	-2.6
Investors Japanese Growth	FgnEq	Japan	-29.6	-7.7	5.5	-16.1	30.4	37.7	-6.7	-	-	-
Investors Latin Amer Grth	FgnEq	Latin	-27.1	-	-	-	-	-	-	-	-	-
Investors Nth American Gth	FgnEq	NrthAm	8.9	24.6	12.4	15.1	5.7	23.7	13.9	7.1	7.9	21.7
Investors Pacific Intl.	FgnEq	PacRim	-51.3	5.0	6.4	4.5	43.6	17.0	26.4	-	-	-
Investors Special	FgnEq	Global	11.9	26.3	11.1	10.6	-0.6	36.4	11.8	9.5	12.0	18.3
Investors World Gth. Port	FgnEq	Global	-2.7	15.1	10.2	5.6	18.5	-	-	-	-	-
Ivy Foreign Equity	FgnEq	Global	21.5	24.2	13.1	17.2	10.2	-	-	-	-	-

% RETURN AT YEAR END

FUND NAME	FUND CATEGORY		JUN98	JUN97	JUN96	JUN95	JUN94	JUN93	JUN92	JUN91	JUN90	JUN89
London Life Intl Equity	FgnEq	IntlEq	6.8	3.7	13.4	-	-	-	-	-	-	-
MAXXUM Global Equity	FgnEq	Global	28.3	14.1	-	-	-	-	-	-	-	-
MB Global Equity	FgnEq	Global	22.6	23.5	10.0	-	-	-	-	-	-	-
MD Emerging Markets	FgnEq	Emerg	-48.0	21.6	-	-	-	-	-	-	-	-
MD Growth Investments	FgnEq	Global	17.1	26.7	16.7	7.4	28.4	14.9	21.3	-9.6	10.1	8.7
MLI Fidelity Int Portf GIF	FgnEq	IntlEq	23.1	-	-	-	-	-	-	-	-	-
MLI Trimark Select Gth GIF	FgnEq	Global	4.2	-	-	-	-	-	-	-	-	-
Mackenzie Sentinel Global	FgnEq	IntlEq	15.8	11.1	14.4	-1.8	27.0	17.2	1.3	-15.3	10.1	-
Manulife Cabot Global Eq.	FgnEq	Global	12.9	18.1	13.1	6.0	-	-	-	-	-	-
Manulife Vistafd1 Glo Eq	FgnEq	IntlEq	9.5	16.7	13.1	-	-	-	-	-	-	-
Manulife Vistafd2 Glo Eq	FgnEq	IntlEq	8.6	15.8	12.2	-	-	-	-	-	-	-
Maritime Life EurAsia A&C	FgnEq	IntlEq	13.5	-	-	-	-	-	-	-	-	-
Maritime Life EurAsia B	FgnEq	IntlEq	13.5	-	-	-	-	-	-	-	-	-
Maritime Life Glo Eq A&C	FgnEq	Global	14.8	16.5	9.9	-	-	-	-	-	-	-
Maritime Life Global Eq B	FgnEq	Global	14.8	-	-	-	-	-	-	-	-	-
Maritime Life Pacif BasinB	FgnEq	PacRim	-43.4	-	12.7	-10.9	-	-	-	-	-	-
Maritime Life Pacif Eq A&C	FgnEq	PacRim	-43.4	6.6	13.3	3.5	26.4	5.1	-	-	-	-
Mawer World Investment	FgnEq	IntlEq	8.8	31.5	-	-	-	-	25.0	0.7	10.1	-
McDonald Asia Plus	FgnEq	PacRim	-35.2	9.6	-	-	-	-	-	-	-	-
McDonald Emerg Economies	FgnEq	Emerg	-21.9	11.8	-	-	-	-	-	-	-	-
McDonald Enhanced Glob	FgnEq	Global	24.6	-	-	-	-	-	-	-	-	-
McDonald Euro Plus	FgnEq	Europe	26.1	15.9	-	-	-	-	-	-	-	-
McDonald New Japan	FgnEq	Japan	-26.9	-9.3	-	-	-	-	-	-	-	-
Merrill Lynch Emerg Mkts	FgnEq	Emerg	-30.8	18.2	-	-	-	-	-	-	-	-
MetLife Mvp Asian-Pac RSP	FgnEq	PacRim	-25.5	-	-	-	-	-	-	-	-	-
MetLife Mvp Global Equity	FgnEq	Global	19.3	-	-	-	-	-	-	-	-	-
Millennia III Intl Eq 1	FgnEq	Global	13.2	11.1	-	-	-	-	-	-	-	-
Millennia III Intl Eq 2	FgnEq	Global	13.1	11.0	-	-	-	-	-	-	-	-
Montrusco Select E.A.F.E.	FgnEq	IntlEq	9.0	13.2	18.3	0.7	25.9	9.4	12.3	-14.7	16.2	5.1
Montrusco Select Emerg Mkt	FgnEq	Emerg	-41.0	13.8	13.4	1.2	47.8	-	-	-	-	-
Mutual Alpine Asian	FgnEq	PacRim	-48.0	-	-	-	-	-	-	-	-	-
Mutual Premier Emerg Mkts	FgnEq	Emerg	-31.4	9.2	-	-	-	-	-	-	-	-
Mutual Premier Intl.	FgnEq	IntlEq	16.3	15.0	14.3	3.4	23.5	-	-	-	-	-
Mutual Summit Foreign Eq	FgnEq	Global	18.8	-	-	-	-	20.7	-	-	-	-
NAL-Global Equity	FgnEq	Global	11.6	14.2	14.5	-0.3	29.5	-	-	-	-	-
NN Can-Asian	FgnEq	PacRim	-34.9	9.7	31.9	-11.1	-	-	-	-	-	-
NN Can-Emerge	FgnEq	Emerg	-38.2	2.3	-	-	-	-	-	-	-	-
NN Can-Euro	FgnEq	Europe	37.7	34.7	19.9	-	-	-	-	-	-	-
National Global Equities	FgnEq	Global	1.7	23.4	16.4	2.2	25.0	13.0	16.3	-1.5	23.8	-
National Trust Emerg Mkts.	FgnEq	Emerg	-37.6	21.4	3.5	-	-	-	-	-	-	-
National Trust Intl Equity	FgnEq	IntlEq	16.6	5.7	18.8	-	-	-	-	-	-	-
Navigator Asia Pacific	FgnEq	PacRim	-26.9	57.5	9.9	-	-	-	-	-	-	-
North West Life Ecoflex E	FgnEq	IntlEq	-36.7	-	-	-	-	-	-	-	-	-

FUND NAME	FUND CATEGORY	JUN89	JUN90	JUN91	JUN92	JUN93	JUN94	JUN95	JUN96	JUN97	JUN98
North West Life Ecoflex I	FgnEq / IntlEq	-	-	-	-	-	-	-	-	-	9.0
Northwest International	FgnEq / Global	-	-	-	-	-	-	-	14.3	9.2	24.4
O'Donnell World Equity	FgnEq / Global	-	-	-	-	-	-	-	-	-	3.7
O.I.Q. Ferique Internation	FgnEq / IntlEq	-	-	-	5.0	20.4	5.3	-5.5	12.3	15.3	25.8
OTGIF Global	FgnEq / Global	-	-	-	-	-	-	9.9	12.9	21.2	15.7
Optima Strat-Intl Equity	FgnEq / Global	-	-	-	-	-	-	1.0	26.5	17.6	4.5
Optimum International	FgnEq / IntlEq	-	-	-	-	-	-	-	10.0	17.6	25.4
Orbit North American Eq.	FgnEq / NrthAm	-	-	-	-	-	-	-	-	25.9	20.7
Orbit World	FgnEq / Global	-	9.7	1.5	6.4	14.0	18.7	-7.0	-2.0	27.4	34.0
PH & N Intl Equity	FgnEq / IntlEq	-	-	-	-	-	-	2.1	11.5	14.5	4.4
PH & N North Amer Equity	FgnEq / NrthAm	-	-	-	-	-	7.3	-4.6	26.4	27.9	7.8
Pret et Revenu Intl	FgnEq / Global	-	-	-	-	-	-	-	13.8	18.0	16.1
Primus EAFE Equity	FgnEq / IntlEq	-	-	-	-	-	-	-	-	-	14.9
Primus Emerging Markets Eq	FgnEq / Emerg	-	-	-	-	-	-	-	-	16.4	-32.0
Pursuit Global Equity	FgnEq / IntlEq	-	-	-	-	-	-	-	-	-	13.2
Pursuit Growth	FgnEq / Global	-	-	-	-	-	-	-	-	-	25.5
Quebec Prof Intl Equity	FgnEq / Global	-	-	-	-	22.6	13.6	6.5	18.0	17.4	5.5
Royal&SunAlliance Balanced	FgnEq / PacRim	3.4	0.3	-11.8	18.9	5.7	24.5	0.2	8.6	-2.2	-50.5
Royal Canadian Money Mkt	FgnEq / Europe	-	-	-	-	-	24.6	10.6	13.3	23.7	41.7
Royal Canadian T-Bill	FgnEq / IntlEq	-	-	-	-	-	-	1.1	14.2	18.5	10.7
Royal Canadian Value	FgnEq / Japan	-6.9	-4.7	-8.5	-16.9	32.8	32.4	-25.0	7.2	-7.0	-17.5
Royal Cdn Strategic Index	FgnEq / Latin	-	-	-	-	-	-	-	-	24.8	-9.5
Royal International Equity	FgnEq / Emerg	-	-	-	-	-	-	-	-	-	-31.1
Royal Latin American	FgnEq / IntlEq	-	-	-	-	-	-	-	12.5	11.8	12.3
Saxon World Growth	FgnEq / Global	29.0	-5.2	-5.3	9.1	32.6	16.0	33.2	13.2	18.0	5.9
Sceptre Asian Growth	FgnEq / PacRim	19.5	19.1	-4.7	23.9	27.0	50.3	-10.8	14.5	4.9	-54.4
Sceptre International	FgnEq / Global	-	-	-	-	-	29.5	0.2	15.9	20.2	-4.9
Scotia Ex. European Gth	FgnEq / Europe	7.3	12.6	-1.3	10.1	19.6	19.5	2.4	10.9	18.6	32.8
Scotia Ex. International	FgnEq / Global	-	-	-	-	-	-	-	-	-	15.1
Scotia Ex. Latin American	FgnEq / Latin	-	-	-	-	-	-	-	32.4	34.8	-17.9
Scotia Ex. Pacific Rim	FgnEq / PacRim	-	-	-	-	-	-	-	12.7	14.4	-32.5
Scudder Emerging Markets	FgnEq / Emerg	-	-	-	-	-	-	-	-	31.7	-15.6
Scudder Global	FgnEq / Global	-	-	-	-	-	-	-	-	21.5	22.3
Scudder Greater Europe	FgnEq / Europe	-	-	-	-	-	-	-	-	23.7	54.4
Scudder Pacific	FgnEq / PacRim	-	-	-	-	-	-	-	-	13.7	-33.7
Special Opportunities	FgnEq / NrthAm	4.0	-8.0	5.8	-11.5	26.1	6.7	12.1	19.9	26.9	-21.7
Spectrum Utd Asian Dynasty	FgnEq / PacRim	-	-	-	-	-	-	-1.8	10.7	-0.1	-49.1
Spectrum Utd Emerging Mkts	FgnEq / Emerg	-	-	-	-	-	-	-6.0	27.9	28.0	-31.1
Spectrum Utd European Gth	FgnEq / Europe	-	-	-	-	-	-	-	27.1	19.7	48.0
Spectrum Utd Global Equity	FgnEq / Global	-	-	-	-	-	-	-3.3	20.4	18.2	18.3
Spectrum Utd Global Growth	FgnEq / Global	-	-	-	-	-	-	-4.1	9.6	-6.1	15.6
Standard Life Gth Equity	FgnEq / NrthAm	11.2	-14.5	-2.5	13.4	13.5	12.5	-	18.4	19.9	18.1
Standard Life Intl Equity	FgnEq / IntlEq	-	-	-	14.5	20.4	21.0	-	13.7	18.0	13.2

% RETURN AT YEAR END

% RETURN AT YEAR END

FUND NAME	FUND CATEGORY		JUN89	JUN90	JUN91	JUN92	JUN93	JUN94	JUN95	JUN96	JUN97	JUN98
Strategic Val Asia Pacific	FgnEq	PacRim	-	-	-	-	-	-	-	5.4	1.5	-39.9
Strategic Val Commonwealth	FgnEq	Global	14.4	6.6	-1.7	11.1	15.8	14.0	5.7	8.8	10.8	12.9
Strategic Val Emerging Mkt	FgnEq	Emerg	-	-	-	-	-	-	-	5.3	17.2	-35.1
Strategic Val Europe	FgnEq	Europe	-	-	-	-	-	-	-	11.3	24.3	39.2
Strategic Val Intl	FgnEq	Global	9.9	9.4	-4.8	8.2	17.7	18.0	5.5	9.9	11.0	13.0
Strategic Value	FgnEq	Global	-	-	-	-	-	-	-	-	22.8	-22.3
Talvest/Hyperion Asian	FgnEq	PacRim	-	-	-	23.6	16.7	42.0	3.7	5.7	5.0	-34.4
Talvest/Hyperion European	FgnEq	Europe	-	-	-11.7	30.8	0.5	17.5	11.8	10.3	27.6	39.4
Talvest Global RRSP	FgnEq	Global	-	-	-	-	-	19.1	-2.7	12.5	18.2	26.6
Templeton Emerging Markets	FgnEq	Emerg	-	-	-	-	19.6	29.5	0.0	11.9	31.4	-30.9
Templeton Glo Smaller Com	FgnEq	Global	-	8.1	-0.9	10.1	23.9	18.1	14.3	17.6	16.0	4.7
Templeton Growth	FgnEq	Global	17.9	14.0	-4.0	28.0	16.3	23.9	11.5	12.3	25.2	8.9
Templeton Intl Stock	FgnEq	IntlEq	-	7.9	-5.7	20.1	24.1	32.8	7.8	15.2	27.2	15.0
Tradex Emerg Mkts Country	FgnEq	Emerg	-	-	-	-	-	-	-	9.1	18.0	-26.4
Trimark Americas	FgnEq	Amrcas	-	-	-	-	-	11.7	1.1	21.7	21.5	-4.4
Trimark Fund	FgnEq	Global	14.9	8.6	0.7	20.0	28.6	23.2	20.1	15.8	22.9	7.4
Trimark Indo-Pacific	FgnEq	PacRim	-	-	-	-	-	-	-	11.0	23.3	-47.7
Trimark Select Growth	FgnEq	Global	-	11.4	0.0	20.3	25.9	19.2	18.4	14.2	20.4	5.4
Universal Americas	FgnEq	Amrcas	19.7	-0.6	0.0	13.6	22.0	12.1	-1.9	14.6	27.1	3.0
Universal Euro Opportunity	FgnEq	Europe	-	-	-	-	-	-	-	37.5	27.6	42.6
Universal Far East	FgnEq	PacRim	-	-	-	-	-	-	1.4	6.0	8.7	-50.7
Universal Growth	FgnEq	Global	-	-	-	-	-	-	-	9.8	27.2	13.7
Universal Intl Stock	FgnEq	IntlEq	2.8	8.5	-14.1	2.0	18.5	29.0	-1.4	15.2	12.1	16.6
Universal Japan	FgnEq	Japan	-	-	-	-	-	-	-24.3	13.1	2.2	-23.9
Universal World Emerg Gth	FgnEq	Emerg	-	-	-	-	-	-	-10.9	17.5	19.9	-24.1
Universal World Gth RRSP	FgnEq	IntlEq	-	-	-	-	-	-	-	20.1	25.5	1.0
Valorem Demographic Trends	FgnEq	NrthAm	-	-	-	-	-	-	-	-	-	29.2
Vision Europe	FgnEq	Europe	-	-	-	-	-2.1	16.4	13.5	15.4	27.9	41.5
YMG International	FgnEq	IntlEq	-	-	-	-	-	24.7	-3.9	12.4	15.0	9.0
ABAX Bradys Obligations	FixInc	GlbBnd	-	-	-	-	-	-	-	-	10.2	2.0
AGF Canadian Bond	FixInc	CdnBnd	12.2	1.4	10.0	21.8	14.4	-3.9	16.9	9.0	13.6	9.8
AGF Global Government Bond	FixInc	GlbBnd	2.6	11.2	4.4	28.5	7.3	7.2	8.3	5.1	6.8	12.5
AGF Intl Grp-S-Term Income	FixInc	IntMkt	-	-	-	-	-	-	-	4.2	-0.2	4.1
AGF Money Market Account	FixInc	CdnMkt	-	-	-	-	-	3.7	5.7	5.0	2.4	2.4
AGF RSP Global Bond	FixInc	GlbBnd	-	-	-	7.3	5.3	-	6.3	5.3	5.7	11.8
AGF U.S. Income	FixInc	GlbBnd	-	-	-	-	-	1.4	6.2	1.9	4.1	14.8
AGF U.S. S-Term High Yield	FixInc	GlbBnd	-	-	-	-	-	-	7.9	2.5	10.3	10.1
AGF US$ Money Mkt Account	FixInc	USMkt	-	-	-	4.5	2.8	2.7	4.5	4.6	4.5	4.7
AIC Money Market	FixInc	CdnMkt	-	-	-	-	-	-	-	4.8	2.6	3.2
AIM Cash Performance	FixInc	CdnMkt	-	-	-	-	-	3.1	5.2	4.6	3.0	2.9
AIM GT Canada Money Market	FixInc	CdnMkt	-	-	-	-	-	-	-	-	-	3.3
AIM GT S-T Income SrA	FixInc	ST Bnd	10.6	12.1	11.3	-	-	-	-	-	3.3	2.0

FUND NAME	FUND CATEGORY		JUN98	JUN97	JUN96	JUN95	JUN94	JUN93	JUN92	JUN91	JUN90	JUN89
			% RETURN AT YEAR END									
AIM GT S-T Income SrB	Fixlnc	ST Bnd	1.4	2.7	-	-	-	-	-	-	-	-
AIM GT World Bond	Fixlnc	GlbBnd	8.0	7.8	12.3	-	-	-	-	-	-	-
AIM Global RSP Income	Fixlnc	GlbBnd	8.3	12.2	8.5	5.4	3.2	26.2	-	-	-	-
APEX Fixed Income	Fixlnc	CdnBnd	7.8	12.2	7.0	13.3	-2.2	19.1	22.2	9.6	6.6	10.0
APEX Money Market	Fixlnc	CdnMkt	2.4	2.3	5.1	5.7	-	-	-	-	-	-
APEX Mortgage	Fixlnc	Mortge	3.5	4.5	6.8	-	-	-	-	-	-	-
Acadia Bond	Fixlnc	ST Bnd	6.8	11.7	6.0	-	-	-	-	-	-	-
Acadia Money Market	Fixlnc	CdnMkt	2.5	2.1	5.1	-	-	-	-	-	-	-
Acadia Mortgage	Fixlnc	Mortge	4.2	3.2	4.2	-	-	-	-	-	-	-
Acuity Pld Fixed Income	Fixlnc	CdnBnd	29.6	17.6	6.7	11.9	-0.1	-	-	-	-	-
Acuity Pld Short Term	Fixlnc	CdnMkt	0.6	8.4	7.0	14.5	2.6	-	-	-	-	-
Allstar Money Market	Fixlnc	CdnMkt	3.0	-	-	-	-	-	-	-	-	-
Altamira Bond	Fixlnc	CdnBnd	22.9	16.3	7.6	24.8	-5.6	19.2	18.2	11.7	3.6	12.0
Altamira Global Bond	Fixlnc	GlbBnd	10.4	5.8	3.6	12.3	-	-	-	-	-	-
Altamira High Yield Bond	Fixlnc	GlbBnd	12.4	18.3	-	-	-	-	-	-	-	-
Altamira Income	Fixlnc	CdnBnd	9.5	11.7	6.5	21.9	-3.0	16.9	21.4	14.8	5.7	13.5
Altamira S-T Global Income	Fixlnc	IntMkt	3.7	1.6	1.4	1.7	11.6	8.8	16.2	-	-	-
Altamira S-Term Cdn Income	Fixlnc	CdnMkt	4.3	-	-	-	-	-	-	-	-	-
Altamira S-Term Govt Bond	Fixlnc	ST Bnd	4.6	7.4	7.6	-	-	-	-	-	-	-
Altamira T-Bill	Fixlnc	CdnMkt	3.5	-	-	-	-	-	-	-	-	-
Atlas American Money Mkt	Fixlnc	USMkt	4.6	4.4	4.7	4.3	2.3	2.2	3.9	6.5	7.9	7.2
Atlas Canadian Bond	Fixlnc	CdnBnd	9.1	12.0	7.9	11.9	0.5	11.4	17.5	11.3	1.6	9.5
Atlas Canadian Money Mkt	Fixlnc	CdnMkt	3.1	2.7	5.2	5.7	3.8	5.1	7.3	11.3	12.2	9.9
Atlas Canadian T-Bill	Fixlnc	CdnMkt	2.5	2.4	4.9	5.6	3.4	4.8	6.9	10.9	12.0	9.9
Atlas Cdn High Yield Bond	Fixlnc	CdnBnd	7.8	16.5	10.3	-	-	-	-	-	-	-
Atlas World Bond	Fixlnc	GlbBnd	6.6	6.5	10.3	10.7	-	-	-	-	-	-
BNP (Canada) Bond	Fixlnc	CdnBnd	10.8	12.4	8.4	14.9	-1.8	11.2	-	-	-	-
BNP (Canada) Cdn. Mny. Mkt	Fixlnc	CdnMkt	2.8	3.0	5.1	5.5	3.6	4.9	-	-	-	-
BPI Canadian Bond	Fixlnc	CdnBnd	9.4	10.9	0.3	12.1	-3.9	10.9	17.0	12.9	1.7	-
BPI Global RSP Bond	Fixlnc	GlbBnd	11.5	10.2	11.3	-	-	-	-	-	-	-
BPI T-Bill	Fixlnc	CdnMkt	3.5	3.4	5.9	5.8	3.9	5.5	7.5	11.4	12.3	10.6
BPI U.S. Money Market	Fixlnc	USMkt	4.8	4.3	-	-	-	-	-	-	-	-
Batirente Sec Marche Monet	Fixlnc	CdnMkt	3.2	2.7	4.9	5.8	3.7	5.5	8.7	12.8	9.7	9.7
Batirente Sec Obligations	Fixlnc	CdnBnd	10.5	16.2	11.1	17.9	-2.2	15.1	20.3	12.8	-0.1	13.7
Beutel Goodman Income	Fixlnc	CdnBnd	10.4	13.9	9.3	16.5	-3.4	11.9	18.5	-	-	-
Beutel Goodman Money Mkt.	Fixlnc	CdnMkt	3.6	3.3	5.9	6.1	4.6	6.2	9.1	-	-	-
Beutel Goodman Private Bd	Fixlnc	CdnBnd	7.2	15.0	8.7	16.2	-2.7	-	-	-	-	-
Bissett Bond	Fixlnc	CdnBnd	10.0	14.4	10.2	15.0	0.3	9.9	17.4	14.4	2.6	11.8
Bissett Money Market	Fixlnc	CdnMkt	3.6	3.8	6.3	6.2	4.5	5.9	-	-	-	-
C.I. Canadian Bond	Fixlnc	CdnBnd	10.0	16.0	10.8	14.0	-1.3	-	-	-	-	-
C.I. Global Bond RSP	Fixlnc	GlbBnd	8.3	7.5	10.7	10.2	-	-	-	-	-	-
C.I. Global High Yield	Fixlnc	GlbBnd	2.8	18.2	20.5	3.0	-	-	-	-	-	-
C.I. Money Market	Fixlnc	CdnMkt	3.3	3.2	5.6	6.2	4.1	5.7	7.8	-	-	-

% RETURN AT YEAR END

FUND NAME	FixInc	FUND CATEGORY	JUN98	JUN97	JUN96	JUN95	JUN94	JUN93	JUN92	JUN91	JUN90	JUN89
C.I. Short-term Sector	FixInc	CdnMkt	4.3	2.8	2.3	3.9	2.4	3.3	4.1	6.8	7.1	5.1
C.I. US Money Market	FixInc	USMkt	4.9	4.8	5.2	-	4.2	-	-	-	-	-
C.I. World Bond	FixInc	GlbBnd	6.9	7.4	9.6	7.5	-	-	-	-	-	-
CCPE Fixed Income	FixInc	CdnBnd	8.6	10.2	9.5	13.9	-0.1	13.7	18.0	12.8	3.9	10.6
CCPE Money Market	FixInc	CdnMkt	5.6	2.9	5.6	-	-	-	-	-	-	-
CDA Bond & Mortgage (C)	FixInc	B & M	7.3	11.6	9.2	15.4	-0.4	10.9	16.9	14.1	6.2	10.6
CDA Money Market (Canagex)	FixInc	CdnMkt	3.5	3.4	5.9	6.7	3.9	5.8	8.0	11.8	12.3	10.6
CIBC Canadian Bond	FixInc	CdnBnd	9.6	13.3	8.7	16.5	-7.2	12.9	20.1	12.8	2.6	11.2
CIBC Canadian S-Term Bond	FixInc	ST Bnd	4.0	9.6	8.9	12.4	-	-	-	-	-	-
CIBC Canadian T-Bill	FixInc	CdnMkt	2.9	2.8	4.9	5.4	3.1	4.6	6.7	-	-	-
CIBC Global Bond	FixInc	GlbBnd	7.6	7.7	2.2	-	-	-	-	-	-	-
CIBC Money Market	FixInc	CdnMkt	3.0	2.8	5.0	5.5	3.3	4.5	7.2	11.2	12.4	-
CIBC Mortgage	FixInc	Mortge	3.1	8.9	7.3	12.8	1.2	9.1	14.5	17.1	7.2	9.4
CIBC Premium Cdn T-Bill	FixInc	CdnMkt	3.5	3.1	5.4	6.1	3.8	5.3	7.3	-	-	-
CIBC US$ Money Market	FixInc	USMkt	4.6	4.4	4.4	4.4	2.3	2.3	4.0	-	-	-
CT Bond	FixInc	CdnBnd	9.4	12.1	8.1	15.0	-2.8	11.4	20.0	12.2	3.0	12.1
CT Canadian Bond Index	FixInc	CdnBnd	9.8	-	-	-	-	-	-	-	-	-
CT International Bond	FixInc	GlbBnd	5.5	1.9	3.3	-	-	-	-	-	-	-
CT Money Market	FixInc	CdnMkt	2.9	2.7	4.9	5.4	3.6	4.6	7.6	11.9	12.6	11.5
CT Mortgage	FixInc	B & M	4.4	6.6	6.6	11.0	3.4	8.6	11.1	15.4	8.4	9.2
CT Premium Money Market	FixInc	CdnMkt	3.4	-	-	-	-	-	-	-	-	-
CT Short Term Bond	FixInc	ST Bnd	4.2	-	-	-	-	-	-	-	-	-
CUMIS Life Canadian Bond	FixInc	CdnBnd	9.3	-	-	-	-	-	-	-	-	-
CUMIS Life Cdn Money Mkt	FixInc	CdnMkt	3.1	-	-	-	-	-	-	-	-	-
Caldwell Canadian Income	FixInc	CdnBnd	9.0	-	-	-	-	-	-	-	-	-
Canada Life Fixed Income	FixInc	CdnBnd	8.9	11.9	7.9	14.4	-3.4	11.4	16.6	12.3	3.4	9.4
Canada Life Intl. Bond	FixInc	GlbBnd	14.7	5.1	3.6	11.1	-	-	-	-	-	-
Canada Life Money Market	FixInc	CdnMkt	2.7	2.9	5.0	5.6	3.1	5.3	7.2	11.7	11.1	9.7
Capstone Cash Management	FixInc	CdnBnd	3.7	3.2	5.4	7.8	3.6	6.0	8.2	11.9	12.3	10.0
CentrePost Bond	FixInc	CdnBnd	7.2	10.4	10.3	15.8	-4.4	13.0	19.1	17.3	-	-
CentrePost Short Term	FixInc	CdnMkt	3.5	2.7	5.5	5.7	4.2	5.8	7.7	12.1	12.8	11.0
Clarington Money Market	FixInc	CdnMkt	3.1	-	-	-	-	-	-	-	-	-
Clean Environment Income	FixInc	CdnBnd	8.7	10.1	4.0	8.5	-2.4	12.2	-	-	-	-
Co-Operators Fixed Income	FixInc	CdnBnd	11.8	14.4	9.3	17.3	-0.2	11.2	-	-	-	-
Colonia Life Bond	FixInc	CdnBnd	8.4	8.7	7.8	14.2	3.2	5.0	-	-	-	-
Colonia Life Money Market	FixInc	CdnMkt	2.7	3.2	5.5	6.1	1.7	6.7	-	-	-	-
Colonia Life Mortgage	FixInc	Mortge	4.4	5.1	8.4	10.0	-	-	-	-	-	-
Cornerstone Bond	FixInc	CdnBnd	10.1	10.5	8.5	15.1	-1.8	11.0	16.1	13.1	7.9	10.4
Cornerstone Govt Money	FixInc	CdnMkt	2.8	2.4	5.2	5.7	3.7	5.1	7.3	11.5	-	-
Desjardins	FixInc	CdnBnd	8.0	11.4	9.1	15.1	-2.4	11.7	14.9	13.9	1.1	10.8
Desjardins Distinct Bond	FixInc	CdnBnd	10.1	13.3	10.8	16.1	-1.9	12.7	21.2	15.5	3.0	15.6
Desjardins Distinct Mtg	FixInc	Mortge	7.5	5.0	9.1	11.1	3.0	7.2	11.2	16.9	8.7	11.6
Desjardins Money Market	FixInc	CdnMkt	2.9	2.4	4.9	5.3	3.7	5.4	7.1	10.9	11.6	-

% RETURN AT YEAR END

FUND NAME		FUND CATEGORY	JUN98	JUN97	JUN96	JUN95	JUN94	JUN93	JUN92	JUN91	JUN90	JUN89
Desjardins Mortgage	FixInc	Mortge	4.6	5.4	7.0	11.8	2.2	7.8	10.7	14.8	8.8	9.0
Dynamic Global Bond	FixInc	GlbBnd	-4.3	6.7	6.7	11.8	11.3	11.4	25.3	-0.7	5.4	2.3
Dynamic Global Income&Gth	FixInc	GlbBnd	2.1	–	–	–	–	–	–	–	–	–
Dynamic Government Income	FixInc	ST Bnd	4.0	10.4	9.7	11.2	–	–	–	–	–	–
Dynamic Income	FixInc	CdnBnd	-0.6	7.8	9.1	8.5	8.5	12.6	16.5	11.6	4.8	13.9
Dynamic Money Market	FixInc	CdnMkt	3.0	2.7	5.0	6.2	3.7	5.2	7.5	12.0	11.7	8.9
Elliott & Page Bond	FixInc	CdnBnd	10.6	9.6	6.0	11.7	-4.9	10.2	16.2	11.7	6.1	11.8
Elliott & Page Global Bond	FixInc	GlbBnd	6.6	4.1	-0.5	–	–	–	–	–	–	–
Elliott & Page Money	FixInc	CdnMkt	3.4	3.1	5.3	6.3	4.3	5.4	8.6	12.4	12.5	10.8
Elliott & Page T-Bill	FixInc	CdnMkt	2.2	1.9	4.0	4.4	–	–	–	–	2.6	11.4
Empire Bond	FixInc	CdnBnd	8.9	11.3	7.8	13.5	-2.0	9.4	17.7	14.0	–	–
Empire Fgn Curr Cdn Bond	FixInc	CdnBnd	6.7	3.8	-3.7	5.3	3.2	4.7	7.5	11.7	10.0	10.6
Empire Money Market	FixInc	CdnMkt	2.7	2.3	4.4	15.7	-1.7	11.8	19.7	15.9	5.2	–
Equitable Life Accum Inc	FixInc	CdnBnd	11.2	13.9	10.0	12.7	-1.9	10.6	–	–	–	–
Equitable Life Cdn Bond	FixInc	CdnBnd	9.4	12.3	8.2	–	–	–	–	–	–	–
Equitable Life Money Mkt	FixInc	CdnMkt	2.8	2.3	4.7	17.0	-2.0	8.6	8.8	12.8	10.0	7.5
Ethical Global Bond	FixInc	GlbBnd	8.6	8.1	5.1	5.4	3.6	5.3	7.2	11.4	12.7	10.5
Ethical Income	FixInc	CdnBnd	10.4	13.3	9.0	10.9	6.5	5.5	–	–	–	–
Ethical Money Market	FixInc	CdnMkt	2.7	2.9	5.1	6.5	4.2	6.1	8.6	11.8	12.0	–
FMOQ Bond	FixInc	GlbBnd	8.8	7.9	4.9	5.2	3.7	5.9	7.5	11.0	2.3	8.8
FMOQ Money Market	FixInc	CdnMkt	3.6	3.7	6.0	15.0	-3.3	9.1	16.8	14.1	4.6	7.0
Ficadre Hypotheques	FixInc	ST Bnd	4.0	7.1	5.7	10.2	0.3	12.5	13.9	6.5	–	–
Ficadre Monetaire	FixInc	CdnMkt	3.0	3.0	5.4	–	–	–	–	–	–	–
Ficadre Obligations	FixInc	CdnBnd	8.6	11.4	8.5	5.4	3.3	4.5	7.4	–	–	–
Fidelity Canadian Bond	FixInc	CdnBnd	9.3	13.0	8.1	5.3	3.3	–	–	–	–	–
Fidelity Canadian Income	FixInc	ST Bnd	5.2	9.4	8.4	-4.5	2.6	–	–	–	–	–
Fidelity Cdn S-Term Asset	FixInc	CdnMkt	2.9	2.3	4.7	–	–	–	–	–	0.9	10.2
Fidelity Emerging Mkts Bnd	FixInc	GlbBnd	4.4	36.3	28.4	15.8	-2.9	11.3	19.2	13.6	–	–
Fidelity N American Income	FixInc	GlbBnd	4.9	5.6	6.4	16.6	3.6	5.1	7.6	11.1	11.3	9.1
Fidelity US Money Market	FixInc	USMkt	4.5	4.3	4.4	5.6	1.0	8.5	13.9	19.1	7.7	8.9
First Canadian Bond	FixInc	CdnBnd	8.1	12.4	8.4	13.8	–	–	–	–	–	–
First Canadian Intl. Bond	FixInc	GlbBnd	7.7	2.3	1.9	5.6	–	–	–	–	–	–
First Canadian Money Mkt	FixInc	CdnMkt	2.9	2.8	5.2	16.8	-1.9	13.0	19.4	14.0	1.4	13.1
First Canadian Mortgage	FixInc	Mortge	3.9	7.8	7.3	6.1	4.0	5.6	7.5	11.6	12.4	–
First Canadian T-Bill	FixInc	CdnMkt	2.8	2.8	5.1	–	–	–	–	–	–	–
Friedberg Foreign Bond	FixInc	GlbBnd	0.5	–	8.7	13.2	-2.8	12.4	18.1	13.6	0.7	11.6
GBC Canadian Bond	FixInc	CdnBnd	9.7	13.3	5.1	6.0	3.5	5.4	8.3	12.2	10.7	8.2
GBC Money Market	FixInc	CdnMkt	3.0	2.6	5.2	9.0	3.7	7.2	13.3	15.3	8.0	8.0
GS International Bond	FixInc	GlbBnd	6.6	2.7	9.1	–	–	–	–	–	–	–
General Trust Bond	FixInc	CdnBnd	8.4	13.4	5.2	–	–	–	–	–	–	–
General Trust Money Market	FixInc	CdnMkt	2.9	2.9	6.3	–	–	–	–	–	–	–
General Trust Mortgage	FixInc	Mortge	5.1	5.7	–	–	–	–	–	–	–	–
Global Mgr-US Bond Index	FixInc	GlbBnd	16.4	5.8	-1.7	–	–	–	–	–	–	–

% RETURN AT YEAR END

FUND NAME	FUND CATEGORY		JUN98	JUN97	JUN96	JUN95	JUN94	JUN93	JUN92	JUN91	JUN90	JUN89
Global Strategy Bond	ST Bnd	Fixinc	3.7	7.4	8.2	9.6	-3.3	14.6	19.9	-	-	-
Global Strategy Diver Bond	GlbBnd	Fixinc	8.1	6.2	11.0	5.3	-	-	-	-	-	-
Global Strategy Divers FgnBd	GlbBnd	Fixinc	9.3	6.0	6.1	-	-	-	-	-	-	-
Global Strategy Money Mkt	CdnMkt	Fixinc	3.0	2.7	5.0	5.7	4.0	5.6	7.6	9.5	11.5	9.8
Global Strategy World Bond	GlbBnd	Fixinc	8.2	6.0	11.3	4.6	-4.3	19.0	20.4	6.9	-0.5	8.4
Great-West Bond (B) A	CdnBnd	Fixinc	8.6	12.2	-	-	-	-	-	-	-	-
Great-West Bond (B) B	CdnBnd	Fixinc	8.9	12.4	-	-	-	-	-	-	-	-
Great-West Bond (S) A	CdnBnd	Fixinc	11.0	12.3	-	-	-	-	-	-	-	-
Great-West Bond (S) B	CdnBnd	Fixinc	11.3	12.6	-	-	-	-	-	-	-	-
Great-West Cdn Bond (G) A	CdnBnd	Fixinc	8.8	12.2	6.9	14.0	-3.6	11.2	17.6	13.3	0.0	10.6
Great-West Cdn Bond (G) B	CdnBnd	Fixinc	9.1	12.5	7.1	-	-	-	-	-	-	-
Great-West Glob Income(A)	GlbBnd	Fixinc	10.5	4.5	-	-	-	-	-	-	-	-
Great-West Glob Income(A)B	GlbBnd	Fixinc	10.8	4.7	-	-	-	-	-	-	-	-
Great-West Govt Bond (G) A	CdnBnd	Fixinc	4.5	8.5	7.0	-	-	-	-	-	-	-
Great-West Govt Bond (G) B	CdnBnd	Fixinc	4.8	8.8	7.2	-	-	-	-	-	-	-
Great-West Income (G) A	CdnBnd	Fixinc	10.8	17.7	8.8	-	-	-	-	-	-	-
Great-West Income (G) B	CdnBnd	Fixinc	11.1	18.0	9.0	-	-	-	-	-	-	-
Great-West Income (M) A	CdnBnd	Fixinc	7.3	14.6	-	-	-	-	-	-	-	-
Great-West Income (M) B	CdnBnd	Fixinc	7.6	14.9	-	-	-	-	-	-	-	-
Great-West Intl Bond (P)A	GlbBnd	Fixinc	1.7	2.4	6.1	-	-	-	-	-	-	-
Great-West Intl Bond (P)B	GlbBnd	Fixinc	2.0	2.7	6.3	-	-	-	-	-	-	-
Great-West Money Mkt (G)A	CdnMkt	Fixinc	2.7	1.9	4.3	5.0	3.1	4.6	6.9	10.9	12.0	9.9
Great-West Money Mkt (G)B	CdnMkt	Fixinc	2.9	2.2	4.5	-	-	-	-	-	-	-
Great-West Mortgage (G)A	Mortge	Fixinc	7.2	10.7	6.8	12.0	-0.6	9.2	15.7	13.3	3.5	10.8
Great-West Mortgage (G)B	Mortge	Fixinc	7.5	11.0	7.0	-	-	-	-	-	-	-
Green Line Canadian Bond	CdnBnd	Fixinc	11.3	15.4	10.6	18.0	-3.3	12.3	18.1	12.2	2.5	-
Green Line Canadian T-Bill	CdnMkt	Fixinc	3.1	3.3	5.4	5.8	3.8	4.9	-	-	-	-
Green Line Cdn Govt Bd Idx	CdnBnd	Fixinc	9.7	12.9	9.5	15.9	-2.4	11.3	14.4	11.4	-0.8	12.8
Green Line Cdn Money Mkt	CdnMkt	Fixinc	3.3	3.4	5.5	5.9	4.2	5.5	8.1	11.7	12.7	-
Green Line Global Govt Bnd	GlbBnd	Fixinc	11.9	4.0	-0.1	13.3	6.6	-	-	-	-	-
Green Line Global RSP Bond	GlbBnd	Fixinc	10.5	12.0	2.0	14.2	-	-	-	-	-	-
Green Line Mortgage	Mortge	Fixinc	3.5	7.0	6.5	12.3	1.0	9.1	12.6	16.2	9.5	9.8
Green Line Mortgage-Backed	B & M	Fixinc	3.9	6.8	6.9	10.7	1.1	6.8	11.6	15.0	11.8	-
Green Line Real Return Bnd	CdnBnd	Fixinc	11.6	12.3	1.7	-	-	-	-	-	-	-
Green Line Short Term Inco	ST Bnd	Fixinc	3.5	6.4	7.9	10.3	-0.4	6.3	8.3	11.3	12.2	-
Green Line US Money Market	USMkt	Fixinc	4.6	4.4	4.5	4.3	2.3	2.4	4.2	6.6	7.8	-
GrowSafe Canadian Bond	CdnBnd	Fixinc	8.8	8.7	4.8	9.5	-	-	-	-	-	-
GrowSafe Cdn Money Markets	CdnMkt	Fixinc	3.2	2.8	4.2	3.4	-	-	-	-	-	-
Guardian Canadian Income C	ST Bnd	Fixinc	4.1	6.8	7.4	-	-	-	-	-	-	-
Guardian Canadian Income M	ST Bnd	Fixinc	3.4	6.2	-	-	-	-	-	-	-	-
Guardian Cdn Money Mkt C	CdnMkt	Fixinc	3.2	2.7	5.0	5.8	3.9	5.5	7.2	11.8	13.0	10.7
Guardian Cdn Money Mkt M	CdnMkt	Fixinc	2.6	2.0	-	-	-	-	-	-	-	-
Guardian Foreign Income A	GlbBnd	Fixinc	16.1	10.2	8.0	-	-	-	-	-	-	-

% RETURN AT YEAR END

FUND NAME		FUND CATEGORY	JUN98	JUN97	JUN96	JUN95	JUN94	JUN93	JUN92	JUN91	JUN90	JUN89
Guardian Foreign Income B	FixInc	GlbBnd	15.3	8.9	9.9	7.7	3.2	16.0	17.2	3.9	3.4	2.1
Guardian Intl Income C	FixInc	GlbBnd	8.5	8.1								
Guardian Intl Income M	FixInc	GlbBnd	7.9	7.1								
Guardian US Money Market C	FixInc	USMkt	4.9	4.4	4.7	4.6	2.7	2.6	4.3	6.7	8.4	13.3
Guardian US Money Market M	FixInc	USMkt	4.2	3.8								
Hongkong Bank Cdn Bond	FixInc	CdnBnd	9.5	13.6	8.5	5.6	3.5	5.0				
Hongkong Bank Global Bond	FixInc	GlbBnd	4.6	4.5	2.8	12.3	7.5	13.7				
Hongkong Bank Money Market	FixInc	CdnMkt	3.2	3.2	5.4							
Hongkong Bank Mortgage	FixInc	Mortge	4.2	9.5	6.5	5.2	-0.2					
ICM Bond	FixInc	CdnBnd	8.8	10.5	8.9	16.4	5.2	12.3	18.9	10.6		
ICM Short Term Investment	FixInc	CdnMkt	4.0	3.9	6.7	6.7		4.9				
IG Sceptre Canadian Bond	FixInc	CdnBnd	12.1	11.4	7.8	15.4	-2.6	10.4	18.8	13.3	1.8	8.9
Ideal Bond	FixInc	CdnBnd	8.3		6.2							
Ideal Money Market	FixInc	CdnMkt	4.7	4.1	4.4	6.7	3.0		6.2	10.8	10.1	
Imperial Gth Money Market	FixInc	CdnMkt	2.4	1.9								
Ind. Alliance Bond 2	FixInc	CdnBnd	3.1									
Ind. Alliance Bonds	FixInc	CdnBnd	8.1	10.7	9.0	14.3	-2.8	4.9	17.0	16.4	3.6	12.6
Ind. Alliance Ecoflex B	FixInc	CdnBnd	7.7	10.2	8.5	13.7	-3.5					
Ind. Alliance Ecoflex G	FixInc	GlbBnd	-1.7									
Ind. Alliance Ecoflex H	FixInc	Mortge	4.4	5.5	6.1	10.5	1.0					
Ind. Alliance Ecoflex M	FixInc	CdnMkt	2.7	2.5	4.7	5.0						
Ind. Alliance Global Bond	FixInc	GlbBnd	-1.5									
Ind. Alliance Money Market	FixInc	CdnMkt	2.5	2.4	4.7	5.0	2.7					
Ind. Alliance Mortgages	FixInc	Mortge	4.7	5.9	6.6	11.1	1.7	7.6	11.2	16.2	7.8	8.9
Industrial Bond	FixInc	CdnBnd	10.0	16.9	7.7	17.1	-5.2	12.4	18.3	12.6	1.2	
Industrial Cash Management	FixInc	CdnMkt	3.3	3.1	5.5	6.3	4.0	5.6	7.5	11.6	12.5	10.7
Industrial Mtge Securities	FixInc	B & M	0.6	11.9	8.6	10.5	-2.2	17.8	13.8	9.8	-1.2	13.1
Industrial Short-Term	FixInc	CdnMkt	2.4	2.2	4.8	5.4	3.1	4.3	6.4			
Infinity T-Bill	FixInc	CdnMkt	3.0									
InvesNat Corp Cash Mgmt	FixInc	CdnMkt	3.6	3.6	5.7	5.6						
InvesNat Intl RSP Bond	FixInc	GlbBnd	9.6	6.7	5.6	11.8	3.7	5.3				
InvesNat Money Market	FixInc	CdnMkt	3.0	3.1	5.2		3.3	8.0				
InvesNat Mortgage	FixInc	Mortge	4.0	6.8	7.5	9.3	0.1	9.2	7.4			
InvesNat S-T Govt. Bond	FixInc	ST Bnd	4.0	8.1	8.8	5.9	3.8	5.5	6.6	14.2	2.6	
InvesNat T-Bill Plus	FixInc	CdnMkt	3.3	3.3	5.5	4.3	2.1	2.2				
InvesNat US Money Market	FixInc	USMkt	4.5	4.4	4.4							
Investors Corporate Bond	FixInc	CdnBnd	9.0	12.8	9.3	9.4	7.1	10.9	16.6	13.3	3.3	11.5
Investors Global Bond	FixInc	GlbBnd	8.8	3.8	-1.8	12.5	-2.6	9.2	13.4	14.2	4.6	
Investors Government Bond	FixInc	CdnBnd	9.6	12.7	8.8	15.8	-1.8	5.0	7.0	11.2	11.8	10.1
Investors Income Portfolio	FixInc	CdnBnd	7.1	10.5	8.0	13.8	3.6	7.8	17.3			
Investors Money Market	FixInc	CdnMkt	3.0	2.5	5.1	6.0			7.5		11.8	9.0
Investors Mortgage	FixInc	Mortge	3.4	7.2	6.5	12.4	-0.7		10.5	15.7	7.1	
Investors N.A. High Yield	FixInc	GlbBnd	7.4									

% RETURN AT YEAR END

FUND NAME	FUND CATEGORY	JUN98	JUN97	JUN96	JUN95	JUN94	JUN93	JUN92	JUN91	JUN90	JUN89
Investors US Money Market	USMkt	4.5									
Ivy Mortgage	Mortge	4.0	8.6	7.1	11.2						
Jones Heward Bond	CdnBnd	7.8	12.1	7.8	13.8	-3.8	11.4	15.6	12.4	2.4	11.5
Jones Heward Money Market	CdnMkt	3.0	2.9	5.4							
Leith Wheeler Fixed Income	CdnBnd	8.9	11.6	9.0	14.3						
Leith Wheeler Money Market	CdnMkt	3.4	2.9	5.4	6.2						
London Life Bond	CdnBnd	8.8	10.8	8.9	15.4	-3.1	11.2	17.7	5.2	3.1	13.2
London Life Money Market	CdnMkt	2.7	2.8	5.8	6.0	3.4	5.2	10.4	11.6	11.5	
London Life Mortgage	Mortge	6.7	7.8	6.9	12.0	1.0	10.6	12.7	15.7	7.3	8.9
Lotus Group Bond	CdnBnd	10.1	13.5	9.3	14.5						
Lotus Group Income	CdnMkt	3.2	3.4	5.6	5.8	4.2	5.2	7.9	12.1	13.2	10.9
MAXXUM Income	CdnBnd	16.0	15.8	8.6	17.2	-3.3	12.3	14.5	12.5	1.7	13.2
MAXXUM Money Market	CdnMkt	3.4	3.5	5.9	6.0	4.4	5.7	8.2	11.9	12.2	10.0
MD Bond	CdnBnd	9.6	13.6	9.9	15.7	-1.0	12.2	18.2	13.5	3.8	11.9
MD Bond & Mortgage	ST Bnd	5.0	7.4								
MD Global Bond	GlbBnd	11.9	3.4	0.0							
MD Money	CdnMkt	3.4	3.4	5.8	6.3	4.0	5.4	7.6	11.4	11.6	9.3
MLI AGF Canadian Bond GIF	CdnBnd	9.1									
MLI E&P Money Market A GIF	CdnMkt	2.7									
MLI E&P Money Market B GIF	CdnMkt	2.2									
MLI Fidelity Cdn Bond GIF	CdnBnd	8.4									
Manulife Cabot Divers Bond	CdnBnd	8.9	5.9	4.1	11.9						
Manulife Cabot Money Mkt	CdnMkt	2.6	2.4	5.0	6.1						
Manulife VistaFd 1 S-T Sec	CdnMkt	2.2	3.0	5.6	6.5	3.1	4.9	7.5	11.6	11.9	10.2
Manulife VistaFd 2 S-T Sec	CdnMkt	1.5	2.3	4.8	5.7	2.3	4.1	6.7	10.7	11.1	9.4
Manulife VistaFund 1 Bond	CdnBnd	8.6	10.9	5.1	15.8	-5.9	14.1	18.1	14.2	3.0	11.8
Manulife VistaFund 2 Bond	CdnBnd	7.8	10.1	4.4	15.0	-6.6	13.3	17.2	13.4	2.2	11.0
Manulife Vistafd1 Gbl Bond	GlbBnd	7.3	1.5	5.3							
Manulife Vistafd2 Gbl Bond	GlbBnd	6.4	0.7	4.5							
Maritime Life Bond A	CdnBnd	8.6	11.1	7.2	14.7	-2.5	11.0	17.0	13.5		
Maritime Life Bond B	CdnBnd	8.4									
Maritime Life Bond C	CdnBnd	8.3									
Maritime Life Money Mkt A	CdnMkt	2.6	2.4	4.3	4.5	3.0	4.5	7.8	10.6	11.0	9.5
Maritime Life Money Mkt B	CdnMkt	2.6									
Maritime Life Money Mkt C	CdnMkt	1.9									
Mawer Canadian Bond	CdnBnd	9.5	12.6	9.5	15.6	-2.5	11.2	15.8			
Mawer Canadian Income	CdnBnd	7.9	15.0	10.5	13.3	-1.0					
Mawer Canadian Money Mkt	CdnMkt	3.5	3.0	5.4	5.9	3.8	5.3	7.3	11.2	12.1	9.9
Mawer Cdn High Yield Bond	CdnBnd	10.5	10.7								
McDonald Enhanced Bond	CdnBnd	9.3	7.2								
McLean Budden Pld Fixd Inc	CdnBnd	11.8	15.3	10.9	17.7	-1.0	13.4	19.6	14.5	4.2	12.0
Mclean Budden Fixed Income	CdnBnd	10.9	13.7	9.7	16.2	-2.4	12.3	17.6	14.3	5.1	
Mclean Budden Money Market	CdnMkt	3.6	3.7	5.5	5.8	3.9	4.9	7.4	11.2	11.9	

% RETURN AT YEAR END

FUND NAME	FUND CATEGORY		JUN98	JUN97	JUN96	JUN95	JUN94	JUN93	JUN92	JUN91	JUN90	JUN89
Merrill Lynch World Bond	FixInc	GlbBnd	9.6	5.2	6.8	11.5	-3.3	9.2	14.5	12.3	3.8	11.2
Metlife Mvp Bond	FixInc	CdnBnd	8.5	9.0	5.0	5.0	3.1	4.1	-	-	-	-
Metlife Mvp Money Market	FixInc	CdnMkt	2.1	2.2	-	-	-	-	-	-	-	-
Middlefield Money Market	FixInc	CdnMkt	3.6	3.8	-	-	-	-	-	-	-	-
Millennia III Income 1	FixInc	CdnBnd	7.0	9.4	-	-	-	-	-	-	-	-
Millennia III Income 2	FixInc	CdnBnd	6.6	2.2	-	-	-	-	-	-	-	-
Millennia III Money Mkt 1	FixInc	CdnMkt	2.5	2.2	-	-	-	-	-	-	-	-
Millennia III Money Mkt 2	FixInc	CdnMkt	2.3	2.0	-	-	-	-	-	-	-	-
Montrusco Select Bd Index+	FixInc	CdnBnd	10.0	13.9	10.4	14.4	0.9	14.2	22.2	14.0	3.9	13.3
Montrusco Select Income	FixInc	CdnBnd	10.5	13.0	6.3	-	-	-	-	-	-	-
Montrusco Select T-Max	FixInc	CdnMkt	4.0	4.0	-	-	-	-	-	-	-	-
Mutual Bond	FixInc	CdnBnd	7.9	10.9	7.3	13.3	-2.0	11.1	16.2	10.7	11.3	9.8
Mutual Money Market	FixInc	CdnMkt	3.1	2.6	5.1	5.9	3.8	5.2	7.0	-	-	-
Mutual Premier Bond	FixInc	CdnBnd	8.8	12.1	7.5	13.7	-2.0	-	-	-	-	-
Mutual Premier Mortgage	FixInc	Mortge	3.9	6.7	6.7	12.1	1.6	-	-	-	-	-
NAL-Canadian Bond	FixInc	CdnBnd	9.5	11.4	8.1	15.2	-1.2	11.0	16.6	12.2	1.8	9.6
NAL-Canadian Money Market	FixInc	CdnMkt	4.8	2.4	5.1	5.2	3.2	5.1	7.3	11.2	12.3	-
NN Bond	FixInc	CdnBnd	12.6	13.8	10.0	14.6	-1.8	11.7	15.5	12.5	3.5	9.6
NN Can-Global Bond	FixInc	GlbBnd	11.3	7.3	-	-	-	-	-	-	-	-
NN Money Market	FixInc	CdnMkt	3.6	3.5	5.7	6.2	4.0	5.7	7.8	11.6	9.8	8.7
NN T-Bill	FixInc	CdnMkt	2.7	2.7	4.5	4.9	3.1	5.0	7.8	11.0	2.9	10.5
National Fixed Income	FixInc	CdnBnd	9.0	12.6	8.1	15.1	-1.6	11.4	17.3	13.7	0.7	10.7
National Money Market	FixInc	CdnMkt	2.3	2.2	4.4	5.2	3.0	4.5	-	-	-	-
National Trust Cdn Bond	FixInc	CdnBnd	9.5	15.2	9.3	16.0	-3.2	11.7	17.0	13.0	-	-
National Trust Intl RSP Bd	FixInc	GlbBnd	8.1	12.7	8.1	-	-	-	-	-	-	-
National Trust Money Mkt.	FixInc	CdnMkt	2.8	3.2	5.3	5.2	3.5	5.3	7.0	12.7	-	-
National Trust Mortgage	FixInc	Mortge	3.3	8.5	7.1	12.7	-0.2	-	-	-	-	-
Navigator Canadian Income	FixInc	CdnBnd	8.1	15.5	11.0	-	-	-	-	-	-	-
North West Life Ecoflex B	FixInc	CdnBnd	7.7	-	-	-	-	-	-	-	-	-
North West Life Ecoflex G	FixInc	GlbBnd	-1.7	-	-	-	-	-	-	-	-	-
North West Life Ecoflex H	FixInc	Mortge	4.4	-	-	-	-	-	-	-	-	-
North West Life Ecoflex M	FixInc	CdnMkt	2.7	-	-	-	-	-	-	-	-	-
Northwest Income	FixInc	CdnBnd	9.1	11.3	7.7	13.7	-2.5	8.0	-	-	-	-
Northwest Money Market	FixInc	CdnMkt	3.2	2.9	5.2	5.7	4.2	4.8	12.8	-	-	-
Northwest Mortgage	FixInc	Mortge	1.9	6.9	5.0	11.0	1.2	9.0	-	-	-	-
O'Donnell High Income	FixInc	CdnBnd	7.9	15.9	-	-	-	-	-	-	-	-
O'Donnell Money Market	FixInc	CdnMkt	2.7	3.1	-	-	-	-	-	-	-	-
O'Donnell Short Term	FixInc	CdnMkt	2.5	2.6	-	-	-	-	-	-	-	-
O.I.Q. Ferique Obligations	FixInc	CdnBnd	8.7	13.3	9.8	14.1	0.4	11.6	20.3	11.1	4.7	11.2
O.I.Q. Ferique Revenu	FixInc	CdnMkt	3.6	3.9	6.1	6.8	4.5	6.0	8.7	11.9	11.9	9.8
OTGIF Fixed Value	FixInc	CdnMkt	3.6	3.6	6.0	6.6	4.3	8.6	8.3	11.1	11.1	9.8
OTGIF Mortgage Income	FixInc	B & M	8.9	9.8	8.3	11.0	3.8	11.4	9.1	10.5	10.3	9.7
Optima Strat-Cdn Fx Income	FixInc	CdnBnd	13.6	17.3	8.9	15.8	-	-	-	-	-	-

% RETURN AT YEAR END

FUND NAME	FUND CATEGORY		JUN98	JUN97	JUN96	JUN95	JUN94	JUN93	JUN92	JUN91	JUN90	JUN89
Optima Strat-Glo Fx Income	GlbBnd	FixInc	11.4	5.4	2.2	14.8	-	-	-	-	-	-
Optima Strat-Short Term	ST Bnd	FixInc	4.6	7.1	7.3	9.0	1.5	-	-	-	-	-
Optimum Epargne	CdnMkt	FixInc	3.3	2.7	4.9	6.1	3.9	5.6	9.0	13.2	9.6	10.0
Optimum Obligations	CdnBnd	FixInc	8.5	15.5	10.4	18.1	-2.6	14.2	20.7	12.5	0.4	12.8
PH & N $US Money Market	USMkt	FixInc	5.1	5.0	5.2	5.0	2.9	2.9	4.7	-	-	-
PH & N Bond	CdnBnd	FixInc	10.0	13.2	10.1	16.6	-0.5	12.9	19.8	15.2	3.4	13.4
PH & N Canadian Money Mkt.	CdnMkt	FixInc	3.7	3.1	5.5	6.3	4.1	5.8	7.9	11.8	12.7	10.4
PH & N S-T Bond & Mortgage	B & M	FixInc	5.3	9.5	9.6	12.5	-	-	-	-	-	-
Perigee Income Fund 2	ST Bnd	FixInc	5.6	11.0	10.1	13.7	1.2	12.7	14.8	13.9	4.2	11.4
Pret et Revenu Hypotheque	Mortge	FixInc	2.7	6.9	6.8	11.0	0.5	9.1	12.0	15.7	7.6	9.2
Pret et Revenu Mond Oblig	GlbBnd	FixInc	5.9	3.4	0.2	-	-	-	-	-	-	-
Pret et Revenu Money Mkt.	CdnMkt	FixInc	3.1	2.9	5.2	5.6	4.1	5.3	7.3	11.4	11.1	-
Pret et Revenu Obligations	CdnBnd	FixInc	9.3	11.6	8.6	15.1	-1.9	9.5	20.0	12.6	4.4	8.6
Primus Cdn Fixed Income	CdnBnd	FixInc	11.7	-	-	-	-	-	-	-	-	-
Primus Prime Credit Mny Mk	CdnMkt	FixInc	4.2	-	-	-	-	-	-	-	-	-
Pursuit Canadian Bond	CdnBnd	FixInc	12.6	10.8	2.1	6.6	4.2	10.8	15.3	8.9	-5.9	4.6
Pursuit Global Bond	GlbBnd	FixInc	3.2	6.3	-	-	-	-	-	-	-	-
Pursuit Money Market	CdnMkt	FixInc	3.5	4.0	6.1	6.2	4.6	6.4	7.7	12.6	11.0	9.5
Quebec Prof Bond	CdnBnd	FixInc	9.5	10.4	9.0	14.3	-2.0	10.4	16.7	15.5	3.7	10.3
Quebec Prof Short Term	CdnMkt	FixInc	3.9	3.9	6.6	7.5	3.9	6.0	9.7	12.8	9.7	9.9
Royal $US Money Market	USMkt	FixInc	4.6	4.4	4.5	4.3	2.2	2.3	4.0	-	-	-
Royal&SunAlliance Glo Emg	CdnBnd	FixInc	11.7	14.1	8.5	13.7	-1.5	11.9	18.4	13.6	1.9	11.0
Royal&SunAlliance US Eq	CdnMkt	FixInc	3.2	2.7	4.8	5.3	3.4	5.1	7.7	11.4	12.3	10.0
Royal Balanced	CdnMkt	FixInc	3.1	2.9	5.2	5.6	3.7	5.2	7.8	-	-	-
Royal Canadian Small Cap	GlbBnd	FixInc	9.1	5.6	1.9	11.5	6.9	20.6	-	-	-	-
Royal Japanese Stock	CdnBnd	FixInc	9.7	13.7	7.9	14.4	-4.1	12.0	13.1	10.0	-	-
Royal LePage Commercial	CdnMkt	FixInc	3.4	3.9	6.5	6.4	5.0	9.4	-	-	-	-
Royal Precious Metals	Mortge	FixInc	4.0	8.0	6.7	11.8	3.4	-	-	-	-	-
Royal Trust Adv. Balanced	CdnMkt	FixInc	3.9	-	-	-	-	-	-	-	-	-
SSQ - Hypotheques	Mortge	FixInc	3.4	8.1	9.6	12.2	4.6	8.1	13.1	18.5	9.5	-
SSQ - Marche Monetaire	CdnMkt	FixInc	4.0	4.0	6.6	7.1	-	-	-	-	-	-
SSQ - Obligations	CdnBnd	FixInc	11.1	14.6	11.6	16.3	-1.4	13.3	19.8	16.6	4.7	13.8
Sceptre Bond	CdnBnd	FixInc	13.3	14.0	8.8	14.3	-2.1	11.4	17.2	16.1	5.8	8.4
Sceptre Money Market	CdnMkt	FixInc	3.3	3.5	5.8	6.0	3.9	5.7	7.4	11.5	12.1	11.0
Scotia CanAm Income	ST Bnd	FixInc	7.3	5.4	2.7	11.0	-2.0	8.8	-	-	-	-
Scotia CanAm Money Market	USMkt	FixInc	4.7	-	-	-	-	-	-	-	-	-
Scotia Ex. Defensive Inc	ST Bnd	FixInc	3.8	6.2	8.1	11.7	0.9	7.9	12.3	12.3	3.7	8.4
Scotia Ex. Global Bond	GlbBnd	FixInc	9.7	4.9	-4.5	-	-	-	-	-	-	-
Scotia Ex. Income	CdnBnd	FixInc	6.5	9.6	9.1	15.5	-0.9	9.7	12.2	11.5	4.4	10.1
Scotia Ex. Money Market	CdnMkt	FixInc	3.1	2.7	5.2	5.7	3.7	4.7	7.3	-	-	-
Scotia Ex. Mortgage	Mortge	FixInc	3.7	8.0	7.3	14.3	1.4	-	-	-	-	-
Scotia Ex. Premium T-Bill	CdnMkt	FixInc	3.4	3.1	5.6	6.0	4.1	-	-	-	-	-
Scotia Ex. T-Bill	CdnMkt	FixInc	2.9	2.6	5.1	5.8	3.8	4.7	-	-	-	-

FUND NAME	FUND CATEGORY		% RETURN AT YEAR END									
			JUN89	JUN90	JUN91	JUN92	JUN93	JUN94	JUN95	JUN96	JUN97	JUN98
Scudder Cdn S-Term Bond	FixInc	ST Bnd	10.3	12.1	11.2	7.2	5.1	3.7	5.6	5.1	8.5	4.5
Spectrum Utd Cdn Money Mkt	FixInc	CdnMkt							15.9	-1.6	2.8	3.1
Spectrum Utd Global Bond	FixInc	GlbBnd		2.3	10.7	19.9	13.8	-5.7	17.5	7.1	5.6	6.5
Spectrum Utd Long-Term Bd	FixInc	CdnBnd	9.8	3.8	12.1	17.1	11.7	-4.6	16.0	8.2	15.3	16.7
Spectrum Utd Mid-Term Bond	FixInc	CdnBnd			11.4	7.3	5.0	8.9	13.1	-0.1	11.3	8.8
Spectrum Utd RSP Intl Bond	FixInc	GlbBnd	10.6	12.3	14.9	9.4	5.0	3.8	5.7	5.2	2.6	5.3
Spectrum Utd Savings	FixInc	CdnMkt	7.1	6.5	4.7	2.5	7.1	-1.4	13.0	6.9	2.8	3.0
Spectrum Utd Short-Term Bd	FixInc	B & M	9.4	7.3	13.8	13.5	2.7	2.9	4.9	4.5	6.5	3.2
Spectrum Utd US$ Money Mkt	FixInc	US$Mkt						-2.6	16.2	8.6	4.1	4.3
Standard Life Bond	FixInc	CdnBnd				15.0		3.4		0.6	11.9	9.1
Standard Life Intl Bond	FixInc	GlbBnd				7.0			10.3	5.5	4.8	15.4
Standard Life Money Market	FixInc	CdnMkt						-0.3	13.5		4.1	3.6
Stone & Co Flagship Mny Mk	FixInc	CdnMkt					8.0	-2.3	5.6			3.3
Strategic Val Govt Bond	FixInc	ST Bnd	10.4	4.7	12.9	17.7	11.0	3.5	15.3	7.4	6.4	4.5
Strategic Val Income	FixInc	CdnBnd	10.7	2.4	13.5	13.7	5.0	-2.4	10.7	8.2	10.4	15.0
Strategic Val Money Market	FixInc	CdnMkt			11.1	8.1	11.2	6.3	11.7	5.0	2.5	2.7
Tal/Hyper High Yield Bond	FixInc	CdnBnd	11.6	11.9	12.9	16.4	10.0	-0.2	6.2	8.7	12.4	11.0
Talvest Bond	FixInc	CdnBnd			13.5	8.1	5.7	4.3	7.8	1.2	9.1	8.9
Talvest Forgn Pay Cdn Bond	FixInc	GlbBnd	9.1	2.3	12.1	16.8	9.2	1.1	9.3	8.5	9.0	10.9
Talvest Income	FixInc	ST Bnd	10.8	5.6	8.6	7.4	11.5	3.3	5.7	5.9	3.4	3.9
Talvest Money	FixInc	CdnMkt			10.0	12.7	5.3	3.9	12.7	6.4	3.4	3.2
Templeton Canadian Bond	FixInc	CdnBnd		12.2	11.4	14.8	10.2	-4.8	10.1	6.8	8.3	5.0
Templeton Global Bond	FixInc	GlbBnd	10.2	9.7	11.3	7.6	6.1	-1.0	6.0	5.1	7.2	2.1
Templeton T-Bill	FixInc	CdnMkt			11.9		5.2	4.5		8.3	2.7	3.0
Tradex Bond	FixInc	CdnBnd			11.2			3.8		4.4	12.4	8.9
Trans-Canada Bond	FixInc	CdnBnd	6.2	12.2				-2.0		5.7	8.2	3.4
Trans-Canada Money Market	FixInc	CdnMkt	3.9					-2.6			4.0	3.2
Trimark Advantage Bond	FixInc	CdnBnd								11.3	15.3	10.2
Trimark Canadian Bond	FixInc	CdnBnd							12.1	10.4	12.2	9.6
Trimark Government Income	FixInc	ST Bnd	9.6	10.8						8.2	7.7	3.6
Trimark Interest	FixInc	CdnMkt						3.8	6.0	5.3	2.9	3.5
Universal US Money Market	FixInc	US$Mkt								3.9	3.8	3.7
Universal World Inc RRSP	FixInc	GlbBnd		12.8			4.9			9.9	10.4	12.8
Universal World Tact. Bond	FixInc	GlbBnd						-3.3		5.3	5.6	12.4
University Avenue Money	FixIntc	CdnMkt									2.8	3.1
Valorem Cdn Bond-Value	FixInc	CdnBnd										9.8
Valorem Government S-Term	FixInc	CdnMkt										2.7
Westbury Cdn Life B	FixInc	CdnBnd	8.6	5.8			12.7	-2.0	15.8	9.5	13.5	10.2
Westbury Cdn Life Bond	FixInc	CdnBnd					10.0	-2.6	12.7	7.6	11.2	8.1
Westbury Cdn Life C	FixInc	CdnMkt	10.2	10.9	10.4	6.1	4.8	4.9	6.2	5.6	3.8	3.5
YMG Income	FixInc	CdnBnd	11.1	2.7	9.8	14.9	11.4	-3.3	15.1	8.3	14.3	-5.3
YMG Money Market	FixInc	CdnMkt	10.5	12.1	11.6	7.5	5.3	4.2	6.1	5.9	3.4	3.4

% RETURN AT YEAR END

FUND NAME	FUND CATEGORY	JUN98	JUN97	JUN96	JUN95	JUN94	JUN93	JUN92	JUN91	JUN90	JUN89
B.E.S.T. Discoveries	Labour LSVC	-3.2	-	-	-	-	-	-	-	-	-
C.I. Covington	Labour LSVC	0.5	9.9	6.4	-	-	-	-	-	-	-
Canadian Medical Discov.	Labour LSVC	2.4	-1.3	10.0	-	-	-	-	-	-	-
Canadian Venture Opportun	Labour LSVC	-9.4	-2.0	-16.4	-17.5	-	-	-	-	-	-
Capital Alliance Ventures	Labour LSVC	1.2	-7.3	17.7	-	-	-	-	-	-	-
Cdn Science & Tech Gth Inc	Labour LSVC	-1.4	-	-	-	-	-	-	-	-	-
Centerfire Growth Fund Inc	Labour LSVC	4.3	-	-	-	-	-	-	-	-	-
Crocus Investment Fund	Labour LSVC	12.5	1.8	7.2	6.1	3.8	-	-	-	-	-
DGC Entertainment Ventures	Labour LSVC	0.3	9.0	8.0	0.8	-	-	-	-	-	-
Enterprise Fund	Labour LSVC	-10.9	7.1	-7.4	-	-	-	-	-	-	-
First Ontario	Labour LSVC	7.1	2.4	2.0	-	-	-	-	-	-	-
Innovacap Capital Corp.	Labour LSVC	-12.3	-	-	-	-	-	-	-	-	-
Retrocom Growth	Labour LSVC	5.6	2.8	2.6	-	-	-	-	-	-	-
Sportfund	Labour LSVC	-6.9	16.9	7.5	-	-	-	-	-	-	-
Triax Growth	Labour LSVC	5.4	1.3	-	-	-	-	-	-	-	-
Trillium Growth Cap Inc.	Labour LSVC	-6.7	-4.8	0.9	-	-	-	-	-	-	-
VenGrowth Fund	Labour LSVC	5.7	10.2	4.2	-	-	-	-	-	-	-
Workers Investment	Labour LSVC	0.0	-	-	-	-	-	-	-	-	-
Working Opportunity (EVCC)	Labour LSVC	8.5	4.1	11.3	3.1	2.0	0.8	-	-	-	-
Working Ventures Canadian	Labour LSVC	3.4	-0.7	5.0	5.8	1.2	2.8	5.0	8.5	-	-
Average All Funds	Avg	7.7	16.1	12.3	9.7	5.1	19.0	9.2	5.9	3.9	10.2
Average Asset Alloc Serv	Avg	9.1	16.1	12.5	11.7	0.9	18.4	12.6	8.5	-	-
Average Balanced Funds	Avg	11.1	19.0	11.1	11.6	2.7	17.1	9.8	7.4	1.9	10.7
Average Cdn Diver Equity	Avg	10.6	25.4	14.3	11.7	2.3	26.3	3.7	4.1	-1.7	12.0
Average Cdn Dividend Funds	Avg	15.6	28.3	13.2	12.5	3.6	14.9	6.2	5.8	-0.1	10.6
Average Cdn Large Cap	Avg	13.0	29.0	11.8	13.9	1.2	17.9	2.4	3.0	-2.2	15.2
Average Cdn Sector Funds	Avg	-24.8	-0.5	28.6	2.2	1.0	92.8	2.6	-5.6	0.1	-3.7
Average Cdn Small Cap	Avg	3.1	18.9	25.8	8.0	5.7	51.1	5.9	1.3	-0.8	9.6
Average Fixed Income Funds	Avg	7.9	9.9	7.3	12.9	-0.6	11.3	16.4	12.8	4.2	10.3
Average LSVC Funds	Avg	0.3	3.3	4.2	-0.3	2.3	1.8	5.0	8.5	-	-
Average Money Market Funds	Avg	3.3	3.1	5.2	5.7	3.7	5.0	7.3	11.1	11.4	9.8
Average Other Country Eq	Avg	-16.6	2.5	8.4	-15.2	25.7	28.0	-12.2	-11.6	3.2	-5.4
Average Regional Eq Funds	Avg	0.6	18.3	13.9	2.7	20.5	17.5	13.5	-3.6	9.3	9.1
Average Specialty Funds	Avg	14.6	10.7	19.7	13.1	5.9	14.4	-2.4	-0.6	9.2	1.2
Average U.S. Equity Funds	Avg	28.9	25.1	19.1	19.4	7.3	20.0	11.9	4.5	9.9	12.4
Avg Americas Equity	Avg	14.4	15.5	21.2	2.2	7.4	21.7	13.1	-0.1	4.7	11.3
Avg Asia-Pacific Rim Eq	Avg	-42.8	8.4	9.0	-1.9	35.5	21.1	15.6	-6.6	18.3	-15.5
Avg Bond & Mortgage	Avg	4.8	9.0	8.0	12.0	0.7	10.4	12.0	13.3	7.0	10.0
Avg Cdn Balanced (S.A.A.)	Avg	10.2	19.6	11.0	12.5	1.6	16.5	9.3	8.4	1.5	11.0
Avg Cdn Balanced (T.A.A.)	Avg	10.8	20.2	10.7	11.9	2.9	19.8	9.5	7.0	1.6	10.6
Avg Cdn Bond	Avg	9.4	12.4	8.2	14.6	-2.2	11.8	17.3	12.8	3.1	11.0
Avg Cdn Consumer Sector	Avg	6.3	16.0	0.1	11.0	5.7	-	-	-	-	-
Avg Cdn Divers -Growth	Avg	15.4	25.0	22.8	9.5	0.2	34.6	13.1	9.0	-4.6	9.5
Avg Cdn Divers -Neutral	Avg	9.8	24.3	13.2	12.3	2.1	25.5	3.2	3.2	-1.6	12.2

% RETURN AT YEAR END

FUND NAME	FUND CATEGORY	JUN98	JUN97	JUN96	JUN95	JUN94	JUN93	JUN92	JUN91	JUN90	JUN89
Avg Cdn Divers -Value	Avg	10.7	32.5	13.1	9.6	7.2	27.7	1.5	10.1	0.4	12.8
Avg Cdn Financial Services	Avg	25.4	82.9	38.9	24.8	10.1	30.3	17.0	14.5	-8.0	11.7
Avg Cdn Gold/Prec Metals	Avg	-33.8	-22.4	39.9	7.3	16.3	53.1	-1.6	-8.8	-0.5	-8.1
Avg Cdn Large Cap -Growth	Avg	15.6	14.0	4.0	14.8	6.6	20.8	19.7	3.1	6.3	12.0
Avg Cdn Large Cap -Neutral	Avg	13.5	29.7	12.1	13.4	0.6	17.8	2.1	3.4	-3.0	15.4
Avg Cdn Large Cap -Value	Avg	10.0	28.0	11.6	16.1	3.0	18.1	-0.6	0.0	2.7	14.7
Avg Cdn Money Market	Avg	3.1	3.0	5.3	5.9	3.7	5.2	7.5	11.4	11.6	9.8
Avg Cdn Real Estate	Avg	2.8	3.9	2.0	3.8	-2.1	-6.1	-1.3	3.2	8.8	10.7
Avg Cdn Resource Sector	Avg	-25.3	7.3	22.3	-3.4	-7.3	116.5	3.3	-5.9	1.3	-3.4
Avg Cdn Science & Tech	Avg										
Avg Cdn Short Term Bond	Avg	4.2	7.5	7.7	11.0	0.1	9.0	13.3	13.2	5.5	9.6
Avg Cdn Small Cap -Growth	Avg	0.6	18.9	27.0	6.6	2.5	50.5	8.0	1.6	1.7	15.9
Avg Cdn Small Cap -Neutral	Avg	4.2	18.7	26.7	11.4	8.6	55.8	7.8	2.9	-2.3	4.6
Avg Cdn Small Cap -Value	Avg	11.1	19.8	15.7	4.6	10.2	43.8	-1.2	-1.8	-2.9	7.9
Avg Chinese Equity	Avg	-29.3	17.0	3.8							
Avg Currency Oriented	Avg	18.5	10.7	22.1	4.1						
Avg Emerging Markets Eq	Avg	-30.4	16.7	9.8	-7.3	33.1	16.5				
Avg European Equity	Avg	37.4	25.6	14.8	10.6	16.8	-0.7	20.6	-14.6	0.3	3.4
Avg German Equity	Avg	41.3	26.2	7.3							
Avg Global/Foreign-Pay Bnd	Avg	7.9	7.1	5.4	9.3	4.4	14.7	21.4	4.9	5.8	3.9
Avg Global Balanced S.A.A.	Avg	13.8	15.6	12.4	7.9	8.7	13.3	12.5	3.4	4.1	7.5
Avg Global Balanced T.A.A.	Avg	19.7	16.2	12.0	3.2	14.8	19.2	18.1	-3.5	7.4	4.0
Avg Global Equity	Avg	14.3	18.1	16.2	5.6	19.5	18.6	13.8	-2.4	10.3	10.1
Avg Global Precious Metals	Avg	-40.0	-13.2	6.7	-10.9	34.6	65.5	-7.8	-1.1	3.4	-20.4
Avg Global Real Estate	Avg	13.3	33.0	42.8							
Avg Global Science & Tech	Avg	28.7	12.8	30.3	26.5	4.4	25.1	-0.4	-11.4	16.4	3.7
Avg Indian Equity	Avg	-16.8	-15.0	-22.0							
Avg International Equity	Avg	11.5	16.5	14.0	-0.9	26.4	14.0	9.4	-10.0	13.1	12.6
Avg Intl Money Market	Avg	3.9	0.7	2.8	1.7	11.6	8.8	16.2	16.2		
Avg Japanese Equity	Avg	-26.5	-6.4	14.0	-22.9	24.0	34.5	-12.2	-11.6	3.2	-5.4
Avg Korean Equity	Avg	-66.2	-20.7	-18.2	-0.1	32.8	8.6				
Avg Latin American Equity	Avg	-20.7	37.6	18.6	-14.0						
Avg Mortgage	Avg	4.3	7.1	6.9	11.8	1.9	8.4	12.6	16.2	7.7	9.4
Avg North American Equity	Avg	16.2	24.3	16.1	10.2	3.7	28.8	9.9	1.6	0.0	14.7
Avg Specialty: Other	Avg	-4.4	13.2	11.9	-1.8						
Avg Strategic A.A.Services	Avg	9.2	16.4	12.7							
Avg Tactical A.A. Services	Avg	3.4	9.1	10.7	11.7	0.9	18.4	12.6	8.5		
Avg U.S. Large Cap	Avg	29.4	26.9	18.3	19.6	7.5	18.1	12.2	4.4	11.3	13.6
Avg U.S. Mid Cap	Avg	29.6	24.4	20.9	17.8	6.4	19.4	10.9	4.5	7.4	13.4
Avg U.S. Money Market	Avg	4.6	4.4	4.6	4.5	2.5	2.5	4.0	6.1	7.9	10.0
Avg U.S. Small Cap	Avg	20.0	13.9	16.0	25.0	9.9	35.7	14.3	6.6	13.1	-17.9
Average 5 Yr GIC	Index	4.5	5.1	6.3	7.8	6.3	7.1	8.7	10.2	10.7	10.4
CPI	Index	1.1	1.5	1.5	2.9	-0.2	1.8	1.4	6.2	4.4	5.0
Canada Savings Bonds	Index	3.0	3.7	5.4	5.2	4.8	6.5	8.6	10.8	10.7	9.8
TSE 300	Index	16.2	30.1	13.9	15.2	3.9	20.8	1.1	1.9	-2.4	13.5

Survey of Fund Volatility and Compound Performance for Periods Ended June 30, 1998

This table shows total return for the year ended June 30, 1998, and compound returns for two, three, five, 10 and 15 years. In addition it indicates RRSP eligibility, volatility, management expense ratio, sales fees, and total assets. Funds are listed by category:

Divers=Diversified;

SC=Small capitalization;

LC=Large capitalization;

FinServ=Financial Services;

PrMet=Precious Metals;

LSVC=Labour Sponsored Investment Fund;

SAA=Strategic Asset Allocation;

TAA=Tactical Asset Allocation.

Table prepared using PAL*Trak*

© Copyright Portfolio Analytics Limited, 1998

FUND NAME	FUND CATEGORY	RRSP ELIGIB.	1 YR	2 YR	3 YR	5 YR	10 YR	15 YR	3 YR VOLATILITY	MER	SALES FEES	ASSETS IN $MIL
20/20 RSP Aggr Smaller Co	CdnEq Growth	Yes	20.7	14.2						2.7	F or B	468.3
20/20 RSP Aggressive Eq	CdnEq Growth	Yes	24.0	12.4	25.7				High	2.5	F or B	345.8
@rgentum Cdn Eq Portfolio	CdnEq Divers	Yes									F or B	1.1
@rgentum Cdn Small Com Pfl	CdnEq SCDivers	Yes									F or B	0.2
ABC Fundamental-value	CdnEq Value	Yes	6.6	18.8	17.9	18.9			Med–	2.0	None	296.9
AGF Canadian Equity	CdnEq Divers	Yes	0.7	5.8	9.5	7.4	5.4	7.8	High	3.0	F or B	613.7
AGF Canadian Growth	CdnEq Divers	Yes	12.7	18.4	13.6	12.5			Med+	2.5	F or B	394.2
AGF Growth Equity	CdnEq Growth	Yes	6.4	13.6	16.2	10.6	11.9	10.7	High	2.8	F or B	923.2
AGF Intl Grp-Canada Class	CdnEq Divers	Fgn	-2.4							2.6	F or B	7.0
AIC Advantage Fund II	CdnEq Divers	Yes	28.2							2.6	F or B	4389.3
AIC Diversified Canada	CdnEq Growth	Yes	32.4	47.6	42.5				Med+	2.4	F or B	2082.3
AIM Canadian Premier	CdnEq Divers	Yes	18.8	17.7	17.0	11.6			High	2.8	F or B	56.7
AIM GT Canada Growth	CdnEq Growth	Yes	25.1	19.3	24.0				High	2.5	F or B	809.0
AIM GT Canada valuee	CdnEq LCValue	Yes								2.9	F or B	22.8
APEX Canadian Growth (AGF)	CdnEq Divers	Yes	3.1	8.9	10.4	10.2	7.6	7.4	High	3.0	F or B	50.7
APEX Canadian Stock	CdnEq Divers	Yes	10.9							2.5	F or B	28.3
Acadia Canadian Equity	CdnEq Divers	Yes									Defer	1.0
Acker Finley QSA Cdn Eq	CdnEq Divers	Yes								1.0	Front	4.7
Acuity Pld Cdn Equity	CdnEq Divers	Yes	31.4	49.4	37.6	23.0			High		None	
All-Canadian Capital Fund	CdnEq Divers	Yes	4.9	2.3	3.2	6.7	6.8	7.3	Low	2.0	Front	13.1
All-Canadian Compound	CdnEq Divers	Yes	4.8	2.3	2.9	6.6	6.7	7.2	Low	0.0	None	11.7
Allstar AIG Canadian Eq	CdnEq LCDivers	Yes	12.9	20.1	16.5	11.1			Low	2.7	Front	4.7
Alpha Quantitative Equity	CdnEq Divers	Yes									F or B	2.1
Alpha Quantitative valuee	CdnEq Value	Yes									F or B	1.7
Altafund Investment Corp.	CdnEq Divers	Yes	-18.6	0.9	7.7	5.1	11.5		High	0.0	None	149.5
Altamira Capital Growth	CdnEq LCGrowth	Yes	15.6	14.8	11.1	10.9	19.0	9.4	Med+	2.3	None	145.2
Altamira Equity	CdnEq Divers	Yes	1.2	6.9	9.2	8.0	19.0		Med+	2.0	None	1549.3
Altamira Special Growth	CdnEq SCGrowth	Yes	2.5	10.6	14.4	5.6	13.4		Med	2.3	None	256.2
Artisan Canadian Equity	CdnEq Divers	Yes								1.8	F or B	0.9
Associate Investors	CdnEq Value	Yes	34.6	36.7	28.6	18.6	12.2	11.8	Low	3.0	None	15.4
Astra Actions canadiennes	CdnEq Divers	Yes								2.4	None	8.0
Atlas Cdn Emerging Growth	CdnEq SCGrowth	Yes	-22.2	-5.8	5.4				Med+	1.8	F or B	55.0
Atlas Cdn Large Cap Growth	CdnEq LCDivers	Yes	20.2	27.0	23.2	16.7	10.3		Med–	2.4	F or B	618.1
Atlas Cdn Large Cap value	CdnEq LCDivers	Yes	14.4	18.0	13.8				Med–	2.5	F or B	54.0
Atlas Cdn Small Cap Growth	CdnEq SCDivers	Yes	5.0							2.5	F or B	127.2
Atlas Cdn Small Cap value	CdnEq SCDivers	Yes	0.8	14.3	12.9				Med+	2.6	F or B	39.8
Azura Growth RSP Pooled	CdnEq Growth	Yes	6.6	12.4						2.7	F or B	29.2
Azura RSP Aggressive Gth	CdnEq Divers	Yes								2.6	F or B	7.1
BNP (Canada) Equity	CdnEq Divers	Yes	14.5	22.3	19.2	13.4			Med–	2.3	None	8.1
BPI Canadian Eq value Sgr	CdnEq Value	Yes								2.3	F or B	6.5
BPI Canadian Equity value	CdnEq Value	Yes	8.9	15.1	17.1	9.9			Med	2.5	F or B	483.6
BPI Canadian Mid-Cap	CdnEq Divers	Yes	3.5							2.9	F or B	37.5
BPI Canadian Mid-Cap Sgr	CdnEq Divers	Yes									F or B	1.5
BPI Cdn Opportunities RSP	CdnEq Divers	Yes	-19.6	-8.5						2.5	F or B	57.8

FUND NAME	FUND CATEGORY		RRSP-ELIGIB.	1 YR	2 YR	3 YR	5 YR	10 YR	15 YR	3 YR VOLATILITY	MER	SALES FEES	ASSETS IN $MIL
BPI Cdn Small Companies	CdnEq	SCDivers	Yes	-24.0	-12.7	5.5	5.1	8.0		High	2.9	F or B	347.6
BPI Dividend Equity	CdnEq	Divers	Yes									F or B	1.8
Batirente Sec Actions	CdnEq	Value	Yes	17.0	24.5	19.6	13.4			Med-	1.5	None	4.4
Beutel Goodman Cdn Equity	CdnEq	Divers	Yes	12.5	18.3	14.6				Low	2.1	Front	60.4
Beutel Goodman Small Cap	CdnEq	SCDivers	Yes	3.4	19.7	21.5				Med+	2.4	Front	14.1
Bissett Canadian Equity	CdnEq	Divers	Yes	23.0	32.0	27.7	19.3	15.0	13.5	Med-	1.4	None	482.8
Bissett Microcap	CdnEq	SCDivers	Yes								2.0	None	26.0
Bissett Small Capital	CdnEq	SCDivers	Yes	6.8	23.7	25.0	17.5			Med-	1.9	None	129.5
C.I. Canadian Growth	CdnEq	Divers	Yes	14.8	13.3	12.1	11.4			Med	2.4	F or B	879.1
C.I. Canadian Sector	CdnEq	Divers	Fgn	11.4	11.2	10.5	10.2	6.3		Med-	2.4	F or B	49.1
C.I. Harbour Explorer Sect	CdnEq	SCGrowth	Fgn								2.3	F or B	1.0
C.I. Harbour Sector	CdnEq	Value	Fgn	4.1							2.3	F or B	32.1
C.I. Harbour Segregated	CdnEq	Value	Yes								3.1	F or B	25.6
CCPE Growth R	CdnEq	LCDivers	Yes	10.5	18.8	15.6	13.3	9.3		Med-	1.4	None	39.3
CDA Aggressive Equity (A)	CdnEq	SCGrowth	Yes	5.9	14.3	15.8				Med	1.0	None	7.7
CDA Canadian Eq (Trimark)	CdnEq	Divers	Yes	1.4							1.5	None	10.3
CDA Common Stock(Altamira)	CdnEq	Divers	Yes	9.3	10.8	10.2	8.7	8.8	10.6	Med+	1.0	None	41.1
CDA Special Equity (KBSH)	CdnEq	SCDivers	Yes	15.0							1.5	None	18.5
CIBC Canadian Equity	CdnEq	Divers	Yes	19.4	22.9	17.4	11.3			Med	2.2	None	1196.0
CIBC Canadian Index	CdnEq	Divers	Yes	15.5							0.9	None	398.6
CIBC Capital Appreciation	CdnEq	Divers	Yes	12.7	16.9	14.0	8.0			High	2.4	None	546.3
CT Canadian Equity Index	CdnEq	Divers	Yes	14.8							0.8	None	32.3
CT Special Equity	CdnEq	SCGrowth	Yes	4.8	11.4	12.2	6.2	9.5		Med	2.2	None	363.3
CT Stock	CdnEq	LCDivers	Yes	12.5	21.4	16.5	11.8			High	1.9	None	1039.9
CUMIS Life Cdn Growth Eq	CdnEq	Divers	Yes	2.4							3.0	Back	2.7
Caldwell Canadian Equity	CdnEq	LCValue	Yes	2.5							0.5	F or B	2.5
Cambridge Growth	CdnEq	SCDivers	Yes	-29.0	-31.8	-16.4	-12.5	0.0	5.8	High	3.5	F or B	11.8
Cambridge Special Equity	CdnEq	SCGrowth	Yes	-22.5	-36.0	-12.4	-12.1	-3.0		High	3.5	F or B	3.7
Canada Life Cdn Equity	CdnEq	LCDivers	Yes	9.6	18.2	16.4	12.1	9.3	10.6	Low	2.3	Defer	699.7
Canada Life S-2	CdnEq	Divers	Yes	10.6	19.0	17.2	12.8	10.2	11.5	Low	1.5	Defer	184.2
Canadian Protected	CdnEq	Divers	Yes	9.6	5.0	4.7	2.9	6.5		Low	2.4	F or B	1.3
Canso Canadian Equity	CdnEq	Divers	Yes									F or B	0.9
Cdn Anaes. Mutual Accum.	CdnEq	Divers	Yes	10.6	17.7	17.3	12.4	8.3	9.5	Med+	1.5	None	39.8
CentrePost Canadian Equity	CdnEq	Divers	Yes	2.6	10.5	13.4	5.8			Med-	1.0	None	21.8
Chou RRSP	CdnEq	SCValue	Yes	43.9	37.1	31.3	19.1	11.5		Low	2.0	Front	2.2
Clarington Canadian Equity	CdnEq	Divers	Yes	8.0							2.8	F or B	52.6
Clarington Cdn Micro-Cap	CdnEq	SCDivers	Yes								3.0	F or B	3.2
Clarington Cdn Small Cap	CdnEq	SCDivers	Yes	3.2							2.8	F or B	24.3
Clean Environment Equity	CdnEq	Growth	Yes	29.0	30.3	26.5	19.0			Med	2.6	F or B	305.7
Co-Operators Canadian Eq	CdnEq	Divers	Yes	20.1	23.8	18.2	14.1			Med	2.1	None	25.4
Colonia Life Equity	CdnEq	Divers	Yes	19.2	25.8	19.1	11.8			Med+	2.3	Defer	33.2
Colonia Life Special Gth	CdnEq	SCGrowth	Yes	6.7	22.4	27.6				High	2.3	Defer	32.9
Comm. Un. Cdn TSE35 Index	CdnEq	LCDivers	Yes								2.6	Defer	9.1
Cornerstone Cdn Growth	CdnEq	Divers	Yes	4.9	10.7	13.5	10.5	9.0		Med+	2.2	None	70.0

FUND NAME	FUND CATEGORY	RRSP. ELIGIB.	1 YR	2 YR	3 YR	5 YR	10 YR	15 YR	3 YR VOLATILITY	MER	SALES FEES	ASSETS IN $MIL
Cote 100 EXP	CdnEq	SCDivers	Yes	15.0	21.6	22.4	-	-	-	Low	2.6	None	48.0
Cote 100 REA - action	CdnEq	SCDivers	Fgn	8.8	11.2	-	-	-	-	-	2.6	None	12.2
Cote 100 REER	CdnEq	Divers	Yes	16.9	23.7	22.1	17.2	-	-	Med+	1.4	None	45.1
Cundill Security A	CdnEq	SCValue	Yes	17.8	20.3	17.0	17.5	9.2	10.2	Low	2.0	Front	31.2
Cundill Security B	CdnEq	SCValue	Yes	17.3	-	-	-	-	-	-	2.4	Front	18.4
Desjardins Distinct Eqty	CdnEq	LCDivers	Yes	11.7	21.5	18.3	14.0	11.0	11.2	Med	2.0	None	36.4
Desjardins Environment	CdnEq	Divers	Yes	16.2	25.6	19.3	14.5	-	-	Med-	2.1	None	147.0
Desjardins Equity	CdnEq	Divers	Yes	9.9	19.1	15.8	11.6	8.9	7.5	Med-	1.9	None	193.0
Desjardins Growth	CdnEq	Growth	Yes	16.9	18.5	16.7	-	-	-	High	2.0	None	113.8
Desjardins High Potential	CdnEq	SCDivers	Yes	-	-	-	-	-	-	-	-	None	18.8
Dynamic Cdn Growth	CdnEq	Divers	Yes	-5.8	6.7	9.0	6.6	13.3	-	High	2.3	F or B	677.6
Dynamic Fund of Canada	CdnEq	Divers	Yes	6.2	16.2	13.0	7.0	10.1	10.2	Med-	2.2	F or B	262.1
Dynamic Quebec	CdnEq	Divers	Yes	11.7	-	-	-	-	-	-	2.5	F or B	22.9
Dynamic Small Cap	CdnEq	SCDivers	Yes	17.0	-	-	-	-	-	-	3.0	F or B	43.3
Elliott & Page Equity	CdnEq	Divers	Yes	3.6	10.4	13.5	11.0	11.6	-	Med	1.9	F or B	834.4
Elliott & Page valuee Eq	CdnEq	LCValue	Yes	-	-	-	-	-	-	-	2.1	F or B	32.1
Empire Elite Equity	CdnEq	LCDivers	Yes	8.1	19.4	17.4	11.7	9.8	10.7	Low	2.4	Defer	653.8
Empire Elite Small Cap Eq	CdnEq	SCDivers	Yes	-	-	-	-	-	-	-	2.6	Defer	8.2
Empire Equity Growth #3	CdnEq	LCDivers	Yes	10.8	22.8	20.2	14.7	11.8	12.1	Med-	1.2	Front	15.3
Empire Premier Equity	CdnEq	LCDivers	Yes	10.0	22.0	19.2	13.7	10.8	11.3	Med-	1.4	Front	225.6
Equitable Life Cdn Stock	CdnEq	Divers	Yes	6.4	15.9	14.3	12.2	-	-	Low	2.3	Defer	85.0
Equitable Life Common Stck	CdnEq	Divers	Yes	6.9	18.4	17.2	15.3	9.7	9.6	Med	1.0	Front	23.0
Ethical Growth	CdnEq	LCDivers	Yes	13.7	22.4	20.0	14.7	11.8	-	Med+	2.1	None	805.0
Ethical Special Equity	CdnEq	SCDivers	Yes	4.5	11.8	14.4	-	-	-	Low	2.7	None	90.0
FIRM Canadian Growth	CdnEq	Divers	Yes	15.7	-	-	-	-	-	-	2.3	None	10.8
FMOQ Canadian Equity	CdnEq	Divers	Yes	30.9	27.6	21.2	-	-	-	Med+	0.8	None	4.8
Ficadre Actions	CdnEq	Divers	Yes	4.8	14.0	14.4	12.4	6.3	-	Med+	2.2	Defer	16.1
Fidelity Capital Builder	CdnEq	Growth	Yes	5.2	10.0	10.9	7.3	8.8	-	Med-	2.5	F or B	394.3
Fidelity Cdn Gth Company	CdnEq	SCGrowth	Yes	22.9	25.6	23.8	-	-	-	Low	2.5	F or B	1582.7
Fidelity True North	CdnEq	Divers	Yes	16.1	-	-	-	-	-	-	2.5	F or B	1414.7
First Canadian Eq Index	CdnEq	Divers	Yes	14.7	21.3	18.2	13.8	9.1	-	Med	1.2	None	412.3
First Canadian Growth	CdnEq	Divers	Yes	16.0	24.1	20.4	-	-	-	Med-	2.2	None	1225.4
First Canadian Special Gth	CdnEq	SCGrowth	Yes	4.9	17.1	18.5	-	-	-	Med-	2.2	None	442.2
Fonds D'Investissement REA	CdnEq	SCDivers	Yes	25.3	27.4	22.0	11.9	-	-	Low	2.8	Defer	63.7
GBC Canadian Growth	CdnEq	SCGrowth	Yes	18.3	25.9	24.5	15.2	-	-	Med-	1.9	None	203.9
GS Canadian Equity	CdnEq	Value	Yes	6.5	17.5	-	-	-	-	-	2.8	FnDf	340.1
General Trust Cdn Equity	CdnEq	LCDivers	Yes	0.0	14.3	13.6	10.7	7.1	7.6	High	2.1	None	34.8
General Trust Growth	CdnEq	SCDivers	Yes	11.8	19.5	16.2	9.8	12.0	-	Med-	2.2	None	17.7
Global Strategy Canada Gth	CdnEq	Value	Yes	7.0	16.3	14.5	10.8	-	-	Low	2.6	F or B	605.1
Global Strategy Cdn Opport	CdnEq	Divers	Yes	14.6	-	-	-	-	-	-	2.6	F or B	155.1
Global Strategy Cdn Sm Cap	CdnEq	SCDivers	Yes	-1.0	19.6	16.7	-	-	-	Med	2.7	F or B	387.9
Goodwood Fund	CdnEq	Value	No	38.6	-	-	-	-	-	-	1.5	Back	2.1
Great-West Cdn Eq (G) A	CdnEq	Growth	Yes	7.6	15.8	14.8	9.2	9.9	-	High	2.6	None	238.6
Great-West Cdn Eq (G) B	CdnEq	Growth	Yes	7.9	16.1	15.1	-	-	-	High	2.4	Defer	142.8

FUND NAME	FUND CATEGORY	RRSP. ELIGIB.	1 YR	2 YR	3 YR	5 YR	10 YR	15 YR	3 YR VOLATILITY	MER	SALES FEES	ASSETS IN $MIL
Great-West Eq Index (G) A	CdnEq	Divers	Yes	13.1	19.6	16.7	12.6	8.5	8.5	Med	2.6	None	70.2
Great-West Eq Index (G) B	CdnEq	Divers	Yes	13.3	19.9	16.9				Med	2.3	Defer	27.4
Great-West Equity (M) A	CdnEq	Divers	Yes	13.4	18.5						2.9	None	41.2
Great-West Equity (M) B	CdnEq	Divers	Yes	13.7	18.8						2.6	Defer	52.5
Great-West Equity (S) A	CdnEq	Value	Yes	10.2	20.2						2.9	None	53.8
Great-West Equity (S) B	CdnEq	Value	Yes	10.5	20.5						2.6	Defer	44.0
Great-West Gth Equity (A)A	CdnEq	Growth	Yes	4.6	13.5						3.2	None	34.4
Great-West Gth Equity (A)B	CdnEq	Growth	Yes	4.9	13.8						3.0	Defer	30.4
Great-West Lg Company(M)A	CdnEq	Divers	Yes	9.8	14.2						2.9	None	10.8
Great-West Lg Company(M)B	CdnEq	Divers	Yes	10.1	14.5						2.7	Defer	12.0
Great-West Mid Cap Cda(G)A	CdnEq	Growth	Yes								2.6	None	3.4
Great-West Mid Cap Cda(G)B	CdnEq	Growth	Yes								2.4	Defer	4.3
Great-West Smaller Co.(M)A	CdnEq	Divers	Yes	12.2	13.5						2.9	None	21.7
Great-West Smaller Co.(M)B	CdnEq	Divers	Yes	12.5	13.8						2.7	Defer	22.9
Green Line Blue Chip Eq.	CdnEq	LCDivers	Yes	10.2	20.2	18.1	12.5	9.2		Med	2.3	None	440.4
Green Line Canadian Equity	CdnEq	Divers	Yes	11.2	23.0	18.3	13.3			Med	2.1	None	949.9
Green Line Canadian Index	CdnEq	Divers	Yes	15.4	21.7	18.6	14.3	9.6		Med	1.1	None	429.7
Green Line Cdn Small-Cap	CdnEq	SCDivers	Yes								2.4	None	40.3
Green Line valuee	CdnEq	Value	Yes	4.5	20.9	21.3				Med+	2.1	None	547.8
GrowSafe Canadian Equity	CdnEq	Value	Yes	3.0	14.3	12.8				Low	2.5	Defer	101.0
Guardian Enterprise C	CdnEq	SCGrowth	Yes	-4.6	12.2	22.4	14.3	10.3	10.4	Med+	2.1	Front	58.5
Guardian Enterprise M	CdnEq	SCGrowth	Yes	-5.3	11.5						2.8	F or B	222.1
Guardian Growth Equity C	CdnEq	Divers	Yes	4.4	18.8	18.8	11.7			Med-	2.2	Front	72.2
Guardian Growth Equity M	CdnEq	Divers	Yes	3.8	18.1						2.8	F or B	245.7
Harbour Explorer	CdnEq	SCGrowth	Yes								2.3	F or B	23.5
Harbour Fund	CdnEq	Value	Yes	5.2							2.3	F or B	779.0
Hartford Aggressive Growth	CdnEq	SCGrowth	Yes								2.8	Defer	3.1
Hartford Canadian Equity	CdnEq	Divers	Yes								2.8	Defer	2.5
Hirsch Canadian Growth	CdnEq	Divers	Yes								2.8	F or B	10.8
Hongkong Bank Equity	CdnEq	Divers	Yes	12.8	21.8	19.4	12.4			Med-	1.9	None	196.7
Hongkong Bank Sml Cap Gth	CdnEq	SCGrowth	Yes	6.5	16.5	19.6				Med+	2.2	None	59.2
ICM Equity	CdnEq	Divers	Yes	8.6	12.6	12.9	12.4	10.1		Low	0.1	None	255.7
IG BG Canadian Small Cap	CdnEq	SCDivers	Yes	1.9							2.8	FnDf	133.7
IG Beutel Goodman Cdn Eq	CdnEq	Divers	Yes	13.3							2.8	FnDf	62.2
IG Sceptre Canadian Equity	CdnEq	Divers	Yes	10.5							2.8	FnDf	351.4
Ideal Equity	CdnEq	Divers	Yes	20.1	23.5	21.8	16.8	11.5		Low	2.0	Defer	232.0
Imperial Gth Cdn Equity	CdnEq	LCDivers	Yes	9.4	18.3	15.4	11.7	10.4	13.0	Med+	2.0	Front	70.3
Ind. Alliance Can Advantag	CdnEq	Divers	Yes								1.5	None	0.0
Ind. Alliance Ecoflex A	CdnEq	LCValue	No	2.2	12.8	11.5	11.9			Med	2.5	Defer	202.4
Ind. Alliance Ecoflex ANL	CdnEq	LCValue	Yes								2.4	Defer	2.7
Ind. Alliance Ecoflex N	CdnEq	Divers	Yes								2.4	Defer	12.4
Ind. Alliance Ecoflex T	CdnEq	Divers	Fgn	4.1							2.4	None	11.4
Ind. Alliance Stock 2	CdnEq	Divers	Yes								2.8	None	2.1
Ind. Alliance Stock ANL	CdnEq	LCValue	No								1.5	None	0.7

FUND NAME	FUND CATEGORY		RRSP-ELIGIB.	1 YR	2 YR	3 YR	5 YR	10 YR	15 YR	3 YR VOLATILITY	MER	SALES FEES	ASSETS IN $MIL
Ind. Alliance Stocks	CdnEq	LCValue	Yes	3.1	13.7	12.3	12.6	11.3	10.4	Med	1.6	None	41.7
Industrial Equity	CdnEq	SCValue	Yes	-29.7	-15.1	-8.3	-5.9	0.4	4.3	Med+	2.4	F or B	79.6
Industrial Growth	CdnEq	Divers	Yes	-5.8	4.8	6.3	6.1	5.4	8.6	High	2.4	F or B	840.2
Industrial Horizon	CdnEq	Divers	Yes	15.4	18.6	15.0	12.6	8.8		Low	2.4	F or B	1063.7
Infinity Canadian	CdnEq	Growth	Yes	25.3							3.0	F or B	435.1
InvesNat Canadian Equity	CdnEq	Divers	Yes	0.5	14.4	13.8	10.7			Med	2.1	None	270.2
InvesNat Cdn Index Plus	CdnEq	Divers	Yes								1.2	None	16.6
InvesNat Protected Cdn Eq	CdnEq	Divers	Yes								3.0	None	15.1
Investors Canadian Equity	CdnEq	Divers	Yes	3.6	14.0	13.5	10.9	10.2		Med-	2.5	FnDf	3825.5
Investors Cdn Enterprise	CdnEq	Divers	Yes	14.6							2.6	FnDf	185.5
Investors Cdn Small Cap	CdnEq	SCDivers	Yes								2.5	FnDf	725.2
Investors Cdn Small Cap II	CdnEq	SCDivers	Yes								2.6	FnDf	192.0
Investors Ret. Gth. Port	CdnEq	Divers	Yes	8.2	15.3	14.6	11.8			Low	2.6	FnDf	2631.7
Investors Retirement	CdnEq	Divers	Yes	5.8	14.7	14.1	11.6	8.5	9.6	Med-	2.4	FnDf	3140.7
Investors Summa	CdnEq	Divers	Yes	17.4	28.1	24.3	17.1	11.4		Low	2.5	FnDf	498.6
Ivy Canadian	CdnEq	LCValue	Yes	13.6	21.4	19.2	15.3			Low	2.4	F or B	5655.6
Ivy Enterprise	CdnEq	SCDivers	Yes	13.2	17.3	18.2				Low	2.5	F or B	368.8
Jones Heward Fund Limited	CdnEq	Divers	Yes	16.2	18.1	14.5	8.8	9.4	10.1	Med+	3.1	F or B	72.2
Lasalle Equity	CdnEq	Divers	Yes	19.9	15.5						1.4	None	1.6
Leith Wheeler Cdn Equity	CdnEq	Value	Yes		32.7	23.6				Med-	2.9	F or B	11.9
Lion Knowledge Industries	CdnEq	SCDivers	Yes	-8.7	-12.8	1.3	12.2			High	2.0	Defer	11.0
London Life Cdn Equity	CdnEq	Divers	Yes	18.2	23.2	19.6	13.1	10.2	10.9	High	2.1	None	1426.2
Lotus Group Cdn Equity	CdnEq	Growth	Yes	5.4	15.8	22.5				High	2.1	None	8.2
MAXXUM Cdn Equity Growth	CdnEq	Divers	Yes	6.6	10.1	12.6	10.0	10.8	10.6	Med	2.1	F or B	146.3
MB Canadian Equity Growth	CdnEq	LCDivers	Yes	12.2	26.8	24.1	17.4	13.4	13.3	High	0.0	None	500.3
MD Equity	CdnEq	Divers	Yes	15.4	21.6	16.9	13.2	10.2	12.1	Med	1.3	None	1934.5
MD Select	CdnEq	Divers	Yes	7.3	19.4	19.3				Low	1.3	None	277.0
MLI AGF Canadian Eq GIF	CdnEq	Divers	Yes	0.5							3.2	F or B	46.4
MLI Cdn Equity Index GIF	CdnEq	Divers	Yes								1.8	None	1.0
MLI E&P Equity GIF	CdnEq	LCDivers	Yes								2.8	F or B	36.1
MLI E&P valuee Equity GIF	CdnEq	LCValue	Yes	4.7							2.8	F or B	7.7
MLI Fidelity Cap Build GIF	CdnEq	Divers	Yes	15.5							3.0	F or B	26.7
MLI Fidelity True NorthGIF	CdnEq	Divers	Yes	24.4							3.0	F or B	256.5
MLI GT Glo Canada Gth GIF	CdnEq	Divers	Yes								3.0	F or B	142.2
MLI Harbour GIF	CdnEq	Value	Yes								3.0	F or B	38.8
MLI O'Donnell Canadian GIF	CdnEq	LCDivers	Yes								3.0	F or B	15.5
MLI O'Donnell Select GIF	CdnEq	Divers	Yes								3.0	F or B	31.5
MLI Trimark Select Cdn Gth	CdnEq	Divers	Yes	0.3							2.9	F or B	187.4
Mackenzie Sentinel Cda Eq	CdnEq	Divers	Yes	-0.7	7.3	7.4	8.2	6.6		Med-	2.0	Front	9.9
Manulife Cabot Blue Chip	CdnEq	LCDivers	Yes	15.9	19.8	18.3				Low	2.5	None	23.7
Manulife Cabot Cdn. Equity	CdnEq	LCDivers	Yes	16.8	20.6	18.8				High	2.5	None	45.3
Manulife Cabot Cdn. Growth	CdnEq	SCDivers	Yes	-0.4	12.4	18.9				Med	2.5	None	15.5
Manulife Cabot Emer Growth	CdnEq	SCGrowth	Yes	-3.9	8.2	15.5				Med-	2.5	None	9.3
Manulife VistaFd 1 Cap.Gns	CdnEq	Divers	Yes	-11.9	-1.8	2.4	2.7	6.7		High	1.6	Front	29.2

FUND NAME	FUND CATEGORY	RRSP-ELIGIB.	1 YR	2 YR	3 YR	5 YR	10 YR	15 YR	3 YR VOLATILITY	MER	SALES FEES	ASSETS IN $MIL
Manulife VistaFd 2 Cap.Gns	CdnEq Divers	Yes	-12.6	-2.5	1.6	1.9	5.9		High	2.4	Defer	135.6
Manulife VistaFnd 1 Equity	CdnEq Divers	Yes	11.3	11.9	11.3	8.8	8.2	7.8	Med	1.6	Front	29.2
Manulife VistaFnd 2 Equity	CdnEq Divers	Yes	10.4	11.1	10.4	8.0	7.3	7.0	Med	2.4	Defer	168.5
Marathon Equity	CdnEq SCGrowth	Yes	-23.6	-5.8	7.4	13.3	19.2		High	2.5	F or B	124.0
Marathon Perf Lg Cap Cdn	CdnEq LCDivers	Yes	7.1							2.2	F or B	12.5
Maritime Life Aggr Eq A&C	CdnEq Growth	Yes	7.1							2.6	None	14.2
Maritime Life Aggr Eq B	CdnEq Growth	Yes	14.8	18.3	16.7				High	2.6	Defer	2.4
Maritime Life Cdn Eq A&C	CdnEq LCDivers	Yes	14.8							2.6	Defer	107.0
Maritime Life Cdn Equity B	CdnEq LCDivers	Yes								2.6	Defer	13.0
Maritime Life Diver Eq A&C	CdnEq Divers	Yes								2.6	None	16.3
Maritime Life Diver Eq B	CdnEq Divers	Yes								2.6	None	2.4
Maritime Life Growth A&C	CdnEq Divers	Yes	10.8	20.7	17.9	12.2	9.2	9.7	Med	2.6	Defer	306.3
Maritime Life Growth B	CdnEq Divers	Yes	10.7							2.6	None	33.4
Mawer Canadian Equity	CdnEq LCDivers	Yes	17.8	23.3	17.2	12.4			Med	1.3	Defer	21.9
Mawer New Canada	CdnEq SCValue	Yes	6.2	14.4	17.8	14.6	15.2		Med	1.5	None	44.5
McElvaine Investment Trust	CdnEq Divers	Yes	31.0								None	3.7
Mclean Budden Equity Gth	CdnEq Divers	Yes	9.9	23.9	21.3	15.2			Med+	1.8	None	22.9
Merrill Lynch Cdn Equity	CdnEq LCDivers	Yes	-1.2	9.0						2.8	FnDf	104.9
Metlife Mvp Equity	CdnEq SCGrowth	Yes	16.2	20.4	16.1	11.6	7.7		Med	2.2	Defer	79.6
Metlife Mvp Growth	CdnEq LCDivers	Yes	16.6	22.5	21.2	15.9			Med-	2.2	Defer	138.7
Millennia III Cdn Eq 1	CdnEq LCDivers	Yes	9.1	17.9						2.8	None	192.4
Millennia III Cdn Eq 2	CdnEq LCDivers	Yes	8.8	17.7						2.9	None	21.5
Millennium Next Generation	CdnEq SCDivers	Yes	13.3	19.3	28.8				High	2.5	Front	35.1
Monarch Canadian	CdnEq Divers	Yes	7.1							2.4	F or B	78.0
Monarch Canadian Sector	CdnEq Divers	Yes	6.8							2.4	F or B	2.6
Montrusco Select Cdn Eq	CdnEq Divers	Yes	10.3	17.6	16.6	14.9	11.5		Med+		None	156.0
Montrusco Select Growth	CdnEq SCDivers	Yes	-1.9	17.7	23.2	16.0	17.0		High		None	306.3
Multiple Opportunities	CdnEq Divers	Yes	-8.4	-11.0	7.8	18.6	11.6		High	2.5	Front	10.6
Mutual Alpine Equity	CdnEq Divers	Yes	0.6								None	23.7
Mutual Equifund	CdnEq Divers	Yes	8.4	17.8	17.3	13.3	8.6		Med+	1.9	Front	120.7
Mutual Premier Blue Chip	CdnEq LCDivers	Yes	11.0	18.8	17.4	13.1			Med-	2.4	None	848.9
Mutual Premier Growth	CdnEq SCGrowth	Yes	-1.8	10.9	13.4	12.2			Med-	2.4	None	1054.0
Mutual Summit Equity	CdnEq Divers	Yes	14.1								None	40.1
NAL-Canadian Equity	CdnEq Divers	Yes	2.2	9.8	13.3	10.1	8.4		Med-	1.8	Defer	71.5
NAL-Equity Growth	CdnEq Divers	Yes	10.6	21.5	19.0				Med-	2.0	Defer	113.7
NN Canadian 35 Index	CdnEq LCDivers	Yes	16.9	22.5	18.7	14.9	8.0	8.0	Med	2.4	Defer	81.2
NN Canadian Growth	CdnEq LCDivers	Yes	14.8	20.9	17.4	11.7	11.0	10.8		2.7	Defer	41.0
National Equities	CdnEq Divers	Yes	15.3	24.8	20.6	15.5	10.1	10.0	Low	2.4	Defer	211.6
National Trust Cdn Equity	CdnEq LCDivers	Yes	15.0	24.1	18.1	12.0			Med+	1.6	None	230.6
National Trust Cdn Index	CdnEq Divers	Yes	16.0							0.9	None	64.6
National Trust Special Eq	CdnEq SCGrowth	Yes	6.1	12.9	13.9	7.9			Med-	2.5	None	47.7
Navigator Canadian Growth	CdnEq Growth	Yes								2.8	F or B	0.6
Navigator valuee Inv Retire	CdnEq SCGrowth	Yes	-21.9	-5.5	7.0	14.4			Med+	3.0	F or B	37.1
North West Life Ecoflex A	CdnEq Divers	Yes	2.2							2.5	Defer	7.2

FUND NAME	FUND CATEGORY		RRSP-ELIGIB.	1 YR	2 YR	3 YR	5 YR	10 YR	15 YR	3 YR VOLATILITY	MER	SALES FEES	ASSETS IN $MIL
North West Life Ecoflex N	CdnEq	Divers	Yes	-	-	-	-	-	-	-	2.4	Defer	1.0
North West Life Ecoflex T	CdnEq	Divers	Fgn	-	-	-	-	-	-	-	2.4	Defer	0.4
North West Life Ecofix ANL	CdnEq	LCValue	No	-	-	-	-	-	-	-	2.4	Defer	0.4
Northwest Growth	CdnEq	Divers	Yes	11.7	17.0	16.6	13.2	-	-	Med+	2.0	F or B	48.5
O'Donnell Canadian	CdnEq	LCDivers	Yes	-	-	-	-	-	-	-	2.8	F or B	81.8
O'Donnell Cdn Emerging Gth	CdnEq	SCGrowth	Yes	-21.1	-6.0	-	-	-	-	-	2.8	F or B	390.6
O'Donnell Growth	CdnEq	SCGrowth	Yes	1.3	8.5	-	-	-	-	-	2.8	F or B	203.0
O'Donnell Select	CdnEq	Divers	Yes	-	-	-	-	-	-	-	2.8	F or B	99.8
O.I.Q. Ferique Actions	CdnEq	LCDivers	Yes	10.9	19.3	16.9	14.0	10.6	10.8	Med	0.5	None	119.0
O.I.Q. Ferique Croissance	CdnEq	Divers	Yes	7.0	9.3	-	-	-	-	-	0.8	None	6.6
OTGIF Diversified	CdnEq	Divers	Yes	16.7	24.1	20.4	14.7	10.0	10.6	Med-	1.0	None	57.4
OTGIF Growth	CdnEq	SCGrowth	Yes	10.7	17.3	14.7	10.7	8.2	9.8	Low	1.0	None	21.6
Optima Strat-Cdn Equity	CdnEq	Value	Yes	15.8	30.5	24.3	-	-	-	Med-	0.4	F or B	762.3
Optimum Actions	CdnEq	Divers	Yes	13.3	23.5	18.9	-	-	-	Med-	1.6	None	4.3
PH & N Canadian Eq Plus	CdnEq	Divers	Yes	9.7	20.5	17.5	15.4	11.6	11.4	Med	1.2	None	226.3
PH & N Canadian Equity	CdnEq	Divers	Yes	11.5	21.5	18.6	15.7	11.5	11.7	Med	1.1	None	803.8
PH & N Cdn Eq Plus Pens Tr	CdnEq	Divers	Fgn	15.6	24.3	21.3	17.2	12.1	12.0	Med	0.5	None	1413.0
PH & N Vintage	CdnEq	Growth	Yes	11.5	25.2	22.9	18.7	16.5	-	Med+	1.8	Front	143.3
Pacific Total Return	CdnEq	Divers	Yes	1.9	-	-	-	-	-	-	2.9	Front	0.0
Perigee Equity Fund B	CdnEq	LCDivers	Yes	22.9	26.8	22.5	16.0	11.1	10.6	High	0.0	None	16.3
Perigee Nth American Eq Tr	CdnEq	LCDivers	Yes	24.7	27.8	23.0	16.6	11.3	10.7	Med+	0.0	None	161.8
Pret et Revenu Canadien	CdnEq	Divers	Yes	8.5	17.1	16.2	12.7	10.6	8.2	Med+	1.9	None	60.1
Primus Canadian Equity	CdnEq	Divers	Yes	13.2	-	-	-	-	-	-	0.2	None	158.2
Pursuit Canadian Equity	CdnEq	Growth	Yes	20.3	29.0	23.0	15.6	10.9	11.3	Med+	1.5	Front	11.8
Quebec Growth Fund Inc.	CdnEq	Growth	Yes	38.0	42.3	34.1	19.0	15.6	-	Med+	2.0	F or B	26.4
Quebec Prof Cdn Equity	CdnEq	Divers	Yes	13.8	20.4	17.6	12.6	9.1	-	Med-	1.0	None	108.8
Resolute Growth	CdnEq	SCGrowth	Yes	14.8	-2.8	16.9	-	-	-	High	2.0	F or B	4.8
Royal&SunAlliance Intl Eq	CdnEq	Divers	Fgn	13.2	18.1	16.1	12.9	9.1	10.1	Low	2.6	Defer	3352.4
Royal&SunAlliance Mny Mrkt	CdnEq	SCGrowth	Yes	0.5	7.4	10.6	6.6	-	-	Med-	1.0	Defer	691.5
Royal Asian Growth	CdnEq	SCGrowth	Fgn	-5.7	0.5	6.4	4.1	-	-	Med-	3.0	None	194.5
Royal Balanced Growth	CdnEq	Value	Yes	-	-	-	-	-	-	-	2.3	None	21.2
Royal Bond	CdnEq	Divers	Yes	-	-	-	-	-	-	-	1.4	None	220.9
Royal European Grth	CdnEq	SCDivers	Fgn	-1.1	7.3	11.7	-	-	-	Med	2.5	None	59.8
Royal Global Bond	CdnEq	Value	Yes	16.1	23.3	19.9	15.1	-	-	Med-	1.9	None	202.7
SSQ - Actions Canadiennes	CdnEq	Divers	Yes	11.9	19.2	17.8	12.7	10.6	8.8	Med-	-	None	47.1
Saxon Small Cap	CdnEq	SCDivers	Yes	21.0	28.2	23.9	15.8	10.9	-	Low	1.8	None	23.7
Saxon Stock	CdnEq	Divers	Yes	13.4	19.4	16.8	14.2	11.2	-	Low	1.8	None	23.5
Sceptre Equity Growth	CdnEq	Divers	Yes	0.3	14.4	21.8	22.3	13.7	-	High	1.4	None	449.3
Scotia Ex. Canadian Growth	CdnEq	Divers	Yes	8.2	15.4	17.9	15.8	10.8	10.1	Med+	2.1	None	992.5
Scotia Ex. Cdn Blue Chip	CdnEq	Divers	Yes	7.4	15.6	13.5	8.9	8.3	-	Med-	1.9	None	417.0
Scudder Canadian Equity	CdnEq	Value	Yes	26.2	36.4	-	-	-	-	-	1.4	None	314.1
Spectrum Utd Canadian Eq	CdnEq	Divers	Yes	12.4	20.5	17.8	13.9	12.6	12.7	Med-	2.4	F or B	1625.4
Spectrum Utd Canadian Gth	CdnEq	SCDivers	Yes	-6.1	5.3	11.7	12.0	11.2	11.0	Med	2.4	F or B	841.7
Spectrum Utd Canadian Inv	CdnEq	LCValue	Yes	18.6	26.3	22.0	15.7	9.8	9.0	Low	2.3	F or B	296.2

FUND NAME	FUND CATEGORY		RRSP-ELIGIB.	1 YR	2 YR	3 YR	5 YR	10 YR	15 YR	3 YR VOLATILITY	MER	SALES FEES	ASSETS IN $MIL
Spectrum Utd Cdn Max Gth P	CdnEq	Divers	Yes	-	-	-	-	-	-	-	2.3	F or B	7.7
Spectrum Utd Cdn Small-Mid	CdnEq	SCDivers	Yes	-	-	-	-	-	-	-	2.4	F or B	13.2
Spectrum Utd Cdn Stock	CdnEq	Divers	Yes	15.6	21.4	17.3	13.1	8.5	-	Low	2.3	F or B	183.1
Standard Life Equity	CdnEq	Divers	Yes	19.5	24.1	20.4	16.0	-	-	Low	2.0	Defer	20.6
Stone & Co Flagship Stock	CdnEq	Divers	Yes	12.8	19.6	-	-	-	-	-	2.9	F or B	131.5
Strategic Val Cdn Eq valuee	CdnEq	Divers	Yes	4.4	-	-	-	-	-	-	2.7	F or B	21.7
Strategic Val Cdn Equity	CdnEq	LCDivers	Yes	13.3	19.8	16.1	11.4	7.9	8.6	Med+	2.7	F or B	278.5
Strategic Val Cdn Small Co	CdnEq	SCGrowth	Yes	15.0	16.7	11.0	11.2	-	-	Med-	2.7	F or B	172.2
Strategic valuee RSP	CdnEq	Divers	Yes	-	-	-	-	-	-	-	4.2	F or B	2.2
Sunfund	CdnEq	Divers	Yes	22.3	26.9	21.2	15.8	10.6	10.7	Low	1.5	Front	45.5
Synergy Cdn. Growth Class	CdnEq	Growth	Yes	-	-	-	-	-	-	-	-	F or B	1.9
Synergy Cdn Momentum Class	CdnEq	Divers	Yes	-	-	-	-	-	-	-	-	F or B	14.1
Synergy Cdn Small Cap Cl.	CdnEq	SCDivers	Yes	-	-	-	-	-	-	-	-	F or B	1.8
Synergy Cdn Style Mgmt Cl.	CdnEq	Divers	Yes	-	-	-	-	-	-	-	-	F or B	22.7
Synergy Cdn valuee Class	CdnEq	Value	Yes	-	-	-	-	-	-	-	-	F or B	2.8
Tal/Hyper Small Cap Cdn Eq	CdnEq	SCGrowth	Yes	10.2	23.4	21.5	-	-	-	Med	2.6	F or B	269.6
Talvest/Hyper Cdn Eq Gth	CdnEq	Growth	Yes	24.5	-	-	-	-	-	-	2.6	F or B	398.8
Talvest Canadian Eq. valuee	CdnEq	Divers	Yes	11.2	17.2	13.8	12.1	9.1	10.1	Med	2.4	F or B	123.9
Talvest New Economy	CdnEq	Growth	Yes	8.2	7.4	10.1	-	-	-	High	2.5	F or B	110.6
Templeton Canadian Stock	CdnEq	Divers	Yes	8.5	18.2	15.8	13.5	-	-	Low	2.4	F or B	483.3
Tradex Canadian Growth	CdnEq	Divers	Yes	7.5	-	-	-	-	-	-	1.5	None	4.8
Tradex Equity	CdnEq	Divers	Yes	12.0	23.3	22.0	17.7	11.6	11.6	Med+	1.4	None	101.8
Trans-Canada valuee	CdnEq	Value	Yes	-18.8	-0.5	3.4	1.1	3.5	8.6	High	3.5	F or B	1.9
Trimark Canadian	CdnEq	Divers	Yes	0.9	12.1	12.6	12.0	11.5	12.1	Low	1.5	Front	2205.7
Trimark Cdn Small Comp	CdnEq	SCDivers	Yes	-	-	-	-	-	-	-	2.4	F or B	14.9
Trimark RSP Equity	CdnEq	Value	Yes	-2.0	9.8	10.1	10.4	-	-	Low	2.0	Defer	2736.0
Trimark Select Cdn Growth	CdnEq	Value	Yes	0.9	12.0	11.5	11.4	-	-	Low	2.3	F or B	5026.6
Universal Canadian Growth	CdnEq	Divers	Yes	12.6	23.2	-	-	-	-	-	2.4	F or B	1904.5
Universal Future	CdnEq	Divers	Yes	12.7	16.1	14.4	13.6	10.2	-	Med-	2.4	F or B	738.7
University Avenue Canadian	CdnEq	Divers	Yes	-0.3	-2.1	4.9	2.8	-	-	High	2.4	F or B	9.6
University Cdn Small Cap	CdnEq	SCDivers	Yes	-	-	-	-	-	-	-	-	F or B	0.3
Valorem Cdn Equity-valuee	CdnEq	Divers	Yes	9.2	-	-	-	-	-	-	-	F or B	3.5
valuee Contrarian Cdn Eq	CdnEq	Divers	Yes	27.0	-	-	-	-	-	-	2.0	None	6.2
Westbury Cdn Life A	CdnEq	LCDivers	Yes	21.0	26.3	21.9	16.5	13.4	13.0	Med-	1.1	Front	2.8
Westbury Cdn Life Eq Gth	CdnEq	LCValue	Yes	15.9	22.6	18.6	12.8	-	-	High	2.4	Defer	72.2
YMG Emerging Companies	CdnEq	SCDivers	Yes	6.2	-	-	-	-	-	-	2.0	Front	6.8
YMG Growth	CdnEq	Divers	Yes	4.4	21.7	17.7	10.1	7.8	-	High	2.0	F or B	7.3
20/20 Canadian Resources	CdnEq	Resource	Yes	-21.9	-4.7	5.3	0.5	7.6	5.3	-	2.9	F or B	223.0
AIC Advantage	CdnEq	FinSer	Yes	25.4	51.5	47.1	34.3	22.9	-	Med-	2.3	F or B	2988.2
All-Canadian ConsumerFund	CdnEq	Consum	Yes	6.3	11.1	7.3	7.7	-	-	Low	2.0	Front	1.0
All-Canadian Resources Co.	CdnEq	Resource	Yes	-11.6	-15.8	-10.3	-2.1	-0.3	-	-	2.0	Front	2.9
Altamira Prec &Strat Metal	CdnEq	PrMetl	Yes	-35.6	-32.3	-13.6	-8.1	-	0.3	Med+	2.8	None	44.2
Altamira Resource	CdnEq	Resource	Yes	-33.6	-17.2	-7.9	-	-	-	-	2.3	None	137.9

FUND NAME	FUND CATEGORY		RRSP-ELIGIB.	1 YR	2 YR	3 YR	5 YR	10 YR	15 YR	3 YR VOLATILITY	MER	SALES FEES	ASSETS IN $MIL
BPI Cdn Resource Fund Inc	CdnEq	Resource	Yes	-31.1	-26.2	-10.0	-9.4	4.2	3.6		3.0	F or B	30.9
C.I. Canadian Resource	CdnEq	Resource	Yes	-26.9							2.4	F or B	2.0
CIBC Canadian Resources	CdnEq	Resource	Yes	-28.0	-12.7						2.3	None	61.6
CIBC Energy	CdnEq	Resource	Yes	-16.6							2.3	None	38.1
CIBC Financial Companies	CdnEq	FinSer	Yes								2.5	None	220.9
CIBC Precious Metal	CdnEq	PrMetl	Yes	-27.5							2.2	None	42.4
Cambridge Precious Metals	CdnEq	PrMetl	Yes	-47.2	-47.9						3.5	None	2.0
Cambridge Resource	CdnEq	Resource	Yes	-45.6	-43.0	-15.7	-16.7	-1.9	1.6		3.4	F or B	7.4
Dominion Equity Resource	CdnEq	Resource	Yes	-18.9	2.0	4.9	-5.2	2.0	-1.2		2.3	None	15.1
Double Gold Plus	CdnEq	PrMetl	Yes	-16.0	-5.3	-5.3	-1.0	-2.9		Low	0.0	Front	0.8
Dynamic Precious Metals	CdnEq	PrMetl	Yes	-37.4	-31.0	-15.3	-5.8	1.0		Med+	2.5	F or B	193.4
First Canadian Resource	CdnEq	Resource	Yes	-32.5	-14.2	-5.6					2.3	None	42.9
First Cdn Precious Metals	CdnEq	PrMetl	Yes	-39.3							2.1	F or B	23.1
First Heritage	CdnEq	Resource	Yes	-19.4	-9.3	-3.0	-1.5	1.7			4.0	Front	3.8
FirstTrust Fin Inst 97	CdnEq	FinSer	Yes								2.6	Front	6.8
FirstTrust Wealth Mgmt 97	CdnEq	FinSer	Yes								2.8	Front	2.6
Global Strategy Gold Plus	CdnEq	PrMetl	Yes	-43.5	-35.1	-15.3	-7.2	-1.2	0.9	High	0.8	Front	51.9
Goldtrust	CdnEq	PrMetl	Yes	-27.5	-25.4	-14.0				Med	2.8	None	6.4
Great-West Cdn Opp (M) A	CdnEq	SciTec	Yes		-7.1						2.6	Defer	0.8
Great-West Cdn Opp (M) B	CdnEq	SciTec	Yes		-6.8						3.3	None	1.8
Great-West Cdn Res (A) A	CdnEq	Resource	Yes	-23.7	-5.5						3.1	Defer	18.7
Great-West Cdn Res (A) B	CdnEq	Resource	Yes	-23.5	-24.3						2.1	None	16.7
Green Line Energy	CdnEq	Resource	Yes	-38.5		-0.5					2.1	None	82.3
Green Line Precious Metals	CdnEq	PrMetl	Yes	-32.1		-3.6				High	2.1	None	92.6
Green Line Resource	CdnEq	Resource	Yes	-35.5	-15.6	-5.2					2.5	None	103.5
Hartford Cdn Advanced Tech	CdnEq	SciTec	Yes								3.0	Defer	1.2
Infinity Wealth Management	CdnEq	FinSer	No	25.3							2.5	FnDf	196.7
Investors Cdn Natural Res	CdnEq	Resource	Yes	-8.1	-23.8	-4.9	-1.3	11.9				F or B	147.9
Lion Natural Resources	CdnEq	Resource	Yes								2.2	F or B	2.4
MAXXUM Natural Resource	CdnEq	Resource	Yes	-31.2	-31.0	-7.0	0.0	4.9		High	2.2	F or B	45.1
MAXXUM Precious Metals	CdnEq	PrMetl	Yes	-34.1							3.1	F or B	11.5
Marathon Resource	CdnEq	Resource	Yes	-38.4							2.6	F or B	22.0
Middlefield Growth	CdnEq	Resource	Yes	-8.0	5.4	7.1	1.0				2.6	F or B	31.1
Mutual Alpine Resources	CdnEq	Resource	Yes	-25.6							2.4	None	17.6
NCE Canadian Energy Gth	CdnEq	Resource	No								2.4	Front	0.7
NCE Precious Metals Gth	CdnEq	PrMetl	No								2.9	Front	0.4
Navigator Cdn Technology	CdnEq	SciTec	Yes								2.2	F or B	4.6
Royal Canadian Growth	CdnEq	Resource	Yes	-14.6	8.4	8.7	1.1	9.6	6.4	Med+	0.3	None	242.4
Royal Premium Money Market	CdnEq	PrMetl	Yes	-30.4	-25.1	0.2	6.4				2.2	None	215.7
Scotia Ex. Precious Metals	CdnEq	PrMetl	Yes	-36.1	-27.9	-9.7				Med+	2.4	None	49.8
Spectrum Utd Cdn Resource	CdnEq	Resource	Yes	-28.6							2.4	F or B	75.7
Standard Life Natural Res	CdnEq	Resource	Yes	-20.1	-7.9	-0.1					2.0	Defer	5.7
Talvest/Hyperion Cdn Res	CdnEq	Resource	Yes								2.5	F or B	0.9
Trimark Canadian Resources	CdnEq	Resource	Yes								2.4	F or B	6.8

FUND NAME	FUND CATEGORY	RRSP. ELIGIB.	1 YR	2 YR	3 YR	5 YR	10 YR	15 YR	3 YR VOLATILITY	MER	SALES FEES	ASSETS IN $MIL
Universal Cdn Resource	CdnEq	Resource	Yes	-25.7	-7.1	1.2	-1.4	5.9	5.6	-	2.4	F or B	163.0
Universal Precious Metals	CdnEq	PrMetl	Yes	-33.0	-27.1	-11.4	-	-	-	High	2.4	F or B	76.2
B.E.S.T. Discoveries	Labour	LSVC	Yes	-3.2							4.3	Defer	13.8
C.I. Covington	Labour	LSVC	Yes	0.5	5.1	5.5					4.6	Defer	134.9
Canadian Medical Discov.	Labour	LSVC	Yes	2.4	0.5	3.6					4.9	Defer	262.3
Canadian Venture Opportun	Labour	LSVC	Yes	-9.4	-5.7	-9.4					6.4	Defer	13.8
Capital Alliance Ventures	Labour	LSVC	Yes	1.2	-3.2	3.3					4.0	Defer	43.4
Cdn Science & Tech Gth Inc	Labour	LSVC	Yes	-1.4							5.5	Defer	18.5
Centerfire Growth Fund Inc	Labour	LSVC	Yes	4.3							1.6	Defer	2.7
Crocus Investment Fund	Labour	LSVC	Yes	12.5	7.0	7.1	6.2				3.8	None	87.4
DGC Entertainment Ventures	Labour	LSVC	Yes	0.3	4.6	5.7					5.6	Defer	7.4
ENSIS Growth Fund Inc.	Labour	LSVC	Yes									None	4.4
Enterprise Fund	Labour	LSVC	Yes	-10.9	-2.3	-4.1					6.6	Defer	7.4
First Ontario	Labour	LSVC	Yes	7.1	4.7	3.8					4.8	Defer	30.8
Innovacap Capital Corp.	Labour	LSVC	Yes	-12.3							12.1	Defer	0.5
Retrocom Growth	Labour	LSVC	Yes	5.6	4.2	3.6					4.2	Defer	49.0
Sportfund	Labour	LSVC	Yes	-6.9	4.3	5.4					4.9	Defer	12.0
Triax Growth	Labour	LSVC	Yes	5.4	3.3						3.6	Defer	176.9
Trillium Growth Cap Inc.	Labour	LSVC	Yes	-6.7	-5.8	-3.6					5.6	Defer	7.5
VenGrowth Fund	Labour	LSVC	Yes	5.7	7.9	6.6					3.9	Defer	200.8
Workers Investment	Labour	LSVC	Yes	0.0								Defer	1.0
Working Opportunity (EVCC)	Labour	LSVC	Yes	8.5	6.2	7.9	5.7				2.7	Defer	201.2
Working Ventures Canadian	Labour	LSVC	Yes	3.4	1.3	2.5	2.9				2.4	Defer	741.7
@rgentum Income Portfolio	CdnEq	Dividend	Yes									F or B	0.4
AGF Dividend	CdnEq	Dividend	Yes	19.1	28.7	22.9	18.1	13.4		High	1.9	F or B	2309.0
AGF High Income	CdnEq	Dividend	Yes	6.6	9.3	9.3	8.4			Low	1.7	F or B	598.3
Acuity Pld High Income	CdnEq	Dividend	Fgn	31.2	22.5	18.7	15.7			Med+		None	
Altamira Dividend	CdnEq	Dividend	Yes	21.3	25.0	21.1				Med	1.6	None	282.4
Astra Dividendes	CdnEq	Dividend	Yes								2.4	None	4.2
Atlas Canadian Income Tr	CdnEq	Dividend	Yes	15.0							1.9	F or B	67.7
Atlas Cdn Dividend Growth	CdnEq	Dividend	Yes	18.3	21.8	19.6	15.1	10.3	9.4	Low	2.3	F or B	77.7
BPI Dividend Income	CdnEq	Dividend	Yes								1.2	F or B	599.1
BPI Dividend Income Segrd	CdnEq	Dividend	Yes	10.7								F or B	19.4
BPI High Income	CdnEq	Dividend	Yes								1.5	F or B	312.7
BPI High Income Segregated	CdnEq	Dividend	Yes							Med		F or B	5.1
Bissett Dividend Income	CdnEq	Dividend	No	17.2	25.3	23.1	17.6	11.5			1.5	None	51.1
Bissett Income Trust	CdnEq	Dividend	Yes	-1.1							1.3	None	13.6
C.I. Dividend	CdnEq	Dividend	Yes	16.9							1.9	F or B	36.2
CIBC Dividend	CdnEq	Dividend	Yes	17.0	20.2	16.5	11.7			Med-	1.9	None	660.9
CT Dividend Income	CdnEq	Dividend	Yes	17.2	22.4	20.3				Med-	1.9	None	485.3
Canada Life Enhanced Divid	CdnEq	Dividend	Yes								2.0	Defer	60.8
Desjardins Dividend	CdnEq	Dividend	Yes	21.2	24.8	20.5				Med	1.9	None	495.9

FUND NAME	FUND CATEGORY	RRSP-ELIGIB.	1 YR	2 YR	3 YR	5 YR	10 YR	15 YR	3 YR VOLATILITY	MER	SALES FEES	ASSETS IN $MIL
Dynamic Dividend	CdnEq	Dividend	Yes	10.9	15.6	14.2	11.2	9.9	-	Low	1.5	F or B	402.1
Dynamic Dividend Growth	CdnEq	Dividend	Yes	6.1	17.2	16.9	13.8	9.7	-	Med-	1.6	F or B	488.7
Elliott & Page Mth High In	CdnEq	Dividend	Yes	-	-	-	-	-	-	-	1.6	F or B	10.5
Empire Elite Dividend Gth	CdnEq	Dividend	Yes	-	-	-	-	-	-	-	2.6	Defer	20.8
First Canadian Div Income	CdnEq	Dividend	Yes	31.7	36.0	28.1	-	-	-	High	1.7	None	1358.5
Great-West Divid/Gth (M) A	CdnEq	Dividend	Yes	-	-	-	-	-	-	-	2.7	None	3.4
Great-West Divid/Gth (M) B	CdnEq	Dividend	Yes	-	-	-	-	-	-	-	2.5	Defer	3.9
Great-West Dividend (G) A	CdnEq	Dividend	Yes	-	-	-	-	-	-	-	2.5	None	11.0
Great-West Dividend (G) B	CdnEq	Dividend	Yes	-	-	-	-	-	-	-	2.3	Defer	7.9
Green Line Dividend	CdnEq	Dividend	Yes	23.5	30.5	22.5	15.0	12.7	-	Med+	2.0	None	502.6
Growsafe Cdn Divid & Inc	CdnEq	Dividend	Yes	-5.6	-	-	-	-	-	-	2.3	F or B	13.3
Guardian Mnthly High Inc C	CdnEq	Dividend	Yes	-6.0	-	-	-	-	-	-	1.5	Front	86.6
Guardian Mnthly High Inc M	CdnEq	Dividend	Yes	0.0	7.7	8.1	6.9	7.2	-	Med-	2.1	F or B	459.4
Guardian Monthly Divid C	CdnEq	Dividend	Yes	-0.6	7.2	-	-	-	-	-	1.3	Front	86.6
Guardian Monthly Divid M	CdnEq	Dividend	Yes	21.1	26.4	22.4	-	-	-	Med	1.9	F or B	279.2
Hongkong Bank Dividend Inc	CdnEq	Dividend	Yes	-	-	-	-	-	-	-	1.9	None	236.6
Ind. Alliance Dividend	CdnEq	Dividend	Yes	-	-	-	-	-	-	-	1.5	None	0.3
Ind. Alliance Ecoflex V	CdnEq	Dividend	Yes	-	-	-	-	-	-	-	1.9	Defer	21.4
Industrial Dividend Growth	CdnEq	Dividend	Yes	21.7	27.4	22.8	17.0	9.7	12.2	Med+	2.4	F or B	947.0
Infinity Income	CdnEq	Dividend	Yes	0.5	-	-	-	-	-	-	2.2	F or B	6.9
InvesNet Dividend	CdnEq	Dividend	Yes	8.9	11.9	11.7	9.4	-	-	Low	1.6	None	106.9
Investors Dividend	CdnEq	Dividend	Yes	21.5	23.8	19.1	13.3	11.4	10.9	Med-	2.4	FnDf	5084.5
MAXXUM Dividend	CdnEq	Dividend	Yes	21.2	27.4	22.9	18.9	13.1	-	Med+	1.7	F or B	270.2
MD Dividend	CdnEq	Dividend	Yes	15.8	17.3	15.5	12.2	-	-	Low	1.3	None	168.3
MLI AGF Dividend GIF	CdnEq	Dividend	Yes	-	-	-	-	-	-	-	2.8	F or B	247.2
MLI AGF High Income GIF	CdnEq	Dividend	Yes	-	-	-	-	-	-	-	2.4	F or B	27.6
MLI Dynamic Divid Gth GIF	CdnEq	Dividend	Yes	-	-	-	-	-	-	-	2.9	F or B	22.8
Maritime Life Divid Inc A	CdnEq	Dividend	Yes	22.1	24.0	18.8	-	-	-	Med	2.1	None	165.3
Maritime Life Divid Inc B	CdnEq	Dividend	Yes	21.3	-	-	-	-	-	-	2.1	Defer	47.4
Maritime Life Divid Inc C	CdnEq	Dividend	Yes	21.9	-	-	-	-	-	-	2.3	Defer	34.1
MetLife-AGF Dividend	CdnEq	Dividend	Yes	-	-	-	-	-	-	-	2.7	Defer	9.6
Millennia III Cdn Divid 1	CdnEq	Dividend	Yes	-	-	-	-	-	-	-	2.3	Defer	28.2
Millennia III Cdn Divid 2	CdnEq	Dividend	Yes	-	-	-	-	-	-	-	2.4	None	4.9
Millennium Income	CdnEq	Dividend	Yes	-4.7	-	-	-	-	-	-	2.5	Front	27.1
Mutual Summit Dividend Gth	CdnEq	Dividend	Yes	19.6	16.4	15.4	-	-	-	Low	2.4	Defer	110.0
NN Dividend	CdnEq	Dividend	Yes	10.7	35.2	27.6	18.1	-	-	Med+	1.8	Defer	287.8
National Trust Dividend	CdnEq	Dividend	Yes	35.1	-	-	-	-	-	-	1.9	None	168.1
North West Life Ecoflex V	CdnEq	Dividend	Yes	-	-	-	-	-	-	-	1.8	Defer	1.2
Northwest Dividend	CdnEq	Dividend	Yes	9.9	24.8	22.9	-	-	-	Med+	1.8	F or B	19.6
PH & N Dividend Income	CdnEq	Dividend	Yes	36.6	42.1	31.6	23.0	15.6	13.8	High	1.2	None	674.8
Pret et Revenu Dividendes	CdnEq	Dividend	Yes	8.6	24.0	23.2	-	-	-	Med+	1.6	None	56.4
Royal Canadian Equity	CdnEq	Dividend	Yes	31.5	36.6	28.0	19.8	-	-	High	2.0	None	2314.5
Royal Mortgage	CdnEq	Dividend	Yes	-	-	-	-	-	-	-	1.6	None	850.9
Saxon High Income	CdnEq	Dividend	Yes	-	-	-	-	-	-	-	1.3	None	5.7

FUND NAME	FUND CATEGORY	RRSP. ELIGIB.	1 YR	2 YR	3 YR	5 YR	10 YR	15 YR	3 YR VOLATILITY	MER	SALES FEES	ASSETS IN $MIL.
Scotia Ex. Dividend	CdnEq	Dividend	Yes	23.1	27.2	22.7	15.9	11.8	-	Med	1.1	None	985.2
Spectrum Utd Dividend	CdnEq	Dividend	Yes	16.6	18.3	15.5	11.9	9.7	-	Med-	1.6	F or B	288.4
Standard Life Cdn Dividend	CdnEq	Dividend	Yes	38.3	41.4	32.5	-	-	-	High	1.5	Defer	44.6
Strategic Val Dividend	CdnEq	Dividend	Yes	15.6	20.2	16.4	12.1	10.1	10.7	Med-	2.7	F or B	515.3
Talvest Dividend	CdnEq	Dividend	Yes	10.8	16.4	-	-	-	-	-	2.3	F or B	200.8
Trans-Canada Dividend	CdnEq	Dividend	Yes	4.5	7.2	10.1	10.4	6.2	9.2	High	3.5	F or B	5.8
ABC Fully-Managed	Balan	CdnSAA	Yes	6.6	16.5	18.4	16.6	16.1	-	High	2.0	None	81.5
AIC Income Equity	Balan	CdnSAA	Yes	-	-	-	-	-	-	-	2.5	F or B	119.4
AIM GT Canada Income	Balan	CdnSAA	Yes	11.9	19.5	-	-	-	-	-	2.1	F or B	886.8
APEX Growth & Income	Balan	CdnSAA	Yes	7.7	-	-	-	-	-	-	2.5	F or B	29.3
Acadia Atlantic	Balan	CdnSAA	Yes	-	-	-	-	-	-	-	-	Defer	0.2
Acadia Balanced	Balan	CdnSAA	Yes	-7.4	6.8	5.8	-	-	-	High	2.4	Defer	18.4
Acadia Diversified	Balan	CdnSAA	Yes	-	-	-	-	-	-	-	-	None	0.3
Acuity Pld Cdn Balanced	Balan	CdnSAA	Yes	30.4	32.5	25.1	19.8	-	-	High	-	None	
Acuity Pld Conserv AA	Balan	CdnSAA	Yes	27.6	26.6	19.2	10.4	-	-	Med+	-	F or B	
Artisan RSP Gth & Income	Balan	CdnSAA	Yes	-	-	-	-	-	-	-	3.0	F or B	16.6
Artisan RSP Income	Balan	CdnSAA	Yes	-	-	-	-	-	-	-	3.0	F or B	2.3
Astra 110	Balan	CdnSAA	Yes	-	-	-	-	-	-	-	2.5	None	10.5
Astra Equilibre	Balan	CdnSAA	Yes	-	-	-	-	-	-	-	2.4	None	28.9
Atlas Canadian Balanced	Balan	CdnSAA	Yes	15.8	19.5	16.8	13.2	-	-	Low	2.2	F or B	329.0
Azura Balanced RSP Pooled	Balan	CdnSAA	Yes	6.4	11.6	-	-	-	-	-	2.3	F or B	49.8
Azura Conservative Pooled	Balan	CdnSAA	Yes	6.9	10.0	-	-	-	-	-	2.0	F or B	18.9
BPI Canadian Balanced	Balan	CdnSAA	Yes	10.0	10.3	10.6	7.1	8.4	-	High	2.2	F or B	72.7
BPI Global Bal RSP Sgr	Balan	CdnSAA	Yes	-	-	-	-	-	-	-	-	F or B	3.7
BPI Global Balanced RSP	Balan	CdnSAA	Yes	19.2	17.0	12.5	11.1	9.5	-	High	2.3	F or B	225.1
BPI Income & Growth	Balan	CdnSAA	Yes	40.3	-	-	-	-	-	-	2.5	F or B	109.5
BPI Income & Growth Segrd	Balan	CdnSAA	Yes	-	-	-	-	-	-	-	-	F or B	8.4
Beutel Goodman Balanced	Balan	CdnSAA	Yes	10.7	14.9	13.0	11.6	10.1	-	Med-	2.1	Front	195.2
Bissett Retirement	Balan	CdnSAA	Yes	16.2	20.9	19.4	14.8	10.4	10.6	Med	0.4	None	201.2
C.I. Canadian Balanced	Balan	CdnSAA	Yes	10.8	10.9	10.7	10.8	10.7	-	Med	2.3	F or B	356.4
C.I. Canadian Income	Balan	CdnSAA	Yes	7.5	12.5	13.0	-	-	-	Low	1.8	F or B	230.5
C.I. Harbour Gth&Inc Sgrd	Balan	CdnSAA	Yes	-	-	-	-	-	-	-	3.0	F or B	35.9
CCPE Diversified	Balan	CdnSAA	Yes	9.0	15.0	14.3	11.5	10.1	-	Med+	1.4	None	36.0
CDA Balanced (KBSH)	Balan	CdnSAA	Yes	9.2	14.8	14.2	11.4	10.4	-	Med	1.0	None	55.6
CGO&V Balanced	Balan	CdnSAA	Yes	8.4	-	-	-	-	-	-	1.7	None	7.3
CT Balanced	Balan	CdnSAA	Yes	10.7	15.5	13.8	10.4	10.7	10.1	Med-	2.1	None	1786.8
CT Retirement Balanced	Balan	CdnSAA	Yes	12.3	-	-	-	-	-	-	1.7	None	149.5
CUMIS Life Balanced	Balan	CdnSAA	Yes	1.1	-	-	-	-	-	-	3.0	Back	2.9
Cambridge Balanced	Balan	CdnSAA	Yes	-28.9	-24.0	-14.1	-9.9	1.2	5.3	High	3.5	F or B	5.5
Canada Life Managed	Balan	CdnSAA	Yes	9.7	14.9	13.8	10.8	9.8	-	Med-	2.3	Defer	1308.3
Capstone Investment Trust	Balan	CdnSAA	Yes	20.1	19.1	18.6	13.1	10.9	10.1	Med	2.1	None	7.7
CentrePost Balanced	Balan	CdnSAA	Yes	4.3	9.9	12.0	8.4	-	-	Med-	1.0	None	2.7
Clarington Canadian Bal	Balan	CdnSAA	Yes	9.0	-	-	-	-	-	-	2.8	F or B	32.3

FUND NAME	FUND CATEGORY	RRSP-ELIGIB.	1 YR	2 YR	3 YR	5 YR	10 YR	15 YR	3 YR VOLATILITY	MER	SALES FEES	ASSETS IN $MIL
Clarington Canadian Income	Balan	CdnSAA	Yes	10.6	-	-	-	-	-	-	2.1	F or B	68.9
Colonia Strategic Balanced	Balan	CdnSAA	Yes	13.2	18.0	-	-	-	-	-	0.3	Defer	24.5
Comm. Un. Asset Allocation	Balan	CdnSAA	Yes	-	-	-	-	-	-	-	2.7	Defer	3.1
Cormel Equilibree	Balan	CdnSAA	Yes	14.4	17.0	14.4	11.6	11.5	-	Med	1.0	None	24.4
Cornerstone Balanced	Balan	CdnSAA	Yes	7.0	10.3	11.8	9.0	8.2	7.1	High	2.4	None	63.3
Desjardins Balanced	Balan	CdnSAA	Yes	9.7	15.1	13.3	10.7	9.8	-	Med+	1.9	None	898.4
Desjardins Distinct Dvrsd	Balan	CdnSAA	Yes	11.2	16.5	14.5	11.6	-	-	Med	1.8	None	42.2
Desjardins Diver Audacious	Balan	CdnSAA	Yes	7.9	11.4	10.9	-	-	-	Low	1.9	None	294.6
Desjardins Divers Moderate	Balan	CdnSAA	Yes	6.5	8.8	8.9	-	-	-	Low	1.8	None	565.2
Desjardins Divers Secure	Balan	CdnSAA	Yes	4.9	5.9	6.3	-	-	-	Low	1.7	None	289.0
Desjardins Divr. Ambitious	Balan	CdnSAA	Yes	10.1	-	-	-	-	-	-	2.0	None	80.0
Desjardins Quebec	Balan	CdnSAA	Yes	23.0	-	-	-	-	-	-	2.2	None	57.9
Empire Balanced	Balan	CdnSAA	Yes	7.2	14.1	12.8	9.9	-	-	Med-	2.4	Defer	276.2
Ethical Balanced	Balan	CdnSAA	Yes	19.9	22.0	17.4	13.7	-	-	Med+	2.1	None	713.6
Fidelity Cdn Asset Alloc	Balan	CdnSAA	Yes	20.0	25.6	21.4	-	-	-	High	2.5	F or B	3016.9
First Capital Income & Gth	Balan	CdnSAA	Yes	-	-	-	-	-	-	-	-	Front	1.6
GS Canadian Balanced	Balan	CdnSAA	Yes	14.8	21.4	-	-	-	-	-	2.7	FnDf	1093.0
General Trust Balanced	Balan	CdnSAA	Yes	5.8	12.5	12.0	9.5	8.8	-	Med+	2.1	None	92.6
Global Strategy Income Pls	Balan	CdnSAA	Yes	16.2	22.6	19.7	15.1	-	-	Low	2.4	F or B	2150.4
Great-West Balanced (B) A	Balan	CdnSAA	Yes	11.5	14.8	-	-	-	-	-	2.8	None	32.6
Great-West Balanced (B) B	Balan	CdnSAA	Yes	11.8	15.1	-	-	-	-	-	2.6	Defer	30.0
Great-West Balanced (M) A	Balan	CdnSAA	Yes	1.9	11.4	-	-	-	-	-	2.9	None	19.1
Great-West Balanced (M) B	Balan	CdnSAA	Yes	2.1	11.7	-	-	-	-	-	2.7	Defer	18.3
Great-West Balanced (S) A	Balan	CdnSAA	Yes	9.2	15.1	-	-	-	-	-	2.9	None	56.4
Great-West Balanced (S) B	Balan	CdnSAA	Yes	9.5	15.4	-	-	-	-	-	2.6	Defer	35.6
Great-West Divers (G) A	Balan	CdnSAA	Yes	12.3	15.0	13.1	9.5	9.1	-	Med-	2.6	None	379.2
Great-West Divers (G) B	Balan	CdnSAA	Yes	12.6	15.3	13.4	-	-	-	Med-	2.4	Defer	115.1
Great-West Equity/Bd (G) A	Balan	CdnSAA	Yes	9.3	14.5	13.1	9.0	9.9	-	High	2.6	None	257.9
Great-West Equity/Bd (G) B	Balan	CdnSAA	Yes	9.6	14.8	13.4	-	-	-	High	2.4	Defer	110.0
Great-West Gth & Inc (A)A	Balan	CdnSAA	Yes	-0.4	4.3	-	-	-	-	-	2.9	None	16.2
Great-West Gth & Inc (A)B	Balan	CdnSAA	Yes	-0.2	4.6	-	-	-	-	-	2.6	None	16.5
Great-West Gth & Inc (M)A	Balan	CdnSAA	Yes	13.4	17.8	-	-	-	-	-	2.8	None	32.2
Great-West Gth & Inc (M)B	Balan	CdnSAA	Yes	13.7	18.1	-	-	-	-	-	2.5	Defer	26.9
Green Line Balanced Growth	Balan	CdnSAA	Yes	12.6	17.5	16.6	11.6	9.6	-	Med+	2.0	None	585.7
Green Line Balanced Income	Balan	CdnSAA	Yes	10.0	16.5	14.8	10.8	-	-	Med+	2.0	None	278.2
Greystone Managed Wealth	Balan	CdnSAA	Yes	17.8	20.4	15.1	-	-	-	Med+	2.5	None	3.2
GrowSafe Canadian Balanced	Balan	CdnSAA	Yes	7.1	10.8	10.3	-	-	-	Low	2.5	Defer	142.8
Guardian Cdn Balanced C	Balan	CdnSAA	Yes	3.3	8.4	8.5	8.0	9.3	9.9	Low	1.7	Front	92.8
Guardian Cdn Balanced M	Balan	CdnSAA	Yes	2.6	7.7	-	-	-	-	-	2.7	Front	287.0
Guardian Gth & Income C	Balan	CdnSAA	Yes	7.1	-	-	-	-	-	-	2.0	F or B	3.6
Guardian Gth & Income M	Balan	CdnSAA	Yes	7.1	-	-	-	-	-	-	2.6	Front	31.9
Harbour Gth & Income	Balan	CdnSAA	Yes	4.4	-	-	-	-	-	-	2.3	F or B	438.0
Hartford Asset Allocation	Balan	CdnSAA	Yes	-	-	-	-	-	-	-	2.5	Defer	2.5
Hemisphere valuee	Balan	CdnSAA	Yes	7.6	10.6	10.0	-	-	-	Med-	1.8	None	1.7

FUND NAME	FUND CATEGORY	RRSP- ELIGIB.	1 YR	2 YR	3 YR	5 YR	10 YR	15 YR	3 YR VOLATILITY	MER	SALES FEES	ASSETS IN $MIL
ICM Balanced	Balan	CdnSAA	Yes	9.2	11.9	12.5	11.4	11.1	-	Low	0.2	None	187.0
IG Beutel Goodman Cdn Bal	Balan	CdnSAA	Yes	11.2	-	-	-	-	-	-	2.7	FnDf	136.1
IG Sceptre Cdn Balanced	Balan	CdnSAA	Yes	9.2	-	-	-	-	-	-	2.7	FnDf	310.9
Ideal Balanced	Balan	CdnSAA	Yes	14.7	17.6	15.0	12.3	10.7	-	Med-	2.0	Defer	504.7
Imperial Gth Diversified	Balan	CdnSAA	Yes	9.1	15.5	13.4	10.6	-	-	High	2.0	Front	12.5
Ind. Alliance Divers DNL	Balan	CdnSAA	No	-	-	-	-	-	-	-	1.5	None	1.0
Ind. Alliance Ecoflex DNL	Balan	CdnSAA	No	-	-	-	-	-	-	-	2.4	None	5.2
Industrial Balanced	Balan	CdnSAA	Yes	3.2	13.3	11.3	9.1	-	-	Med+	2.4	F or B	345.5
Industrial Inc $0.40 units	Balan	CdnSAA	Yes	-	-	-	-	-	-	-	1.9	F or B	34.7
Industrial Income Class A	Balan	CdnSAA	Yes	5.8	11.7	10.4	8.4	9.1	11.2	Low	1.9	F or B	2628.2
Industrial Pension	Balan	CdnSAA	Yes	14.6	23.3	19.5	16.4	8.0	10.4	Med+	2.4	F or B	321.4
InvesNat Protected Gth Bal	Balan	CdnSAA	Yes	-	-	-	-	-	-	-	3.0	None	17.5
InvesNat Protected Ret Bal	Balan	CdnSAA	Yes	-	-	-	-	-	-	-	3.1	None	29.8
InvesNat Retirement Bal	Balan	CdnSAA	Yes	5.8	13.0	12.1	9.1	-	-	Med	2.1	None	807.9
Investors Income Plus Port	Balan	CdnSAA	Yes	11.8	13.6	11.8	9.1	-	-	Low	2.3	FnDf	1593.8
Investors Mutual	Balan	CdnSAA	Yes	13.2	17.1	14.4	11.5	10.3	9.7	Med+	2.4	FnDf	1178.9
Investors Ret. Plus Port	Balan	CdnSAA	Yes	8.2	11.7	10.8	9.3	-	-	Low	2.1	FnDf	1935.9
Ivy Growth & Income	Balan	CdnSAA	Yes	16.6	20.2	19.5	14.0	-	-	Low	2.4	F or B	2473.9
Jones Heward Cdn Balanced	Balan	CdnSAA	Yes	10.4	12.7	10.5	7.7	9.0	-	Med+	2.4	F or B	54.7
Lasalle Balanced	Balan	CdnSAA	Yes	9.9	14.8	12.3	9.8	9.8	-	Med+	2.3	F or B	4.2
Leith Wheeler Balanced	Balan	CdnSAA	Yes	15.4	20.6	16.6	13.5	11.1	-	Low	1.1	None	175.8
London Life Diversified	Balan	CdnSAA	Yes	14.6	16.7	14.9	10.9	10.3	-	Med+	2.0	Defer	2662.5
Lotus Group Balanced	Balan	CdnSAA	Yes	13.1	16.6	14.9	10.2	9.9	-	Med	2.2	None	36.2
MAXXUM Canadian Balanced	Balan	CdnSAA	Yes	9.2	15.0	13.4	10.0	11.0	-	Med+	2.1	F or B	116.9
MB Balanced Growth Pension	Balan	CdnSAA	No	12.8	18.8	17.6	14.0	12.8	-	Med	-	None	294.4
MD Balanced	Balan	CdnSAA	Yes	12.1	17.4	15.6	13.0	-	-	High	1.3	None	891.2
MLI AGF Gth & Income GIF	Balan	CdnSAA	Yes	2.0	-	-	-	-	-	-	3.0	F or B	128.0
MLI E&P Balanced GIF	Balan	CdnSAA	Yes	-	-	-	-	-	-	-	2.8	F or B	30.1
MLI Fidelity Cdn AA GIF	Balan	CdnSAA	Yes	19.3	-	-	-	-	-	-	3.0	F or B	500.4
MLI Harbour Gth & Inc GIF	Balan	CdnSAA	Yes	-	-	-	-	-	-	-	3.0	F or B	46.5
MLI Talvest Cdn Asset GIF	Balan	CdnSAA	Yes	-	-	-	-	-	-	-	3.0	F or B	44.8
MLI Trimark Select Bal GIF	Balan	CdnSAA	Yes	3.7	-	-	-	-	-	-	2.9	F or B	256.0
Manulife VistaFd 1 Divers	Balan	CdnSAA	Yes	8.9	10.4	9.9	8.1	8.5	8.7	Med+	1.6	Front	33.5
Manulife VistaFd 2 Divers	Balan	CdnSAA	Yes	8.1	9.6	9.0	7.3	7.6	7.9	Med+	2.4	Defer	296.0
Marathon Perf Cdn Balanced	Balan	CdnSAA	Yes	-	-	-	-	-	-	-	2.2	F or B	0.9
Maritime Life Balanced A&C	Balan	CdnSAA	Yes	13.2	15.7	13.9	11.1	9.5	-	Low	2.5	None	428.5
Maritime Life Balanced B	Balan	CdnSAA	Yes	13.1	-	-	-	-	-	-	2.5	Defer	45.5
Mawer Cdn Balanced RSP	Balan	CdnSAA	Yes	13.7	18.2	15.4	12.1	11.0	-	Med-	1.0	None	80.4
McDonald Canada Plus	Balan	CdnSAA	Yes	8.0	9.8	9.4	-	-	-	High	2.9	Front	1.7
Mclean Budden Balanced	Balan	CdnSAA	Yes	11.6	18.0	16.4	12.7	-	-	Med+	1.8	None	21.7
Members Mutual	Balan	CdnSAA	Yes	-5.2	-	-	-	-	-	-	3.4	None	2.8
Metlife Mvp Balanced	Balan	CdnSAA	Yes	11.8	14.8	12.6	9.4	8.2	-	Med	2.2	Defer	106.7
Millennia III Cdn Bal 1	Balan	CdnSAA	Yes	8.6	14.3	-	-	-	-	-	2.7	Defer	171.1
Millennia III Cdn Bal 2	Balan	CdnSAA	Yes	8.4	14.1	-	-	-	-	-	2.9	None	22.5

FUND NAME	FUND CATEGORY	RRSP-ELIGIB.	1 YR	2 YR	3 YR	5 YR	10 YR	15 YR	3 YR VOLATILITY	MER	SALES FEES	ASSETS IN $MIL
Millennium Diversified	Balan	CdnSAA	Yes	15.6	18.4	17.4	-	-	-	High	2.5	Front	10.2
Montrusco Select Balanced	Balan	CdnSAA	Yes	9.0	14.1	14.0	12.4	11.7	-	Med	-	None	73.3
Montrusco Select Balanced+	Balan	CdnSAA	Yes	12.5	19.8	18.5	17.3	-	-	Med+	-	None	352.4
Mutual Summit Growth & Inc	Balan	CdnSAA	Yes	14.0	-	-	-	-	-	-	-	None	81.0
NAL-Balanced Growth	Balan	CdnSAA	Yes	10.6	17.3	15.4	-	-	-	Med	2.0	Defer	135.1
NN-Canadian Diversified	Balan	CdnSAA	Yes	6.5	10.5	12.4	9.6	9.0	-	High	1.8	Defer	81.2
NN Asset Allocation	Balan	CdnSAA	Yes	13.9	17.2	15.8	12.0	9.5	-	Med-	2.7	Defer	143.5
National Balanced	Balan	CdnSAA	Yes	11.6	17.7	15.5	11.7	-	-	Med-	2.4	Defer	222.4
National Trust Balanced	Balan	CdnSAA	Yes	15.5	19.7	16.5	12.2	-	-	Med	1.7	None	332.9
Navigator Cdn Gth & Income	Balan	CdnSAA	Yes	-	-	-	-	-	-	-	2.8	F or B	0.7
North West Life Ecofix DNL	Balan	CdnSAA	No	-	-	-	-	-	-	-	2.4	Defer	0.6
O'Donnell Balanced	Balan	CdnSAA	Yes	3.6	-	-	-	-	-	-	2.4	F or B	128.2
O.I.Q. Ferique Equilibre	Balan	CdnSAA	Yes	20.6	22.0	18.3	14.4	12.7	12.1	High	0.3	None	369.6
OTGIF Balanced	Balan	CdnSAA	Yes	12.8	17.7	15.5	12.1	10.8	-	Med-	1.0	None	69.9
Optimum Croissance et Reve	Balan	CdnSAA	Yes	-	-	-	-	-	-	-	-	None	6.2
Optimum Equilibre	Balan	CdnSAA	Yes	10.8	13.6	12.5	10.4	9.9	-	Low	1.5	None	28.9
PH & N Balance Pension Tr	Balan	CdnSAA	Yes	12.3	17.3	15.9	13.4	-	-	Med-	0.0	None	2390.9
PH & N Balanced	Balan	CdnSAA	Yes	10.7	16.1	14.7	12.6	-	-	Med-	0.9	None	560.7
Quebec Prof Balanced	Balan	CdnSAA	Yes	9.0	11.6	11.2	9.2	9.9	10.2	Low	1.0	None	488.1
Quebec Prof Gth & Income	Balan	CdnSAA	Yes	8.1	12.1	11.5	-	-	-	Med-	1.0	None	65.6
Royal&SunAlliance Equity	Balan	CdnSAA	Yes	-	-	-	-	-	-	-	2.4	Defer	81.1
Royal Energy	Balan	CdnSAA	Yes	12.4	17.0	14.3	11.1	-	-	Med	2.3	None	260.6
Royal Trust Adv. Growth	Balan	CdnSAA	Yes	11.6	14.8	13.1	10.4	10.0	-	Med-	1.9	None	492.3
Royal Trust Adv. Income	Balan	CdnSAA	Yes	9.5	13.3	12.6	9.9	9.3	-	Med+	1.6	None	187.7
Royal U.S. Equity	Balan	CdnSAA	Fgn	10.9	13.6	11.9	9.6	9.9	-	Low	2.1	None	163.1
Saxon Balanced	Balan	CdnSAA	Yes	10.7	15.6	13.6	12.2	10.0	-	Med-	1.8	None	11.4
Sceptre Balanced Growth	Balan	CdnSAA	Yes	8.2	16.2	17.8	14.2	11.5	-	High	1.4	None	252.0
Scotia Ex. Balanced	Balan	CdnSAA	Yes	9.0	12.3	12.3	10.5	-	-	Med-	1.9	None	735.2
Spectrum Utd Cdn Bal Port	Balan	CdnSAA	Yes	9.3	13.1	13.7	11.1	-	-	Med	2.2	F or B	539.7
Spectrum Utd Cdn Conserv P	Balan	CdnSAA	Yes	-	-	-	-	-	-	-	2.0	F or B	24.1
Spectrum Utd Cdn Gth Port	Balan	CdnSAA	Yes	-	-	-	-	-	-	-	2.2	F or B	13.6
Spectrum Utd Cdn Income Pf	Balan	CdnSAA	Yes	-	-	-	-	-	-	-	1.9	F or B	12.8
Spectrum Utd Diversified	Balan	CdnSAA	Yes	12.6	17.0	14.3	10.5	9.2	-	Med	2.1	F or B	232.6
Standard Life Balanced	Balan	CdnSAA	Yes	14.5	18.2	16.2	12.3	-	-	Med	2.0	Defer	22.0
Stone & Co Flagship Gth&In	Balan	CdnSAA	Yes	8.7	-	-	-	-	-	-	2.9	F or B	17.5
Strategic Val Cdn Balanced	Balan	CdnSAA	Yes	9.4	14.8	12.7	9.7	-	-	Med+	2.7	F or B	177.5
Talvest Canadian Asset All	Balan	CdnSAA	Yes	16.1	18.5	15.4	11.9	10.0	-	High	2.4	F or B	349.1
Templeton Balanced	Balan	CdnSAA	Yes	8.9	17.5	14.8	12.8	-	-	Med	2.4	Front	64.4
Transamerica Bal Inv Gth	Balan	CdnSAA	Yes	7.1	10.9	10.3	9.4	9.4	9.6	Low	1.8	None	70.8
Trimark Income Growth	Balan	CdnSAA	Yes	0.8	10.1	10.5	10.8	10.7	-	Med	1.6	Front	886.1
Trimark Select Balanced	Balan	CdnSAA	Yes	4.4	12.7	12.4	11.5	-	-	Med	2.2	F or B	4803.6
Universal Canadian Bal	Balan	CdnSAA	Yes	19.4	-	-	-	-	-	-	2.4	F or B	459.7
University Avenue Balanced	Balan	CdnSAA	Yes	-	-	-	-	-	-	-	2.3	F or B	1.1
Valorem Diversified	Balan	CdnSAA	Yes	13.3	-	-	-	-	-	-	-	F or B	3.4

FUND NAME	FUND CATEGORY	RRSP-ELIGIB.	1 YR	2 YR	3 YR	5 YR	10 YR	15 YR	3 YR VOLATILITY	MER	SALES FEES	ASSETS IN $MIL.
YMG Balanced	Balan	CdnSAA	Yes	-1.7	8.2	8.2	7.1	7.0	8.1	High	1.8	F or B	18.6
AGF Cdn T.A. Asset Alloc	Balan	CdnTAA	Yes	15.5	18.7	15.8	12.3	-	-	High	2.4	F or B	1036.2
AGF Growth & Income	Balan	CdnTAA	Yes	2.4	7.3	13.1	11.5	9.1	9.4	High	2.5	F or B	688.4
AIM Canadian Balanced	Balan	CdnTAA	Yes	13.8	13.7	12.0	9.5	-	-	Med+	2.7	F or B	6.5
APEX Balanced (AGF)	Balan	CdnTAA	Yes	5.9	7.2	7.5	8.1	7.9	7.9	Low	3.0	F or B	94.2
Altamira Balanced	Balan	CdnTAA	Yes	11.3	11.4	10.0	7.1	7.7	-	Med	2.0	None	78.1
Altamira Growth & Income	Balan	CdnTAA	Yes	-2.9	0.5	2.4	4.5	8.2	-	High	1.4	None	126.1
Asset Builder I	Balan	CdnTAA	Yes	17.4	21.2	17.2	-	-	-	Low	2.3	Defer	55.0
Asset Builder II	Balan	CdnTAA	Yes	22.8	26.7	20.9	-	-	-	Med-	2.3	Defer	82.9
Asset Builder III	Balan	CdnTAA	Yes	24.3	28.6	22.4	-	-	-	Med	2.3	Defer	75.4
Asset Builder IV	Balan	CdnTAA	Yes	23.5	28.3	22.2	-	-	-	Med	2.3	Defer	37.9
Asset Builder V	Balan	CdnTAA	Yes	22.6	28.0	22.1	-	-	-	Med	2.3	Defer	15.2
CIBC Balanced	Balan	CdnTAA	Yes	16.9	19.0	15.6	11.1	9.9	-	Med+	2.2	None	1279.0
Caldwell Associate	Balan	CdnTAA	Yes	3.7	13.7	13.0	14.2	-	-	High	2.4	F or B	114.3
Clean Environment Balanced	Balan	CdnTAA	Yes	23.5	26.2	20.8	16.1	-	-	High	2.6	F or B	111.2
Co-Operators Balanced	Balan	CdnTAA	Yes	17.9	20.4	17.3	14.3	-	-	Low	2.1	None	73.3
Dynamic Partners	Balan	CdnTAA	Yes	5.1	11.3	10.1	9.3	-	-	Low	2.3	F or B	1898.2
Dynamic Team	Balan	CdnTAA	Yes	-0.8	7.0	9.3	7.3	9.2	-	Med	0.5	F or B	216.2
Elliott & Page Balanced	Balan	CdnTAA	Yes	5.9	10.2	11.4	10.1	10.5	-	Med+	1.8	F or B	301.0
Empire Asset Allocation	Balan	CdnTAA	Yes	7.9	14.6	12.8	-	-	-	Low	2.5	Defer	182.0
Equitable Life Asset Allc	Balan	CdnTAA	Yes	10.1	14.0	11.8	-	-	-	Med	2.3	Defer	73.4
Ficadre Equilibre	Balan	CdnTAA	Yes	7.3	11.8	12.2	10.7	8.6	9.4	Med-	2.2	Defer	71.2
First Canadian Asset Alloc	Balan	CdnTAA	Yes	9.8	14.4	12.9	9.3	8.5	-	Low	1.9	None	421.3
Hongkong Bank Balanced	Balan	CdnTAA	Yes	10.4	15.5	14.9	10.9	-	-	Med-	1.8	None	380.9
Ind. Alliance Divers 2	Balan	CdnTAA	Yes	1.8	-	-	-	-	-	-	2.8	None	2.0
Ind. Alliance Diversified	Balan	CdnTAA	Yes	8.8	13.9	12.2	11.1	10.9	-	Med-	1.6	None	275.2
Ind. Alliance Ecoflex D	Balan	CdnTAA	Yes	7.8	13.0	11.4	10.4	-	-	Med-	2.5	Defer	776.2
Investors Asset Allocation	Balan	CdnTAA	Yes	13.2	17.5	16.9	-	-	-	High	2.7	FnDf	1899.5
MLI Dynamic Partners GIF	Balan	CdnTAA	Yes	-	-	-	-	-	-	-	3.4	F or B	12.5
Mawer Canadian Diver Invst	Balan	CdnTAA	No	11.5	16.5	14.4	11.3	10.3	-	Low	1.1	None	30.6
Mutual Diversifund 40	Balan	CdnTAA	Yes	12.3	16.2	14.9	11.6	9.5	-	Med-	1.9	Front	312.8
Mutual Premier Diversified	Balan	CdnTAA	Yes	10.2	15.5	14.8	-	-	-	Med-	2.4	None	674.4
North West Life Ecoflex D	Balan	CdnTAA	Yes	7.8	-	-	-	-	-	-	2.5	Defer	15.4
Northwest Balanced	Balan	CdnTAA	Yes	11.2	13.3	13.1	-	-	-	Med	2.0	F or B	46.6
Pret et Revenu Eq Retraite	Balan	CdnTAA	Yes	8.2	12.8	13.4	11.0	10.6	10.1	Med+	2.0	None	83.0
Protected American	Balan	CdnTAA	Yes	10.5	3.3	3.7	2.4	-	-	Low	2.3	F or B	2.7
Royal&SunAlliance Cdn Gwth	Balan	CdnTAA	Yes	11.9	14.6	13.2	10.6	10.3	-	Med-	2.4	Defer	7741.9
SSO - Equilibre	Balan	CdnTAA	Yes	12.4	16.2	15.4	11.9	-	-	Med	-	None	35.7
Scotia Ex. Total Return	Balan	CdnTAA	Yes	8.1	15.8	14.4	12.3	-	-	Med+	2.3	None	940.7
Spectrum Utd Asset Alloc	Balan	CdnTAA	Yes	13.3	15.9	13.8	10.7	-	-	Med-	2.2	F or B	541.6
Templeton Cdn Asset Alloc	Balan	CdnTAA	Yes	6.7	13.1	12.4	-	-	-	Low	2.2	F or B	128.0
Trans-Canada Pension	Balan	CdnTAA	Yes	-0.4	19.3	11.4	9.3	8.6	9.9	High	3.5	F or B	2.3
Westbury Cdn Life Balanced	Balan	CdnTAA	Yes	12.9	17.3	14.7	11.7	-	-	Med+	2.4	Defer	34.4

FUND NAME	FUND CATEGORY	RRSP-ELIGIB.	1 YR	2 YR	3 YR	5 YR	10 YR	15 YR	3 YR VOLATILITY	MER	SALES FEES	ASSETS IN $MIL
AGF Canadian Bond	FixInc	CdnBond	Yes	9.8	11.7	10.8	8.8	10.3	11.3	High	1.9	F or B	808.1
AIM GT S-T Income SrA	FixInc	ST Bond	Fgn	2.0	2.6						1.6	Front	3.5
AIM GT S-T Income SrB	FixInc	ST Bond	Fgn	1.4	2.1						2.2	Defer	9.8
APEX Fixed Income	FixInc	CdnBond	Yes	7.8	10.0	9.0	7.5	10.4	10.1	Med	2.3	F or B	50.1
Acadia Bond	FixInc	ST Bond	Yes	6.8	9.2	8.1					2.2	Defer	3.3
Acuity Pld Fixed Income	FixInc	CdnBond	Yes	29.6	23.4	17.6	12.7			High		None	
Altamira Bond	FixInc	CdnBond	Yes	22.9	19.6	15.4	12.6	12.7		High	1.3	None	410.1
Altamira Income	FixInc	CdnBond	Yes	9.5	10.6	9.2	9.0	11.7	11.4	Med+	1.0	None	539.9
Altamira S-Term Govt Bond	FixInc	ST Bond	Yes	4.6	6.0	6.5					1.3	None	70.0
Astra Obligations	FixInc	CdnBond	Yes								2.2	None	3.9
Atlas Canadian Bond	FixInc	CdnBond	Yes	9.1	10.6	9.7	8.2	9.2		Med	2.0	F or B	49.5
Atlas Cdn High Yield Bond	FixInc	CdnBond	Yes	7.8	12.1	11.5				Low	1.9	F or B	469.7
BNP (Canada) Bond	FixInc	CdnBond	Yes	10.8	11.6	10.5	8.8			High	1.7	None	5.6
BPI Canadian Bond	FixInc	CdnBond	Yes	9.4	10.1	6.7	5.5			High	1.5	F or B	29.2
BPI Canadian Bond Segrd	FixInc	CdnBond	Yes									F or B	1.8
BPI Corporate Bond	FixInc	CdnBond	Yes								1.5	F or B	5.6
Batirente Sec Obligations	FixInc	CdnBond	Yes	10.5	13.3	12.6	10.5	11.3		Med	1.5	None	41.3
Beutel Goodman Income	FixInc	CdnBond	Yes	10.4	12.1	11.2	9.1			Med+	0.7	Front	57.2
Beutel Goodman Private Bd	FixInc	CdnBond	Yes	7.2	11.0	10.2	8.7			Med+	0.7	None	5.5
Bissett Bond	FixInc	CdnBond	Yes	10.0	12.2	11.5	9.8	10.5		Med-	0.8	None	173.3
C.I. Canadian Bond	FixInc	CdnBond	Yes	10.0	13.0	12.2	9.7			Med-	1.7	F or B	151.0
CCPE Fixed Income	FixInc	CdnBond	Yes	8.6	9.4	9.4	8.3	10.0		Low	1.4	Defer	17.0
CIBC Canadian Bond	FixInc	CdnBond	Yes	9.6	11.4	10.5	7.9	9.8		Med	1.6	None	804.4
CIBC Canadian Bond Index	FixInc	CdnBond	Yes								0.9	None	86.9
CIBC Canadian S-Term Bond	FixInc	ST Bond	Yes	4.0	6.7	7.5					0.9	None	147.4
CT Bond	FixInc	CdnBond	Yes	9.4	10.7	9.8	8.2	9.9		Med	1.4	None	736.8
CT Canadian Bond Index	FixInc	CdnBond	Yes	9.8							0.8	None	19.7
CT Short Term Bond	FixInc	ST Bond	Yes	4.2							1.4	None	290.5
CUMIS Life Canadian Bond	FixInc	CdnBond	Yes	9.3							3.0	Back	1.6
Caldwell Canadian Income	FixInc	CdnBond	Yes	9.0							0.5	F or B	7.4
Canada Life Fixed Income	FixInc	CdnBond	Yes	8.9	10.4	9.6	7.8	9.1	9.7	Med-	2.0	Defer	433.1
Canso valuee Bond	FixInc	CdnBond	Yes									F or B	1.9
CentrePost Bond	FixInc	CdnBond	Yes	7.2	8.8	9.3	7.6			Low	1.0	None	39.5
Clean Environment Income	FixInc	CdnBond	Yes	8.7	9.4	7.6				Low	2.0	F or B	17.1
Co-Operators Fixed Income	FixInc	CdnBond	Yes	11.8	13.1	11.8	9.9			High	2.1	None	11.1
Colonia Life Bond	FixInc	CdnBond	Yes	8.4	8.5	8.3	7.7			Med-	1.6	Defer	14.9
Comm. Un. Cdn Bond Index	FixInc	CdnBond	Yes								2.4	Defer	2.9
Cornerstone Bond	FixInc	CdnBond	Yes	10.1	10.3	9.7	8.3	10.0		Med-	1.4	None	41.3
Desjardins Bond	FixInc	CdnBond	Yes	8.0	9.7	9.5	8.1	9.2	9.6	Med-	1.6	None	145.4
Desjardins Distinct Bond	FixInc	CdnBond	Yes	10.1	11.7	11.4	9.5	11.5	12.1	Med-	1.7	None	30.6
Dynamic Dollar-Cost Avging	FixInc	CdnBond	Yes									Defer	15.1
Dynamic Government Income	FixInc	ST Bond	Yes	4.0	7.1	8.0	6.6	9.2	10.0	Med-	0.9	Front	15.0
Dynamic Income	FixInc	CdnBond	Yes	-0.6	3.5	5.4	6.4	9.2		Med-	1.6	F or B	326.4
Elliott & Page Bond	FixInc	CdnBond	Yes	10.6	10.1	8.7		8.8		High	1.9	F or B	21.7

FUND NAME	FUND CATEGORY		RRSP-ELIGIB.	1 YR	2 YR	3 YR	5 YR	10 YR	15 YR	3 YR VOLATILITY	MER	SALES FEES	ASSETS IN $MIL
Empire Bond	FixInc	CdnBond	Yes	8.9	10.1	9.3	7.7	9.3	-	Med	2.1	Defer	71.3
Empire Fgn Curr Cdn Bond	FixInc	CdnBond	Yes	6.7	5.2	2.2	-	-	-	Med+	2.1	Defer	3.0
Equitable Life Accum Inc	FixInc	CdnBond	Yes	11.2	12.5	11.7	9.6	11.1	11.5	Med-	0.4	Front	14.3
Equitable Life Cdn Bond	FixInc	CdnBond	Yes	9.4	10.8	10.0	8.0	-	-	Med+	2.0	Defer	39.5
Ethical Income	FixInc	CdnBond	Yes	10.4	11.8	10.9	9.3	9.4	9.8	High	1.6	None	191.4
Ficadre Hypotheques	FixInc	ST Bond	Yes	4.0	5.6	5.6	-	-	-	-	1.6	Defer	1.2
Ficadre Obligations	FixInc	CdnBond	Yes	8.6	10.0	9.5	7.9	9.0	-	Med	1.6	Defer	19.0
Fidelity Canadian Bond	FixInc	CdnBond	Yes	9.3	11.1	10.1	8.1	8.5	-	Med-	1.4	F or B	169.9
Fidelity Canadian Income	FixInc	ST Bond	Yes	5.2	7.3	7.6	-	-	-	-	1.3	F or B	63.3
First Canadian Bond	FixInc	CdnBond	Yes	8.1	10.2	9.6	8.2	9.5	-	Med-	1.5	None	1529.4
GBC Canadian Bond	FixInc	CdnBond	Yes	9.7	11.5	10.6	9.2	10.6	-	Med+	1.1	None	50.4
General Trust Bond	FixInc	CdnBond	Yes	8.4	10.9	10.3	8.1	9.6	10.6	Med-	1.6	None	42.2
Global Strategy Bond	FixInc	ST Bond	Yes	3.7	5.5	6.4	-	-	-	-	1.5	F or B	16.3
Great-West Bond (B) A	FixInc	CdnBond	Yes	8.6	10.4	-	-	-	-	-	2.3	None	3.3
Great-West Bond (B) B	FixInc	CdnBond	Yes	8.9	10.7	-	-	-	-	-	2.1	Defer	3.8
Great-West Bond (S) A	FixInc	CdnBond	Yes	11.0	11.6	-	-	-	-	-	2.4	None	8.3
Great-West Bond (S) B	FixInc	CdnBond	Yes	11.3	11.9	-	-	-	-	-	2.1	Defer	8.8
Great-West Cdn Bond (G) A	FixInc	CdnBond	Yes	8.8	10.5	9.3	7.5	8.9	9.6	Med+	2.1	None	50.7
Great-West Cdn Bond (G) B	FixInc	CdnBond	Yes	9.1	10.8	9.5	-	-	-	Med+	1.8	Defer	31.1
Great-West Govt Bond (G) A	FixInc	CdnBond	Yes	4.5	6.5	6.7	-	-	-	Low	2.1	None	13.4
Great-West Govt Bond (G) B	FixInc	CdnBond	Yes	4.8	6.8	6.9	-	-	-	Low	1.8	Defer	7.5
Great-West Income (G) A	FixInc	CdnBond	Yes	10.8	14.2	12.4	-	-	-	Med	2.2	None	34.3
Great-West Income (G) B	FixInc	CdnBond	Yes	11.1	14.5	12.6	-	-	-	Med	1.9	Defer	33.5
Great-West Income (M) A	FixInc	CdnBond	Yes	7.3	10.9	-	-	-	-	-	2.5	None	6.3
Great-West Income (M) B	FixInc	CdnBond	Yes	7.6	11.2	-	-	-	-	-	2.2	Defer	7.6
Green Line Canadian Bond	FixInc	CdnBond	Yes	11.3	13.3	12.4	10.1	-	-	Med+	0.9	None	952.3
Green Line Cdn Govt Bd Idx	FixInc	CdnBond	Yes	9.7	11.3	10.7	8.9	9.3	-	Med-	1.0	None	216.5
Green Line Monthly Income	FixInc	CdnBond	Yes	-	-	-	-	-	-	-	1.3	None	15.9
Green Line Real Return Bnd	FixInc	CdnBond	Yes	11.6	12.0	8.4	-	-	-	High	1.5	None	22.0
Green Line Short Term Inco	FixInc	ST Bond	Yes	3.5	4.9	5.9	5.5	-	-	-	1.1	None	184.6
GrowSafe Canadian Bond	FixInc	CdnBond	Yes	8.8	8.7	7.4	-	-	-	Low	2.3	Defer	25.3
Guardian Canadian Income C	FixInc	ST Bond	Yes	4.1	5.5	6.1	-	-	-	-	1.1	Front	10.2
Guardian Canadian Income M	FixInc	ST Bond	Yes	3.4	4.8	-	-	-	-	-	1.9	F or B	8.7
Hartford Canadian Income	FixInc	CdnBond	Yes	-	-	-	-	-	-	-	2.4	Defer	2.1
Hongkong Bank Cdn Bond	FixInc	CdnBond	Yes	9.5	11.5	10.5	8.8	-	-	Med	1.1	None	75.4
ICM Bond	FixInc	CdnBond	Yes	8.8	9.6	9.4	-	-	-	Low	0.2	None	66.4
IG Sceptre Canadian Bond	FixInc	CdnBond	Yes	12.1	-	-	-	-	-	-	2.1	Defer	45.8
Ideal Bond	FixInc	CdnBond	Yes	8.3	9.9	9.2	7.9	9.4	-	Med+	2.0	Defer	41.3
Ind. Alliance Bond 2	FixInc	CdnBond	No	3.1	-	-	-	-	-	-	1.7	None	0.7
Ind. Alliance Bond BNL	FixInc	CdnBond	Yes	-	-	-	-	-	-	-	1.5	None	0.7
Ind. Alliance Bonds	FixInc	CdnBond	Yes	8.1	9.4	9.3	7.7	9.8	10.3	Low	1.5	None	39.7
Ind. Alliance Ecoflex B	FixInc	CdnBond	Yes	7.7	9.0	8.8	7.2	-	-	Low	1.9	Defer	67.0
Ind. Alliance Ecoflex BNL	FixInc	CdnBond	No	-	-	-	-	-	-	-	2.0	Defer	0.6
Ind. Alliance Ecoflex R	FixInc	CdnBond	Yes	-	-	-	-	-	-	-	1.9	Defer	3.7

FUND NAME	FUND CATEGORY		RRSP-ELIGIB.	1 YR	2 YR	3 YR	5 YR	10 YR	15 YR	3 YR VOLATILITY	MER	SALES FEES	ASSETS IN $MIL
Ind. Alliance Income	FixInc	CdnBond	Yes	-	-	-	-	-	-	-	1.5	None	0.1
Industrial Bond	FixInc	CdnBond	Yes	10.0	13.4	11.5	9.0	-	-	High	1.9	F or B	505.8
InvesNat Protected Cdn Bd	FixInc	CdnBond	Yes	-	-	-	-	-	-	-	2.1	None	5.3
InvesNat S-T Govt. Bond	FixInc	ST Bond	Yes	4.0	6.0	7.0	6.0	-	-	-	1.3	None	155.3
Investors Corporate Bond	FixInc	CdnBond	Yes	9.0	10.9	10.3	-	-	-	Med-	1.9	Defer	967.5
Investors Government Bond	FixInc	CdnBond	Yes	9.6	11.1	10.3	8.7	9.8	10.3	Med+	1.9	Defer	1680.9
Investors Income Portfolio	FixInc	CdnBond	Yes	7.1	8.8	8.6	7.4	-	-	Low	2.1	Defer	811.2
Jones Heward Bond	FixInc	CdnBond	Yes	7.8	9.9	9.2	7.3	8.9	-	Med-	1.8	F or B	4.6
Leith Wheeler Fixed Income	FixInc	CdnBond	Yes	8.9	10.3	9.8	-	-	-	Low	0.8	None	8.9
London Life Bond	FixInc	CdnBond	Yes	8.8	9.8	9.5	8.0	9.0	10.6	Med-	2.0	Defer	1429.8
Lotus Group Bond	FixInc	CdnBond	Yes	10.1	11.8	11.0	-	-	-	Med	0.8	None	1.3
MAXXUM Income	FixInc	CdnBond	Yes	16.0	15.9	13.4	10.6	10.7	10.9	High	1.7	F or B	119.5
MD Bond	FixInc	CdnBond	Yes	9.6	11.6	11.0	9.4	10.6	-	Med	1.0	None	505.9
MD Bond & Mortgage	FixInc	ST Bond	Yes	5.0	6.2	-	-	-	-	-	1.1	None	83.0
MLI AGF Canadian Bond GIF	FixInc	CdnBond	Yes	9.1	-	-	-	-	-	-	2.4	F or B	69.4
MLI Fidelity Cdn Bond GIF	FixInc	CdnBond	Yes	8.4	-	-	-	-	-	-	2.2	F or B	24.4
MLI Talvest Income GIF	FixInc	CdnBond	Yes	-	-	-	-	-	-	-	2.3	F or B	4.5
Manulife Cabot Divers Bond	FixInc	CdnBond	Yes	8.9	7.4	6.3	-	-	-	Low	2.0	None	13.7
Manulife VistaFund 1 Bond	FixInc	CdnBond	Yes	8.6	9.8	8.2	6.7	9.4	9.9	High	1.6	Front	10.2
Manulife VistaFund 2 Bond	FixInc	CdnBond	Yes	7.8	8.9	7.4	5.9	8.5	9.1	High	2.4	Defer	75.2
Maritime Life Bond A	FixInc	CdnBond	Yes	8.6	9.8	9.0	7.7	-	-	Low	1.8	None	51.7
Maritime Life Bond B	FixInc	CdnBond	Yes	8.4	-	-	-	-	-	-	1.8	Defer	11.1
Maritime Life Bond C	FixInc	CdnBond	Yes	8.3	-	-	-	-	-	-	2.2	Defer	17.2
Mawer Canadian Bond	FixInc	CdnBond	Yes	9.5	11.0	10.5	8.8	-	-	Med-	1.0	None	36.3
Mawer Canadian Income	FixInc	CdnBond	No	7.9	11.4	11.1	9.0	-	-	Low	1.0	None	28.6
Mawer Cdn High Yield Bond	FixInc	CdnBond	Yes	10.5	10.6	-	-	-	-	-	1.5	None	8.2
McDonald Enhanced Bond	FixInc	CdnBond	Yes	9.3	8.3	-	-	-	-	-	1.0	Front	1.0
McLean Budden Pld Fxd Inc	FixInc	CdnBond	Yes	11.8	13.5	12.6	10.8	11.7	11.9	Med+	0.0	None	621.3
McLean Budden Fixed Income	FixInc	CdnBond	Yes	10.9	12.3	11.4	9.4	8.2	-	Med+	1.0	None	17.8
Metlife Mvp Bond	FixInc	CdnBond	Yes	8.5	8.8	8.1	6.4	-	-	Low	2.2	Defer	36.4
Millennia III Income 1	FixInc	CdnBond	Yes	7.0	8.2	-	-	-	-	-	2.2	Defer	47.1
Millennia III Income 2	FixInc	CdnBond	Yes	6.6	8.0	-	-	-	-	-	2.4	Defer	5.9
Montrusco Select Bd Index+	FixInc	CdnBond	Yes	10.0	11.9	-	-	-	-	-	-	None	157.5
Montrusco Select H-Yld Bd	FixInc	CdnBond	Yes	-	-	-	-	-	-	-	-	None	3.2
Montrusco Select Income	FixInc	CdnBond	Yes	10.5	11.7	11.3	9.7	11.5	-	Med-	-	None	113.1
Mutual Bond	FixInc	CdnBond	Yes	7.9	9.4	8.7	7.4	-	-	Med-	1.9	Front	18.6
Mutual Premier Bond	FixInc	CdnBond	Yes	8.8	10.4	9.5	7.9	-	-	Med	2.0	None	251.6
NAL-Canadian Bond	FixInc	CdnBond	Yes	9.5	10.4	9.6	8.4	9.3	-	High	1.8	Defer	21.2
NN Bond	FixInc	CdnBond	Yes	12.6	13.2	12.1	9.7	10.1	-	High	2.2	Defer	46.3
National Fixed Income	FixInc	CdnBond	Yes	9.0	10.8	9.9	8.5	9.8	10.2	Med+	2.0	Defer	66.4
National Trust Cdn Bond	FixInc	CdnBond	Yes	9.5	12.3	11.3	9.2	9.8	10.3	Med+	1.2	None	217.0
Navigator Canadian Income	FixInc	CdnBond	Yes	8.1	11.7	11.5	-	-	-	Low	2.5	F or B	22.1
North West Life Ecoflex B	FixInc	CdnBond	Yes	7.7	-	-	-	-	-	-	1.9	Defer	2.1
North West Life Ecoflex R	FixInc	CdnBond	Yes	-	-	-	-	-	-	-	1.9	Defer	0.1

FUND NAME	FUND CATEGORY		RRSP-ELIGIB.	1 YR	2 YR	3 YR	5 YR	10 YR	15 YR	3 YR VOLATILITY	MER	SALES FEES	ASSETS IN $MIL
North West Life Ecofix BNL	FixInc	CdnBond	No	9.1	10.2	9.4	7.7				2.0	Defer	0.1
Northwest Income	FixInc	CdnBond	Yes	7.9	11.8					Med	1.8	F or B	6.6
O'Donnell High Income	FixInc	CdnBond	Yes	8.7	11.0						2.0	F or B	387.8
O.I.Q. Ferique Obligations	FixInc	CdnBond	Yes	13.6	15.4	10.6	9.2	10.4	10.7	Low	0.5	None	55.8
Optima Strat-Cdn Fx Income	FixInc	CdnBond	Yes	4.6	5.8	13.2	5.9			High	0.4	F or B	452.4
Optima Strat-Short Term	FixInc	ST Bond	Yes	8.5	11.9	6.3					0.3	F or B	186.2
Optimum Obligations	FixInc	CdnBond	Yes	10.0	11.6	11.4	9.7	10.8		Med+	1.4	None	5.0
PH & N Bond	FixInc	CdnBond	Yes	5.6	8.3	11.1	9.7	11.3		Med-	0.6	None	2020.8
Perigee Income Fund 2	FixInc	ST Bond	Yes	9.3	10.4	8.9	8.2	9.8	11.9		0.0	None	4.3
Pret et Revenu Obligations	FixInc	CdnBond	Yes	11.7	11.7	9.8	8.4	9.6	10.8	Med	1.6	None	52.9
Primus Cdn Fixed Income	FixInc	CdnBond	Yes	12.6	10.0	8.4					0.2	None	164.6
Pursuit Canadian Bond	FixInc	CdnBond	Yes	9.5	12.9	9.7	7.2	6.8			0.8	Front	24.3
Quebec Prof Bond	FixInc	CdnBond	Yes	11.7	11.7	11.4	8.1	9.7		High	1.0	None	63.9
Royal&SunAlliance Glo Emg	FixInc	CdnBond	Fgn	9.7	12.9	10.4	9.1	10.2	10.3	Low		None	2580.7
Royal Japanese Stock	FixInc	CdnBond	Fgn	11.1	13.6	12.4	8.1		10.7	High	2.8	Defer	44.4
SSQ - Obligations	FixInc	CdnBond	Yes	13.3	6.3	12.0	10.3	11.9	12.4	Med		None	61.5
Sceptre Bond	FixInc	CdnBond	Yes	7.3	5.0	5.1	9.5	10.6		Med	1.0	None	49.8
Scotia CanAm Income	FixInc	ST Bond	Yes	3.8	8.1	6.0	4.8			Med+	1.6	None	18.1
Scotia Ex. Defensive Inc	FixInc	ST Bond	Yes	6.5	6.5	8.4	6.1	7.5			1.4	None	121.3
Scotia Ex. Income	FixInc	CdnBond	Yes		16.0	13.0	7.8	8.7			1.0	None	373.1
Scudder Canadian Bond	FixInc	CdnBond	Yes	4.5	10.5	9.4				Low	0.6	None	11.5
Scudder Cdn S-Term Bond	FixInc	ST Bond	Yes	16.7	5.4	9.8					1.7	None	12.8
Spectrum Utd Long-Term Bd	FixInc	CdnBond	Yes	8.8	12.7	6.1	9.8	9.2		High	1.6	F or B	159.4
Spectrum Utd Mid-Term Bond	FixInc	CdnBond	Yes	9.1	10.6	11.2	7.7			Med+	1.5	F or B	423.4
Standard Life Bond	FixInc	CdnBond	Yes	4.5	6.4	10.0	8.4		10.4	High	2.2	F or B	8.4
Strategic Val Govt Bond	FixInc	ST Bond	Yes	15.0	6.6	7.1	5.6				2.2	Defer	56.5
Strategic Val Income	FixInc	CdnBond	Yes		10.6	6.6	8.8	9.5		Med+		F or B	170.3
Synergy Cdn ST Income Cl.	FixInc	CdnBond	Yes		5.8	9.9					2.1	F or B	1.2
Tal/Hyper High Yield Bond	FixInc	CdnBond	Yes	11.0	12.7	5.3	8.4	9.7	10.7		2.0	F or B	89.9
Talvest Bond	FixInc	CdnBond	Yes	8.9	10.9	12.2	6.5	8.4	9.0	Med	1.7	F or B	100.6
Talvest Income	FixInc	ST Bond	Yes	3.9	5.6	10.7	5.7				1.7	F or B	97.2
Templeton Canadian Bond	FixInc	CdnBond	Yes	5.0	11.8	6.5	7.3	6.7		Low	1.0	F or B	43.2
Tradex Bond	FixInc	CdnBond	Yes	8.9	9.6	11.0	4.9			Med+	2.9	None	12.4
Trans-Canada Bond	FixInc	CdnBond	Yes	3.4	4.0	8.9				Med-	1.2	F or B	0.8
Trimark Advantage Bond	FixInc	CdnBond	Yes	10.2		5.5	9.2	9.9		Med	1.2	F or B	674.2
Trimark Canadian Bond	FixInc	CdnBond	Yes	9.6			7.3	7.7	10.1	Med-	1.2	F or B	146.4
Trimark Government Income	FixInc	ST Bond	Yes	3.6			5.5				1.2	F or B	257.4
Valorem Cdn Bond-valuee	FixInc	CdnBond	Yes	9.8								F or B	6.8
Westbury Cdn Life B	FixInc	CdnBond	Yes	10.2						Med	1.1	Front	1.4
Westbury Cdn Life Bond	FixInc	CdnBond	Yes	8.1						Med	2.1	Defer	11.4
YMG Income	FixInc	CdnBond	Yes	-5.3						High	1.7	F or B	5.7
APEX Mortgage	FixInc	Mortgage	Yes	3.5	4.0	4.9				Med	2.0	F or B	5.6
Acadia Mortgage	FixInc	Mortgage	Yes	4.2	3.7	3.9				Low	2.0	Defer	6.7

FUND NAME	FUND CATEGORY		RRSP-ELIGIB.	1 YR	2 YR	3 YR	5 YR	10 YR	15 YR	3 YR VOLATILITY	MER	SALES FEES	ASSETS IN $MIL
CIBC Mortgage	FixInc	Mortgage	Yes	3.1	6.0	6.4	6.6	9.0	9.3	High	1.7	None	1471.7
Colonia Life Mortgage	FixInc	Mortgage	Yes	4.4	4.7	5.9	5.9			Med+	1.9	Defer	2.7
Desjardins Distinct Mtg	FixInc	Mortgage	Yes	7.5	6.2	7.2	7.1	9.1	10.0	Med+	1.7	None	13.6
Desjardins Mortgage	FixInc	Mortgage	Yes	4.6	5.0	5.7	6.1	9.0	9.0	Low	1.6	None	166.4
First Canadian Mortgage	FixInc	Mortgage	Yes	3.9	5.8	6.3	6.7	8.2	9.8	High	1.4	None	1364.7
General Trust Mortgage	FixInc	Mortgage	Yes	5.1	5.4	5.7	5.9	9.1	9.3	Med-	1.6	None	42.7
Great-West Mortgage (G)A	FixInc	Mortgage	Yes	7.2	9.0	8.2	7.1	8.1	9.2	High	2.4	None	105.0
Great-West Mortgage (G)B	FixInc	Mortgage	Yes	7.5	9.2	8.5		8.8		High	2.2	Defer	65.2
Green Line Mortgage	FixInc	Mortgage	Yes	3.5	5.2	5.6	6.0	8.7	9.0	Med-	1.6	None	665.5
Hongkong Bank Mortgage	FixInc	Mortgage	Yes	4.2	6.8	6.7	8.0			High	1.5	None	219.3
Ind. Alliance Ecoflex H	FixInc	Mortgage	Yes	4.4	4.9	5.3	5.4			High	1.9	Defer	13.7
Ind. Alliance Mortgages	FixInc	Mortgage	Yes	4.7	5.3	5.8	6.0	8.1	9.4	Low	1.5	None	6.0
InvesNat Mortgages	FixInc	Mortgage	Yes	4.0	5.4	6.1	6.6			Med-	1.6	None	237.3
Investors Mortgage	FixInc	Mortgage	Yes	3.4	5.3	5.7	5.7	7.8	8.8	Med-	1.9	Defer	2292.0
Ivy Mortgage	FixInc	Mortgage	Yes	4.0	6.3	6.5				Med	1.9	F or B	287.4
London Life Mortgage	FixInc	Mortgage	Yes	6.7	7.3	7.1	6.8	8.9	9.9	Low	2.0	Defer	470.5
Mutual Premier Mortgage	FixInc	Mortgage	Yes	3.9	5.3	5.8	6.1			Med	1.7	None	160.6
National Trust Mortgage	FixInc	Mortgage	Yes	3.3	5.8	6.3	6.2			Med	1.6	None	69.0
North West Life Ecoflex H	FixInc	Mortgage	Yes	4.4							1.9	Defer	0.4
Northwest Mortgage	FixInc	Mortgage	Yes	1.9	4.4	4.6	5.1			Med+	1.8	F or B	3.5
Pret et Revenu Hypotheque	FixInc	Mortgage	Yes	2.7	4.8	5.5	5.5	8.1	8.9	Med	1.7	None	69.3
Royal Precious Metals	FixInc	Mortgage	Yes	4.0	6.0	6.2	6.8			Med+	2.4	None	1355.7
SSQ - Hypotheques	FixInc	Mortgage	Yes	3.4	5.7	7.0	7.5			Med-		None	2.1
Scotia Ex. Mortgage	FixInc	Mortgage	Yes	3.7	5.9	6.3	6.9			Med+	1.6	None	427.9
CDA Bond & Mortgage (C)	FixInc	B & M	Yes	7.3	9.4	9.3	8.5	10.1	10.4		1.0	None	41.1
CT Mortgage	FixInc	B & M	Yes	4.4	5.5	5.9	6.4	8.4	9.2		1.6	None	501.0
Green Line Mortgage-Backed	FixInc	B & M	Yes	3.9	5.3	5.9	5.8				1.6	None	78.7
Industrial Mtge Securities	FixInc	B & M	Yes	0.6	6.1	6.9	5.7	8.1	10.4		1.9	F or B	514.5
OTGIF Mortgage Income	FixInc	B & M	Yes	8.9	9.3	9.0	8.3	9.3	9.6		0.8	None	111.3
PH & N S-T Bond & Mortgage	FixInc	B & M	Yes	5.3	7.3	8.1					0.6	None	172.3
Spectrum Utd Short-Term Bd	FixInc	B & M	Yes	3.2	4.8	5.5	5.5	7.2	8.0		1.5	F or B	28.5
@rgentum S-Term Asset Pfl	FixInc	CdnMMkt	Yes									F or B	0.2
AGF Money Market Account	FixInc	CdnMMkt	Yes	2.4	2.4	3.3	3.8		7.4	Med+	1.4	F or B	634.2
AIC Money Market	FixInc	CdnMMkt	Yes	3.2	2.9	3.5				Low	1.0	F or B	175.1
AIM Cash Performance	FixInc	CdnMMkt	Yes	2.9	2.9	3.5	3.7			Low	1.0	F or B	13.5
AIM GT Canada Money Market	FixInc	CdnMMkt	Yes	3.3							0.8	F or B	41.3
APEX Money Market	FixInc	CdnMMkt	Yes	2.4	2.4	3.3				Med+	1.6	F or B	7.4
Acadia Money Market	FixInc	CdnMMkt	Yes	2.5	2.3	3.2				High	1.6	Defer	0.4
Acuity Pld Short Term	FixInc	CdnMMkt	Yes	0.6	4.4	5.3	6.5			High		None	
Allstar Money Market	FixInc	CdnMMkt	Yes	3.0							1.2	Front	2.6
Alpha Money Market	FixInc	CdnMMkt	Yes								0.0	F or B	0.6
Altamira S-Term Cdn Income	FixInc	CdnMMkt	Yes	4.3							0.4	None	25.9

FUND NAME	FUND CATEGORY		RRSP. ELIGIB.	1 YR	2 YR	3 YR	5 YR	10 YR	15 YR	3 YR VOLATILITY	MER	SALES FEES	ASSETS IN $MIL
Altamira T-Bill	FixInc	CdnMMkt	Yes	3.5	-	-	-	-	-	-	0.2	None	51.0
Astra Marche monetaire	FixInc	CdnMMkt	Yes	-	-	-	-	-	-	-	1.3	None	1.1
Atlas Canadian Money Mkt	FixInc	CdnMMkt	Yes	3.1	2.9	3.7	4.1	6.6	-	Med-	1.1	F or B	292.2
Atlas Canadian T-Bill	FixInc	CdnMMkt	Yes	2.5	2.5	3.3	3.8	6.3	-	Med	1.3	F or B	272.9
BNP (Canada) Cdn. Mny. Mkt	FixInc	CdnMMkt	Yes	2.8	2.9	3.6	4.0	-	-	Med-	1.3	None	5.0
BPI T-Bill	FixInc	CdnMMkt	Yes	3.5	3.4	4.3	4.5	6.9	7.7	Med	0.7	F or B	173.0
BPI T-Bill Segregated	FixInc	CdnMMkt	Yes	-	-	-	-	-	-	-	-	F or B	3.0
Batirente Sec Marche Monet	FixInc	CdnMMkt	Yes	3.2	3.0	3.6	4.1	6.6	-	Med+	0.8	None	1.1
Beutel Goodman Money Mkt.	FixInc	CdnMMkt	Yes	3.6	3.4	4.3	4.7	-	-	Med	0.6	Front	65.8
Bissett Money Market	FixInc	CdnMMkt	Yes	3.6	3.7	4.6	4.9	-	-	Med+	0.5	None	52.3
C.I. Money Market	FixInc	CdnMMkt	Yes	3.3	3.3	4.1	4.5	-	-	Med	0.8	F or B	291.7
C.I. Money Market Sgrd	FixInc	CdnMMkt	Yes	-	-	-	-	-	-	-	1.5	F or B	3.3
C.I. Short-term Sector	FixInc	CdnMMkt	Fgn	4.3	3.6	3.1	3.1	4.2	-	High	0.1	F or B	73.0
CCPE Money Market	FixInc	CdnMMkt	Yes	5.6	4.2	4.7	-	-	-	High	0.8	None	15.3
CDA Money Market (Canagex)	FixInc	CdnMMkt	Yes	3.5	3.4	4.3	4.7	7.1	7.8	High	0.7	None	23.7
CIBC Canadian T-Bill	FixInc	CdnMMkt	Yes	2.9	2.8	3.5	3.8	-	-	Low	1.0	None	484.7
CIBC Money Market	FixInc	CdnMMkt	Yes	3.0	2.9	3.6	3.9	-	-	Low	1.0	None	1817.5
CIBC Premium Cdn T-Bill	FixInc	CdnMMkt	Yes	3.5	3.3	4.0	4.4	-	-	Low	0.6	None	1904.7
CT Money Market	FixInc	CdnMMkt	Yes	2.9	2.8	3.5	3.9	6.7	-	Low	1.0	None	887.3
CT Premium Money Market	FixInc	CdnMMkt	Yes	3.4	-	-	-	-	-	-	0.6	None	384.7
CUMIS Life Cdn Money Mkt	FixInc	CdnMMkt	Yes	3.1	-	-	-	-	-	-	0.8	Back	1.2
Canada Life Money Market	FixInc	CdnMMkt	Yes	2.7	2.8	3.5	3.9	6.4	6.9	High	1.3	Defer	159.8
Capstone Cash Management	FixInc	CdnMMkt	Yes	3.7	3.5	4.1	4.7	7.2	-	High	0.6	None	2.2
CentrePost Short Term	FixInc	CdnMMkt	Yes	3.5	3.1	3.9	4.3	7.1	-	Med+	0.8	None	59.9
Clarington Money Market	FixInc	CdnMMkt	Yes	3.1	-	-	-	-	-	-	0.8	F or B	7.7
Co-Operators Money Market	FixInc	CdnMMkt	Yes	-	-	-	-	-	-	-	1.9	None	1.1
Colonia Life Money Market	FixInc	CdnMMkt	Yes	2.7	3.0	3.8	4.1	-	-	High	1.0	None	1.9
Comm. Un. Cdn Money Market	FixInc	CdnMMkt	Yes	-	-	-	-	-	-	-	1.2	Defer	0.7
Cornerstone Govt Money	FixInc	CdnMMkt	Yes	2.8	2.6	3.5	4.0	-	-	Med+	1.1	None	39.7
Desjardins Money Market	FixInc	CdnMMkt	Yes	2.9	2.6	3.4	3.8	-	-	Med	1.1	None	75.5
Dynamic Money Market	FixInc	CdnMMkt	Yes	3.0	2.9	3.6	4.1	6.5	-	Med	0.8	F or B	187.6
Elliott & Page Money	FixInc	CdnMMkt	Yes	3.4	3.2	3.9	4.4	7.1	-	Med+	0.3	Front	460.0
Elliott & Page T-Bill	FixInc	CdnMMkt	Yes	2.2	2.1	2.7	-	-	-	Med+	1.8	Defer	20.6
Empire Money Market	FixInc	CdnMMkt	Yes	2.7	2.5	3.1	3.6	-	-	Med	1.4	None	26.0
Equitable Life Money Mkt	FixInc	CdnMMkt	Yes	2.8	2.6	3.3	-	-	-	High	1.8	Defer	5.0
Ethical Money Market	FixInc	CdnMMkt	Yes	2.7	2.8	3.6	3.9	6.6	7.5	Med-	1.3	None	107.6
FMOQ Money Market	FixInc	CdnMMkt	Yes	3.6	3.6	4.4	4.8	-	-	Med+	0.8	None	4.6
Ficadre Monetaire	FixInc	CdnMMkt	Yes	3.0	3.0	3.8	4.1	-	-	Med	1.1	None	3.9
Fidelity Cdn S-Term Asset	FixInc	CdnMMkt	Yes	2.9	2.6	3.3	3.7	-	-	Low	1.3	F or B	355.1
First Canadian Money Mkt	FixInc	CdnMMkt	Yes	2.9	2.9	3.6	4.0	6.4	-	Med-	1.1	None	1038.5
First Canadian T-Bill	FixInc	CdnMMkt	Yes	2.8	2.8	3.5	-	-	-	Med-	1.1	None	743.4
First Cdn Premium Mny Mkt	FixInc	CdnMMkt	Yes	-	-	-	-	-	-	-	0.4	None	412.1
GBC Money Market	FixInc	CdnMMkt	Yes	3.0	2.8	3.6	4.1	-	-	Med	0.8	None	17.9
General Trust Money Market	FixInc	CdnMMkt	Yes	2.9	2.9	3.7	4.1	6.5	-	Med	1.2	None	20.0

FUND NAME	FUND CATEGORY	RRSP-ELIGIB.	1 YR	2 YR	3 YR	5 YR	10 YR	15 YR	3 YR VOLATILITY	MER	SALES FEES	ASSETS IN $MIL
Global Strategy Money Mkt	FixInc	CdnMMkt	Yes	3.0	2.9	3.6	4.1	6.4	-	Low	0.8	F or B	112.3
Great-West Money Mkt (G)A	FixInc	CdnMMkt	Yes	2.7	2.3	2.9	3.4	6.1	6.9	Med-	1.6	None	83.9
Great-West Money Mkt (G)B	FixInc	CdnMMkt	Yes	2.9	2.6	3.2	-	-	-	Med-	1.4	Defer	30.5
Green Line Canadian T-Bill	FixInc	CdnMMkt	Yes	3.1	3.2	3.9	4.3	-	-	Med-	0.9	None	353.7
Green Line Cdn Money Mkt	FixInc	CdnMMkt	Yes	3.3	3.4	4.1	4.5	-	-	Low	0.8	None	3787.7
Green Line Premium Mny Mkt	FixInc	CdnMMkt	Yes	-	-	-	-	-	-	-	0.3	None	1316.3
GrowSafe Cdn Money Markets	FixInc	CdnMMkt	Yes	3.2	3.0	3.4	-	-	-	Low	1.0	Defer	25.7
Guardian Cdn Money Mkt C	FixInc	CdnMMkt	Yes	3.2	3.0	3.6	4.1	6.8	7.6	Low	0.9	Front	58.0
Guardian Cdn Money Mkt M	FixInc	CdnMMkt	Yes	2.6	2.3	-	-	-	-	-	1.5	F or B	25.3
Hartford Money Market	FixInc	CdnMMkt	Yes	-	-	-	-	-	-	-	1.8	Defer	0.3
Hongkong Bank Money Market	FixInc	CdnMMkt	Yes	3.2	3.2	3.9	4.2	-	-	Low	0.9	None	385.3
ICM Short Term Investment	FixInc	CdnMMkt	Yes	4.0	4.0	4.9	5.3	-	-	Med+	0.1	None	180.2
Ideal Money Market	FixInc	CdnMMkt	Yes	4.7	4.4	5.0	-	-	-	High	1.0	Defer	49.5
Imperial Gth Money Market	FixInc	CdnMMkt	Yes	2.4	2.2	2.9	3.4	-	-	Med	1.5	Front	2.3
Ind. Alliance Ecoflex M	FixInc	CdnMMkt	Yes	2.7	2.6	3.3	-	-	-	Med+	1.4	Defer	10.6
Ind. Alliance Ecoflex M	FixInc	CdnMMkt	Yes	2.5	2.4	3.2	3.4	-	-	Med+	1.5	None	7.8
Industrial Cash Management	FixInc	CdnMMkt	Yes	3.3	3.2	4.0	4.4	7.0	-	Med	0.5	Front	460.5
Industrial Short-Term	FixInc	CdnMMkt	Yes	2.4	2.3	3.1	3.6	-	-	Med+	1.3	Defer	274.2
Infinity T-Bill	FixInc	CdnMMkt	Yes	3.0	-	-	-	-	-	-	1.0	Front	6.0
InvesNat Corp Cash Mgmt	FixInc	CdnMMkt	Yes	3.6	3.6	4.3	-	-	-	Low	0.5	None	246.6
InvesNat Money Market	FixInc	CdnMMkt	Yes	3.0	3.0	3.8	4.1	-	-	Low	1.1	None	391.0
InvesNat Presumed Sound In	FixInc	CdnMMkt	Yes	-	-	-	-	-	-	-	1.1	None	21.6
InvesNat T-Bill Plus	FixInc	CdnMMkt	Yes	3.3	3.3	4.0	4.4	-	-	Med-	0.8	None	258.6
InvesNat Treasury Mgmt	FixInc	CdnMMkt	No	-	-	-	-	-	-	-	0.3	None	173.1
Investors Money Market	FixInc	CdnMMkt	Yes	3.0	2.8	3.6	4.0	6.5	-	Med	1.1	None	547.7
Jones Heward Money Market	FixInc	CdnMMkt	Yes	3.0	3.0	3.8	-	-	-	Med+	1.0	Front	2.7
Leith Wheeler Money Market	FixInc	CdnMMkt	Yes	3.4	3.1	3.9	-	-	-	Med-	0.6	None	9.0
London Life Money Market	FixInc	CdnMMkt	Yes	2.7	2.8	3.8	4.1	7.1	-	High	1.3	Defer	76.5
Lotus Group Income	FixInc	CdnMMkt	Yes	3.2	3.3	4.1	4.4	7.1	-	Med-	0.8	None	2.7
MAXXUM Money Market	FixInc	CdnMMkt	Yes	3.4	3.4	4.2	4.6	6.8	7.4	Med	0.8	None	51.2
MD Money	FixInc	CdnMMkt	Yes	3.4	3.4	4.2	4.6	-	-	Med+	0.5	None	335.5
MLI E&P Money Market A GIF	FixInc	CdnMMkt	Yes	2.7	-	-	-	-	-	-	1.3	F or B	38.8
MLI E&P Money Market B GIF	FixInc	CdnMMkt	Yes	2.2	-	-	-	-	-	-	1.4	None	50.5
Manulife Cabot Money Mkt	FixInc	CdnMMkt	Yes	2.6	2.5	3.3	4.1	6.6	-	Med+	1.3	None	4.4
Manulife VistaFd 1 S-T Sec	FixInc	CdnMMkt	Yes	2.2	2.6	3.6	3.3	5.8	-	High	1.6	Front	4.8
Manulife VistaFd 2 S-T Sec	FixInc	CdnMMkt	Yes	1.5	1.9	2.8	-	-	-	High	2.4	Defer	40.0
Marathon Perf Cdn Cash	FixInc	CdnMMkt	Yes	-	-	-	-	-	-	-	0.8	F or B	0.9
Maritime Life Money Mkt A	FixInc	CdnMMkt	Yes	2.6	2.5	3.1	3.4	6.0	6.8	Low	1.0	None	51.7
Maritime Life Money Mkt B	FixInc	CdnMMkt	Yes	2.6	-	-	-	-	-	-	1.0	Defer	6.3
Maritime Life Money Mkt C	FixInc	CdnMMkt	Yes	1.9	-	-	-	-	-	-	2.0	Defer	12.5
Mawer Canadian Money Mkt	FixInc	CdnMMkt	Yes	3.5	3.3	4.0	4.3	6.7	-	Med-	0.7	None	47.9
Mclean Budden Money Market	FixInc	CdnMMkt	Yes	3.6	3.7	4.3	4.5	-	-	Med	0.8	None	7.3
Metlife Mvp Money Market	FixInc	CdnMMkt	Yes	2.1	2.2	3.1	3.5	-	-	High	1.7	Defer	13.5
Middlefield Money Market	FixInc	CdnMMkt	Yes	3.6	3.7	-	-	-	-	-	0.6	F or B	24.2

FUND NAME	FUND CATEGORY		RRSP. ELIGIB.	1 YR	2 YR	3 YR	5 YR	10 YR	15 YR	3 YR VOLATILITY	MER	SALES FEES	ASSETS IN $MIL
Millennia III Money Mkt 1	FixInc	CdnMMkt	Yes	2.5	2.3	-	-	-	-	-	1.5	Defer	5.9
Millennia III Money Mkt 2	FixInc	CdnMMkt	Yes	2.3	2.1	-	-	-	-	-	1.6	None	8.1
Montrusco Select T-Max	FixInc	CdnMMkt	Yes	4.0	4.0	4.7	-	-	-	-	-	None	317.7
Mutual Money Market	FixInc	CdnMMkt	Yes	3.1	2.8	3.6	4.1	6.4	-	Med+	1.1	None	239.1
NAL-Canadian Money Market	FixInc	CdnMMkt	Yes	4.8	3.6	4.1	4.1	-	-	Med-	1.3	Defer	15.3
NN Money Market	FixInc	CdnMMkt	Yes	3.6	3.6	4.3	4.6	-	-	High	0.8	Defer	10.5
NN T-Bill	FixInc	CdnMMkt	Yes	2.7	2.7	3.3	3.6	6.0	-	Med	1.3	Defer	25.1
National Money Market	FixInc	CdnMMkt	Yes	2.3	2.2	3.0	3.4	-	-	Low	1.6	Defer	10.2
National Trust Money Mkt.	FixInc	CdnMMkt	Yes	2.8	3.0	3.7	4.0	-	-	Med	1.1	None	120.0
North West Life Ecoflex M	FixInc	CdnMMkt	Yes	2.7	-	-	-	-	-	Med-	1.4	Defer	0.4
Northwest Money Market	FixInc	CdnMMkt	Yes	3.2	3.1	3.8	4.2	-	-	-	1.0	F or B	6.3
O'Donnell Money Market	FixInc	CdnMMkt	Yes	2.7	2.9	-	-	-	-	Med-	1.1	Front	29.6
O'Donnell Short Term	FixInc	CdnMMkt	Yes	2.5	2.5	-	-	-	-	-	1.4	Defer	13.9
O.I.Q. Ferique Revenu	FixInc	CdnMMkt	Yes	3.6	3.8	4.5	5.0	7.3	8.0	Med+	0.4	None	37.1
OTGIF Fixed valuee	FixInc	CdnMMkt	Yes	3.6	3.6	4.4	4.8	7.3	7.8	Med	0.5	None	20.8
Optimum Epargne	FixInc	CdnMMkt	Yes	3.3	3.0	3.7	4.2	6.8	-	Med-	0.7	None	1.7
PH & N Canadian Money Mkt.	FixInc	CdnMMkt	Yes	3.7	3.4	4.1	4.5	7.1	-	Low	0.5	None	923.0
Pret et Revenu Money Mkt.	FixInc	CdnMMkt	Yes	3.1	3.0	3.7	4.2	-	-	Med-	1.1	None	53.5
Primus Prime Credit Mny Mk	FixInc	CdnMMkt	Yes	4.2	-	-	-	-	-	-	0.1	None	28.4
Pursuit Money Market	FixInc	CdnMMkt	Yes	3.5	3.7	4.5	4.9	7.1	-	Med-	0.5	None	1.6
Quebec Prof Short Term	FixInc	CdnMMkt	Yes	3.9	3.9	4.8	5.1	7.3	-	High	0.3	None	25.9
Royal&SunAlliance US Eq	FixInc	CdnMMkt	Fgn	3.2	3.0	3.6	3.9	6.6	-	Low	-	Defer	1661.1
Royal Balanced	FixInc	CdnMMkt	Yes	3.1	3.0	3.7	4.1	-	-	Low	2.2	None	2932.9
Royal LePage Commercial	FixInc	CdnMMkt	Yes	3.4	3.7	4.6	5.0	-	-	High	3.4	None	34.7
Royal Trust Adv. Balanced	FixInc	CdnMMkt	Yes	3.9	-	-	-	-	-	-	1.8	None	1485.6
SSQ - Marche Monetaire	FixInc	CdnMMkt	Yes	4.0	4.0	4.9	-	-	-	High	-	None	8.5
Sceptre Money Market	FixInc	CdnMMkt	Yes	3.3	3.4	4.2	4.5	7.0	-	Med	0.8	None	38.8
Scotia Ex. Money Market	FixInc	CdnMMkt	Yes	3.1	2.9	3.6	4.1	-	-	Med-	1.0	None	505.7
Scotia Ex. Premium T-Bill	FixInc	CdnMMkt	Yes	3.4	3.3	4.1	4.5	-	-	Med-	0.5	None	775.0
Scotia Ex. T-Bill	FixInc	CdnMMkt	Yes	2.9	2.8	3.5	4.0	-	-	Med	1.0	None	330.4
Scudder Canadian Money Mkt	FixInc	CdnMMkt	Yes	-	-	-	-	-	-	-	0.0	None	62.6
Spectrum Utd Cdn Money Mkt	FixInc	CdnMMkt	Yes	3.1	3.0	3.7	4.1	6.6	-	Med-	0.9	None	184.5
Spectrum Utd Savings	FixInc	CdnMMkt	No	3.0	2.9	3.7	4.1	6.7	-	Med+	1.0	None	9.8
Standard Life Money Market	FixInc	CdnMMkt	Yes	3.6	3.8	4.4	4.5	-	-	High	0.9	Defer	8.7
Stone & Co Flagship Mny Mk	FixInc	CdnMMkt	Yes	3.3	-	-	-	-	-	-	1.0	F or B	7.9
Strategic Val Money Market	FixInc	CdnMMkt	Yes	2.7	2.6	3.4	3.8	6.4	-	Med+	1.0	None	30.6
Talvest/Hyperion Cash Mgmt	FixInc	CdnMMkt	Yes	-	-	-	-	-	-	-	1.0	F or B	3.5
Talvest Money	FixInc	CdnMMkt	Yes	3.2	3.3	4.2	4.6	7.1	-	Med+	0.8	Front	110.4
Templeton T-Bill	FixInc	CdnMMkt	Yes	3.0	2.8	3.6	4.1	6.6	-	Med	0.8	None	344.6
Trans-Canada Money Market	FixInc	CdnMMkt	Yes	3.2	3.6	4.3	4.6	6.2	6.7	Low	0.7	F or B	10.9
Trimark Interest	FixInc	CdnMMkt	Yes	3.5	3.2	3.9	4.3	6.8	-	Low	0.8	Front	819.2
University Avenue Money	FixInc	CdnMMkt	Yes	3.1	2.9	-	-	-	-	-	0.8	None	3.8
Valorem Government S-Term	FixInc	CdnMMkt	Yes	2.7	-	-	-	-	-	-	-	F or B	0.3
Westbury Cdn Life C	FixInc	CdnMMkt	Yes	3.5	3.6	4.3	4.8	6.6	-	High	0.1	Front	0.1

FUND NAME	FUND CATEGORY		RRSP. ELIGIB.	1 YR	2 YR	3 YR	5 YR	10 YR	15 YR	3 YR VOLATILITY	MER	SALES FEES	ASSETS IN $MIL
YMG Money Market	FixInc	CdnMMkt	Yes	3.4	3.4	4.2	4.6	7.0	-	Med+	0.6	Front	9.2
20/20 Aggressive Growth	USEq	Divers	Fgn	28.8	13.0	17.4	17.5	-	-	High	2.6	F or B	308.9
@rgentum Mkt Neutral Pfl	USEq	Divers	No	-	-	-	-	-	-	-	-	F or B	2.9
@rgentum U.S. Master Pfl	USEq	Divers	No	-	-	-	-	-	-	-	-	F or B	1.4
AGF Intl Grp-American Gth	USEq	LgCap	Fgn	44.9	39.9	32.1	25.9	18.1	14.6	High	2.8	F or B	641.0
AGF Intl Grp-Special U.S.	USEq	Divers	Fgn	6.7	4.6	7.4	9.5	10.7	9.8	High	2.9	F or B	131.2
AIC American Advantage	USEq	Divers	Fgn	28.4	42.0	36.7	28.1	-	-	Med	2.7	F or B	232.4
AIC valuee	USEq	LgCap	Fgn	-	-	-	-	-	-	-	2.4	F or B	1466.2
AIM American Aggress Gth	USEq	Divers	Fgn	37.5	31.7	17.7	14.8	-	-	Med+	2.7	F or B	11.2
AIM American Premier	USEq	LgCap	Fgn	32.8	17.5	13.8	-	-	-	High	2.8	F or B	3.9
AIM GT America Growth	USEq	LgCap	Fgn	32.4	-	-	-	-	-	Med+	2.9	F or B	34.7
APEX U.S. Equity	USEq	Divers	Fgn	17.2	12.1	15.8	16.9	-	-	High	2.8	F or B	20.7
Altamira Select American	USEq	SmCap	Fgn	32.4	24.7	23.1	-	-	-	Med+	2.3	None	215.2
Altamira US Larger Company	USEq	LgCap	Fgn	-	-	-	-	-	-	-	2.3	None	132.5
Artisan U.S. Equity	USEq	Divers	Fgn	-	-	-	-	-	-	-	3.0	F or B	0.3
Astra Actions americanines	USEq	Divers	No	23.4	29.0	26.4	20.4	14.4	-	Med-	2.5	None	2.0
Atlas Amer Large Cap Gth	USEq	LgCap	Fgn	21.4	25.0	23.0	-	-	-	Low	2.6	F or B	51.4
Atlas American Advan valuee	USEq	LgCap	Fgn	25.0	-	-	-	-	-	-	2.5	F or B	46.3
Atlas American RSP Index	USEq	Divers	Yes	-	-	-	-	-	-	-	1.5	F or B	26.1
BPI American Eq valuee Sgr	USEq	LgCap	No	42.8	33.9	28.6	22.0	-	-	Med	2.4	F or B	4.6
BPI American Equity valuee	USEq	LgCap	Fgn	10.8	17.4	18.5	20.6	15.0	-	Med+	2.6	F or B	105.2
BPI American Small Comp	USEq	SmCap	Fgn	18.2	21.1	17.6	16.2	-	-	Low	2.5	Front	169.9
Beutel Goodman American Eq	USEq	LgCap	Fgn	31.9	32.7	27.4	21.9	-	-	Low	1.1	None	8.4
Beutel Goodman Private Fgn	USEq	Divers	Fgn	22.1	21.8	21.2	18.1	13.4	-	Med-	1.5	None	25.9
Bissett American Equity	USEq	LgCap	Fgn	24.7	24.0	23.0	21.4	-	-	Med-	2.4	F or B	27.7
C.I. American	USEq	LgCap	Fgn	27.9	25.3	21.8	20.5	-	-	Med-	2.4	F or B	266.1
C.I. American RSP	USEq	LgCap	Yes	22.5	22.4	-	-	-	-	-	2.4	F or B	66.3
C.I. American Sector	USEq	LgCap	Fgn	-	-	-	-	-	-	-	3.2	F or B	70.2
C.I. American Segregated	USEq	LgCap	Fgn	35.7	36.0	26.8	-	-	-	Med	1.8	F or B	6.2
CCPE US Equity	USEq	Divers	Fgn	24.3	-	-	-	-	-	-	1.2	None	42.9
CDA U.S. Equity (KBSH)	USEq	Divers	Fgn	41.4	-	-	-	-	-	-	2.5	None	2.8
CIBC North Amer Demograph	USEq	Divers	Fgn	36.2	-	-	-	-	-	-	0.9	None	80.3
CIBC U.S. Index RRSP	USEq	Divers	Yes	19.8	12.3	-	-	-	-	-	2.5	None	272.0
CIBC U.S. Small Companies	USEq	SmCap	Fgn	35.0	27.5	26.5	18.6	-	-	Med	0.9	None	26.0
CIBC US Equity	USEq	LgCap	Fgn	26.0	27.3	26.3	20.4	-	-	Med	1.4	None	379.4
CT AmeriGrowth	USEq	LgCap	Yes	22.3	23.1	18.8	15.0	-	-	Med-	2.3	None	801.7
CT U.S. Equity	USEq	LgCap	Fgn	35.9	-	-	-	-	-	-	0.9	None	281.8
CT U.S. Equity Index	USEq	Divers	Fgn	16.0	-	-	-	-	-	-	0.5	None	26.5
Caldwell American Equity	USEq	LgCap	Fgn	14.2	21.3	6.4	5.3	-	-	High	3.6	F or B	1.8
Cambridge American Growth	USEq	SmCap	Fgn	4.4	4.7	5.2	4.2	-	-	Low	0.8	Front	0.7
Century DJ	USEq	LgCap	Fgn	36.1	-	-	-	5.8	-	-	3.0	F or B	0.4
Clarington U.S. Equity	USEq	Divers	Fgn	32.9	-	-	-	-	-	-	3.0	F or B	35.2
Clarington US SmallerCo Gw	USEq	Divers	Fgn	-	-	-	-	-	-	-	-	F or B	10.3

FUND NAME	FUND CATEGORY		RRSP. ELIGIB.	1 YR	2 YR	3 YR	5 YR	10 YR	15 YR	3 YR VOLATILITY	MER	SALES FEES	ASSETS IN $MIL
Co-Operators U.S. Equity	USEq	LgCap	Fgn	30.1	34.3	30.9	-	-	-	High	2.1	None	13.6
Comm. Un. U.S. Eq Index	USEq	Divers	No	-	-	-	-	-	-	-	2.6	Defer	5.4
Cornerstone US	USEq	LgCap	Fgn	34.2	34.1	28.9	22.0	15.9	11.3	Med	2.2	None	49.5
Cote 100 US	USEq	Divers	No	-6.5	-	-	-	-	-	-	2.0	None	10.4
Desjardins American Market	USEq	Divers	Yes	29.4	26.6	-	-	-	-	-	2.1	None	98.5
Dynamic Americas	USEq	Divers	Fgn	28.8	30.7	32.7	20.2	14.6	14.2	Med	2.4	F or B	144.1
Elliott & Page Amer Gth	USEq	LgCap	Fgn	35.6	36.0	27.2	21.2	15.0	11.3	Med-	1.4	F or B	151.7
Elliott & Page US Mid-Cap	USEq	Divers	No	-	-	-	-	-	-	-	3.4	F or B	8.3
Empire Elite S&P 500 Index	USEq	Divers	Yes	-	-	-	-	-	-	-	2.6	Defer	21.7
Ethical North Amer Equity	USEq	LgCap	Fgn	55.9	46.0	36.2	26.3	15.6	12.9	High	2.5	None	211.7
Fidelity Focus Consum Ind	USEq	Divers	Fgn	43.8	-	-	-	-	-	-	2.5	F or B	12.1
Fidelity Focus Financ Serv	USEq	Divers	Fgn	49.5	-	-	-	-	-	-	2.5	F or B	38.1
Fidelity Growth America	USEq	LgCap	Fgn	34.5	29.7	25.3	22.1	-	-	Med-	2.3	F or B	1738.3
Fidelity Small Cap America	USEq	SmCap	Fgn	27.5	26.1	20.8	-	-	-	High	2.5	F or B	112.9
First Canadian US Growth	USEq	LgCap	Fgn	34.8	34.2	21.7	-	-	-	Med+	2.2	F or B	202.1
First Canadian US valuee	USEq	Divers	Fgn	36.1	-	-	-	-	-	-	2.1	None	34.6
First Cdn US Eq Index RSP	USEq	Divers	Yes	25.6	-	-	-	-	-	-	1.2	None	195.8
First Cdn US Special Gth	USEq	Divers	Fgn	28.3	-	-	-	-	-	-	1.9	None	29.0
FirstTrust DJIATarget10 96	USEq	Divers	Fgn	21.5	27.5	-	-	-	-	-	1.0	Front	5.8
FirstTrust DJIATarget10 97	USEq	Divers	Fgn	20.4	-	-	-	-	-	-	1.1	Front	11.2
FirstTrust DJIATarget10 98	USEq	Divers	Fgn	-	-	-	-	-	-	-	-	Front	5.3
Fonds de Croissance Select	USEq	Divers	No	26.6	30.5	27.9	-	-	-	Med-	1.0	None	21.5
Formula Growth	USEq	Divers	Fgn	35.5	22.8	28.3	24.9	20.5	14.8	High	1.0	Fr&Bk	385.1
Franklin US Small Cap Gth	USEq	SmCap	Fgn	24.5	-	-	-	-	-	-	2.5	F or B	48.3
GS American Equity	USEq	Divers	Fgn	30.9	31.7	-	-	-	-	-	2.8	FnDf	74.5
Global Mgr-US Bear	USEq	Divers	Fgn	-21.6	-20.5	-19.0	-	-	-	Med-	1.8	Front	1.4
Global Mgr-US Geared	USEq	Divers	Fgn	49.3	52.9	48.8	-	-	-	High	1.8	Front	3.1
Global Mgr-US Index	USEq	Divers	Fgn	27.9	28.6	26.4	-	-	-	Med-	1.8	Front	13.9
Global Strategy US Equity	USEq	Divers	Fgn	28.8	25.8	25.3	-	-	-	Med-	2.6	F or B	15.3
Great-West Amer Gth(A) A	USEq	Divers	No	-	-	-	-	-	-	-	3.0	None	3.7
Great-West Amer Gth(A) B	USEq	Divers	No	-	-	-	-	-	-	-	2.7	Defer	4.4
Great-West US Equity (G) A	USEq	LgCap	Fgn	30.8	27.5	22.7	-	-	-	Low	2.8	None	42.1
Great-West US Equity (G) B	USEq	LgCap	Fgn	31.1	27.9	23.0	-	-	-	Low	2.6	Defer	33.5
Green Line DJIA Index	USEq	LgCap	Fgn	-	-	-	-	-	-	-	0.8	None	14.3
Green Line U.S. RSP Index	USEq	Divers	Yes	-	-	-	-	-	-	-	0.8	None	79.1
Green Line U.S. Small-Cap	USEq	SmCap	No	36.0	-	-	-	-	-	-	2.4	None	20.6
Green Line US Blue Chip Eq	USEq	LgCap	Fgn	29.1	31.2	28.9	21.8	16.8	-	Med	2.3	None	155.1
Green Line US Index	USEq	Divers	Fgn	37.3	26.2	26.8	-	-	-	Med	0.7	None	150.0
Green Line US Mid-Cap Gth	USEq	Divers	Fgn	45.2	-	-	-	-	-	-	2.3	None	236.2
GrowSafe US 21st Century	USEq	Divers	Yes	34.6	33.1	-	-	-	-	-	2.1	Defer	52.6
GrowSafe US 500 Index	USEq	Divers	Yes	18.2	19.9	18.1	17.7	15.4	11.1	Med	2.1	Defer	107.4
Guardian American Equity C	USEq	LgCap	Fgn	17.4	19.2	-	-	-	-	-	2.2	Front	42.0
Guardian American Equity M	USEq	LgCap	Fgn	33.0	33.2	27.8	-	-	-	Med-	2.8	F or B	21.1
Hongkong Bank U.S. Equity	USEq	Divers	Fgn	-	-	-	-	-	-	-	2.2	None	57.4

FUND NAME	FUND CATEGORY		RRSP-ELIGIB.	1 YR	2 YR	3 YR	5 YR	10 YR	15 YR	3 YR VOLATILITY	MER	SALES FEES	ASSETS IN $MIL.
Ind. Alliance Ecoflex S	USEq	Divers	Fgn	42.9	-	-	-	-	-	-	3.0	Defer	56.1
Ind. Alliance Ecoflex U	USEq	Divers	Yes	-	-	-	-	-	-	-	2.4	Defer	18.5
Ind. Alliance US Advantage	USEq	Divers	Yes								1.5	None	0.4
Ind. Alliance US Equity	USEq	Divers	Fgn	44.0							2.2	None	1.4
Industrial American	USEq	LgCap	Fgn	21.0	21.6	18.2	15.4	12.1	12.2	Low	2.4	F or B	329.2
Infinity International	USEq	Divers	No	30.2							3.0	F or B	193.3
InvesNat Amer Index Plus	USEq	Divers	Fgn								1.2	None	10.8
Investors US Growth	USEq	LgCap	Fgn	44.0	40.6	32.9	25.2	19.6	15.3	Low	2.4	FnDf	1821.2
Investors US Opportunities	USEq	Divers	Fgn	27.7							2.5	FnDf	626.8
Jones Heward American	USEq	LgCap	Fgn	35.9	32.0	24.6	15.1	13.9	12.6	Med+	2.5	F or B	24.7
Leith Wheeler US Equity	USEq	Divers	Fgn	17.6	20.0	18.4				Low	1.3	None	7.2
London Life US Equity	USEq	Divers	Fgn	36.7	36.2	30.1	19.9	13.5		Med+	2.0	Defer	405.3
MAXXUM American Equity	USEq	LgCap	Fgn	41.0	33.6	32.6				Med+	2.5	F or B	32.2
MB American Equity	USEq	LgCap	No	27.3	34.0	29.7	24.6	19.9		Med+	0.0	None	182.7
MD US Equity	USEq	LgCap	Fgn	57.2	44.8	36.4	28.0			High	1.3	None	358.5
MLI AGF American Grth GIF	USEq	Divers	Yes	43.7							3.3	F or B	149.7
MLI E&P American Gth GIF	USEq	Divers	Yes								3.1	F or B	43.8
MLI Fidelity Gth Amer GIF	USEq	Divers	Yes								3.2	F or B	113.7
MLI GT Glo America Gth GIF	USEq	Divers	Yes								3.2	F or B	18.2
MLI Hyper Val Line US EqGl	USEq	Divers	Yes								3.2	F or B	14.9
MLI U.S. Equity Index GIF	USEq	Divers	Yes								1.8	None	1.9
Manulife Vistafd1 Am Stock	USEq	Divers	Fgn	23.3	19.9	19.3				Med+	1.6	Front	9.7
Manulife Vistafd2 Am Stock	USEq	Divers	Fgn	22.4	19.0	18.4				Med+	2.4	Defer	57.8
Marathon Perf Large Cap US	USEq	LgCap	Fgn								2.2	F or B	6.5
Margin of Safety	USEq	Divers	No	17.8	23.7	21.8	16.3			Low	1.9	None	6.0
Maritime Life Am Gth&IncAC	USEq	LgCap	Fgn	26.3	25.8	23.7				Low	2.6	None	255.7
Maritime Life Am Gth&Inc B	USEq	LgCap	Fgn	26.2							2.6	Defer	29.3
Maritime Life Discovery AC	USEq	SmCap	Fgn	22.6							2.6	None	19.4
Maritime Life Discovery B	USEq	SmCap	Fgn	23.3							2.6	Defer	4.3
Maritime Life S&P 500 A&C	USEq	Divers	Yes	24.7	26.3	25.6				Med	2.2	None	309.1
Maritime Life S&P 500 B	USEq	Divers	Yes	24.7							2.2	Defer	39.7
Mawer US Equity	USEq	LgCap	Fgn	34.3	31.7	27.7	20.6			Low	1.3	None	30.6
McDonald New America	USEq	LgCap	No	16.2	15.4						2.0	Front	1.0
Mclean Budden American Gth	USEq	Divers	Fgn	27.3	31.6	27.4	22.0			Med+	1.8	None	23.8
MetLife-Fidelity Sm Cap Am	USEq	SmCap	Yes								2.7	Defer	4.0
Metlife Mvp US Equity	USEq	Divers	No	41.9	36.3	31.2	22.5			Med+	2.2	Defer	32.6
Millennia III Amer Eq 1	USEq	LgCap	Fgn	24.9	20.7						2.8	Defer	39.1
Millennia III Amer Eq 2	USEq	LgCap	Fgn	24.5	20.4						2.6	Defer	8.1
Montrusco Select NTx US Eq	USEq	Divers	No	30.2	32.4	27.8	20.4	16.1		Med+		None	144.7
Montrusco Select Strat US	USEq	Divers	No	18.8	26.1							None	12.0
Montrusco Select Tax US Eq	USEq	Divers	No	18.1	25.6	22.6	18.1	14.9		Med+		None	15.5
Montrusco Select U.S. Gth	USEq	Divers	No	0.8								None	12.6
Mutual Amerifund	USEq	LgCap	Fgn	30.1	32.2	26.6	20.3	13.3		Med	2.1	Front	8.6
Mutual Premier American	USEq	LgCap	No	28.4	30.8	25.4	19.3			Med-	2.4	None	118.8

FUND NAME	FUND CATEGORY		RRSP. ELIGIB.	1 YR	2 YR	3 YR	5 YR	10 YR	15 YR	3 YR VOLATILITY	MER	SALES FEES	ASSETS IN $MIL
NAL-U.S. Equity	USEq	Divers	Fgn	34.9	35.4	26.2	-	-	-	Med	2.3	FnDf	42.9
NN Can-Am	USEq	Divers	Yes	24.1	25.6	24.7	19.3	-	-	Med	2.7	Defer	248.7
NN Can-Daq 100	USEq	Divers	Yes	33.7	33.4	28.3	-	-	-	-	2.7	Defer	39.5
National Trust American Eq	USEq	LgCap	Fgn	40.7	33.4	28.3	19.8	-	-	Med	2.3	None	48.2
National Trust U.S. Index	USEq	Divers	Fgn	37.1	-	-	-	-	-	-	0.9	None	30.0
Navigator American Growth	USEq	Divers	Fgn	25.3	-	-	-	-	-	-	3.0	F or B	1.4
Navigator American valuee	USEq	LgCap	Fgn	28.4	26.4	23.9	-	-	-	Low	3.0	F or B	1.9
North West Life Ecoflex S	USEq	Divers	Fgn	42.9	-	-	-	-	-	-	3.0	Defer	5.4
North West Life Ecoflex U	USEq	Divers	Yes	-	-	-	-	-	-	-	2.4	Defer	1.8
O'Donnell Amer Sector Grth	USEq	LgCap	Fgn	21.5	13.2	-	-	-	-	-	2.9	F or B	25.4
O'Donnell U.S. Mid-Cap	USEq	Divers	Fgn	34.9	25.8	-	-	-	-	-	2.9	F or B	58.7
O.I.Q. Ferique America	USEq	Divers	Yes	37.0	35.2	-	-	-	-	-	0.4	None	24.0
Optima Strat-US Equity	USEq	LgCap	Fgn	38.5	39.2	36.2	-	-	-	Med-	0.4	F or B	296.3
PH & N Pooled US Pension	USEq	LgCap	Fgn	26.7	29.3	29.6	23.0	16.0	-	Low	0.1	None	602.9
PH & N US Equity	USEq	LgCap	Fgn	24.8	27.6	27.9	21.5	14.3	-	Low	1.1	None	691.4
Pret et Revenu Americain	USEq	Divers	Fgn	18.0	8.5	17.8	15.2	11.3	-	High	2.0	None	7.3
Primus U.S. Equity	USEq	Divers	Fgn	39.5	-	-	-	-	-	-	0.2	None	44.9
Royal Monthly Income	USEq	Divers	Yes	40.3	37.5	-	-	-	-	-	1.1	None	52.7
Royal US Gth Strategic Idx	USEq	LgCap	No	20.7	26.3	21.6	18.5	12.9	-	Med-	1.5	None	602.3
Royal US valuee Strat Index	USEq	Divers	No	-	-	-	-	-	-	-	1.5	None	38.7
Royla&SunAlliance Income	USEq	Divers	Yes	-	-	-	-	-	-	-	1.9	Defer	42.8
SSQ - Actions Americaines	USEq	LgCap	Fgn	25.9	26.3	27.2	21.4	-	-	Med+	-	None	8.1
Scotia CanAm Growth	USEq	LgCap	Yes	25.4	27.2	26.2	-	-	-	Med	1.3	None	315.6
Scotia Ex. American Gth	USEq	Divers	Fgn	30.5	24.1	19.4	17.2	12.1	-	Med+	2.2	None	126.1
Scudder US Growth & Income	USEq	Divers	Fgn	27.1	-	-	-	-	-	Med	1.3	None	27.2
Spectrum Utd American Eq	USEq	LgCap	Fgn	31.7	28.0	28.6	21.2	16.2	15.2	Med	2.3	F or B	386.8
Spectrum Utd American Gth	USEq	Divers	Fgn	40.4	25.0	29.2	24.5	19.0	16.1	High	2.4	F or B	649.0
Spectrum Utd Optimax USA	USEq	Divers	Fgn	30.3	24.5	21.6	-	-	-	Low	2.4	F or B	22.2
Standard Life US Equity	USEq	LgCap	Fgn	30.7	30.7	26.2	-	-	-	Med-	2.0	Defer	6.1
Strategic Val American Eq	USEq	LgCap	Fgn	29.1	23.1	20.4	17.7	12.6	12.8	Med-	2.7	F or B	155.9
Tal/Hyper valuee Line US Eq	USEq	LgCap	Fgn	26.5	24.6	24.3	19.6	-	-	High	3.0	F or B	125.1
Templeton Mutual Beacon	USEq	Divers	Fgn	22.0	-	-	-	-	-	-	2.5	F or B	205.3
Universal US Emerg Growth	USEq	SmCap	Fgn	20.2	5.9	17.1	18.8	-	-	High	2.4	F or B	338.7
University Avenue Growth	USEq	Divers	Fgn	33.0	21.8	19.1	13.1	7.0	-	Med+	2.4	F or B	1.0
University U.S. Small Cap	USEq	Divers	Fgn	26.5	-	-	-	-	-	-	2.4	F or B	0.7
Valorem U.S. Equity-valuee	USEq	Divers	Fgn	22.0	-	-	-	-	-	-	-	F or B	0.7
Zweig Strategic Growth	USEq	Divers	Fgn	29.0	22.8	21.4	17.3	-	-	Low	2.5	None	243.8
20/20 Aggr Global Stock	FgnEq	Global	Fgn	27.3	16.8	-	-	-	-	-	3.6	F or B	74.4
20/20 Emerging Mkts valuee	FgnEq	Emerg	Fgn	-43.8	-18.3	-11.4	-	-	-	High	3.6	F or B	23.6
20/20 India	FgnEq	India	Fgn	-16.8	-15.9	-18.0	-	-	-	Med+	3.7	F or B	30.4
20/20 Latin America	FgnEq	Latin	Fgn	-35.9	3.5	5.5	-	-	-	-	3.2	F or B	176.6
@rgentum Intl Master Pfl	FgnEq	IntlEq	No	-	-	-	-	-	-	-	-	F or B	1.4
ABC American-valuee	FgnEq	NrthAm	Fgn	34.4	32.9	-	-	-	-	-	2.0	None	34.9

FUND NAME	FUND CATEGORY		RRSP-ELIGIB.	1 YR	2 YR	3 YR	5 YR	10 YR	15 YR	3 YR VOLATILITY	MER	SALES FEES	ASSETS IN $MIL
AGF International valuee	FgnEq	Global	Fgn	18.2	24.5	20.8	17.7			Med+	2.8	F or B	2201.6
AGF Intl Grp-Asian Growth	FgnEq	PacRim	Fgn	-53.6	-30.6	-20.3	-4.7			Med+	3.0	F or B	176.2
AGF Intl Grp-China Focus	FgnEq	China	Fgn	-47.4	-16.9	-12.3				Med+	3.5	F or B	12.0
AGF Intl Grp-European Gth	FgnEq	Europe	Fgn	52.1	32.5	27.1				Med+	3.0	F or B	268.5
AGF Intl Grp-Germany	FgnEq	German	Fgn	43.8	39.9	31.0				Low	3.0	F or B	64.7
AGF Intl Grp-Germany M	FgnEq	German	Fgn	46.8	42.5	33.1				Low	1.6	None	56.3
AGF Intl Grp-Intl Stock	FgnEq	IntlEq	Fgn	15.4							3.0	F or B	128.4
AGF Intl Grp-Japan	FgnEq	Japan	Fgn	-13.7	-3.1	1.4	-0.3	0.3	9.5		3.1	F or B	100.0
AGF Intl Grp-World Equity	FgnEq	Global	Fgn	16.2	17.9	14.8				Low	3.1	F or B	77.8
AGF RSP Intl Equity Alloc	FgnEq	Global	Yes	15.2	15.8	19.4				High	2.5	F or B	333.6
AIC World Equity	FgnEq	IntlEq	Fgn	33.6	30.4	22.3				Med+	2.7	F or B	296.3
AIM Europa	FgnEq	Europe	Fgn	56.7	44.4	28.9	19.0			Med+	2.9	F or B	18.5
AIM GT Glbl Ntrl Res	FgnEq	Global	Fgn	-7.6	-1.4	9.1				High	3.0	F or B	20.6
AIM GT Global Theme Class	FgnEq	Global	Fgn	29.6							2.9	F or B	296.8
AIM GT Latin Amer Growthh	FgnEq	Latin	Fgn	-21.1	6.5	13.2					2.9	F or B	21.7
AIM GT Pacific Growth	FgnEq	PacRim	Fgn	-48.2	-19.5	-9.3				Med+	3.0	F or B	14.8
AIM Global RSP Index	FgnEq	Global	Yes	20.2							1.9	F or B	1.7
AIM International	FgnEq	Global	Fgn	17.8	21.4	15.1	14.4	10.1		High	3.0	F or B	29.6
AIM Korea	FgnEq	Korean	Fgn	-66.2	-48.2	-39.7	-21.9			High	3.3	F or B	13.6
AIM Nippon	FgnEq	Japan	Fgn	-29.5	-17.0	-1.1	-5.3				3.3	F or B	5.1
AIM Tiger	FgnEq	PacRim	Fgn	-55.6	-27.7	-22.2	-10.8			High	3.4	F or B	14.0
APEX Asian Pacific	FgnEq	PacRim	Fgn	-39.4	-23.0	-13.6				Med-	2.8	F or B	8.1
APEX Global Equity	FgnEq	Global	Fgn	25.3							2.8	F or B	23.3
Acadia International Eq	FgnEq	IntlEq	No									Defer	0.2
Acuity Pld Global Equity	FgnEq	Global	Fgn	24.3	29.0	28.0	18.5			High		None	0.7
Allstar AIG Asian	FgnEq	PacRim	Fgn	-53.7							3.5	Front	71.4
Altamira Asia Pacific	FgnEq	PacRim	Fgn	-38.5	-23.7	-18.0	-9.5			Low	2.3	None	291.5
Altamira European Equity	FgnEq	Europe	Fgn	40.6	32.3	26.7				Med-	2.3	None	50.6
Altamira Glo Small Company	FgnEq	Global	Fgn	10.1							2.4	None	15.6
Altamira Global Discovery	FgnEq	Emerg	Fgn	-30.4	-6.2	-0.8				Med-	3.0	None	13.0
Altamira Japanese Opp	FgnEq	Japan	Fgn	-26.9	-17.4	-5.5					2.4	None	108.8
Altamira Nth Amer Recovery	FgnEq	NrthAm	Yes	12.2	22.0	17.2					2.3	None	1.1
Artisan International Eq	FgnEq	IntlEq	Fgn								3.0	F or B	0.6
Astra Actions intl	FgnEq	IntlEq	No								2.9	None	1.6
Astra Tendances demograph	FgnEq	Global	Fgn	38.3	33.0	27.2				Low	2.7	F or B	66.3
Atlas European valuee	FgnEq	Europe	Fgn	9.6	13.5	12.6	12.7			Med-	2.8	F or B	16.6
Atlas Global valuee	FgnEq	Global	Fgn	-10.7							3.5	F or B	12.6
Atlas Intl Emerg Mkts Gth	FgnEq	Emerg	Fgn	27.9							2.8	F or B	72.9
Atlas Intl Large Cap Gth	FgnEq	IntlEq	Fgn	11.9							2.0	F or B	39.7
Atlas Intl RSP Index	FgnEq	IntlEq	Yes	-11.4	9.5	13.3					3.0	F or B	11.7
Atlas Latin American valuee	FgnEq	Latin	Fgn	-20.2	-14.5	-7.0				Low	2.9	F or B	6.6
Atlas Pacific Basin valuee	FgnEq	PacRim	Fgn	6.9	11.1						2.3	F or B	25.8
Azura Growth Pooled	FgnEq	Global	Fgn	-44.5							3.3	F or B	10.9
BPI Asia Pacific	FgnEq	PacRim	Fgn										

FUND NAME	FUND CATEGORY		RRSP-ELIGIB.	1 YR	2 YR	3 YR	5 YR	10 YR	15 YR	3 YR VOLATILITY	MER	SALES FEES	ASSETS IN $MIL
BPI Emerging Markets	FgnEq	Emerg	Fgn	-15.9	5.0	-	-	-	-	-	3.0	F or B	7.0
BPI Global Eq valuee Sgr	FgnEq	Global	No	-	-	-	-	-	-	-	-	F or B	6.9
BPI Global Equity valuee	FgnEq	Global	Fgn	29.3	26.7	22.6	18.9	14.2	-	Med	2.4	F or B	479.7
BPI Global Opportunities	FgnEq	Global	Fgn	49.2	43.6	33.8	-	-	-	High	2.6	F or B	82.9
BPI Global Small Companies	FgnEq	Global	Fgn	7.6	14.5	11.7	15.2	-	-	Med+	2.5	F or B	100.5
BPI Intl Equity valuee	FgnEq	IntlEq	Fgn	37.3	-	-	-	-	-	-	2.4	F or B	21.2
BPI Intl Equity valuee Sgr	FgnEq	IntlEq	No	-	-	-	-	-	-	-	-	F or B	2.9
Beutel Goodman Intl Equity	FgnEq	IntlEq	Fgn	1.5	8.6	10.4	12.3	-	-	Low	2.6	Front	14.9
Bissett International Eq	FgnEq	IntlEq	No	14.3	15.0	12.9	-	-	-	Med	2.5	None	31.5
Bissett Multinational Gth	FgnEq	Global	Fgn	27.4	32.4	29.2	-	-	-	Med-	1.5	None	80.5
C.I. Emerging Markets	FgnEq	Emerg	Fgn	-8.9	2.7	3.5	5.2	-	-	Low	2.7	F or B	239.2
C.I. Emerging Mkts Sector	FgnEq	Emerg	Fgn	-9.2	2.2	3.0	4.8	-	-	Low	2.8	F or B	39.5
C.I. Glo Consumer Prod Sec	FgnEq	Global	Fgn	24.0	-	-	-	-	-	-	2.4	F or B	9.4
C.I. Glo Financial Ser Sec	FgnEq	Global	Fgn	40.3	-	-	-	-	-	-	2.4	F or B	119.4
C.I. Global	FgnEq	Global	Fgn	24.3	22.2	19.3	15.2	12.9	-	Med	2.5	F or B	1045.1
C.I. Global Equity RSP	FgnEq	Global	Yes	14.9	15.8	16.2	-	-	-	Med+	2.4	F or B	314.4
C.I. Global Resource Sect	FgnEq	Global	Fgn	-21.6	-	-	-	-	-	-	2.4	F or B	7.0
C.I. Global Sector	FgnEq	Global	Fgn	23.4	21.2	18.4	14.6	12.4	-	Med	2.5	F or B	224.0
C.I. Global Segregated	FgnEq	Global	Fgn	-	-	-	-	-	-	-	3.3	F or B	9.3
C.I. Hansberger valuee Sgrd	FgnEq	Global	No	-	-	-	-	-	-	-	3.3	F or B	9.0
C.I. Latin American	FgnEq	Latin	Fgn	-25.1	-3.6	1.7	-	-	-	-	2.8	F or B	184.3
C.I. Latin American Sector	FgnEq	Latin	Fgn	-25.5	-4.1	1.3	-	-	-	-	2.9	F or B	19.0
C.I. Pacific	FgnEq	PacRim	Fgn	-49.3	-21.6	-13.5	-3.2	3.5	10.5	Med	2.5	F or B	342.1
C.I. Pacific Sector	FgnEq	PacRim	Fgn	-49.7	-22.2	-14.1	-3.7	3.1	-	Med	2.6	F or B	59.1
CCPE Global Equity	FgnEq	Global	Fgn	12.4	13.6	14.1	-	-	-	High	1.8	None	63.7
CDA Emerging Markets(KBSH)	FgnEq	Emerg	Fgn	-35.8	-20.2	-12.5	-	-	-	Med+	1.5	None	0.4
CDA European (KBSH)	FgnEq	Europe	Fgn	37.6	27.7	25.4	-	-	-	Med+	1.5	None	4.7
CDA Global (Trimark)	FgnEq	Global	Fgn	7.4	-	-	-	-	-	-	1.6	None	4.1
CDA Intl Equity (KBSH)	FgnEq	IntlEq	Fgn	3.6	7.6	11.9	-	-	-	High	1.5	None	4.4
CDA Pacific Basin (KBSH)	FgnEq	PacRim	Fgn	-24.9	-9.2	0.5	-	-	-	Low	1.5	None	1.1
CGO&V International	FgnEq	IntlEq	No	2.0	-	-	-	-	-	-	1.9	None	11.0
CIBC Emerging Economies	FgnEq	Emerg	Fgn	-12.6	3.9	-	-	-	-	-	2.7	None	19.0
CIBC European Equity	FgnEq	Europe	Fgn	33.2	22.9	-	-	-	-	-	2.5	None	60.8
CIBC Far East Prosperity	FgnEq	PacRim	Fgn	-35.0	-18.3	-9.9	-	-	-	Med-	2.7	None	88.3
CIBC Global Equity	FgnEq	Global	Fgn	27.5	23.9	19.6	14.9	11.2	-	Med+	2.5	None	327.7
CIBC International Index	FgnEq	IntlEq	No	-	-	-	-	-	-	-	0.9	None	37.2
CIBC Intl Index RRSP	FgnEq	IntlEq	Yes	11.2	-	-	-	-	-	-	0.9	None	59.9
CIBC Intl Small Companies	FgnEq	IntlEq	No	-	-	-	-	-	-	-	2.8	None	19.4
CIBC Japanese Equity	FgnEq	Japan	Fgn	-5.4	3.5	-	-	-	-	-	2.5	None	23.7
CIBC Latin American	FgnEq	Latin	Fgn	-19.4	-	-	-	-	-	-	2.7	None	10.5
CT AsiaGrowth	FgnEq	PacRim	Yes	-35.1	-20.3	-7.3	-	-	-	Med-	2.5	None	90.7
CT Emerging Markets	FgnEq	Emerg	Fgn	-38.3	-14.7	-8.4	-	-	-	Med	3.2	None	67.7
CT EuroGrowth	FgnEq	Europe	Yes	32.3	31.8	26.7	-	-	-	High	2.2	None	242.1
CT GlobalGrowth	FgnEq	Global	Yes	9.0	-	-	-	-	-	-	2.1	None	114.5

FUND NAME	FUND CATEGORY		RRSP- ELIGIB.	1 YR	2 YR	3 YR	5 YR	10 YR	15 YR	3 YR VOLATILITY	MER	SALES FEES	ASSETS IN $MIL
CT International	FgnEq	IntlEq	Fgn	26.0	20.1	18.2	13.9	12.8		Low	2.6	None	502.6
CT International Eq Index	FgnEq	IntlEq	Fgn	12.1							0.5	None	17.0
CT North American	FgnEq	NrthAm	Fgn	13.7	19.0	15.8	9.9	9.5	9.2		2.3	None	44.4
Cambridge Americas	FgnEq	Amrcas	Fgn	44.6	19.1	21.8	13.8	11.4		High	3.5	F or B	1.5
Cambridge China	FgnEq	China	Fgn	-16.7	-19.0	-11.9	-15.9	-6.2	0.7	Med+	3.5	F or B	0.6
Cambridge Global	FgnEq	Global	Fgn	-39.5	-42.4	-28.8	-15.3	-11.5	-6.3	High	3.7	F or B	0.6
Cambridge Pacific	FgnEq	PacRim	Fgn	-45.6	-36.0	-27.5				High	3.7	F or B	0.6
Canada Life AsiaPacific Eq	FgnEq	PacRim	Fgn	-28.2	-14.3						2.4	Defer	14.5
Canada Life European Eq	FgnEq	Europe	Fgn	32.2	29.1	21.2	18.8	16.5		Med+	2.4	Defer	86.8
Canada Life US & Intl	FgnEq	Global	Fgn	18.4	23.4	15.8	13.2	12.7		High	2.4	Defer	773.7
Capstone Intl Invest Tr	FgnEq	Global	Fgn	23.1	10.4	19.1	19.6			Med+	2.1	None	2.5
CentrePost Foreign Equity	FgnEq	Global	Fgn	23.1	25.5	22.0	20.5	16.0			1.8	None	3.0
Champion Growth	FgnEq	NrthAm	Fgn	20.5	26.9	28.4					2.5	FnDf	4.3
Chou Associates	FgnEq	NrthAm	Fgn	22.9	32.2	28.3	16.1	13.2			1.9	Front	11.0
Clarington Asia Pacific	FgnEq	PacRim	No								3.0	F or B	4.2
Clarington Global Oppor	FgnEq	Global	Fgn	27.3						Med-	3.0	F or B	18.3
Clean Environment Intl Eq	FgnEq	NrthAm	Fgn	43.1	34.1	17.1	18.2				2.6	F or B	42.0
Comm. Un. Intl G7 Index	FgnEq	IntlEq	No								2.8	Defer	2.8
Cornerstone Global	FgnEq	Global	Fgn	14.4	17.0	20.1	15.9	13.2			2.4	None	19.9
Cote 100 Amerique	FgnEq	NrthAm	Fgn	12.7	16.8	6.6				Med-	1.4	None	27.6
Cote 100 Excel	FgnEq	Global	Fgn								2.6	None	10.6
Cundill valuee A	FgnEq	Global	Fgn	-5.8	3.7		10.7	9.2	10.7	Low	2.0	Front	359.2
Cundill valuee B	FgnEq	Global	Fgn	-6.2							2.4	Front	30.7
Desjardins International	FgnEq	Global	Fgn	12.2	12.9	14.2	13.6	12.9	11.1	Med+	2.3	None	59.4
Dynamic Europe	FgnEq	Europe	Fgn	39.0	39.7	31.8	24.8			High	2.5	F or B	355.6
Dynamic Far East	FgnEq	PacRim	Fgn	-28.9	-6.3	-1.7				Low	2.8	F or B	8.6
Dynamic Global Resource	FgnEq	Global	Fgn	-17.8	-2.8	14.1				High	2.6	F or B	60.9
Dynamic International	FgnEq	Global	Fgn	11.1	18.2	18.1	13.7	10.0		High	2.6	F or B	130.1
Dynamic Latin American	FgnEq	Latin	Fgn	-17.1		-7.5					3.5	F or B	8.4
Elliott & Page Asian Gth	FgnEq	PacRim	Fgn	-31.0	-15.2	-2.7				Low	3.8	F or B	4.7
Elliott & Page Emerg Mkt	FgnEq	Emerg	Fgn	-27.3	-5.6	17.7				Med+	4.7	F or B	6.1
Elliott & Page Global Eq	FgnEq	Global	Fgn	17.0	18.0	15.9				Med	2.0	F or B	40.1
Empire International Gth	FgnEq	Global	Fgn	11.5	18.7	20.1				Med	2.5	Defer	129.7
Equitable Life Intl	FgnEq	Global	Yes	16.4	16.6					Med-	2.8	Defer	30.9
Ethical Pacific Rim	FgnEq	PacRim	Fgn	-57.9	-25.7	-15.2				High	3.2	Defer	24.8
FMOQ International Equity	FgnEq	Global	Yes	27.6	23.0	19.2				Med+	0.8	None	11.3
Fidelity Emerg Mkts Ptl	FgnEq	Emerg	Fgn	-47.7	-32.1	-15.8				High	3.6	Defer	40.6
Fidelity European Growth	FgnEq	Europe	Fgn	45.4	34.8	28.6	24.6			Low	2.7	F or B	2328.0
Fidelity Far East	FgnEq	PacRim	Fgn	-38.7	-14.1	-4.6	3.3			High	2.8	F or B	773.2
Fidelity Focus Nat Resourc	FgnEq	NrthAm	Fgn	6.9						High	2.5	F or B	4.5
Fidelity Intl Portfolio	FgnEq	Global	Fgn	24.1	25.2	22.5	18.2	14.8		Med-	2.7	F or B	3517.4
Fidelity Japanese Growth	FgnEq	Japan	Fgn	-21.1	-11.9	-5.0					3.0	F or B	101.8
Fidelity Latin Amer Growth	FgnEq	Latin	Fgn	-19.2	7.6	13.0					3.1	F or B	108.9
First American	FgnEq	NrthAm	Yes	6.6	0.5	1.5					2.8	Back	10.7

FUND NAME	FUND CATEGORY		RRSP. ELIGIB.	1 YR	2 YR	3 YR	5 YR	10 YR	15 YR	3 YR VOLATILITY	MER	SALES FEES	ASSETS IN $MIL
First Canadian Emerg Mkt	FgnEq	Emerg	Fgn	-28.2	-7.5	-3.5	-	-	-	Med-	2.2	None	109.9
First Canadian Europe Gth	FgnEq	Europe	Fgn	35.1	29.3	22.8	-	-	-	Low	2.1	None	97.4
First Canadian FarEast Gth	FgnEq	PacRim	Fgn	-43.8	-20.5	-10.3	-	-	-	Med	2.4	None	12.6
First Canadian Intl. Gth	FgnEq	IntlEq	Fgn	12.3	9.9	12.3	-	-	-	Med	2.0	None	379.6
First Canadian Japan Gth	FgnEq	Japan	Fgn	-34.2	-23.7	-13.3	11.0	-	-		2.2	None	19.1
First Canadian NAFTA Adv	FgnEq	NrthAm	Fgn	15.1	20.0	18.3	-	-	-		2.1	None	51.3
First Cdn Latin America	FgnEq	Latin	Fgn	-28.6	-	-	-	-	-		2.1	None	8.4
FirstTrust Glo Target15 97	FgnEq	IntlEq	Fgn	-3.6	-	-	-	-	-		1.1	Front	3.2
FirstTrust Pharma 96	FgnEq	Global	Fgn	49.8	-	-	-	-	-		1.1	Front	30.7
FirstTrust Pharma 97	FgnEq	Global	Fgn	44.8	-	-	-	-	-		1.2	Front	32.0
FirstTrust Technology 97	FgnEq	NrthAm	Fgn	19.7	-	-	-	-	-		1.2	Front	10.4
GBC International Growth	FgnEq	IntlEq	Fgn	11.7	10.5	10.2	6.3	-	-	Low	1.9	None	20.5
GBC North American Growth	FgnEq	NrthAm	Fgn	18.7	14.3	17.1	14.7	13.8	11.5	Med	2.0	None	106.0
GFM Emerg Mkts Country $US	FgnEq	Emerg	Fgn	-29.9	-8.5	-3.1	-	-	-		1.5	None	40.3
GS International Equity	FgnEq	Global	Fgn	16.8	16.3	-	-	-	-		2.8	FnDf	378.6
Global Mgr-German Bear	FgnEq	German	Fgn	-38.7	-39.4	-34.8	-	-	-	Med+	1.8	Front	0.3
Global Mgr-German Geared	FgnEq	German	Fgn	107.9	88.1	63.0	-	-	-	High	1.8	Front	1.5
Global Mgr-German Index	FgnEq	German	Fgn	46.7	36.2	25.9	-	-	-	Low	1.8	Front	9.6
Global Mgr-Hong Kong Bear	FgnEq	China	Fgn	35.4	0.1	-6.6	-	-	-	High	1.8	Front	0.5
Global Mgr-Hong Kong Geard	FgnEq	China	Fgn	-75.7	-36.8	-21.7	-	-	-	High	1.8	Front	0.2
Global Mgr-Hong Kong Index	FgnEq	China	Fgn	-42.1	-11.0	-3.0	-	-	-	Med+	1.8	Front	0.8
Global Mgr-Japan Bear	FgnEq	Japan	Fgn	4.7	0.4	-21.7	-	-	-		1.8	Front	0.1
Global Mgr-Japan Geared	FgnEq	Japan	Fgn	-58.9	-44.9	-18.2	-	-	-		1.8	Front	0.2
Global Mgr-Japan Index	FgnEq	Japan	Fgn	-37.1	-26.3	-13.1	-	-	-		1.8	Front	0.6
Global Mgr-UK Bear	FgnEq	Europe	Fgn	-19.1	-14.9	-13.3	-	-	-	High	1.8	Front	0.2
Global Mgr-UK Geared	FgnEq	Europe	Fgn	52.2	55.9	42.6	-	-	-	High	1.8	Front	0.9
Global Mgr-UK Index	FgnEq	Europe	Fgn	29.6	33.1	25.1	-	-	-	Med-	1.8	Front	6.0
Global Strategy Asia	FgnEq	PacRim	Fgn	-53.8	-31.0	-19.6	-	-	-	High	2.8	Front	10.9
Global Strategy Diver Asia	FgnEq	PacRim	Yes	-49.8	-29.8	-20.5	-	-	-	Med+	2.7	F or B	7.3
Global Strategy Diver Euro	FgnEq	Europe	Yes	39.6	34.1	26.9	-	-	-	Med	2.5	F or B	149.9
Global Strategy Diver Jap	FgnEq	Japan	Yes	-30.8	-22.3	-12.8	-	-	-		2.5	F or B	8.5
Global Strategy Divr Latin	FgnEq	Latin	Yes	-20.1	8.0	9.0	-	-	-		3.0	F or B	13.9
Global Strategy Divr World	FgnEq	Global	Yes	18.6	19.3	17.6	-	-	-	Med	2.4	F or B	49.8
Global Strategy Euro Plus	FgnEq	Europe	Fgn	33.9	28.8	24.5	-	-	-	Low	2.8	F or B	129.5
Global Strategy Japan	FgnEq	Japan	Fgn	-34.0	-25.0	-14.9	-	-	-		2.8	F or B	10.4
Global Strategy Latin Amer	FgnEq	Latin	Fgn	-19.4	6.3	9.2	-	-	-		3.0	F or B	6.8
Global Strategy World Comp	FgnEq	Global	Fgn	14.6	14.0	22.1	-	-	-	Med+	2.9	F or B	153.0
Global Strategy World Eq	FgnEq	Global	Fgn	17.5	16.7	17.8	-	-	-	Med-	2.8	F or B	145.7
Globeinvest Emerg Mkt Ctry	FgnEq	Emerg	Fgn	-30.8	-10.0	-	-	-	-		2.7	Front	7.1
Great-West Asian Gth (A) A	FgnEq	PacRim	No	-	-	-	-	-	-		2.9	None	0.8
Great-West Asian Gth (A) B	FgnEq	PacRim	No	-	-	-	-	-	-		2.6	Defer	0.5
Great-West European (S) A	FgnEq	Europe	No	-	-	-	-	-	-		2.9	None	6.7
Great-West European (S) B	FgnEq	Europe	No	-	-	-	-	-	-		2.6	Defer	5.5
Great-West Intl Eq (P) A	FgnEq	IntlEq	Fgn	20.0	19.9	18.2	-	-	-	Med	2.9	None	96.8

FUND NAME	FUND CATEGORY		RRSP ELIGIB.	1 YR	2 YR	3 YR	5 YR	10 YR	15 YR	3 YR VOLATILITY	MER	SALES FEES	ASSETS IN $MIL
Great-West Intl Eq (P) B	FgnEq	IntlEq	Fgn	20.3	20.2	18.5	-	-	-	Med	2.7	Defer	83.6
Great-West Intl Opp (P) A	FgnEq	IntlEq	No	-	-	-	-	-	-	-	2.8	None	1.9
Great-West Intl Opp (P) B	FgnEq	IntlEq	No	-	-	-	-	-	-	-	2.5	Defer	2.1
Great-West Nth Amer Eq(B)A	FgnEq	NrthAm	Yes	15.2	19.7	-	-	-	-	-	2.8	None	21.7
Great-West Nth Amer Eq(B)B	FgnEq	NrthAm	Yes	15.5	20.0	-	-	-	-	-	2.6	Defer	18.6
Green Line Asian Growth	FgnEq	PacRim	Fgn	-49.9	-25.3	-16.6	-	-	-	Med+	2.6	None	41.9
Green Line Emerging Mkts	FgnEq	Emerg	Fgn	-31.3	-12.0	-4.7	0.3	-	-	Med	2.7	None	97.6
Green Line European Growth	FgnEq	Europe	Fgn	38.7	32.8	29.4	-	-	-	Med	2.6	None	219.7
Green Line European Index	FgnEq	Europe	Fgn	-	-	-	-	-	-	-	0.9	None	43.8
Green Line Global Select	FgnEq	Global	Fgn	14.3	14.8	16.8	-	-	-	Med+	2.3	None	250.5
Green Line Intl Equity	FgnEq	IntlEq	Fgn	8.0	10.5	11.1	10.5	-	-	Med+	2.3	None	125.5
Green Line Intl RSP Index	FgnEq	IntlEq	Yes	-	-	-	-	-	-	-	1.3	None	45.0
Green Line Japanese Growth	FgnEq	Japan	Fgn	-25.4	-14.7	-7.0	-	-	-	-	2.6	None	33.0
Green Line Japanese Index	FgnEq	Japan	Fgn	-	-	-	-	-	-	-	0.9	None	7.4
Green Line Latin Amer Gth.	FgnEq	Latin	Fgn	-12.7	6.9	10.2	-	-	-	-	2.7	None	42.7
Greystone Managed Global	FgnEq	Global	Fgn	31.0	26.5	25.4	-	-	-	Low	2.5	None	51.6
GrowSafe European 100	FgnEq	Europe	Yes	37.3	-	-	-	-	-	-	2.1	Defer	63.3
GrowSafe Japanese 225	FgnEq	Japan	Yes	-35.8	-	-	-	-	-	-	2.1	Defer	7.5
Guardian Asia Pacific C	FgnEq	PacRim	Fgn	-40.8	-22.3	-12.6	-	-	-	Med-	1.7	Front	1.7
Guardian Asia Pacific M	FgnEq	PacRim	Fgn	-41.3	-22.9	-	-	-	-	-	3.0	F or B	1.1
Guardian Emerging Mkts C	FgnEq	Emerg	Fgn	-28.7	-11.2	-3.8	-	-	-	Med-	0.8	Front	1.1
Guardian Emerging Mkts M	FgnEq	Emerg	Fgn	-29.3	-11.7	-	-	-	-	-	2.9	Front	4.2
Guardian Global Equity C	FgnEq	Global	Fgn	15.4	14.5	15.5	15.1	8.6	9.2	Med	1.4	Front	3.0
Guardian Global Equity M	FgnEq	Global	Fgn	15.1	14.0	-	-	-	-	-	2.9	F or B	10.7
Hansberger Asian	FgnEq	PacRim	Fgn	-59.8	-36.2	-25.3	-	-	-	High	2.8	F or B	23.7
Hansberger Asian Sector	FgnEq	PacRim	Fgn	-60.1	-36.6	-25.8	-	-	-	Med+	2.8	F or B	4.7
Hansberger Dev Markets Sec	FgnEq	Emerg	Fgn	-42.4	-19.4	-	-	-	-	-	2.9	F or B	3.8
Hansberger Developing Mkts	FgnEq	Emerg	Fgn	-41.7	-	-	-	-	-	-	2.8	F or B	10.7
Hansberger European	FgnEq	Europe	Fgn	25.2	26.3	19.5	15.8	-	-	Med+	2.4	F or B	143.1
Hansberger European Sector	FgnEq	Europe	Fgn	23.6	25.0	18.6	15.1	-	-	Med	2.5	F or B	65.0
Hansberger Glo Small Cap	FgnEq	Global	Fgn	-6.7	4.2	-	-	-	-	-	2.7	F or B	29.2
Hansberger Glo Small Cap S	FgnEq	Global	Fgn	-7.5	-	-	-	-	-	-	2.7	F or B	11.5
Hansberger International	FgnEq	IntlEq	Fgn	-8.1	3.5	-	-	-	-	-	2.5	F or B	118.2
Hansberger Intl Sector	FgnEq	IntlEq	Fgn	-8.7	-	-	-	-	-	-	2.5	F or B	36.4
Hansberger valuee	FgnEq	Global	Fgn	-9.7	5.8	-	-	-	-	-	2.5	F or B	646.5
Hansberger valuee Sector	FgnEq	Global	Fgn	-10.3	-	-	-	-	-	-	2.5	F or B	182.1
Hartford Select World Econ	FgnEq	Global	No	-	-	-	-	-	-	-	-	Defer	0.6
Hongkong Bank Asian Growth	FgnEq	PacRim	Fgn	-47.0	-25.6	-16.0	-	-	-	Med	2.3	None	26.6
Hongkong Bank Emerging Mkt	FgnEq	Emerg	Fgn	-32.8	-13.0	-8.5	-	-	-	Med	2.6	None	7.3
Hongkong Bank European Gth	FgnEq	Europe	Fgn	44.7	35.2	28.9	-	-	-	Med-	2.2	None	101.2
Hongkong Bank Global Eq	FgnEq	Global	Fgn	-	-	-	-	-	-	-	-	None	27.7
ICM International	FgnEq	IntlEq	Fgn	7.9	14.3	14.7	14.3	-	-	Med-	0.4	None	48.1
Imperial Gth N.A. Equity	FgnEq	NrthAm	No	24.2	22.1	19.8	18.0	10.8	10.8	-	1.6	Front	4.0
Ind. Alliance Ecoflex E	FgnEq	Emerg	Fgn	-36.7	-	-	-	-	-	-	3.8	Defer	7.2

FUND NAME	FUND CATEGORY	RRSP. ELIGIB.	1 YR	2 YR	3 YR	5 YR	10 YR	15 YR	3 YR VOLATILITY	MER	SALES FEES	ASSETS IN $MIL
Ind. Alliance Ecoflex I	FgnEq	IntlEq	Fgn	9.0	16.2	-	-	-	-	-	3.0	Defer	120.6
Ind. Alliance Emerging Mkt	FgnEq	Emerg	Fgn	-36.2	-	-	-	-	-	-	3.1	None	0.8
Ind. Alliance Intl.	FgnEq	IntlEq	Fgn	9.8	17.0	-	-	-	-	-	2.2	None	14.4
India Excel	FgnEq	India	Yes	-	-	-	-	-	-	-	-	F or B	0.3
InvesNat European Equity	FgnEq	Europe	Fgn	45.9	32.3	25.2	22.4	-	-	Med-	2.3	None	43.3
InvesNat Far East Equity	FgnEq	PacRim	Fgn	-42.2	-20.0	-9.9	-	-	-	Med-	2.5	None	11.9
InvesNat Japanese Equity	FgnEq	Japan	Fgn	-30.5	-22.5	-13.1	-	-	-	-	2.5	None	10.3
InvesNat Protected Intl	FgnEq	IntlEq	Yes	-	-	-	-	-	-	-	3.2	None	6.7
Investors European Growth	FgnEq	Europe	Fgn	38.3	31.1	25.0	21.3	-	-	Med	2.5	FnDf	1683.6
Investors Global	FgnEq	Global	Fgn	22.9	19.2	18.5	16.6	12.0	-	Low	2.4	FnDf	1799.6
Investors Growth Portfolio	FgnEq	Global	Fgn	19.9	21.7	19.5	16.6	-	-	Low	2.6	FnDf	867.7
Investors Japanese Growth	FgnEq	Japan	Fgn	-29.6	-19.4	-11.8	-5.6	-1.8	6.7	-	2.5	FnDf	427.2
Investors Latin Amer Grth	FgnEq	Latin	Fgn	-27.1	-	-	-	-	-	-	2.9	FnDf	125.0
Investors Nth American Gth	FgnEq	NrthAm	Fgn	8.9	16.5	15.1	13.1	13.9	12.5	Med	2.4	FnDf	1756.9
Investors Pacific Intl.	FgnEq	PacRim	Fgn	-51.3	-28.5	-18.3	-4.0	-	-	Med	2.5	FnDf	522.6
Investors Special	FgnEq	NrthAm	Fgn	11.9	18.9	16.2	11.6	14.3	10.9	-	2.4	FnDf	542.1
Investors World Gth. Port	FgnEq	Global	Fgn	-2.7	5.8	7.3	9.1	-	-	Med	2.6	FnDf	829.5
Ivy Foreign Equity	FgnEq	Global	Fgn	21.5	22.9	19.5	17.1	-	-	Low	2.4	F or B	668.3
London Life Intl Equity	FgnEq	IntlEq	Fgn	6.8	5.2	-	-	-	-	-	2.5	Defer	171.1
MAXXUM Global Equity	FgnEq	Global	Fgn	28.3	21.0	18.4	-	-	-	Med+	2.5	F or B	21.0
MB Global Equity	FgnEq	Global	No	22.6	23.1	-	-	-	-	-	-	None	69.0
MD Emerging Markets	FgnEq	Emerg	Fgn	-48.0	-20.5	-11.4	-	-	-	High	3.0	None	39.3
MD Growth Investments	FgnEq	Global	Fgn	17.1	21.8	20.1	19.0	13.7	15.0	Med-	1.3	None	3519.7
MLI Fidelity Int Portf GIF	FgnEq	IntlEq	Yes	23.1	-	-	-	-	-	-	3.4	F or B	280.0
MLI Trimark Select Gth GIF	FgnEq	Global	Yes	4.2	-	-	-	-	-	-	3.3	F or B	133.2
Mackenzie Sentinel Global	FgnEq	IntlEq	Fgn	15.8	13.4	13.8	12.9	-	-	Med+	0.5	None	6.7
Manulife Cabot Global Eq.	FgnEq	Global	Fgn	12.9	15.5	14.7	-	-	-	Low	2.5	None	69.3
Manulife Vistafd1 Glo Eq	FgnEq	IntlEq	Fgn	9.5	13.0	13.0	-	-	-	Med-	1.6	Front	7.4
Manulife Vistafd2 Glo Eq	FgnEq	IntlEq	Fgn	8.6	12.1	12.2	-	-	-	Med-	2.4	Defer	46.6
Maritime Life EurAsia A&C	FgnEq	IntlEq	Yes	13.5	-	-	-	-	-	-	2.4	None	24.1
Maritime Life EurAsia B	FgnEq	IntlEq	Yes	13.5	-	-	-	-	-	-	2.4	Defer	4.0
Maritime Life Europe A&C	FgnEq	Europe	Yes	-	-	-	-	-	-	-	2.4	None	23.3
Maritime Life Europe B	FgnEq	Europe	Yes	-	-	-	-	-	-	-	2.4	Defer	6.8
Maritime Life Glo Eq A&C	FgnEq	Global	Fgn	14.8	15.6	13.7	-	-	-	High	2.8	None	18.3
Maritime Life Global Eq B	FgnEq	Global	Fgn	14.8	-	-	-	-	-	-	2.8	Defer	2.6
Maritime Life Pacif BasinB	FgnEq	PacRim	Fgn	-43.4	-	-	-	-	-	-	2.8	Defer	0.3
Maritime Life Pacif Eq A&C	FgnEq	PacRim	Fgn	-43.4	-22.4	-12.1	-	-	-	Med-	2.8	Defer	8.7
Mawer World Investment	FgnEq	IntlEq	Fgn	8.8	19.6	17.5	16.2	-	-	Med	1.4	None	50.9
McDonald Asia Plus	FgnEq	PacRim	No	-35.2	-15.8	-	-	-	-	-	2.2	Front	0.3
McDonald Emerg Economies	FgnEq	Emerg	No	-21.9	-6.5	-	-	-	-	-	2.5	Front	0.7
McDonald Enhanced Glob	FgnEq	Global	Yes	24.6	-	-	-	-	-	-	2.8	Front	1.7
McDonald Euro Plus	FgnEq	Europe	No	26.1	20.9	-	-	-	-	-	2.2	Front	2.2
McDonald New Japan	FgnEq	Japan	No	-26.9	-18.6	-	-	-	-	-	2.2	Front	0.6
Merrill Lynch Emerg Mkts	FgnEq	Emerg	Fgn	-30.8	-9.5	-	-	-	-	-	3.0	FnDf	71.7

FUND NAME	FUND CATEGORY		RRSP. ELIGIB.	1 YR	2 YR	3 YR	5 YR	10 YR	15 YR	3 YR VOLATILITY	MER	SALES FEES	ASSETS IN $MIL
MetLife-Fidelity Euro Gth	FgnEq	Europe	Yes	-	-	-	-	-	-	-	2.7	Defer	4.1
MetLife Mvp Asian-Pac RSP	FgnEq	PacRim	Fgn	-25.5	-	-	-	-	-	-	2.7	Defer	2.6
MetLife Mvp Asian-P nonRSP	FgnEq	PacRim	Fgn	-	-	-	-	-	-	-	2.7	Defer	0.1
MetLife Mvp Global Equity	FgnEq	Global	Fgn	19.3	-	-	-	-	-	-	2.9	Defer	6.0
Millennia III Intl Eq 1	FgnEq	Global	Fgn	13.2	12.2	-	-	-	-	-	3.1	None	53.7
Millennia III Intl Eq 2	FgnEq	Global	Fgn	13.1	12.0	-	-	-	-	-	2.9	Defer	8.4
Millennia III NA Sml Co 1	FgnEq	NrthAm	Yes	-	-	-	-	-	-	-	3.1	Defer	1.6
Millennia III NA Sml Co 2	FgnEq	NrthAm	Yes	-	-	-	-	-	-	-	-	None	17.8
Montrusco Select Cont Euro	FgnEq	Europe	No	9.0	11.1	13.4	13.1	9.0	-	High	-	None	317.4
Montrusco Select E.A.F.E.	FgnEq	IntlEq	No	-41.0	-18.1	-8.7	2.6	-	-	Med+	0.3	None	7.4
Montrusco Select Emerg Mkt	FgnEq	Emerg	No	-	-	-	-	-	-	-	-	None	8.6
Montrusco Select U.K. Eq	FgnEq	Europe	Fgn	-	-	-	-	-	-	-	-	None	6.8
Mutual Alpine Asian	FgnEq	PacRim	Fgn	-48.0	-13.4	-	-	-	-	-	3.4	None	16.3
Mutual Premier Emerg Mkts	FgnEq	Emerg	No	-31.4	15.7	15.2	14.3	-	-	Med-	2.4	None	76.0
Mutual Premier Intl.	FgnEq	IntlEq	Fgn	16.3	-	-	-	-	-	-	-	None	18.8
Mutual Summit Foreign Eq	FgnEq	Global	Fgn	18.8	12.9	13.4	13.5	-	-	High	2.5	FnDf	63.7
NAL-Global Equity	FgnEq	Global	Fgn	11.6	-	-2.0	-	-	-	Med	2.7	Defer	71.0
NN Can-Asian	FgnEq	PacRim	Yes	-34.9	-15.5	-	-	-	-	-	2.7	Defer	16.5
NN Can-Emerge	FgnEq	Emerge	Yes	-38.2	-20.5	30.5	-	-	-	High	2.7	Defer	164.7
NN Can-Euro	FgnEq	Europe	Fgn	37.7	36.2	13.5	-	-	-	Med	2.8	Defer	71.7
National Global Equities	FgnEq	Global	Yes	1.7	12.0	-	13.3	-	-	High	2.7	None	8.5
National Trust Emerg Mkts.	FgnEq	Emerg	Fgn	-37.6	-13.0	-7.8	-	-	-	High	2.4	None	16.8
National Trust Intl Equity	FgnEq	IntlEq	Fgn	16.6	11.0	13.6	-	-	-	Med+	3.0	F or B	6.6
Navigator Asia Pacific	FgnEq	PacRim	Fgn	-26.9	7.3	8.2	-	-	-	-	3.8	Defer	0.6
North West Life Ecoflex E	FgnEq	IntlEq	Fgn	-36.7	-	-	-	-	-	-	3.0	Defer	5.5
North West Life Ecoflex I	FgnEq	IntlEq	Fgn	-	-	-	-	-	-	-	2.3	F or B	6.5
Northwest International	FgnEq	Global	Fgn	9.0	16.6	15.8	-	-	-	Med-	2.8	F or B	2.1
O'Donnell World Equity	FgnEq	Global	Fgn	24.4	20.4	17.7	-	-	-	Med-	0.6	None	23.0
O.I.Q. Ferique Internation	FgnEq	IntlEq	Yes	3.7	18.4	16.5	-	-	-	Med-	1.0	None	11.7
OTGIF Global	FgnEq	Global	Fgn	25.8	10.9	15.9	12.9	-	-	Med	0.5	F or B	224.9
Optima Strat-Intl Equity	FgnEq	IntlEq	Fgn	15.7	-	17.5	-	-	-	Med-	2.0	None	6.0
Optimum International	FgnEq	IntlEq	Fgn	4.5	-	-	-	-	-	-	2.7	Front	4.5
Orbit North American Eq.	FgnEq	NrthAm	Fgn	25.4	21.4	-	13.1	-	-	-	2.7	Front	7.5
Orbit World	FgnEq	Global	Fgn	20.7	23.3	18.7	-	-	-	Med	1.5	None	538.2
PH & N Intl Equity	FgnEq	IntlEq	Fgn	34.0	30.6	10.0	12.2	-	-	Med+	1.2	None	81.3
PH & N North Amer Equity	FgnEq	NrthAm	Fgn	4.4	9.3	20.3	-	-	-	Low	1.3	None	23.3
Pret et Revenu Intl	FgnEq	Global	Fgn	7.8	17.4	16.0	-	-	-	-	0.2	None	44.5
Primus EAFE Equity	FgnEq	IntlEq	No	16.1	17.1	-	-	-	-	-	0.2	None	6.8
Primus Emerging Markets Eq	FgnEq	Emerg	Fgn	14.9	-	-	-	-	-	-	1.8	Front	2.8
Pursuit Growth	FgnEq	IntlEq	Fgn	-32.0	14.8	-	-	-	-	-	1.8	Front	2.7
Quebec Prof Intl Equity	FgnEq	Global	Fgn	13.2	11.3	13.5	12.1	-	-	Low	1.3	None	87.1
Royal&SunAlliance Balanced	FgnEq	PacRim	Fgn	-50.5	-30.4	-19.3	-	-	-	Med+	2.3	Defer	59.2
Royal Canadian Money Mkt	FgnEq	Europe	Yes	41.7	32.4	25.7	22.3	12.1	-	Med+	1.0	None	554.5

FUND NAME	FUND CATEGORY		RRSP. ELIGIB.	1 YR	2 YR	3 YR	5 YR	10 YR	15 YR	3 YR VOLATILITY	MER	SALES FEES	ASSETS IN $MIL
Royal Canadian T-Bill	FgnEq	IntlEq	Yes	10.7	14.5	14.4	13.5	-	-	Low	0.9	None	228.7
Royal Canadian valuee	FgnEq	Japan	Yes	-17.5	-12.4	-6.3	-4.0	-3.1	-	-	2.0	None	35.4
Royal Cdn Strategic Index	FgnEq	Latin	Yes	-9.5	6.3	-	-	-	-	-	1.5	None	30.8
Royal Internationl Equity	FgnEq	Emerg	Fgn	-31.1	-	-	-	-	-	-	2.7	None	4.0
Royal Latin American	FgnEq	IntlEq	Fgn	12.3	12.0	12.2	-	-	-	Med+	3.0	None	18.6
Saxon World Growth	FgnEq	Global	Fgn	5.9	11.8	12.3	16.9	13.9	-	Med-	1.8	None	53.4
Sceptre Asian Growth	FgnEq	PacRim	Fgn	-54.4	-30.8	-18.2	-6.0	-	-	High	2.5	None	7.6
Sceptre International	FgnEq	Global	Fgn	-4.9	6.9	9.8	11.4	13.9	-	High	2.1	None	152.8
Scotia Ex. European Gth	FgnEq	Europe	Fgn	32.8	-	-	-	-	-	-	2.3	None	103.5
Scotia Ex. International	FgnEq	Global	Fgn	15.1	16.9	14.9	13.1	11.3	-	Med	2.2	None	226.0
Scotia Ex. Latin American	FgnEq	Latin	Fgn	-17.9	5.2	13.6	-	-	11.7	-	2.4	None	48.7
Scotia Ex. Pacific Rim	FgnEq	PacRim	Fgn	-32.5	-12.1	-4.5	-	-	-	Low	2.4	None	29.5
Scudder Emerging Markets	FgnEq	Emerg	Fgn	-15.6	5.4	-	-	-	-	-	2.1	None	18.0
Scudder Global	FgnEq	Global	Fgn	22.3	21.9	-	-	-	-	-	1.8	None	44.1
Scudder Greater Europe	FgnEq	Europe	Fgn	54.4	38.2	-	-	-	-	-	1.9	None	88.8
Scudder Pacific	FgnEq	PacRim	Fgn	-33.7	-13.2	-	-	-	-	-	1.8	None	3.7
Special Opportunities	FgnEq	NrthAm	Fgn	-21.7	-0.3	6.0	7.4	4.9	-	-	2.1	Front	4.5
Spectrum Utd Asian Dynasty	FgnEq	PacRim	Fgn	-49.1	-28.7	-17.5	-	-	-	Med-	2.6	F or B	10.9
Spectrum Utd Emerging Mkts	FgnEq	Emerg	Fgn	-31.1	-6.1	4.1	-	-	-	Med	2.7	F or B	39.9
Spectrum Utd European Gth	FgnEq	Europe	Fgn	48.0	33.1	31.1	-	-	-	Med-	2.6	F or B	156.9
Spectrum Utd Global Equity	FgnEq	Global	Fgn	18.3	18.3	19.0	12.9	-	-	Med+	2.3	F or B	61.0
Spectrum Utd Global Growth	FgnEq	Global	Fgn	15.6	4.2	6.0	6.7	5.9	6.1	Med+	2.4	F or B	15.5
Spectrum Utd Global Gth Pf	FgnEq	IntlEq	No	-	-	-	-	-	-	-	2.0	F or B	2.7
Standard Life Gth Equity	FgnEq	NrthAm	Yes	18.1	19.0	18.8	-	-	-	Med+	2.0	Defer	10.0
Standard Life Intl Equity	FgnEq	IntlEq	Fgn	13.2	15.6	14.9	-	-	-	-	2.0	Defer	8.5
Strategic Val Asia Pacific	FgnEq	PacRim	Fgn	-39.9	-21.9	-13.7	-	-	-	Low	2.7	F or B	6.1
Strategic Val Commonwealth	FgnEq	Global	Fgn	12.9	11.9	10.8	10.4	9.7	11.1	Low	2.7	F or B	293.0
Strategic Val Emerging Mkt	FgnEq	Emerg	Fgn	-35.1	-12.7	-7.1	-	-	-	Med-	3.0	F or B	3.6
Strategic Val Europe	FgnEq	Europe	Fgn	39.2	31.6	24.4	-	-	-	Low	2.7	F or B	53.1
Strategic Val Intl	FgnEq	Global	Fgn	13.0	12.0	11.3	11.4	9.6	10.5	Med	2.7	F or B	175.9
Strategic valuee	FgnEq	Global	Fgn	-22.3	-2.3	-	-	-	-	-	3.1	F or B	5.4
Tal/Hyper Global Small Cap	FgnEq	Global	No	-	-	-	-	-	-	-	2.8	F or B	5.5
Tal/Hyper Global Eq	FgnEq	Global	Fgn	-	-	-	-	-	-	-	2.8	F or B	8.1
Talvest/Hyperion Asian	FgnEq	PacRim	Fgn	-34.4	-17.0	-10.0	1.4	-	-	Med-	3.3	F or B	52.8
Talvest/Hyperion China Pls	FgnEq	China	Fgn	-	-	-	-	-	-	-	2.8	F or B	1.0
Talvest/Hyperion European	FgnEq	Europe	Fgn	39.4	33.4	25.2	20.8	-	-	Med	3.0	F or B	82.3
Talvest Global RRSP	FgnEq	Global	Yes	26.6	22.3	19.0	14.3	-	-	Med-	2.5	F or B	39.2
Templeton Emerging Markets	FgnEq	Emerg	Fgn	-30.9	-4.7	0.5	5.6	-	-	Med+	3.2	F or B	827.6
Templeton Glo Smaller Com	FgnEq	Global	Fgn	4.7	10.2	12.6	14.0	-	-	Low	2.6	F or B	361.7
Templeton Growth	FgnEq	Global	Fgn	8.9	16.8	15.3	16.2	15.0	-	Low	2.0	F or B	10636.0
Templeton Intl Stock	FgnEq	IntlEq	Fgn	15.0	21.0	19.0	19.3	-	14.7	Low	2.5	F or B	5860.9
Tradex Emerg Mkts Country	FgnEq	Emerg	Fgn	-26.4	-6.8	-1.8	-	-	-	Low	2.5	None	2.5
Trimark Americas	FgnEq	Amrcas	Fgn	-4.4	7.8	12.2	9.8	-	-	Med	2.7	F or B	341.0
Trimark Europlus	FgnEq	Europe	Fgn	-	-	-	-	-	-	-	2.5	F or B	90.3

FUND NAME	FUND CATEGORY	RRSP. ELIGIB.	1 YR	2 YR	3 YR	5 YR	10 YR	15 YR	3 YR VOLATILITY	MER	SALES FEES	ASSETS IN $MIL
Trimark Fund	FgnEq	Global	Fgn	7.4	14.9	15.2	17.7	15.9	15.2	Med-	1.5	Front	3087.4
Trimark Indo-Pacific	FgnEq	PacRim	Fgn	-47.7	-19.7	-10.5				Med	3.0	F or B	141.3
Trimark Select Growth	FgnEq	Global	Fgn	5.4	12.7	13.2	15.4			Med-	2.3	F or B	5941.9
Universal Americas	FgnEq	Amrcas	Fgn	3.0	14.4	14.5	10.5	10.5	11.4	Med-	2.6	F or B	102.0
Universal Euro Opportunity	FgnEq	Europe	Fgn	42.6	34.9	35.8				Med-	2.5	F or B	896.3
Universal Far East	FgnEq	PacRim	Fgn	-50.7	-26.8	-17.2				Med+	2.6	F or B	37.9
Universal Growth	FgnEq	Global	Fgn	13.7	20.3	16.6					2.4	F or B	386.1
Universal Intl Stock	FgnEq	IntlEq	Fgn	16.6	14.3	14.6	13.9	8.3		Low	2.4	F or B	244.7
Universal Japan	FgnEq	Japan	Fgn	-23.9	-11.8	-4.2				High	2.5	F or B	18.4
Universal World Emerg Gth	FgnEq	Emerg	Fgn	-24.1	-4.6	2.3				Low	2.5	F or B	125.2
Universal World Gth RRSP	FgnEq	IntlEq	Yes	1.0	12.6	15.0				High	2.4	F or B	424.1
Universal World valuee	FgnEq	Global	No									F or B	9.7
University Avenue World	FgnEq	Global	Fgn	29.2							2.4	F or B	0.8
Valorem Demographic Trends	FgnEq	NrthAm	Fgn									F or B	7.6
Valorem Glo Equity-valuee	FgnEq	Global	Fgn									F or B	0.3
Vision Europe	FgnEq	Europe	Fgn	41.5	34.5	27.8	22.5			Med+	1.7	Defer	43.6
YMG International	FgnEq	IntlEq	Fgn	9.0	12.0	12.1	11.1			Med	1.8	F or B	79.1
20/20 Managed Futures Val.	Spclty	Other	Yes	-34.2	-14.5	-4.6					3.7	F or B	47.6
AIM GT Glbl Infrstructure	Spclty	GlobST	Fgn	12.0	12.1	15.5					2.8	F or B	68.3
AIM GT Global Health Care	Spclty	GlobST	Fgn	18.8	19.0						2.8	F or B	361.7
AIM GT Global Telecom	Spclty	GlobST	Fgn	27.2	12.1	21.2					2.8	F or B	474.6
AIM Global Health Sciences	Spclty	GlobST	Fgn	27.9	20.7	31.9	30.4				2.9	F or B	296.7
AIM Global Technology	Spclty	GlobST	Fgn	30.9							2.9	F or B	39.5
Acuity Pld Envir Sc & Tech	Spclty	GlobST	Fgn	30.3	22.6	20.0	13.8					None	-
Allstar Adrian Day Gold Pl	Spclty	GlPrMt	Fgn	-54.2							5.3	Front	0.2
Altamira Science & Tech	Spclty	GlobST	Fgn	45.7	23.4						2.3	None	90.1
C.I. Glo Health Sci Sector	Spclty	GlobST	Fgn	17.6							2.4	F or B	111.0
C.I. Glo Technology Sector	Spclty	GlobST	Fgn	40.6							2.4	F or B	57.8
C.I. Glo Telecom Sector	Spclty	GlobST	Fgn	71.1							2.4	F or B	74.7
CIBC Canadian Real Estate	Spclty	CdnRE	Yes								2.3	None	30.5
CIBC Global Technology	Spclty	GlobST	Fgn	32.0	23.0						2.6	None	100.4
Caratax LP - 1997	Spclty	Other	Fgn	43.1								Front	8.1
Clarington Glo Communica.	Spclty	GlobST	Yes	6.1							3.0	F or B	36.6
Dynamic Cdn Real Estate	Spclty	CdnRE	Yes	-9.0	8.6	16.3	6.3	6.1			2.7	F or B	245.8
Dynamic Global Millennia	Spclty	GlobST	Fgn	-32.8	-18.7						2.4	F or B	17.5
Dynamic Global Prec Metal	Spclty	GlPrMt	Fgn	13.0	26.0	31.4					2.9	F or B	26.7
Dynamic Real Estate Equity	Spclty	GlobRE	Fgn	34.4							2.7	F or B	223.4
Fidelity Focus Health Care	Spclty	GlobST	Fgn	22.9							2.5	F or B	60.4
Fidelity Focus Technology	Spclty	GlobST	Fgn	42.2							2.5	F or B	35.1
First Cdn Global Sci & Tec	Spclty	GlobST	Fgn	46.5	27.3	25.6					2.0	None	108.5
Friedberg Currency	Spclty	Crrncy	No	-8.2							4.2	None	59.0
Friedberg Diversified	Spclty	Crrncy	No								5.1	None	3.9
Friedberg Futures	Spclty	Crrncy	No								2.4	None	1.5

FUND NAME	FUND CATEGORY	RRSP-ELIGIB.	1 YR	2 YR	3 YR	5 YR	10 YR	15 YR	3 YR VOLATILITY	MER	SALES FEES	ASSETS IN $MIL
Friedberg Toronto Eq-Hedge	Spclty	Other	No	-	-	-	-	-	-	-	3.0	Back	3.5
Friedberg Toronto Tr Intl	Spclty	Other	No	-	-	-	-	-	-	-	2.0	Back	1.0
Goldfund Limited	Spclty	GlPrMt	Fgn	-32.1	-28.6	-18.4	-8.2	-2.1	-0.1	-	1.0	Front	2.7
Great-West Real Estate(G)A	Spclty	CdnRE	Yes	14.0	8.6	6.6	2.6	1.0	3.8	-	2.9	None	124.3
Great-West Real Estate(G)B	Spclty	CdnRE	Yes	14.3	8.8	6.8	-	-	-	-	2.7	Defer	50.4
Green Line Entertn & Comm	Spclty	GlobST	No	24.3	-	-	-	-	-	-	2.6	None	103.9
Green Line Health Sciences	Spclty	GlobST	Fgn	22.1	16.4	18.7	-	-	-	-	2.6	None	283.1
Green Line Science & Tech	Spclty	GlobST	Fgn	-	-	-	-	-	-	-	2.6	None	210.7
Hartford Real Est Income	Spclty	CdnRE	Yes	17.1	-	-	-	-	-	-	2.8	Defer	1.3
Hillsdale LS American Eq	Spclty	Crrncy	No	1.1	7.9	6.9	-	-	-	-	1.0	None	6.3
Horizons Multi-Asset	Spclty	Other	No	-	-	-	-	-	-	-	2.0	F or B	21.6
Horizons RRSP Hedge	Spclty	Other	Yes	-	-	-	-	-	-	-	3.6	F or B	6.1
Investors Real Property	Spclty	CdnRE	Yes	8.9	6.6	5.8	3.9	4.3	-	-	2.4	FnDf	564.1
Middlefield Cdn Realty	Spclty	CdnRE	Yes	-2.1	-	-	-	-	-	-	2.7	F or B	0.6
NCE Real Estate Securities	Spclty	CdnRE	No	-	-	-	-	-	-	-	2.4	Front	0.7
O'Donnell World Prec Metal	Spclty	GlPrMt	Yes	-40.7	-	-	-	-	-	-	2.9	F or B	10.0
Optima Strat-Real Estate	Spclty	GlobRE	No	13.7	19.5	-	-	-	-	-	0.4	F or B	171.7
REIT & Real Est Gth Tr 98	Spclty	CdnRE	Yes	-	-	-	-	-	-	-	-	Front	1.0
Royal Dividend	Spclty	CdnRE	Yes	-24.6	-11.4	-8.3	-3.4	-	-	-	1.8	None	10.3
Royal Life Science & Tech	Spclty	GlobST	Fgn	14.2	16.5	-	-	-	-	-	2.8	None	405.3
Spectrum Utd Glo Telecomm	Spclty	GlobST	Fgn	31.8	16.3	17.0	-	-	-	-	2.6	F or B	99.4
Tal/Hyper Glo Health Care	Spclty	GlobST	Fgn	16.7	-	-	-	-	-	-	3.3	F or B	7.8
Tal/Hyper Glob Sci & Tech	Spclty	GlobST	Fgn	44.6	-	-	-	-	-	-	2.3	F or B	23.1
Trimark Discovery	Spclty	GlobST	Fgn	12.8	13.0	-	-	-	-	-	2.7	F or B	346.1
Universal World Real Estat	Spclty	GlobRE	No	34.3	-	-	-	-	-	-	-	Front	9.5
Universal World Sci & Tech	Spclty	GlobST	Fgn	19.8	-	-	-	-	-	-	2.4	F or B	209.6
YMG Hedge	Spclty	Other	Fgn	-	-	-	-	-	-	-	2.3	Front	6.8
AIM GT Global Growtth & Inc	Balan	GblSAA	Fgn	26.3	21.2	17.6	-	-	-	Med-	2.9	F or B	46.9
Acuity Pld Global Balanced	Balan	GblSAA	Fgn	45.7	23.0	19.0	12.7	-	-	High	-	None	-
Altamira Glo Diversified	Balan	GblSAA	Fgn	12.1	10.7	14.6	12.3	6.3	-	High	2.0	None	46.3
Artisan Aggressive Growth	Balan	GblSAA	Fgn	-	-	-	-	-	-	-	3.0	F or B	2.0
Artisan Growth	Balan	GblSAA	Fgn	-	-	-	-	-	-	-	3.0	F or B	5.0
Artisan Growth & Income	Balan	GblSAA	Fgn	-	-	-	-	-	-	-	3.0	F or B	3.9
Artisan Income	Balan	GblSAA	Fgn	-	-	-	-	-	-	-	3.0	F or B	1.3
Artisan Maximum Growth	Balan	GblSAA	Fgn	-	-	-	-	-	-	-	3.0	F or B	1.1
Artisan RSP Aggressive Gth	Balan	GblSAA	Yes	-	-	-	-	-	-	-	3.0	F or B	14.0
Artisan RSP Growth	Balan	GblSAA	Yes	-	-	-	-	-	-	-	3.0	F or B	23.8
Artisan RSP Maximum Growth	Balan	GblSAA	Yes	-	-	-	-	-	-	-	3.0	F or B	8.7
Azura Balanced Pooled	Balan	GblSAA	Fgn	8.8	11.9	19.4	15.2	-	-	Med-	2.3	F or B	19.3
Beutel Goodman Private Bal	Balan	GblSAA	No	18.5	22.8	17.0	-	-	-	-	1.1	None	65.7
C.I. International Bal	Balan	GblSAA	Fgn	18.7	18.3	17.0	-	-	-	Med	2.4	F or B	163.0
C.I. Intl. Balanced RSP	Balan	GblSAA	Yes	14.5	15.8	15.5	-	-	-	Med	2.4	F or B	244.4
CGO&V Hazelton	Balan	GblSAA	No	9.7	-	-	-	-	-	-	1.8	None	8.6

FUND NAME	FUND CATEGORY	RRSP-ELIGIB.	1 YR	2 YR	3 YR	5 YR	10 YR	15 YR	3 YR VOLATILITY	MER	SALES FEES	ASSETS IN $MIL
CT Global Asset Alloc	Balan	GblSAA	Yes	-	-	-	-	-	-	-	1.9	None	184.9
CUMIS Life Global Balanced	Balan	GblSAA	Yes	6.6	-	-	-	-	-	-	3.0	Back	3.0
Caldwell International	Balan	GblSAA	Fgn	1.4	3.9	6.2	9.9	-	-	High	2.6	F or B	4.0
Co-Operators US Diversfied	Balan	GblSAA	Fgn	-	-	-	-	-	-	-	2.4	None	2.5
Elliot & Page Global Bal	Balan	GblSAA	Fgn	10.6	11.1	9.4	-	-	-	Med+	2.7	F or B	11.9
FMOQ Fonds De Placement	Balan	GblSAA	Yes	30.4	28.2	24.0	18.1	15.3	-	High	0.6	None	30.8
FMOQ Omnibus	Balan	GblSAA	Yes	21.8	21.6	18.2	14.6	12.4	-	Med+	0.6	None	235.6
Fidelity Glob Asset Alloc	Balan	GblSAA	Fgn	20.1	22.3	19.7	14.0	-	-	Med+	2.7	F or B	434.8
Global Strategy World Bal	Balan	GblSAA	Fgn	14.6	12.0	11.0	-	-	-	Low	2.3	F or B	11.9
GrowSafe Intl Balanced	Balan	GblSAA	Yes	12.1	12.8	12.6	-	-	-	Med-	2.8	Defer	46.7
Guardian Intl Balanced C	Balan	GblSAA	Yes	4.4	8.7	10.5	-	-	-	Med	2.1	Front	6.1
Guardian Intl Balanced M	Balan	GblSAA	Yes	3.7	7.9	-	-	-	-	-	2.9	F or B	59.1
Investors Growth Plus Port	Balan	GblSAA	Fgn	17.2	17.6	16.0	13.0	-	-	Low	2.5	FnDf	407.6
Merrill Lynch Cap Asset	Balan	GblSAA	Fgn	21.7	20.4	-	-	-	-	-	2.8	FnDf	68.0
Merrill Lynch World Alloc	Balan	GblSAA	Fgn	5.7	12.2	-	-	-	-	-	2.8	FnDf	112.5
NN Elite	Balan	GblSAA	Yes	5.2	8.2	7.5	-	-	-	Defer	2.1	Defer	77.1
Spectrum Utd Global Diver	Balan	GblSAA	Fgn	15.2	12.8	13.2	10.7	-	-	Low	2.3	F or B	32.1
Strategic Val Glo Bal RSP	Balan	GblSAA	Yes	4.4	-	-	-	-	-	Med-	2.8	F or B	2.1
Strategic Val Global Bal	Balan	GblSAA	Fgn	15.1	13.1	11.4	10.0	-	-	Med-	2.7	F or B	25.5
Talvest Global Asset Alloc	Balan	GblSAA	Fgn	9.0	10.5	10.1	9.9	8.9	-	Med+	2.8	F or B	54.7
Templeton Global Balanced	Balan	GblSAA	Fgn	8.5	14.0	13.2	-	-	-	Low	2.6	F or B	73.6
Templeton Intl Balanced	Balan	GblSAA	Fgn	5.6	11.8	11.7	-	-	-	Med	2.6	F or B	46.5
Universal World Bal RRSP	Balan	GblSAA	Yes	5.7	14.1	15.2	-	-	-	Med+	2.4	F or B	266.8
Zweig Global Managed Asset	Balan	GblSAA	Fgn	20.9	17.2	-	-	-	-	-	2.8	None	58.2
AGF American T.A. Alloc	Balan	GblTAA	Fgn	24.5	20.8	17.4	14.7	-	-	-	2.6	F or B	424.1
AGF European Asset Alloc	Balan	GblTAA	Fgn	45.9	36.5	28.0	-	-	-	-	2.6	F or B	102.7
AGF World Balanced	Balan	GblTAA	Fgn	17.2	15.8	15.9	11.7	9.2	-	-	2.5	F or B	124.9
Desjardins World Balanced	Balan	GblTAA	Yes	9.8	11.2	11.4	-	-	-	-	2.2	None	54.5
Dynamic Global Partners	Balan	GblTAA	Fgn	2.9	10.7	-	-	-	-	-	2.5	F or B	66.2
Global Mgr-Tactical Growth	Balan	GblTAA	Fgn	15.3	-	-	-	-	-	-	-	Front	17.4
Universal World Asst Alloc	Balan	GblTAA	Fgn	22.3	13.8	11.7	-	-	-	-	2.5	F or B	169.7
ABAX Bradys Obligations	FixInc	GlbBond	Fgn	2.0	6.0	8.1	7.9	9.2	-	-	6.3	Front	1.7
AGF Global Government Bond	FixInc	GlbBond	Fgn	12.5	9.6	7.6	-	-	-	Med-	1.9	F or B	158.8
AGF RSP Global Bond	FixInc	GlbBond	Yes	11.8	8.7	6.8	5.6	-	-	Med-	2.0	F or B	86.7
AGF U.S. Income	FixInc	GlbBond	Fgn	14.8	9.3	7.6	-	-	-	Med-	2.5	F or B	14.4
AGF U.S. S-Term High Yield	FixInc	GlbBond	Fgn	10.1	10.2	7.6	-	-	-	Med-	2.5	F or B	24.1
AIM GT World Bond	FixInc	GlbBond	Fgn	8.0	7.9	9.3	-	-	-	Med-	2.5	F or B	6.8
AIM Global RSP Income	FixInc	GlbBond	Yes	8.3	10.2	9.7	7.5	-	-	Med-	2.4	F or B	28.3
Altamira Global Bond	FixInc	GlbBond	Fgn	10.4	8.0	6.5	-	-	-	High	1.8	None	28.4
Altamira High Yield Bond	FixInc	GlbBond	Yes	12.4	15.3	-	-	-	-	-	2.0	None	18.8
Atlas World Bond	FixInc	GlbBond	Fgn	6.6	6.5	7.8	-	-	-	Low	2.1	F or B	24.2
BPI Global RSP Bond	FixInc	GlbBond	Yes	11.5	10.8	11.0	-	-	-	Med	1.5	F or B	9.2

FUND NAME	FUND CATEGORY		RRSP-ELIGIB.	1 YR	2 YR	3 YR	5 YR	10 YR	15 YR	3 YR VOLATILITY	MER	SALES FEES	ASSETS IN $MIL
C.I. Global Bond RSP	FixInc	GlbBond	Yes	8.3	7.9	8.8	-	-	-	Low	2.1	F or B	82.6
C.I. Global High Yield	FixInc	GlbBond	Fgn	2.8	10.2	13.6	-	-	-	High	2.2	F or B	15.8
C.I. World Bond	FixInc	GlbBond	Fgn	6.9	7.2	8.0	7.1	-	-	Low	2.1	F or B	75.2
CIBC Global Bond	FixInc	GlbBond	Yes	7.6	7.7	5.8	-	-	-	Low	2.0	None	81.1
CIBC Global Bond Index	FixInc	GlbBond	Yes	-	-	-	-	-	-	-	0.9	None	16.7
CT International Bond	FixInc	GlbBond	Yes	5.5	3.7	3.6	-	-	-	Med	2.1	None	166.8
Canada Life Int. Bond	FixInc	GlbBond	Yes	14.7	9.8	7.7	-	-	-	Med	2.0	Defer	38.1
Dynamic Global Bond	FixInc	GlbBond	Yes	-4.3	1.0	2.9	6.3	7.3	-	Med+	1.8	F or B	239.0
Dynamic Global Income&Gth	FixInc	GlbBond	Fgn	2.1	-	-	-	-	-	-	2.7	F or B	57.7
Elliott & Page Global Bond	FixInc	GlbBond	Fgn	6.6	5.3	3.4	-	-	-	Med	2.0	F or B	12.6
Ethical Global Bond	FixInc	GlbBond	Yes	8.6	8.3	7.2	-	-	-	Low	2.6	None	17.3
FMOQ Bond	FixInc	GlbBond	Yes	8.8	8.4	7.2	7.8	-	-	Med-	1.0	None	3.9
Fidelity Emerging Mkts Bnd	FixInc	GlbBond	Fgn	4.4	19.3	22.2	-	-	-	High	2.2	F or B	55.9
Fidelity N American Income	FixInc	GlbBond	Fgn	4.9	5.3	5.6	2.9	-	-	Low	1.8	F or B	68.0
First Canadian Intl. Bond	FixInc	GlbBond	Fgn	7.7	5.0	3.9	-	-	-	High	2.0	None	241.3
Friedberg Foreign Bond	FixInc	GlbBond	Fgn	0.5	-	-	-	-	-	-	0.9	Back	51.4
GS International Bond	FixInc	GlbBond	Yes	6.6	4.6	-	-	-	-	-	2.7	Defer	8.6
Global Mgr-US Bond Index	FixInc	GlbBond	Fgn	16.4	11.0	6.6	-	-	-	High	1.8	Front	0.4
Global Strategy Diver Bond	FixInc	GlbBond	Yes	8.1	7.2	8.4	5.4	-	-	Low	2.2	F or B	257.3
Global Strategy Divr FgnBd	FixInc	GlbBond	Yes	9.3	7.6	7.1	-	-	-	Med	2.4	F or B	6.2
Global Strategy World Bond	FixInc	GlbBond	Fgn	8.2	7.1	8.5	5.0	7.7	-	Low	2.1	F or B	187.3
Great-West Glob Income(A)	FixInc	GlbBond	Yes	10.5	7.4	-	-	-	-	-	2.8	None	5.9
Great-West Glob Income(A)B	FixInc	GlbBond	Yes	10.8	7.7	-	-	-	-	-	2.5	Defer	6.9
Great-West Intl Bond (P)A	FixInc	GlbBond	Fgn	1.7	2.1	3.4	-	-	-	-	3.1	None	7.4
Great-West Intl Bond (P)B	FixInc	GlbBond	Fgn	2.0	2.3	3.7	-	-	-	Med+	2.8	Defer	6.2
Green Line Global Govt Bnd	FixInc	GlbBond	Fgn	11.9	7.9	5.1	7.0	-	-	Med+	2.1	None	99.3
Green Line Global RSP Bond	FixInc	GlbBond	Yes	10.5	11.3	8.1	-	-	-	Med+	2.0	None	268.0
Guardian Foreign Income A	FixInc	GlbBond	Yes	16.1	13.1	11.4	-	-	-	Med-	1.7	Front	4.2
Guardian Foreign Income B	FixInc	GlbBond	Yes	15.3	12.1	-	-	-	-	-	2.6	Defer	6.3
Guardian Intl Income C	FixInc	GlbBond	Yes	8.5	8.3	8.8	7.5	7.9	-	Low	2.1	Front	41.3
Guardian Intl Income M	FixInc	GlbBond	Yes	7.9	7.5	-	-	-	-	-	2.8	F or B	118.4
Hongkong Bank Global Bond	FixInc	GlbBond	Fgn	4.6	4.5	4.0	-	-	-	High	2.1	None	8.4
Ind. Alliance Ecoflex G	FixInc	GlbBond	Fgn	-1.7	-	-	-	-	-	-	1.9	Defer	3.3
Ind. Alliance Global Bond	FixInc	GlbBond	Fgn	-1.5	-	-	-	-	-	-	1.7	None	0.1
InvesNat Intl RSP Bond	FixInc	GlbBond	Yes	9.6	8.1	7.3	-	-	-	Med	2.0	None	7.3
Investors Global Bond	FixInc	GlbBond	Fgn	8.8	6.2	3.5	5.9	-	-	Med	2.2	Defer	245.4
Investors N.A. High Yield	FixInc	GlbBond	Fgn	7.4	-	-	-	-	-	-	2.2	Defer	95.2
MD Global Bond	FixInc	GlbBond	Fgn	11.9	7.5	5.0	-	-	-	Med+	1.2	None	41.8
MLI AGF Global Govt Bd GIF	FixInc	GlbBond	Yes	-	-	-	-	-	-	-	2.4	F or B	4.3
MLI Dynamic Global Bd GIF	FixInc	GlbBond	Yes	-	-	-	-	-	-	-	2.5	F or B	0.7
Manulife Vistafd1 Gbl Bond	FixInc	GlbBond	Fgn	7.3	4.3	4.6	-	-	-	High	1.6	Front	1.3
Manulife Vistafd2 Gbl Bond	FixInc	GlbBond	Fgn	6.4	3.5	3.8	-	-	-	High	2.4	Defer	7.3
Merrill Lynch World Bond	FixInc	GlbBond	Yes	9.6	7.4	-	-	-	-	-	2.3	Defer	22.7
NN Can-Global Bond	FixInc	GlbBond	Yes	11.3	9.2	-	-	-	-	-	2.5	Defer	23.4

FUND NAME	FUND CATEGORY	RRSP-ELIGIB.	1 YR	2 YR	3 YR	5 YR	10 YR	15 YR	3 YR VOLATILITY	MER	SALES FEES	ASSETS IN $MIL
National Trust Intl RSP Bd	GlbBond	Fixinc	Yes	8.1	10.4	9.6				High	1.8	None	17.6
North West Life Ecoflex G	GlbBond	Fixinc	Fgn	-1.7							1.9	Defer	0.3
O'Donnell US High Income	GlbBond	Fixinc	Yes								2.0	F or B	2.5
Optima Strat-Glo Fx Income	GlbBond	Fixinc	Fgn	11.4	8.3	6.3				Med+	0.5	F or B	123.1
Pret et Revenu Mond Oblig	GlbBond	Fixinc	Fgn	5.9	4.7	3.2				Med	1.9	None	0.3
Pursuit Global Bond	GlbBond	Fixinc	Fgn	3.2	4.8						1.3	Front	14.8
Royal Canadian Small Cap	GlbBond	Fixinc	Yes	9.1	7.4	5.5	7.0			Med+	2.2	None	238.9
Scotia Ex. Global Bond	GlbBond	Fixinc	Fgn	9.7	7.3	3.2				Med+	2.0	None	14.9
Spectrum Utd Global Bond	GlbBond	Fixinc	Fgn	6.5	6.0	3.4				Med	2.0	F or B	13.6
Spectrum Utd RSP Intl Bond	GlbBond	Fixinc	Yes	5.3	3.9	2.6	5.8			Med	2.0	F or B	47.5
Standard Life Intl Bond	GlbBond	Fixinc	Yes	15.4	10.0	6.8				Med+	2.0	Defer	6.3
Talvest Forgn Pay Cdn Bond	GlbBond	Fixinc	Yes	10.9	10.0	7.0	7.6			Med-	2.2	F or B	69.4
Templeton Global Bond	GlbBond	Fixinc	Fgn	2.1	4.6	5.4	5.7			Low	2.3	F or B	44.6
Universal World High Yield	GlbBond	Fixinc	No									F or B	4.5
Universal World Inc RRSP	GlbBond	Fixinc	Yes	12.8	11.6	11.0				Med-	2.2	F or B	569.6
Universal World Tact. Bond	GlbBond	Fixinc	Fgn	12.4	9.0	7.7				High	2.3	F or B	43.2
AGF US$ Money Mkt Account	USMkt	Fixinc	Fgn	4.7	4.6	4.6	4.2				0.8	Front	20.2
Atlas American Money Mkt	USMkt	Fixinc	Fgn	4.6	4.5	4.6	4.1	4.8			1.1	F or B	79.9
BPI U.S. Money Market	USMkt	Fixinc	Yes	4.8	4.5						0.7	F or B	5.7
C.I. US Money Market	USMkt	Fixinc	Fgn	4.9	4.9	5.0					0.5	F or B	31.0
CIBC US$ Money Market	USMkt	Fixinc	Fgn	4.6	4.5	4.5	4.0				1.1	None	134.3
Fidelity US Money Market	USMkt	Fixinc	Fgn	4.5	4.4	4.4					1.3	F or B	31.7
Green Line US Money Market	USMkt	Fixinc	Yes	4.6	4.5	4.5	4.0				1.2	None	316.4
Guardian US Money Market C	USMkt	Fixinc	Yes	4.9	4.6	4.7	4.2	5.6			0.9	Front	12.6
Guardian US Money Market M	USMkt	Fixinc	Yes	4.2	4.0						1.5	F or B	0.9
Hongkong Bank US$ Mny Mkt	USMkt	Fixinc	Yes								1.1	None	17.5
InvesNat US Money Market	USMkt	Fixinc	Yes	4.5	4.5	4.4	3.9				1.1	None	11.7
Investors US Money Market	USMkt	Fixinc	Yes	4.5							1.1	None	21.7
PH & N $US Money Market	USMkt	Fixinc	No	5.1	5.1	5.1	4.6				0.5	None	57.5
Royal $US Money Market	USMkt	Fixinc	Yes	4.6	4.5	4.5	4.0				1.1	None	217.0
Scotia CanAm Money Market	USMkt	Fixinc	No	4.7							1.0	None	27.6
Spectrum Utd US$ Money Mkt	USMkt	Fixinc	No	4.3	4.2	4.3	4.1	4.7			1.2	None	4.7
Universal US Money Market	USMkt	Fixinc	No	3.7	3.7	3.8					1.3	F or B	5.0
AGF Intl Grp-S-Term Income	IntMkt	Fixinc	Fgn	4.1	1.9	2.7				High	2.7	F or B	10.3
Altamira S-T Global Income	IntMkt	Fixinc	Yes	3.7	2.7	2.2	3.9			High	1.2	None	22.9
Average 5 Yr GIC	Index			4.5	4.8	5.3	6.0	7.7	8.6				
CPI	Index			1.1	1.3	1.4	1.4	2.5	3.1				
Canada Savings Bonds	Index			3.0	3.4	4.0	4.4	6.8	7.2				
TSE 300	Index			16.2	22.9	19.9	15.6	11.0	10.9				
TSE 35	Index			19.9	26.4	21.7	17.9						
Average All Funds	Avg			7.7	11.1	11.3	10.0	9.5	9.7		2.1		215.5

FUND NAME	FUND CATEGORY	RRSP. ELIGIB.	1 YR	2 YR	3 YR	5 YR	10 YR	15 YR	3 YR VOLATILITY	MER	SALES FEES	ASSETS IN $MIL
Average Asset Alloc Serv	Avg	-	9.1	12.0	11.6	7.1	-	-	-	2.1	-	48.3
Average Balanced Funds	Avg	-	11.1	15.0	13.8	11.1	9.8	9.3	-	2.2	-	306.4
Average Cdn Diver Equity	Avg	-	10.6	17.5	16.6	12.1	9.9	10.0	-	2.2	-	336.6
Average Cdn Dividend Funds	Avg	-	15.6	23.0	20.0	14.3	10.8	11.0	-	2.0	-	350.0
Average Cdn Large Cap	Avg	-	13.0	20.8	17.8	13.5	10.3	10.6	-	2.1	-	281.8
Average Cdn Sector Funds	Avg	-	-24.8	-14.6	-2.8	-0.5	4.7	2.8	-	2.4	-	111.2
Average Cdn Small Cap	Avg	-	3.1	9.8	14.5	9.7	9.2	8.6	-	2.4	-	151.8
Average Fixed Income Funds	Avg	-	7.9	8.9	8.4	7.7	9.4	10.1	-	1.7	-	155.3
Average LSVC Funds	Avg	-	0.3	2.2	2.7	4.9	-	-	-	4.8	-	96.1
Average Money Market Funds	Avg	-	3.3	3.2	3.8	4.2	6.5	7.4	-	1.0	-	205.8
Average Other Country Eq	Avg	-	-16.6	-9.2	-5.2	-7.4	-1.5	8.1	-	2.4	-	30.7
Average Regional Eq Funds	Avg	-	0.6	7.8	9.6	11.8	10.4	9.8	-	2.4	-	211.2
Average Specialty Funds	Avg	-	14.6	10.2	12.0	6.5	2.3	1.9	-	2.7	-	101.2
Average U.S. Equity Funds	Avg	-	28.9	26.6	24.1	19.4	14.9	13.3	-	2.1	-	130.8
Avg Americas Equity	Avg	-	14.4	13.8	16.2	11.4	11.0	11.4	-	2.9	-	148.2
Avg Asia-Pacific Rim Eq	Avg	-	-42.8	-21.7	-13.1	-5.2	-1.6	2.1	-	2.7	-	56.5
Avg Bond & Mortgage	Avg	-	4.8	6.8	7.2	6.7	8.6	9.5	-	1.3	-	206.8
Avg Cdn Balanced (S.A.A.)	Avg	-	10.2	14.7	13.6	11.0	9.8	9.4	-	2.2	-	319.0
Avg Cdn Balanced (T.A.A.)	Avg	-	10.8	15.5	13.8	10.4	9.3	9.3	-	2.2	-	499.4
Avg Cdn Bond	Avg	-	9.4	10.9	10.0	8.4	9.8	10.6	-	1.6	-	172.8
Avg Cdn Consumer Sector	Avg	-	6.3	11.1	7.3	7.7	-	-	-	2.0	-	1.0
Avg Cdn Divers -Growth	Avg	-	15.4	19.8	21.8	14.2	12.3	11.0	-	2.5	-	272.2
Avg Cdn Divers -Neutral	Avg	-	9.8	16.6	15.7	11.9	9.7	9.9	-	2.1	-	324.6
Avg Cdn Divers -valuee	Avg	-	10.7	20.5	17.3	12.0	7.8	10.2	-	2.1	-	479.1
Avg Cdn Financial Services	Avg	-	25.4	51.5	47.1	34.3	22.9	-	-	2.6	-	683.1
Avg Cdn Gold/Prec Metals	Avg	-	-33.8	-28.4	-9.5	-1.5	0.5	0.9	-	2.2	-	57.9
Avg Cdn Large Cap -Growth	Avg	-	15.6	14.8	11.1	10.9	11.5	9.4	-	2.0	-	145.2
Avg Cdn Large Cap -Neutral	Avg	-	13.5	21.3	18.3	13.5	10.3	10.8	-	2.0	-	207.6
Avg Cdn Large Cap -valuee	Avg	-	10.0	19.4	16.7	13.7	10.5	9.7	-	2.1	-	528.1
Avg Cdn Money Market	Avg	-	3.1	3.0	3.8	4.2	6.6	7.4	-	1.0	-	226.0
Avg Cdn Real Estate	Avg	-	2.8	3.2	2.7	1.0	2.7	3.8	-	2.7	-	102.9
Avg Cdn Resource Sector	Avg	-	-25.3	-11.2	-2.4	-3.9	4.5	3.1	-	2.6	-	55.3
Avg Cdn Science & Tech	Avg	-	-	-	-	-	-	-	-	2.7	-	2.1
Avg Cdn Short Term Bond	Avg	-	4.2	5.9	6.8	6.1	8.5	9.9	-	1.3	-	79.0
Avg Cdn Small Cap -Growth	Avg	-	0.6	9.0	14.4	9.0	9.6	10.1	-	2.3	-	230.1
Avg Cdn Small Cap -Neutral	Avg	-	4.2	10.0	14.6	10.0	9.0	8.4	-	2.5	-	106.1
Avg Cdn Small Cap -valuee	Avg	-	11.1	14.2	14.4	11.3	9.1	7.3	-	2.1	-	35.2
Avg Chinese Equity	Avg	-	-29.3	-16.7	-11.1	-	-	-	-	2.5	-	2.5
Avg Currency Oriented	Avg	-	18.5	27.3	25.6	-	-	-	-	3.2	-	17.7
Avg Emerging Markets Eq	Avg	-	-30.4	-9.9	-4.7	3.7	-	-	-	2.7	-	52.7
Avg European Equity	Avg	-	37.4	31.4	25.9	20.7	12.1	-	-	2.4	-	209.0
Avg German Equity	Avg	-	41.3	33.5	23.7	-	-	-	-	2.0	-	26.5
Avg Global/Foreign-Pay Bnd	Avg	-	7.9	7.8	6.9	6.4	8.0	-	-	2.1	-	60.9
Avg Global Balanced S.A.A.	Avg	-	13.8	15.0	14.2	12.8	10.7	-	-	2.5	-	74.6

FUND NAME	FUND CATEGORY	RRSP. ELIGIB.	1 YR	2 YR	3 YR	5 YR	10 YR	15 YR	3 YR VOLATILITY	MER	SALES FEES	ASSETS IN $MIL
Avg Global Balanced T.A.A.	-	-	19.7	18.1	16.9	13.2	9.2	-	-	2.5	-	137.1
Avg Global Equity	-	-	14.3	15.7	16.1	13.9	11.4	10.5	-	2.4	-	398.5
Avg Global Precious Metals	-	-	-40.0	-23.6	-18.4	-8.2	-2.1	-0.1	-	3.0	-	9.9
Avg Global Real Estate	-	-	13.3	22.7	31.4	-	-	-	-	1.6	-	134.9
Avg Global Science & Tech	-	-	28.7	17.0	20.1	16.8	6.1	-	-	2.6	-	150.9
Avg Indian Equity	-	-	-16.8	-15.9	-18.0	-	-	-	-	3.7	-	15.4
Avg International Equity	-	-	11.5	14.3	14.5	13.0	10.0	-	-	2.2	-	178.0
Avg Intl Money Market	-	-	3.9	2.3	2.5	3.9	-	-	-	2.0	-	16.6
Avg Japanese Equity	-	-	-26.5	-16.9	-9.8	-3.8	-1.5	8.1	-	2.4	-	43.3
Avg Korean Equity	-	-	-66.2	-48.2	-39.7	-21.9	-	-	-	3.3	-	13.6
Avg Latin American Equity	-	-	-20.7	4.7	9.0	-	-	-	-	2.9	-	54.5
Avg Mortgage	-	-	4.3	5.7	6.1	6.4	8.5	9.3	-	1.8	-	366.3
Avg North American Equity	-	-	16.2	19.8	17.7	12.4	11.9	11.0	-	2.2	-	121.5
Avg Specialty: Other	-	-	-4.4	-3.3	1.2	-	-	-	-	2.8	-	13.5
Avg Strategic A.A.Services	-	-	9.2	12.2	12.0	-	-	-	-	2.1	-	30.4
Avg Tactical A.A. Services	-	-	3.4	6.2	7.7	7.1	-	-	-	-	-	495.7
Avg U.S. Large Cap	-	-	29.4	28.1	25.4	20.2	15.3	13.3	-	2.1	-	223.1
Avg U.S. Mid Cap	-	-	29.6	26.1	23.5	18.8	14.4	13.3	-	2.1	-	76.6
Avg U.S. Money Market	-	-	4.6	4.5	4.5	4.1	5.0	-	-	1.0	-	58.6
Avg U.S. Small Cap	-	-	20.0	15.8	15.7	15.4	15.0	-	-	2.6	-	87.3

Index